THE MURDER OF AL-HUSAYN

Sayyed Abd Al-Razzaq
Al-Musawi Al-Muqarram

Fatima Books

Copyright © 2016 Fatima Books
All rights reserved. This book or any portion thereof may not be reproduced or used in any manner whatsoever without the express written permission of the publisher except for the use of brief quotations in a book review.

Printed in the United States of America

First Printing, March 2016

ISBN: 0692587055
ISBN-13: 978-0692587058

Fatima Books
Orangevale, California

alFatimahBookstore@gmail.com

Word of Grace

I would like to thank **Fatima Books** for publishing this book. I also would like to thank my family members and friends who encouraged me throughout this personal endeavor. Special thanks and appreciation to the English speaking brothers for their valuable input and encouragement. I am also grateful to my wife's effort in editing my work, and putting up with my absence in the hope of finishing this book. I ask Allah, the Exalted, to reward all of them from His bounties in this life and in the next.

-RLM

CONTENTS

The Author's Life	xiii
The Author	xiii
The Author's Teachers	xiii
The Author's Remarkable Education and Knowledge	xiv
The Author's Style	xv
The Author's First Book	xv
This Book (Maqtal Al-Husayn, or The Murder of Al-Husayn)	xvi
The Author's Work Printed	xviii
Commentaries and Discussions on the following books	xviii
Manuscripts	xviii
The Author's Dedication to the Cause of the Prophet's Household	xix
The Author's Life in Brief	xx
Translator's Introduction	xxiii

PART I: INTRODUCTION

Al-Husayn's Uprising	1
The Prophets and Al-Husayn	19
Self-Sacrifice	23
Introduction	23
The Verse of Self-Destruction	33
Conclusion	39
Al-Husayn's Knowledge of His Own Martyrdom	45
Al-Husayn's Victory	49
Al-Husayn with His Companions	57
Introduction	57
Al-Husayn on the Day of Ashura	66
Relief of Duty	69
Conclusion	74
Al-Husayn is The Preserver of Faith	79

Weeping on Al-Husayn	83
Mock Weeping (Tabaki)	84
Prostrating on Clay from Karbala	89
Legislating the Visitation Ritual (Ziyara)	91
The Infallible Leaders' Selflessness (Eethaar)	95
Commemorating the Prophet's Household in Poetry	99
The Predicament of Exposing the Family	103
The Uprisings of Ali's Descendants	107

PART II: THE STORY OF KARBALA

Yazeed after Mu'awiya	113
People Fearing for Al-Husayn	119
Omar Al-Atraf	119
Bin Al-Hanafiyya	119
Umm Salama	120
The Women of Bani Hashim	121
Abdullah Bin Omar	121
The Will	122
Dearting Medina	123
In Mecca	125
The Letters from the Kufans	127
Al-Husayn's Response	128
The Martyr of Kufa	129
Muslim's Trip	129
The Pledge of Allegiance	130
Muslim's Reaction	132
Hani's Reaction	133
Muslim's Uprising	135
Imprisoning Al-Mukhtar	136
Muslim in Tawaa's House	137

Muslim Facing Bin Ziyad	138

Al-Husayn Departing to Iraq — 145
Al-Husayn's Speech in Mecca — 145

Attempts at Convincing Al-Husayn to Stay — 146
Facts behind the Departure — 147

Al-Husayn's Journey — 151
Al-Tan'eem — 151
Al-Ssifaah — 151
Al-Haajir — 153
Ba'adh Al-Uyoun — 153
Al-Khuzaymiyya — 153
Zuroud — 153
Al-Tha'alabiyya — 154
Al-Shuquq — 155
Zubalah — 155
Batn Al-Aqaba — 156
Sharaaf — 156
Al-Baydha — 158
Al-Raheema — 159
Al-Qadisiyya — 159
Al-Uthayb — 160
Qasr Bani Maqatil — 161
The Villages of Al-Taff — 162
Karbala — 164

Al-Husayn and Bin Ziyad — 167

Bin Ziyad's Speech — 169

The Kufans' View of Al-Husayn — 171
The Armies — 172

The Seventh of Muharram — 175
Bin Sa'ad's Arrogance — 176
Bin Sa'ad's Fabrication — 177
Al-Shimr's Tyranny — 178
Invitation to Safety — 179
The Tribe of Banu Assad — 180

The Ninth of Muharram — 183

True Freedom of the Souls — 184
The Eve of Ashura — 186

PART III: THE DAY OF ASHURA

The Tenth of Muharram (Ashura) — 195
- Al-Husayn on the Day of Ashura — 196
- Al-Husayn's Supplication — 197
- Al-Husayn's First Speech — 198
- Bliss and Guidance — 200
- The Speech of Zuhayr Bin Al-Qayn — 201
- Burayr's Speech — 202
- Al-Husayn's Second Speech — 203
- Bin Sa'ad's Aberration — 205
- Al-Hurr's Repentance — 205
- Al-Hurr Advises the Kufans — 206

The Battle of Karbala — 209
- The First Attack — 209
- Fighting in Small Groups — 210
- Appeal and Subsequent Guidance — 210
- Steadfastness of the Right Flank — 211
- Muslim Bin Ausaja — 212
- The Left Wing — 212
- Uzra Requests Reinforcement — 213
- Abu Al-Sha'thaa' — 214
- Noontime — 214
- Habeeb Bin Muthahir — 215
- Al-Hurr Al-Riyahi — 215
- Noon Prayers — 216
- Disabling the Horses — 217
- Abu Thumama — 217
- Zuhayr and Bin Madharib — 217
- Amr Bin Qartha Al-Ansari — 218
- Nafi' Al-Jamali — 218
- Wadhih and Aslam — 219
- Burayr Bin Khudayr — 219
- Hanthala Al-Shabami — 220
- A'abiss — 220
- John — 221
- Anass Al-Kahili — 222
- Amr Bin Janada — 222
- Al-Hajjaj Al-Ja'afi — 222
- Siwar — 223

Suwayd	223

The Martyrdom of the Prophet's Household — 225
Ali Al-Akbar	225
Abdullah Bin Muslim	228
The Raid of Abu Talib's Family	228
Al-Qassim and His Brother	229
Al-Abbass' Brothers	230
Al-Abbass' Martyrdom	230

The Master of Martyrs in the Battlefield — 235
The Nursing Infant	235
The Second Farewell	237
Mohammed Bin Abu Sa'iid	240
Abdullah Bin Al-Hasan	240
The Supplication	241
The Horse	242
Robbing Al-Husayn	243

PART IV: EVENTS AFTER AL-HUSAYN'S MARTYRDOM

The Eleventh Night of Muharram — 249
Visiting Al-Husayn on the Eleventh Night of Muharram	254
Looting	256
The Horses	258
The Heads	258

Leaving Karbala — 263

In Kufa — 267
Zaynab's Speech	267
The Speech of Fatima Bint Al-Husayn	269
Umm Kulthoum's Speech	271
Al-Sajjad's Speech	272
The Burial	273
In The Governor's Palace	276
Bin Afeef	279
Al-Mukhtar Al-Thaqafi	281
Words from the Holy Head	282
Al-Ashdaq's Tyranny	285
Umm Al-Baneen	287
Abdullah Bin Ja'afar	289

Abdullah Bin Abbass	291
The Captives to Syria	297
In Syria	299
Yazeed and Imam Al-Sajjad	301
The Holy Head	304
A Syrian Man and Fatima	305
Zaynab's Speech	306
The Dilapidated Structure	309
To Medina	313
The Head with the Body	317
The Fortieth Day	319
Conclusion on the Signs of the Believer	325
In Medina	329

The Author's Life

The Author

The author of this book descended, through both of his parents, from the seventh infallible leader. He was known as Abd Al-Razzaq Al-Musawi. His great-grandfather was nicknamed "Al-Muqarram." Before then, the author's forefathers were known as "Al-Sa'iidi "family in reference to their great great-grandfather, Sa'iid Bin Thabet. The author was born in Najaf in the year 1316 A.H. (1894 A.D.). His father, Mohammed Bin Al-Sayyed Abbass, spent most of his time worshipping Allah in the great mosque of Kufa. His maternal grandfather, Sayyed Husayn Al-A'alim, looked after him and encouraged him through his early childhood education. Sayyed Husayn Al-A'alim's sudden death took an emotional toll on the author, who was eighteen years of age at the time. Despite the financial difficulties and intense grief, the author continued his studies and excelled in the fields of language, Islamic dogma, and jurisprudence. The author was attached to his father and frequently commended him. His mother was very pious and, in addition to taking care of him, influenced his pursuit of knowledge. The author's paternal uncle, Sayyed Mehdi, was an advocate of justice, and activist against the Ottomans and their oppressive policies. Sayyed Mehdi was eventually captured and hanged in the city of Al-Kut.

The author's maternal and paternal grandfathers and great grandfathers were prominent scholars and respected teachers in Najaf. Many of them had the honor of being the leaders (Imams) of congregational prayers in the Holy Shrines of Najaf and Kufa.

The Author's Teachers

1. His maternal grandfather, Sayyed Husayn (d.1334 A.H. = 1912 A.D.) This pious man looked after the author and navigated

him through the early stages of his studies.
2. Al-Allama Al-Sheykh Mohammed Ridha Al-Kashif Al-Ghita' (d.1366 A.H. = 1942 A.D.), was the author's teacher in the fundamental Islamic principles (Usul).
3. Al-Allama Al-Sheykh Husayn Al-Hilli taught the author Islamic jurisprudence.
4. The highest authority (Marja') in Najaf, Sayyed Muhsin Al-Hakeem (d. 1390 A.H. = 1970 A.D.) was the author's teacher in advanced discussions on jurisprudence.
5. Al-Sheykh Dhi'a Al-Deen Al-Iraqi (d.1361 A.H. = 1936 A.D.) was the author's teacher in matters that pertained to advanced studies in jurisprudence.
6. The highest authority (Marja') in Najaf, Sayyed Abu Al-Hasan Al-Isfahani (d.1365 A.H. = 1941 A.D.) was also the author's teacher in the field of jurisprudence. The author had the exclusive privilege of documenting Al-Isfahani's advanced discussions.
7. Al-Mirza Mohammed Husayn Al-Na'ieni (d.1355 A.H. = 1930 A.D.) was the author's teacher in jurisprudence and fundamental Islamic principles (Usul).
8. The highest authority (Marja') in Najaf, Al-Sayyed Abu, Al-Qassim Al-Kho'ie, was the author's teacher in jurisprudence and fundamental Islamic principles (Usul).
9. Al-Sheykh Mohammed Jawad Al-Balaghi (d.1352 A.H.= 1927 A.D.), an activist and a strong advocate of the infallible leaders' path, was the mentor and the most influential figure in the author's life. The author was, extremely impressed and fond of Sheykh Al-Balaghi's dedication and loyalty to the Prophet's household. The author attended his lectures and developed a close relationship with him. Al-Balaghi's moral character and activism influenced the author immensely. Al-Balaghi's company shaped the motive and goal to which the author dedicated the rest of his life.

THE AUTHOR'S REMARKABLE EDUCATION AND KNOWLEDGE

The author was an intellectual and well read. He earned a

written permission (Ijaza, which is equivalent to a diploma) from all of his teachers. Sitting next to his manuscripts, these permissions entitled him to teach and discuss matters that pertained to the advanced stages of jurisprudence (Ijtihad). Sayyed Abd Al-Razzaq was an exceptional expert in many fields, and could have easily become the highest religious authority (Marja') in Najaf. However, he dedicated his life to writing biographies (Seera) of the Prophet's household and their loyal supporters. It suffices to read some of his published books (many of his books were never published) in order to sense his vast knowledge and exceptional education.

THE AUTHOR'S STYLE

Sayyed Abd Al-Razzaq was very thorough in his investigation of authentic traditions. He was an authority in the field that pertains to the channel of transmission of narrated traditions (Ilm al-Rijal). Furthermore, he examined and intellectually analyzed each tradition prior to reaching a conclusion. He was very critical of historians and scrupulous in purging their work. He vehemently rejected any narration that contradicted logic and basic common sense. He was very clear and straightforward. To the dismay of his contemporaries, he disposed of the conventional poetic, complicated writing style that authors adhered to at the time. He bravely refuted any narration that did not withstand his thorough examination. He was scrupulous in arguing a point or illustrating his view. He adopted a practical approach. He employed simple and clear literature to convey his ideas. His reasoning and writing style were riveting. He intelligently presented his conclusion and successfully convinced his audience. We recommend reading some of his important books, such as Sayyeda Sukayna, Tanzeeh Al-Mukhtar Al-Thaqafi and Naqd Al-Tareekh (Criticizing History) to form a better idea about the author's unique writing style.

THE AUTHOR'S FIRST BOOK

Sayyed Abd Al-Razzaq's first literary work was his commentary on Sheykh Sabti's *Al-Kalem Al-Tayyib*. Soon after, he wrote a book and titled it *Zayd Al-Shaheed*. Shortly after finishing his first book, he wrote another and titled it *Tanzeeh Al-Mukhtar Al-Thaqafi*. It is highly possible that his love for Al-Husayn, in addition to the relevance between the uprising of the Prophet's grandson and that of Al-Mukhtar, compelled him to write a book about the latter (It is important to know that Al-Mukhtar avenged Al-Husayn). Moreover, in his book about Al-Mukhtar, the author corrected the distortions that many historians stated as facts, and successfully argued against the fabrications of the Umayyads and their supporters. This book was published in the early thirties of the twentieth century, when influential scholars, such as Sayyed Abd Al-Razzaq, were shunned for developing any scholastic interest or inclination to any subject matter that was unrelated to jurisprudence. In addition to its academic value, Sayyed Abd Al-Razzaq's second book obliterated the dominant stigma and biased definition of "true scholars." Encouraged by Sayyed Abd Al-Razzaq's brave initiative, renowned scholars broke out of the conventional circle of scholastic inhibition. Sheykh Abd Al-Husayn Al-Amini published his work *Shuhada' Al-Fadheela*, after which Agha Buzurk published his invaluable encyclopedia, *Al-Tharee'a*. It is worth mentioning that the first few volumes of Agha Buzurk's work were printed in Najaf. Sheykh Abbass Al-Qummi published his exquisite work *Al-Kina Wa Al-Alqaab* while Muntada Al-Nashr, a printing press, commented on Sayyed Al-Radhiyy's *Haqa'iq Al-Ta'weel* and published it. These publications were widely welcomed. Before long, the scholastic shackles were irreversibly broken, and the previously mentioned intellectual restrictions permanently vanished.

THIS BOOK (MAQTAL AL-HUSAYN, OR THE MURDER OF AL-HUSAYN)

The magnitude of the catastrophic tragedy of Karbala was immeasurable. In addition to the pain of captivity and exile, the atrocities that were inflicted on the Prophet's household scarred the hearts of their followers. The infallible leaders focused on Al-Husayn's uprising and urged their followers to continuously remember, and remind others, of the atrocities of Ashura and the subsequent plight of the Prophet's family. The details of events before, during, and after the Battle of Karbala invoke feelings of empathy towards the Prophet's household on one hand, and resentment of the criminals on the other. The believers were, and still are, deeply anxious to learn every aspect and component of Al-Husayn's uprising and all of its associated details. Historians documented what they heard about Ashura without any logical examination or scrutiny. Consequently, they stated in their books some unbelievable stories. Some of these historians deliberately distorted the truth. Others, failing to investigate and assess the sources of these stories, inadvertently blurred the true picture of some historical events. The tragedy of Karbala occurred centuries ago, but the agony of the day of Ashura is everlasting. Therefore, it was prudent to annul the distortions and reconstruct the true image of this epic.

Sayyed Abd Al-Razzaq may have felt duty-bound to purge history books in order to unveil the truth. He, in this book, deliberately omitted the fabrications. Moreover, he eloquently argued against any narration that violated common sense or contradicted the teachings of the infallible leaders. For instance, Hameed Bin Muslim witnessed the Battle of Karbala. Historians portrayed Hameed as a kind gentleman, and considered him a trustworthy source of information. Contrary to this common belief, Hameed was an active soldier in Bin Sa'ad's Army. This man fought against the Prophet's household in Karbala, and was one of the men who transported Al-Husyan's head to Damascus. Abu Al-Faraj Al-Isfahani, a historian and an adamant supporter of the Umayyads, relied on the enemies of the Prophet's household as a primary source for his work. In his *Aghani*, Abu Al-Faraj fabricated that Umm Al-Baneen was alive and mourned Al-Husayn in Al-Baqee' cemetery of Medina every day. He also fabricated that Marwan Bin Al-Hakam wept along as he listened to her moans. Abu Al-Faraj was the source of this dominant misconception. His goal in fabricating this story was to gloss up Marwan's immoral and cruel character. Furthermore, Al-Tabari in his history relied on Mujahid and Al-Saddi, both of whom were untrustworthy narrators. In this book, Sayyed Abd Al-Razzaq, in addition to his immaculate analyses, undermined these common misconceptions on one hand, and exquisitely highlighted the truth on the other. He eloquently argued against these fallacies and proved, beyond reasonable doubt, that some of the stories that people have believed over the past centuries were nothing but fabrications.

THE AUTHOR'S WORK PRINTED:
1. Zayd Al-Shaheed
2. Al-Mukhtar Bin Abu Obeyd Al-Thaqafi
3. Al-Sayyeda Sukayna
4. Maqtal Al-Husayn (this book)
5. Al-Siddiqa Al-Zahra'
6. Al-Imam Zayn Al-Abideen
7. Al-Imam Al-Ridha
8. Al-Imam Al-Jawad
9. Qamar Bani Hashim *(Al-Abbass)*
10. Ali Al-Akbar
11. Al-Shaheed Muslim Bin Aqeel
12. Sirr Al-Iman fi Al-Shahada Al-Thalitha
13. Yawm Al-Arba'een I'nd Al-Husayn
14. Al-Muhadharat fi Al-Fiqh Al-Ja'afari

COMMENTARIES AND DISCUSSIONS ON THE FOLLOWING BOOKS:
1. Dala'il Al-Imama (Bin Jareer Al-Tabari)
2. Al-Amali (Al-Sheykh Al-Mufeed)
3. Al-Khasa'is (Al-Sayyed Al-Radhiyy)
4. Al-Malahim (Al-Sayyed Ahmed Bin Tawouss)
5. Farhat Al-Ghariyy (Al-Sayyed Abd Al-Kareem Bin Tawouss)
6. Ithbaat Al-Wassiyya (Al-Mas'oudi)
7. Al-Kashkoul (Al-Sayyed Haydar Bin Ali)
8. Bisharat Al-Mustafa (Imad Al-Deen Al-Ameli)
9. Al-Jamal (Al-Sheykh Al-Mufeed)

MANUSCRIPTS:
1. Al-Munqith Al-Akbar, Mohammed
2. Al-Hasan Bin Ali
3. Ashura fi Al-Islam
4. Al-A'yaad fi Al-Islam
5. Thikra Al-Ma'soumeen
6. Zaynab Al-A'qeela
7. Maytham Al-Tammar

8. Abu Tharr Al-Ghafari
9. Ammar Bin Yasser
10. Naql Al-Amwaat
11. Naqd Al-Tareekh
12. Halq Al-Lihya
13. Dirasaat fi Al-Fiqh wa Al-Tareekh
14. Raba'ib Al-Rassoul
15. Al-Kina wa Al-Alqaab
16. Hashiya ala Al-Kifaya
17. Hashiya ala Al-Makassib
18. Nawadir Al-Aathar
19. Yawm Al-Ghadeer, Hijjat Al-Widaa'

THE AUTHOR'S DEDICATION TO THE CAUSE OF THE PROPHET'S HOUSEHOLD

Nothing in this life rivals, in its significance, the believer's attachment to the Prophet's household. Loving the infallible leaders in this life is the most rewarding asset in the next. The believer should adopt a lifestyle that assures him the intercession of the Prophet's household on the Day of Judgement. Some believers are content with being an audience in the gatherings that commemorate the infallible leaders. Others exhaust their resources and energy to organize such religious events in order to promulgate or defend the true path. Some have embraced the responsibility of maintaining the Holy shrines and providing for the visitors (Zuwwar). It is worth noting that millions of people visit the Holy Sites every year. Visitors travel from all over the world to convey their high regard to the infallible leaders.

The author was born and raised in a house that was a central location for religious ceremonies. He grew up watching his parents and grandparents organize events to commemorate the infallible members of the Prophet's household. Sayyed Abd Al-Razzaq tirelessly maintained the tradition of his family. However, he further contributed to these gatherings by expounding on the moral lifestyle and the impeccable code of ethics of the infallible leaders. The author's house was rarely empty throughout the year. He frequently organized intellectual discussions on many issues that pertained to the true path. These discussions, especially in the Holy nights of Ramadhan, and the lectures in these organized events, enlightened many of his friends and visitors. Sayyed Abd Al-Razzaq was a prolific writer and active advocate of the true path. The numerous books he left behind reflect his strong loyalty to the Prophet's household, and his sincerity in serving them. *Al-Munqith Al-Akbar*, *Al-Hasan Bin Ali* and *Naqd Al-Tareekh* were probably his most significant achievements. During his life, he frequently referred to his book, *Naqd Al-Tareekh*. We supplicate to Allah to enable us to publish these three books in the near future.

THE AUTHOR'S LIFE IN BRIEF

Sayyed Abd Al-Razzaq suffered financial difficulties throughout his life. He intentionally refrained from pursuing any materialistic goal. He embraced the path of righteousness and upheld its values. He renounced the luxuries of this life to ensure himself eternal comfort in the next. Contemporary religious authorities (Maraj'i), such as Sayyed Abu Al-Hasan Al-Isfahani, frequently asked him to become their representative in one of the big cities of Iraq. Despite their insistence, Sayyed Abd Al-Razzaq strongly rejected their offers. He was totally content with the simple life that Allah, the Exalted, ordained for him. He devoted his life to studying and teaching and spent a great deal of his time worshipping (I'tikaf) the Divine. He informed his family and friends of these offers. He explained that accepting any of them entailed being trapped in the luxury of a comfortable life. He often commented that one should be always alert and watchful against being sucked into an endless spiral of desires in this immortal life. This was about all he said about these opportunities, and his subsequent refusal of them. He was very secretive about all the issues that pertained to his personal life.

Regarding his physical appearance, Sayyed Abd Al-Razzaq was very thin with average height. He suffered many physical illnesses at the end of his life, and struggled very hard to maintain his normal and straight posture. He frequently supplicated to Allah in the Holy shrines of the infallible leaders during disasters, illnesses and hardships. Allah, the Generous, answered his supplication and granted his wishes numerously. He occasionally confessed to others that Allah healed him and stretched his life to serve the cause of the Prophet's household. Sayyed Abd Al-Razzaq was very intuitive and always alert. He was vocally critical of any idea that violated logic and basic common sense. He was also intellectually thorough in defending his point of view. Generally, he was very compassionate but tearfully so, upon listening to the crimes and atrocities inflicted on the Prophet's household. He adopted the infallible leaders' path of honor and dignity all of his life until he died on the 17th of Muharram in the year 1391 A.H. (March 15th, 1971). We ask Allah to generously reward him and bestow mercy upon his soul.

(Written by the author's son, Sayyed Mohammed Husayn Al-Muqarram)

Translator's Introduction

This book contains the best compilation of the authentic events that occurred before, during and after the Battle of Karbala. The author thoroughly purged history books and selected the most reliable narrations in order to construct a clear image of Al-Husayn's Holy uprising. Sayyed Abd Al-Razzaq examined each and every narration and strictly rejected whatever contradicted logic and basic common sense.

This book is composed of an exquisite and intellectual introduction, followed by the story of Karbala. In this book, Sayyed Abd Al-Razzaq documented the details that pertained to Ashura sequentially.

Books about Al-Husayn and his uprising are numerous, but none rival this in value and accuracy. After he carefully investigated a wide selection of historic sources, Sayyed Abd Al-Razzaq depicted the tragedy of Karbala and presented it to readers with very little elaboration. The statements and speeches of Al-Husayn, Sayyeda Zaynab, Umm Kulthoum or Imam Zayn Al-Abideen were, of course, eloquent, but contained metaphors and words that were commonly used back then. The Arabic language nowadays is very different than that used fourteen centuries ago. We relied on language books, like *Taj Al-Arous* and *Lissan Al-Arab*, to learn the meaning of many of the statements and speeches in order to accurately translate them into English. We, in both sections of the book (the introduction and the story of Karbala), appropriately incorporated some of the author's footnotes into the text, and added some footnotes of our own. We clearly labeled them to spare the reader any confusion. We also felt that it was essential to elucidate some points or statements to maintain the coherence of an idea or the relevance of a certain incident. We, however, strictly confined our words to parentheses throughout the whole book.

We independently verified most of the quotes and narrated

traditions. The reader should be aware that some of the sources of this book were reprinted and published many times in the past fifty years. The page or, in a rare situation, the volume number of a certain book might be different in the newly printed edition. We fell short from verifying all the narrated traditions, or updating page numbers in the footnotes. Our shortcoming was due to our crippling lack of resources, and because some of the sources on which the author relied were manuscripts. Yet to be published, these manuscripts sit on the shelves of the libraries in Najaf. The author, in the story of Karbala, inserted Arabic poetry between paragraphs. We omitted these poems and their associated linguistic discussions. The author included a large collection of poetry in the end section of his book. We also omitted this whole section. Nevertheless, we translated all of the poetry and the chants of Al-Husayn, his family members, and his companions. We also translated the poetry and chants of Al-Husayn's enemies. All the translated poetry and chants appear as regular statements. We were extremely selective in our omission. The deleted material was mostly linguistic discussions that would have been meaningless upon translation. Omitting this part of the text neither disrupted the author's presentation of events, nor altered the true story of Karbala. Excluding what has been confined to parentheses, this book, from beginning to end, must be entirely attributed to Sayyed Abd Al-Razzaq Al-Musawi Al-Muqarram.

We adopted a liberal style in translating this book in order to maintain the coherence of the presented ideas, and the integrity of the depicted events. We presented samples of our translations to some native English speakers, and based on their feedback, we adopted this liberal style of translation. In doing so, our goal was to preserve the clarity of the author's work. This goal, in addition to the input of native English speakers, delineated our approach. In achieving the desired result, we integrated some paragraphs into others, and placed some ahead of others. We also interchanged some sentences and statements, or relocated discussions and conclusions. In exception to the previously mentioned omissions, we neither added nor deleted a sentence throughout the whole book. A person, who is fluent in both languages, Arabic and English, would have to agree with us that a translator might sometimes be compelled to write a whole English sentence to translate an Arabic word or a term. For instance,

Bismala is a term that can only be translated as *In the name of Allah, the Most Gracious and the Most Merciful*. In contrast, some details of some incidents, mainly in the second section of the book, consumed fewer words in English than they did in Arabic. Moreover, some Arabic words have no perfect match in the English language. *Al-Ghayb* is one of these words. *Al-Ghayb* can be best defined as the realm of existence that lies beyond the senses of average human beings. We chose *the unseen* in translating *Al-Ghayb* because it is the closest match and the most practical word. These are just two of many examples throughout this book. All in all, we accurately and carefully translated the contents of this book.

We independently matched the lunar years in this book with their approximate solar counterparts. We did so to provide the western reader with a more familiar time frame of Ashura, and the relevant discussions of famous scholars throughout the centuries. The author quoted many scholars in this book. In his own discussions, and the scholars' quoted material, there were many verses from the Holy Qur'an. The author or the publisher of the original text did not indicate the number of the verse, or the name of the Surah of the subject verse. We independently located the verses and placed in parentheses the number of the Surah followed by the number of the associated verse. The published Arabic copy of this book had a few printing errors. The publishing press inadvertently misprinted some narrated traditions. We researched these traditions at their sources and corrected the errors.

The translation of this book was an individual effort. This work was completed independently and was published at no allocated budget or sponsorship. The translator, as well as the publisher, widely welcomes any criticism and feedback. You can contact the printing press at any time via electronic or regular mail.

-RLM

PART I:

INTRODUCTION

In the Name of Allah, the Most Gracious and the Most Merciful

"And those who strive on the straight path, We will surely guide them, and Allah is verily on the side of the righteous"
(29:69)

"Do not consider those who were slain on the way of Allah dead, they're alive enjoying the bounties of their Lord. They rejoice in what Allah bestowed upon them and are anxiously awaiting their peers in faith as they experience neither fear nor grief"
(3:169-170)

"Allah has bought the souls and possessions of the believers for the price of paradise; they slay and get slain fighting on the way of Allah, it is a Divine promise in Taurat, Bible and Qur'an, and none will fulfill his promise like Allah, so rejoice over this transaction. It is indeed the greatest bargain"
(9:111)

AL-HUSAYN'S UPRISING

The sole goal in the mind of the Martyr of Faith and the protector of Islam, Al-Husayn Bin Ali, was to abolish the Umayyads' false claims to power. The Master of Martyrs, through his Holy uprising, destroyed the shameful innovations, transgressions and harsh policies that the Umayyads falsely attributed to the Divine path. Al-Husayn rose up and successfully fulfilled his mission. He exposed the moral decadence of Yazeed and his Umayyad entourage. Imam Husayn's strife stimulated the masses. People, from that point on, dreaded the Umayyads, and disputes over the legitimacy of their rule evolved into military conflicts. The driving force of the late revolutions against the Umayyads was sometimes religious and sometimes cultural. The Umayyad rule was eventually destroyed. This achievement can be attributed to Imam Husayn, whose reputation and honor coupled with his uprising paved the way to this victory. *"Do not consider those who were slain on the way of Allah dead, they are alive enjoying the bounties of their Lord (3:169)."*

Dear reader, when you carefully gaze into history, you will definitely see the radiance of Imam Husayn with his Divinely inspired foresight, righteous intentions, and unrivaled self-sacrifice. Al-Husayn adhered to the Divine code of ethics and amicably treaded the true path throughout his life. I don't see a need to expound on Imam Husayn's lifestyle, because I assume that you have heard or learned about his impeccable character and great deeds. You, above all else, will discover how vile and evil his enemy (Yazeed) was. If we exclude our belief that Imam Husayn was the Divinely appointed leader and the most pious Muslim in his time, it will still be quite ridiculous to compare him to his contemporary, the tyrant Yazeed. Al-Husayn was completely aware of Yazeed's incompetence in all aspects of life. The truth is that the Prophet's grandson never intended to sink down to Yazeed's level, let alone compare the tyrant's evil forefathers (Umayyads) to his. It is inconceivable that Al-Husayn would compare the Prophet to Abu Sufyan, Mu'awiya to the Commander of the Faithful (Imam Ali), the cannibal (Hind) to Umm Al-Mu'mineen Khadija, Maysoon (Yazeed's mother) to the Lady of All Women (Fatima Al-Zahra). Al-Husayn would never compare the decadence of pre-Islamic idolatry to the purity of Islam, absolute ignorance to his abundant knowledge, or extreme corruption to his faithfulness and devotion.

It is quite pathetic that some people were, and still are, unable to understand, or recognize, the relation between Allah and His appointees over people. These people were blinded by prejudice, and to defend their unjustified bias, they daringly fabricated traditions and falsely preached that Mohammed, the greatest of all Prophets, approved of the Umayyads' crimes. These ignorant and biased individuals stated, "Al-Husayn was killed by his grandfather's sword because he revolted against his leader (Imam) Yazeed. Yazeed's leadership was not at all controversial. The foremost of the Community (Ummah) endorsed his leadership. Yazeed was a legitimate leader, and there is no evidence that he was unfit or incompetent."[1]

These people uttered this nonsense due to their ignorance of Yazeed's real image. Mu'awiya's son was vile throughout his life. He was nursed and raised by Maysoon Al-Kalbiyya, whose family was famous for its moral decadence.

In his *Majma' Al-Zawai'd (V.5, P.241)*, Bin Hijr narrated that the Prophet said, "An Umayyad man, called Yazeed, will shatter the prevailing peace and justice in my Community." Also, in his *Al-Sawai'q Al-Muhriqa (p.131)*, Bin Hijr narrated that the Prophet said, "An Umayyad man, called Yazeed, will be the first to distort and alter my path." Moreover, the Prophet had cursed Yazeed's father (Mu'awiya)[2] and ordered the Muslim Community (Ummah) to kill him if they ever saw him on the pulpit in Medina[3] Had the Muslims implemented the Prophet's order, they would have avoided most, if not all, of the subsequent atrocities that the Umayyads committed. The Community disobeyed the Prophet and the outcome was a long suffering on the hands of the desire-driven Umayyad tyrants. Ecstatic at presumably becoming the undisputed leader of the Community, Yazeed publicly expressed his malevolent intention and enmity towards Islam and Allah's Messenger.

In his commentary on the Qur'an, *Ruh Al-Ma'ani (V.26, P.73)*, Al-Allama Al-Alloussi wrote:

> "Whoever thinks that Yazeed was not a transgressor, and shouldn't be cursed, is considered a follower of Yazeed. I think that in addition to the crimes he committed, this vicious man never believed in the Prophet's Message. He committed heinous crimes against the inhabitants of Allah's sanctuary (Mecca), the Prophet's sanctuary (Medina), and the pure members of the Prophet's family during their lives and after their death. He threw a piece of the Holy Qur'an in filth. The Muslims were aware of all this, but they were brutally smothered and could do nothing but persevere. If we ever think that this evil man was a Muslim, then his great sins are beyond being inscribed or described. I think that people of his caliber, even though difficult to find, deserve the wrath of Allah, since the possibility that he repented is very low and the possibility that he ever was a believer is even lower.
>
> Bin Ziyad, Bin Sa'ad and their followers can be added to the same category. We ask Allah, the Exalted, to condemn all of them until the Day of Judgement, and for as long as eyes shed tears on Abu Abdullah Al-Husayn. When asked about cursing Yazeed, Abdul Baqi Afandi, a famous poet, answered, "Yazeed receives as many curses as time allows me to unload."
>
> Whoever is reluctant to curse such a criminal, can generally ask Allah to condemn those who were pleased with the killing of Imam Husayn, and those who unjustifiably hurt the Holy Prophet's family and usurped their rights. Yazeed would definitely fit in this category, and no one disagrees with this except the previously mentioned Bin Al-Arabi and his peers. These extremists disallow cursing the people who were pleased with the killing of Imam Husayn. Such an opinion leads its holder to transgression no less detrimental than that of Yazeed's."

After stating the above, Al-Alloussi quoted from Al-Barzanji's *Al-Isha'aa* and Al-Haythami's *Al-Sawa'iq* that when Abdullah asked his father about cursing Yazeed, Imam Ahmed Bin Hanbal replied, "How could we not curse someone Allah had already cursed in His

Holy book?" Perplexed at his father's response, Abdullah commented, "I read the Holy book and never found Yazeed being cursed in it." Imam Ahmed explained, "Allah says in His Qur'an that *it is not expected of you when you're in charge to spread corruption and cut ties with your relatives, Allah had cursed such people (47:22-23)*. There can be no greater corruption and cutting ties with relatives than what Yazeed did."

Al-Alloussi continued:

> "A group of scholars, like Al-Qadhi Abu Ya'ala and Al-Hafez Bin Al-Jawzi, stated that Yazeed was an atheist or an idolater, and both scholars publicly cursed him. Al-Taftazani ruled him as a non-believer and asked Allah to curse him and condemn his followers and supporters. Al-Suyuti had also expressed a similar opinion."

Al-Alloussi then quoted from Al-Wardi's *History* and Al-Safadi's *Al-Wafi Bi Al-Wafiyyat* that Yazeed anxiously waited on his balcony in Jeeron to watch the Prophet's grand-daughters in the caravan of captives. As Al-Husayn's family and children, and the martyrs' heads atop the spears, appeared in the horizon, a crow screamed. Responding to the crow, Yazeed said, "When the caravan appeared and the heads radiated towards Jeeron, a crow yelled. I told the crow that yelling is pointless, because I have avenged from the Prophet." Al-Alloussi commented that in this statement (poetry in Arabic), Yazeed marked the day he avenged his Umayyad forefathers, like Utbah and Al-Waleed, who were killed fighting against the Muslims in the Battle of Badr. Al-Alloussi added that, in addition to expressing his vindication towards the Prophet, Yazeed further asserted his idolatrous and atheistic beliefs. Mu'awiya's son joyously quoted the poetry that Bin Al-Zaba'ari uttered after the Battle of Uhud. Yazeed said, "I wish my leaders who were killed in Badr could see us cheering our victory today." Considering all of this, and much more, Yazeed deserves the wrath of Allah, His Messenger, His Angels and all the believers to rain down upon him until the Day of Judgement. People who think otherwise are prejudiced and thus blind to distinguish between right and wrong.

Other scholars have also emphasized that Yazeed was a non-believer and an atheist. Bin Khaldoun in his *Muqaddima (P. 254 &255)* stated:

"Bin Al-Arabi Al-Maliki was totally wrong to state that Al-Husayn was justifiably killed. Bin Al-Arabi ignored the fact that the leader of the Muslim Community must be just, and no one at the time could have been more just and qualified to fight the transgressors than Imam Husayn. There was a consensus in the Community (Ummah) that Yazeed was a transgressor, and therefore unfit to be the leader. For this reason Imam Husayn felt duty-bound to rise up against Yazeed. The Prophet's companions and their junior compatriots (Tabi'een) remained neutral to avoid bloodshed. However, their neutrality was by no means a tactic to undermine the legitimacy of Al-Husayn's uprising. Their inaction was never an encouragement to others to support Yazeed in killing Imam Husayn. Murdering Al-Husayn proves that Yazeed was an abominable transgressor, while the Prophet's grandson was a blessed Martyr."

In his *Furu' (V3, P.548)*, Bin Muflih Al-Hanbali wrote:

"Based on Imam Husayn's action against Yazeed, Bin Aqeel and Bin Al-Jawzi approved rising up for reform against an unjust ruler. Bin Al-Jawzi, in his *Al-Ssir Al-Masoon*, belittled the people who believe that Yazeed was right and Imam Husayn was wrong. Bin Al-Jawzi attributed this belief to extremists who claimed to be from the mainstream Sunni sect. He stated that had these extremists looked carefully into history, they would have understood how Yazeed was selected, and how he forced people to pledge allegiance to him. After he held power, Yazeed destroyed the Ka'aba with cannons, looted Medina, killed Imam Husayn and his family, carried his head on a spear and repeatedly hit it with a stick in public. If we assume that Yazeed's leadership was legitimate at the time of his selection, then his actions would have been a good enough reason for people to renounce the pledge of allegiance they'd given him. People who propagate that Yazeed was just are ignorant, and their goal in articulating such a belief is to anger the Opponents (Shi'as)."

In his *Sharh Al-A'qa'id Al-Nassfiyya (P.181)*, Al-Taftazani wrote:

"Yazeed's pleasure in killing Imam Husayn and insulting the family of the Holy Prophet, even though the details of these events are somehow sketchy, are compelling enough a reason to rule him as an infidel. I ask Allah to condemn him along with his followers and supporters."

In his *Muhalla (V.11, P.98)*, Bin Hazm wrote:

"Yazeed only sought worldly gains. His actions were totally oppressive and can never be justified."

In his *Nayl Al-Awtar (V.7, P.147)*, Al-Shawkani wrote:

"Some have gone totally astray, and said that Al-Husayn, may Allah be pleased with him, unjustifiably rose up against Yazeed Bin Mu'awiya, may Allah curse both of them. The ignorance behind such statements is unbelievable. Yazeed was an alcoholic and a transgressor who violated every code of Islamic jurisprudence."

In his *Rasa'il (P.298)*, Al-Jahez wrote:

"Yazeed committed many heinous crimes. He killed Al-Husayn, dragged the Prophet's daughters as captives, struck Al-Husayn's face with a stick, terrorized the people of Medina and destroyed the Ka'aba. Yazeed was an apostate and a hypocrite, and these crimes indicate how cruel, ruthless, and wicked he was. The transgressor should be cursed. Whoever forbids to curse him should be cursed too."

In his *Al-Seera Al-Halabiyya,* Al-Burhan Al-Halabi

"Emulating his father, Sheykh Bakri cursed Yazeed and always asked Allah to chastise him in the worst pits of hellfire."

Al-Kayahrasi cursed Yazeed, and said, "Yazeed's moral decadence is indescribable."[4] Quoting Al-Kayahrasi's description of Yazeed, Bin Al-Imad, in his *Shatharat Al-Thahab (V.3, P.179)*, wrote:

"The man is not considered a companion of the Prophet because he was born during the time of Omar Bin Al-Khattab. Ahmad, Abu Hanifa and Malik were sometimes straightforward and others vague in describing Yazeed, however, I am always straightforward. The transgressor was a gambler and an alcoholic. His poetry describing his passion for intoxicants is known to everyone."

In his *Tareekh Al-Islam (P. 270)*, Dr. Ali Ibraheem Hasan wrote:

"Yazeed was famous for his alcohol consumption, messing around and wasting time in hunting expeditions."

Al-Thahabi, in his *Sayr A'alam Al-Nubala,* wrote:

"Yazeed Bin Mu'awiya was an enemy of the Prophet and his household (Nassibiyy). He was an evil transgressor and an alcoholic. He started his reign with killing Imam Husayn, and ended it with the Battle of Al-Harra (in which Medina was looted and thousands of its inhabitants were slaughtered). People hated him and he was condemned throughout his short life."

In his Commentary on the Qur'an, *Al-Manar (V.1, P.367)*, Sheykh Mohammed Abdu wrote:

"If there is a just government abiding by the Divine codes, and an unjust one breaking them, then it is a duty upon every Muslim to support the first. This was Imam Husayn's motive when he rose up against Yazeed Bin Mu'awiya, the tyrant who forcefully and unjustly became the leader of the Muslims. I ask Allah to chastise him along with those who hated the Prophet and his household."

In his *Al-Nujoum Al-Zahira (V.1, P.16 3)*, Bin Tagherbardi Al-Hanafi wrote:

"Yazeed was a transgressor and an alcoholic."

In the same book *(V.6, P.134)*, he added:

"Scholars ordered Omar Al-Qazweeni expelled from Baghdad for referring to Yazeed as the commander of the faithful."

In his Rijal Al-Qarnayn (P.6), Abu Shama wrote:

"While in Baghdad, people asked Ahmad Al-Qazweeni to curse Yazeed on the day of Ashura. He refused, and added that Yazeed was a just leader (Imam). A person immediately hit him. He fell off the pulpit and almost died. Later on, he was expelled to Qazween where he died in the year 590 A.H. (1194 C.E)."

Sibt Bin Al-Jawzi said, "When asked about cursing Yazeed, Bin Al-Jawzi said that Imam Ahmed allowed it. We, on the other hand, don't like Yazeed because of what he did to our Prophet's grandson. He captured and dragged his family on camels to Syria. If saying we don't like him is not enough, then we curse him as Imam Ahmed did."[5] Quoting Omar Bin Al-Dhahhak, Abu Al-Qassim Al-Zujaji narrated, "Yazeed Bin Mu'awiya befriended a monkey. He saddled it on a zebra and had it race with horses. The zebra died and Yazeed lamented the loss in his poetry."[6]

Bin Al-Atheer narrated from Abu Ya'ala who in turn narrated that Imam Zayn Al-Abideen said, "I don't say that Yazeed was an infidel, because the Prophet asked Allah to empower only a family member over his family, and Allah granted him his wish."[7] (This tradition implies that Yazeed and Al-Husayn were both from Quraysh, and thus relatives. It also implies that the Prophet expressed his contentment with the alleged family feud and the subsequent bloodshed). Abu Ya'ala was honorable and trustworthy, and I find it difficult that a prominent scholar like him would narrate such a fabrication. Al-Rafi'e narrated this tradition when he wrote about the scholars of Qazween.[8] If we assume that Imam Zayn Al-Abideen said this, then it should definitely be a precautionary dissimulation statement (Taqiyya). Most of the respected scholars, like Sheykh Al-Sadouq, praised Abu Ya'ala. Also, Sheykh Abdullah Afandi, Al-Majlisi's student, ferociously defended Abu Ya'ala.[9] Al-Khateeb Al-Baghdadi, as prejudiced as he was, edited Abu Ya'ala's work and intentionally ignored this tradition.[10] Therefore, it is fair to conclude that Al-Rafi'e and Bin Al-Atheer fabricated this narration and attributed it to Abu Ya'ala.

After viewing these great scholars' opinions of Yazeed, we turn the table on Abdul Mugheeth Bin Zuhair Bin Alawi Al-Harbi, and question the sources of his book *Yazeed's Merits*.[11] When and where was a single merit in Yazeed to be documented? Was his life anything but a sham? Did he not break every code of Islamic Jurisprudence? Scholars ridiculed this book. In his *Shatharat Al-Thahab*, under the events of 583 A.H. (1187 C.E.), Bin Al-Imad stated that the book is full of fabrications. Bin Katheer in his *Bidaya* stated that

Bin Al-Jawzi eloquently argued against it. Bin Al-Atheer in his *Kamel*, and Al-Mas'oudi in his *Muruj Al-Thahab* stated that the book is full of lies. Bin Rajah in his *Tabaqat Al-Hanabila* stated that Bin Al-Jawzi wrote a book and titled it *Response to the Prejudice, The Wicked Who Forbids Cursing Yazeed* in response to Al-Barbi's book.

When asked about Yazeed, Abdul Ghani Al-Maqdissi's answer was quite disturbing. He said, "Yazeed's leadership was legitimate, since sixty companions of the Prophet pledged allegiance to him. Those who do not like him shouldn't condemn him just because he wasn't a Prophet's companion (Sahabiyy). We forbid cursing him because we're afraid that people will extend the curse to his father, and we do need to shut the door of sectarianism (Fitna)."[12] More disturbing was Bin Hijr Al-Haythami's rejection of Yazeed's approval or involvement in killing Imam Husayn. Bin Hijr, blinded by prejudice, ignored the consensus amongst the scholars on Yazeed's overt joy for killing Al-Husayn.[13] Bin Jareer and Al-Suyuti asserted that Yazeed was very happy, and rewarded Bin Ziyad for killing Al-Husayn, but later regretted it.[14] Furthermore, Al-Khawarizmi narrated that Yazeed told Al-Nu'maan Bin Basheer, "I thank Allah because He killed Al-Husayn."[15]

People who denied Yazeed's approval of killing Al-Husayn aimed to cover up facts in order to protect Yazeed the way they protected his father. It is evident that Mu'awiya was extremely firm in his enmity towards Allah's Messenger. When Abu Sufyan fearfully became a Muslim, Mu'awiya told him, "Sakhr (Abu Sufyan)! Do not become a Muslim and thus disgrace us. Keep in mind the men we lost in Badr. If you reject (Islam), we shall too. Do not quit worshipping Allat and Al-Uzza (names of two idols)."[16] In his commentary on Nahj Al-Balagha (V.1, P.463), Bin Abi Al-Hadeed wrote:

> "So many scholars were suspicious of Mu'awiya's faith. They construed, from his words and statements, that he was an atheist who never believed in the Prophet's Message."

Yazeed's grandfather, Sakhr (Abu Sufyan), told Al-Abbass on the Day of Victory (the day the Muslims liberated Mecca from the idolaters), "This is a kingship." Al-Abbass replied, "You are doomed! This is Prophethood."[17] Al-Bayhaqi narrated, "During the Prophet's life, Mu'awiya became a hypocrite after being an infidel. However, he reclaimed his infidel beliefs later on."[18]

Maysoon's son (Yazeed) was a vile extension of his Umayyad forefathers. He was a loser and too incompetent a leader (Khalifa). The Muslim Community, at the time, enjoyed Al-Husayn's blissful presence in its ranks. The Community knew that Al-Husayn's status was equivalent to that of the Qur'an. They knew that Al-Husayn was the Prophet's sweetheart and the Master of Youth in Heaven. People also knew Al-Husayn's father, Ali Bin Abu Talib, and his insurmountable sacrifices on the way of Allah. They knew that his mother was the Lady of All Women, and that he was the fifth member of the cloak (Al-Kissa).

Imam Husayn, the Divinely appointed guardian of the Community (Ummah), possessed an unrivaled knowledge, and a great moral character. The Prophet's grandson occasionally articulated the superior qualities Allah had instilled in him. When Al-Waleed, the governor of Medina, asked him to pledge allegiance to Yazeed, Imam Husayn said, "We are the members of the Prophet's household, the core of this Message, the congregational medium of angels. Allah started (creation) with us and shall seal it all with us. Yazeed is a shameless transgressor, an alcoholic and a murderer. A man of my rank can never pledge allegiance to someone like him."[19]

Let us now respond to the clueless individual who said, "Al-Husayn rose up after Yazeed had already been selected." How did this selection happen, and when did the foremost of the Community agree to it? The truth is that Mu'awiya terrorized some, and bribed others, to accept it.[20] Yazeed's subordinates coerced people to accept his leadership, but Imam Husayn and the Hashimites adamantly rejected it. Bin Al-Zubayr escaped from Medina to Mecca, while Bin Umar hid in his house, to avoid the pressure.[21]

Voicing his objection to Yazeed's leadership, Abdurrahman Bin Abu Bakr publicly said, "It has become a Roman style leadership, in which a Hercules takes over after another."[22]

He also said, "Having a leader has become like having a Caesar.[23] Mu'awiya sent Abdurrahman one hundred thousand Dirhams to buy his silence. He sent it back and said, "I shall never sell my faith in favor of this life."[24]

A'abiss Bin Sa'iid urged Abdullah Bin Amr Bin Al-A'as to accept Yazeed's leadership. Abdullah told A'abiss, "I know Yazeed very well. You have favored this life and given up your faith."[25] Marwan Bin Al-Hakam sent a person from Al-Sham to Sa'iid Al-Adawi, urging him to accept Yazeed. Sa'iid exclaimed, "How dare Marwan ask me to pledge allegiance to people (Umayyads) I fought to become Muslims? By Allah! They never accepted Islam, but were forced to."[26]

Ziyad Bin Abeeh told Obeyd Bin Ka'ab Al-Numayri, "Mu'awiya asked me to propagate Yazeed's leadership. Looking after Islam is a great responsibility. I believe that Yazeed is careless, ruthless and hunting is his only passion in life. Convey my concerns, and remind Mu'awiya of Yazeed's indecency and faithlessness."[27]

Sa'iid Bin Othman Bin Affan condemned the choice, and wrote Mu'awiya the following: "My father is better than Yazeed's, my mother is better than his and I am better than him."[28]

Al-Ahnaf Bin Qays condemned the choice, and wrote to Mu'awiya that Yazeed could not become the leader because the righteous and popular Al-Hasan and Al-Husayn were by far more qualified for such a position. He also reminded Mu'awiya of the conditions of his truce with Al-Hasan, and of the clause stating that no one shall be placed ahead of the Prophet's grandson for the position of leadership (Khilafa). Al-Ahnaf warned Mu'awiya that the people of Iraq never disliked Al-Hasan and Al-Husayn, but instead their hearts were still attached to them, and resentful of Mu'awiya.[29]

The Master of Martyrs reminded Mu'awiya of Yazeed's abominable lifestyle, and advised him against choosing his son to succeed him. Al-Husayn also asserted his superiority to Yazeed in all aspects of life. Al-Husayn wrote Mu'awiya: "My mother is better than his, and my father is better than his." Mu'awiya replied: "Your mother is the Prophet's daughter, and she is undeniably better than a woman from the tribe of Kalb, however, my love for Yazeed is priceless. Your father and his, on the other hand, accepted Allah's judgement (in Siffeen), and the outcome was in his father's favor, not yours."[30] Realizing that it was useless to reason with the son of Hind, the cannibal (Hind, Mu'awiya's mother, chewed Hamza's liver after the Battle of Uhud), Imam Husayn ended the dialogue at this point. Mu'awiya tactfully avoided comparing himself directly to Ali, because everyone was familiar with the latter's dedication and devotion. Nevertheless, Mu'awiya inserted the judgement event (of Siffeen) in his letter as a diversion. Linguists call this method of distortion "gradual entrapment."

In another correspondence, Imam Husayn wrote Mu'awiya: "You propose Yazeed as if he is the perfect person to lead Mohammed's Community. You are so deceitful! You mention Yazeed as if you're describing an unknown, or promoting an underdog. Yazeed has already told us about himself. His only merit is his passion for jewelry-decorated wild dogs, racing pigeons, dancing maids and musical instruments. Drop your scheme, and don't be accountable for more than what you've already done. You've always promoted transgression through oppression, and hatred through repression. Soon you'll die and be with your well documented deeds to be witnessed in an eventful day (Day of Judgement)."[31]

Imam Husayn wrote Mu'awiya a third time: "You should know that Allah documents every minor or major act of yours in His book. The Exalted never forgets that you prosecuted people on suspicion, and executed or sent into exile some of His guardians on baseless accusations. Didn't you murder Hijr, the brother of Kinda, and the devoted worshippers who condemned oppression, rejected innovation and feared nothing on the way of Allah? Didn't you murder Amr Bin Al-Hamaq, the Prophet's companion, who became so emaciated and pale from devoutly serving Allah? You murdered him after you falsely pledged to grant him safety. Don't think lightly of violating such a pledge, with which a flying bird would have felt safe enough to land on your hand. You're too bold in breaking the Divine rules. Didn't you adjoin the newborn (Ziyad) of Thaqeef's servant to your family, after claiming that he was your father's son? The Prophet said that an infant belongs to the household in which he was born, while the adulterer gets the stone. You, devoid of any guidance from Allah, intentionally ignored the Prophet's teachings to serve your own interest. You then appointed him (Ziyad) in Iraq to torture, cut off limbs, poke eyes and crucify the Muslims. You act as if you were a bitter enemy to this Community (Ummah). Didn't you order Ziyad to kill the followers of Ali Bin Abi Talib? Ziyad implemented your orders. He killed them and mutilated their bodies. Ali was a firm believer in Allah's Message. Ali fought you and your father to propagate this religion; the very same religion you used to assume your current position (Khaleefa). You are propagating the leadership of your immature, alcoholic and dog-loving son Yazeed. You have squandered your life and your faith. You have betrayed the entrustment."[32]

When Ziyad Bin Abeeh killed Muslim Bin Zaymar and Abdullah Bin Najiyy Al-Hadhrami, both of whom were Ali's followers, and hung them for days on their own doorsteps in Kufa, Imam Husayn wrote Mu'awiya again to condemn such atrocities.

Al-Husayn wrote: "Didn't you order Ziyad to kill Hijr and the two Hadhrami men because they were Imam Ali's followers? You ordered him to kill the people who adhere to the religion of Ali and his cousin (the Prophet). It is the same religion for which Ali fought you and your father. You, in the name of this religion, became what you are; otherwise your highest honor would have remained confined to the two trips (Surah 106). Nonetheless, Allah relieved you from this burden because of us." This is only an excerpt of a long letter in which Imam Husayn condemned Mu'awiya for adjoining and appointing Ziyad to govern Iraq.[33] Terrorism and greed had sealed Mu'awiya's heart, and Al-Husayn's advice never found a way to it. Mu'awiya was a ruthless schemer. He knew that it was politically inappropriate and self-destructive to hurt Al-Husayn physically, and that the outcome of such an act could provoke instability and factionalism. He also knew that Al-Husayn would never compromise any of his principles at any cost.

The followers of the Prophet's household had already witnessed and experienced the crimes that the Umayyad governors, (Mu'awiya's appointees), committed. Mu'awiya was quite aware that Al-Husayn's followers, having suffered under the Umayyad reign of terror, were not as complacent as they had been during Al-Hasan's life. The situation at that time was extremely difficult, to the extent that a man would prefer being accused of fire worshipping (Zindeeq) rather than being called Turabi (Ali's follower). Despite their trust in him and their knowledge that the truce he signed was Divinely ordained to spare bloodshed, Imam Al-Hasan's followers often verbally abused the infallible leader for putting up with Mu'awiya's violations. These people, anxious to wage war against Mu'awiya, often urged Imam Husayn (after his brother's martyrdom) to rise up, but he did not, in observance of the truce conditions. Al-Husayn refused to initiate any action before the specified time his grandfather and father had foretold.

Mu'awiya knew that if Al-Husayn were hurt under these circumstances, the followers of the Prophet's household would gather around him, and the rivalry between the two would eventually escalate into a military confrontation. In his will, Mu'awiya urged Yazeed to seek peaceful channels, no matter how firm Al-Husayn was in his opposition. Mu'awiya told Yazeed, "The people of Iraq will urge Al-Husayn to rise up against you. If he did, and you were victorious, honor his superior status and let him go free because of his kinship to the Prophet (Rahiman Massa)."[34] Yazeed was conceited and incredibly ruthless. He did not heed his father's instructions.

The so-called victory backfired on Yazeed, and invoked his own demise soon after the Battle of Karbala. People, including non-Muslims, cursed and condemned the Umayyad tyrant for his savagery and brutality.

The dialogue between the Roman emperor's messenger and Yazeed shook up the forum in which the latter repeatedly struck Al-Husayn's face with a stick. At that point, Yazeed realized that he could no longer deceive people and distort facts. How could he, after the attendants of that forum heard Imam Husayn's head speaking loudly? When Yazeed ordered the execution of the Roman emperor's messenger, Imam Husayn's head loudly uttered, "There is no power and strength except that from Allah (La Hawla Wala Quwwata Illa Billah)."[35] No one until that time had heard such eloquence from a human head that had been separated from its body. Could Maysoon's son (Yazeed) halt Allah's Power or overshadow the Divine radiance? Yazeed's entourage and women protested his actions. His wife Hind saw Al-Husayn's head radiating light from her doorstep to the skies. Blood dripped from the head and its fragrance filled the air.[36] Unveiled, she hysterically stormed into the main assembly and screamed, "How could you hang the head of the Prophet's grandson on my doorstep?" Yazeed covered her and urged her to weep on Al-Husayn. He told her, "Bani Hashim are bereaved for him. Bin Ziyad hastily killed him."[37]

Attempting to camouflage the truth, Yazeed accused his governor of acting independently. He unsuccessfully tried his best to distance himself from the crime. Historical evidence proves that he was directly responsible for the murder. Historians mentioned an attachment to the letter he sent to Al-Waleed Bin Utba, his governor in Medina. In the letter, he ordered Al-Waleed to acquire a pledge of allegiance from the people of Medina. In the attachment, Yazeed wrote: "Be extremely harsh with Al-Husayn. Shall he refuse, behead him and send his head to me."[38] Yazeed forced the people into accepting his leader ship because he was aware that the foremost of the Community were adamantly opposed to it.

Yazeed also knew that the few who had complied did so under pressure and threats during Mu'awiya's reign. The attachment to the letter was a preemptive tactic, in case the Umayyad governor killed Al-Husayn. Yazeed could then claim that he had nothing to do with the crime, because the main letter didn't include such a daring order. Yazeed schemed to assure himself a safe way out and a venue of excuses. All along he planned to use his governor as a scapegoat for his crime. Some historians were indeed deceived by this scheme.

Notes & References

1. Al-A'wassim (P.232)
2. Tareekh Al-Tabari (V.11, P.357); Tareekh Abu Al-Fida (V.2, P.57); Siffeen (P.247); Tathkirat Al-Khawass (P.115)
3. Tareekh Baghdad (V.12, P357); Tahtheeb Al-Tahtheeb (V.2, P.248 & V.5, P.110); Tareekh Al-Tabari (V.11, P.357); Siffeen (P. 243 & 248); Al-La'ali al-Masnou'a (V. l, P.320); Mizan Al-I'tidal (V.1, P.268); Sayr A'laam Al-Nubala' (V.2, P.99); Tareekh Abu Al-Fida (V.2, P.57).
4. Wafiyyat Al-A'yaan (Biography of al-Kayahrasi); Mar'at Al-Janan (V.3, P.179).
5. Mar'at Al-Zaman (V.8, P.496)
6. Amali Al-Zujaji (P.45)
7. Al-Kamil (V.4, P.51)
8. Al-Tadween Fi Ulama' Qazween (V.2, P.184)
9. Riyadh Al-Ulama' (handwritten copy in al-Hakeem's Library in Najaf)
10. Tareekh Baghdad (V.8, P.184)
11. Tabaqat Al-Hanabila (V.1, P.356)
12. Tabaqat Al-Hanabila (V.2, P.34)
13. Al-Fatawa Al-Hadeethiyya (P.193)
14. Tareekh Al-Tabari (V.7, P.19) & Tareekh Al-Khulafa' (V.1, P.139)
15. Maqtal Al-Khawarizmi (V.2, P.59)
16. Tathkirat Al-Khawass (P.115) & Al-Ta'ajjub (P.39)
17. Al-Kamel (V.2, P.93) & Tareekh Al-Tabari (V.3, P.117)
18. Hadiyyat Al-Ahbaab (P.111)

19. Al-Luhuf
20. Tareekh al-Tabari (V.6, P.135)
21. Tareekh al-Tabari (V.6, P.170)
22. Al-Kamel (V.3, P.199) & Al-Fa'iq (V.2, P.203)
23. Salas Al-Ghaniyat (P.41)
24. Tahtheeb Al-Asma' (V.1, P.294)
25. Al-Qudhat (P.310)
26. Tahtheeb Tareekh Bin Asakir (V.6, P.128)
27. Tareekh Al-Tabari (V.6, P.169)
28. Nawadir Al-Makhtoutat (P.165)
29. Al-Imama Wa Al-Siyasa (V.1, P.141)
30. Al-Mathal Al-Sa'ir (V.1, P.71)
31. Al-Imama Wa Al-Siyasa (V.1, P.154)
32. Rijal Al-Kashshi (P.32)
33. Al-Mihbar (P.479)
34. Tareekh Al-Tabari (V.6, P.179)
35. Maqtal Al-Awalim (P.150)
36. Al-Khatat (V.3, P.284)
37. Tareekh Al-Tabari (V.6, P.267)
38. Tareekh Al-Tabari (V.6, P.188)

The Prophets and Al-Husayn

Imam Husayn's martyrdom was a Divine secret. The story of his martyrdom was an entrustment that was handed down to the Prophets. His self-sacrifice was the Prophets' daily talk, and a frequent discussion amongst their vicegerents. The Prophets' mission was to pave the way and train the people to accept the seal and the last of all Messages. Allah informed them that Al-Husayn, a bliss for all creatures, has unrivaled significance because his uprising would preserve the seal of all the Divine Messages. The Prophets were deeply touched by this painful tragedy. The Benevolent consoled their hearts, and rewarded them for mourning and weeping on Al-Husayn.

Prophet Adam, Al-Khalil (Prophet Ibraheem), and Prophet Musa wept on Al-Husayn. Prophet Isa wept and ordered the Israelis of his time to curse the murderer who kills Al-Husayn. He urged them to join Al-Husayn's uprising if they happened to be living at the time. Prophet Isa said, "Being martyred with Al-Husayn is equivalent to being martyred with the Prophets." He continued, "I look at his spot (Karbala), and I see that all the Prophets have visited it. I see a blessed piece of land in which the brightest light of guidance will be buried."[1] Assured that the awaited infallible leader shall avenge him, Prophet Isma'eel, the truthful (Sadiq Al-Wa'd), accepted Al-Husayn as his role model.[2] Prophet Yahya embraced Al-Husayn's path, and chose that his head be shown around in public.

Long before Al-Husayn's birth, Prophet Mohammed wept for his grandson's martyrdom.[3] One can only imagine the Prophet's reaction, had he seen the radiant faces of Al-Husayn and his family members as they lay slaughtered in Karbala after they were deprived of what is normally offered to animals, water. Prophet Mohammed did witness these atrocities, which touched the heavens. He saw his beloved grandson in such a wretched condition, and watched the murderers trying to eradicate his family from the face of the earth.

Some of the people who witnessed the battle saw the Prophet staring at Karbala for a moment, and gazing into the sky another. These people described that the look on the Prophet's face expressed complete submission to Allah's Will.[4]

Imam Ali rested in Karbala on his way to Siffeen. He pointed with his hand to a piece of land, and said, "Here is their encampment after a long journey." He then pointed to another piece of land and said, "Here is where their blood will be spilled. Loved ones from Mohammed's household will end up here." He continued exclaiming, "What a piece of land! A group of people will be resurrected immediately to paradise from this land."[5] He then wept and so did his companions. He later informed his intimate associates that his son Husayn would be murdered along with his family and companions on this piece of land, and that they are the Masters of Martyrs of all times.[6]

In another narration, after he pointed to the land in which Mohammed's family would be murdered, Imam Ali said, "Earth and heaven will shed tears on them."[7] He continued, "I weep on the one who has no supporter except Allah."[8] He also said, "The Umayyads will maintain their transgression until they spill the Holy blood in the Holy month. I see a man from Quraysh, unjustifiably slaughtered and drenched in his blood. Once they do it (kill Al-Husayn), their kingdom will be destroyed."[9]

While in Karbala, on his way to Al-Mada'in, Salman Al-Farisi said, "Here is where they will rest and get slaughtered. The son of the best man ever will be murdered on this piece of land."[10] Prophet Isa passed through Karbala. While there, a deer told him, "We're grazing and sniffing the dust on which the blessed son of Prophet Ahmed will be martyred. We feel very secure in this land." Isa sniffed its stools and supplicated, "Oh Allah! Preserve it and console Al-Husayn's father when he smells it." When Imam Ali arrived to Karbala he smelled it and wept. He gave some to Bin Abbass to keep. He told him, "This will turn into blood when Al-Husayn is martyred." In the afternoon of the day of Ashura, Bin Abbass saw it bubbling with blood.[11]

Notes & References

1. Kamel Al-Ziyarat (P.67)
2. Kamel Al-Ziyarat (P.65)
3. Al-Khasa'is Al-Kubra (V.2, P.125) & Majma' Al-Zawa'id (V.9, P.188)
4. Kamel Al-Ziyarat
5. Siffeen (Ps. 157 & 159)
6. Kamel Al-Ziyarat (P.27)
7. Dala'il Al-Nubuwwa (V.3, P.211)
8. Ussud Al-Ghaba (V.4, P.169)
9. Sharh Al-Nahj (V.4, P.363)
10. Rijal Al-Kashshi (P.13)
11. Ikmal Al-Deen (P.295)

Self-Sacrifice

Introduction

Human societies, subject to corruption and wrongdoing, are always in need of a reformer whose main goal is improving the condition of his society. This reformer must be able to identify arising problems and prescribe the solutions that would restore law and order. In the absence of a reformer, the Community (Ummah) is bound to plunge into disputes and rivalries; criminals would fear no one, trust would be lost, and humans would become victims of greed.

Allah knows best the purity of the souls He created, and He accordingly selects the fittest for this task. The selected character must be highly remarkable for its rejection of oppression, and of all forms of wrongdoing which displease the Lord of the Worlds. The reformer (in this discussion) must be infallible, and spiritually above and beyond the sins and violations that common people commit on a regular basis. If this reformer were fallible, he would be incapable of guiding people, demonstrating righteousness and identifying wrongdoing. As a result, the social condition would deteriorate, and the Community would further drown in its problems.

Allah created the soul of our great Prophet from His light, and blessed him with a perfect character. Prophet Mohammed is undeniably superior to all of Allah's creatures. The Prophet, in addition to acquiring the utmost blessing of receiving the Divine Revelation, was a manifestation of the Divine Ethics. One can never fully describe the Prophet's superb character, however we can reflect on the depth of the following tradition (Hadeeth), in which the Prophet described himself. He told Imam Ali, "No one really knows Allah except me and you, no one really knows me except Allah and you, and no one really knows you except Allah and me."[1]

The Prophet was a human and thus mortal. Much of his preaching and many of his teachings were codes waiting to be implemented. Therefore, the position of leadership was a vital component of the Divine Message, and it was prudent and dutiful of the Messenger of Righteousness, whose goal was to guide humans, to appoint a devout vicegerent whose moral character was similar (but not equivalent) to the Prophet's. Allah created the souls, and only He knows the most private feelings of each one. Humans are in continuous need of guidance, and thus unable to identify or select their leader on their own. Allah, the Kind One, never intended for His creatures to live through hardship while helplessly struggling to choose a qualified leader. At the same time, people's failure to select the right leader would cause more chaos and corruption, and the lingering disputes would eventually escalate into hostilities and bloody conflicts.

Allah says, *"And your Lord creates what He wants, and chooses whom He wants, they have no right to choose (28:68)."* The Exalted also says, *"When a matter has been ordained by Allah and His Messenger, the believers, males and females, are not supposed to prefer their own choice regarding the same matter, those who disobey are totally astray (33:36)."*

The position of supreme leadership (Khilafa) is Divinely designated. Allah, the Exalted, selects a qualified man to carry on the responsibility of Prophethood in the absence of the Prophet. This responsibility includes guiding people and expounding on the details of jurisprudence laid by the Seal of All Prophets (Mohammed). It also includes teaching the ignorant, warning the heedless, punishing the aggressor and implementing matters the Prophet only stated, or intentionally ignored, due to their inapplicability during his time. Imam Ali was the Divinely appointed extension of the Prophet's leadership. Al-Hasan came next; then his brother Al-Husayn; then his son Zayn Al-Abideen; then Al-Baqir Mohammed; then Al-Sadiq Ja'afar; then Al-Kathim Musa; then Al-Ridha Ali; then Al-Jawad Mohammed, then Al-Hadi Ali; then Al-A'skari Al-Hasan. Last is the awaited Abu Al-Qassim Mohammed, may Allah hasten his return.

The infallible leader must be a role model of piety and a source of guidance to, all humans. There is a consensus in the narrated traditions that Allah, the Exalted, blessed the infallible leader (Imam) with a power of enlightenment by which he could contact all of His creatures, and know all the events in the universe. It is narrated that upon birth, Allah erects a pillar of light with which the infallible leader can see the deeds of all humans, and the scope of all events throughout the world.² This power, bestowed upon them by the Divine, enables them to verify all realities and know beyond doubt what has been said or done throughout the universe. Also, possessing this power, no ignorance or heedlessness can ever be attributed to the infallible leaders, since everything is equidistant to their special souls. Moreover, this pillar of light obliterates every form of darkness or veil that might obstruct their vision. Abu Abdullah Al-Sadiq described this special bounty that the Exalted bestowed upon them. He explained that this power verifies, or uncovers, to them all matters that relate to humans, earth and heavens. This power enables the infallible leaders to clearly see whatever happens, just as others can easily see things in front of their eyes.³ Imam Al-Sadiq said, "Allah, the Exalted, blessed us with everything He blessed the Prophet with, except the Prophethood and the number of wives."⁴ This claim is not an exaggeration, especially when we realize how generous Allah is, and how fit the infallible leaders' souls are to receive such a bounty. Praising these pure souls in His Holy Book, Allah revealed, "*Allah shall definitely keep filth away from you, the people of the Messenger's household, and purify you (33:33)."*

No believer can deny that Allah's generosity is limitless. Allah is generous even to the tyrants and oppressors; His mercy is inclusive and His bounties are continuously flowing upon all humans. Allah's Kindness encompasses the nonbelievers, who willfully violate His codes and daringly express their enmity towards Him. If the Benevolent is this generous to these sinners, we should try to contemplate His flow of bounties and blessings for His devoted servants, whose souls were extracted from Mohammed's light, who in turn was created from Divine Radiance (Nour). In brief, Allah is The Generous Source who poured ultimate blessings into receptive souls. Therefore, it is never an exaggeration to attribute to them (Ahl Al-Bayt) the knowledge of the unseen; that is the knowledge of all human actions and events of the past, present and future throughout the universe. This knowledge of the unseen attributed to them is different than that attributed to Allah. His is a Divine matter, but that of the appointed leaders (Imams) is a special form of knowledge that He instilled in their hearts. It is Allah's Bounty and Kindness that enabled them to see the details of all things and events.

The unknown or the unseen is of two types. One belongs in

its entirety to Allah, and another connected to a cause. Allah, the Exalted, enlightened the hearts of His Prophets and their vicegerents with the knowledge of the second type. Our belief in the knowledge of the unseen matches what Al-Alloussi stated in his commentary on the Qur'an, *Rouh Al-Ma'ani*. Allah says, *"Say no one knows, whether in heavens or earth, the unseen except Allah (27:65)."* Commenting on this verse in his *Ruh Al-Ma'ani (V.20, P.11)*, Al-Alloussi wrote:

> "The fact is that Allah denounced any knowledge of the unseen, if He is not its source. The claim to independently know the unseen is equivalent to atheism, but because Allah taught His devoted servants and informed them of the unseen, this verse does not negate such knowledge of the select few."

The following tradition attests to this point. Imam Al-Jawad told his wife, Umm Al-Fadhl, Al-Ma'moun's daughter, that her mood swing was due to the onset of her menstrual cycle. She replied, "Only Allah knows the unseen." Al-Jawad emphasized, "And I know it from Allah."[5]

The infallible leaders (Imams) are always in need of a supply from the Divine to replenish their knowledge. Any disruption to this continuous flow would result in the dissipation of their knowledge. Imam Al-Sadiq said, "We get replenished every Friday eve, otherwise our knowledge would vanish."[6] This means that all of their knowledge is a gift from their Creator, and to maintain it they're always in need of Allah's Kindness and Mercy. More blissful than other nights, Friday eve is the time in which the Divine bestows His bounties upon them. Elaborating on the bounty of this special knowledge, Imam Al-Ridha said, "We know (the unseen) when we are taught, and we don't when it is withheld from us."[7]

Allah favored Prophet Mohammed over all of His creatures, and there is no doubt that he is the messenger meant in the following verse: *"The Knower of the unseen informs no one of the unseen, except a Messenger with whom He is very pleased (72:26-27)."* Commenting on this verse, Imam Abu Ja'afar Al-Baqir said, "By Allah! Mohammed was the one with whom He is pleased."[8] Allah blessed the Prophet with this incredible bounty, and similarly blessed his infallible descendants. Imam Al-Ridha's answer to Amr Bin Haddab, who rejected the infallible leaders' knowledge of the unseen, further attests to this point.

Expounding on the previously mentioned verses (26 and 27 of Surah Al-Jinn), Imam Al-Ridha told Amr, "Mohammed was the Messenger with whom Allah, the Exalted, is pleased, and we inherited the knowledge of the unseen from him. Therefore, we know the events of the past and the future, until Day of Judgement."[9]

Prophet Mohammed was Allah's most beloved creature. It is absurd to suggest that anyone but him could have been meant in this verse. Allah, the Exalted, honored and loved our Prophet, such that He conveyed messages to him without an intermediary. Zurara narrated that he once inquired about the Prophet's condition when he seemed totally overwhelmed by the intensity of revelation (Ghashya). Zurara asked, "Was that during the revelations?" Imam Al-Sadiq replied, "Not necessarily. The Prophet experienced such a thing only when Allah, the Exalted, spoke to him without an intermediary. Jabra'eel, on the other hand, always waited for permission to enter the Prophet's house and once he did, he sat in front of the Prophet like a humble servant.[10] When the Prophet wasn't ready to receive him, Jabra'eel waited by the spout for permission.[11] The following scholars agree that the Prophet received some revelations without an intermediary: Burhan Al-Deen Al-Halabi[12], Al-Suhayli[13] Bin Sayyed Al-Nass[14], Al-Suyuti[15] and Al-Zarqani.[16]

There are many traditions explaining the incredible proximity bet ween Allah and His Messenger, Mohammed. Sheykh Al-Sadouq and Sheykh Al-Mufeed relied on these traditions to explain the overwhelming spiritual intensity the Prophet experienced upon receiving the Divine revelations. They stated that revelations were either direct or through angels.[17] Sheykh Mohammed Taqi Al-Isfahani, known as Agha Najafi, agreed with them, but added that the Prophet knew the Qur'an inside out, and the details of all things and events long before he publicly announced his Prophethood. Nonetheless, Allah ordered him not to inform anyone of it until he was instructed to do so. Allah says, *'Do not hastily deliver the Qur'an before the revelations ordain so (20:114).*"[18] Had the Prophet's heart not possessed the knowledge and secrets of the Holy Book, the Divine order in the above verse would have been redundant. We conclude that the Prophet knew the details of all events, and that Jabra'eel was not the primary source of information. Allah, the Exalted, lavished His Divine Blessings upon the Prophet, and verified all realities before his eyes long before the creation of Jabra'eel.

The Prophet's character had more dimensions than our simple understanding can encounter. He, before receiving the first revelations, earned the highest position of perfection any human can attain. The Prophet knew how to write and read all of the existing languages. Arguing otherwise means that the Prophet would need the help of another human to teach him something he didn't know. This means that another human is superior to our Prophet, and this is a clear violation of the Prophet's unrivaled perfection. Renowned Muslim scholars, from all sects, have arrived at a similar conclusion.

The verse *"You do not write it with your right hand (29:48)"* negates the Prophet's writing, and not his knowledge of writing. This verse was revealed because contemporary idolaters rejected the Divine revelations and accused the Prophet of writing the Qur'an. Deliberately and tactfully, the Prophet did not write anything throughout his life in order to shut the door of suspicion, and fend off what the Qur'an describes as "troublemakers." The followers of the Prophet's household believe that Allah blessed the infallible leaders with the same qualities and bounties with which He blessed their Holy grandfather, except Prophethood and the number of wives. (Allah allowed the seal of the Prophets to concurrently have more than four wives).

Unable to comprehend the true meaning of the unseen, some people completely rejected the concept. They ruled that the Muslims, who believed that the Prophet and his vicegerents were blessed with the knowledge of the unseen, were infidels. Sheykh Zadeh Al-Hanafi said that Qassim Al-Saffar issued the following edict: "A person who believes in Allah and His Messenger, but also believes that the Prophet knew the unseen, is considered an infidel." The Tatarkhaniyya preacher, however, was more moderate. He rejected this edict, saying that the Prophet's soul did encounter the unseen, and the Prophet might have known some of it in accordance with the following verse: *"The Knower of the unseen informs no one of the unseen, except a Messenger with whom He is very pleased (72:26&27)."*[19]

These people rejected the Prophet's knowledge of the unseen, either because of their ill understanding of the true meaning of the unseen (Al-Ghayb), or because they underestimated the Prophet's immense devotion. Their demented intellect led them to such a flawed and unfounded conclusion. After this clarification, the reader should be doubtless that the knowledge of the unseen is a real bounty that Allah bestows upon the select few. It is worth repeating that this special knowledge of the select few is by no means a denial that there is a kind of knowledge of the unseen that belongs in its entirety to Allah. Moreover, the Exalted never shared this kind of knowledge with anyone. Knowing the onset of the Day of Judgement is an example of the exclusively Divine knowledge.

We have traditions from our infallible leaders in which they denied their knowledge of the unseen. Imam Al-Sadiq once said, "It is amazing! How could some people claim that we know the unseen? I was about to punish my maid. She hid and I didn't see (or know) where she was."[20] This tradition is an example of how the infallible leaders (Imams) practiced precautionary dissimulation (Taqiyya). Imam Al-Sadiq denied his knowledge of the unseen because the attendants at the time, like Dawood Al-Raqqi, Yahya Al-Bazzaz and Abu Baseer, were not capable of handling this reality. Imam Al-Sadiq tactfully articulated his denial to spare them any confusion.

Looking at the full picture attests to the fact that the infallible leaders appropriately practiced precautionary dissimulation, and selectively confessed their special knowledge. Sadeer Al-Sayrafi, the narrator of the previously mentioned tradition, visited Imam Al-Sadiq later, and expressed his confusion at the infallible leader's denial of knowing the unseen. Imam Al-Sadiq assured Sadeer that he had a full knowledge of the Holy Book, which is more significant than that of the unseen. Moreover, Al-Majlisi in his *Mar'aat Al-Uqoul* stated that the tradition in which Imam Al-Sadiq denied his knowledge of the unseen is unreliable, because the men in its channel of transmission were unknown. It is also possible that Imam Al-Sadiq denied seeing the maid but did not deny knowing where she was. He said, "Ma A'limt." In the Arabic language this can be interpreted as "I didn't know" or "I didn't see" where she went. The latter is definitely the suitable interpretation, because not knowing where the maid really was contradicts Imam Al-Sadiq's following statement in describing his own knowledge: "I know what has happened, and I know the things that happen away from me."

It was also narrated that someone knocked at Imam Al-Baqir's door. The man firmly held the maid's hand while she was opening the door. Imam Al-Baqir yelled from inside, "Mubasher!

You are doomed! Come in." (All this happened while Mubasher was still behind the door). Mubasher apologized, and explained to Imam Al-Baqir that he intended no harm, but instead he came to learn. Imam Al-Baqir told him, "Walls never obstruct our vision. If they did, we would have been equal to you."[21] Furthermore, Imam Al-Baqir told Mohammed Bin Muslim, "If we didn't have full knowledge of your whereabouts, and of your life affairs, we wouldn't have been spiritually superior to people." Imam Al-Baqir further asserted his knowledge of the unseen, and accurately reiterated to Bin Muslim the discussion of leadership that had taken place between the latter and his companion in Rabatha.[22]

Allah revealed to His Messenger, *"Say, had I known the unseen, I would have sought only goodness (7:188)."* This verse emphasizes that all of the Prophet's knowledge was from Allah, and he had no way to acquire any of it on his own. The verse also implies that the Prophet was in continuous need of Allah's Kindness to maintain his special knowledge. The interpretation of this verse further proves our belief that Allah blessed the Prophet, and his infallible descendants (Imams), with a special power by which they can see everything in the universe.[23]

While in Mecca, Imam Ja'afar Al-Sadiq asked his companions to double check whether or not a private eye followed them. His companions assured him that there was no one. Imam Ja'afar then said, "By the Lord of this Building! (Ka'aba)," repeating his oath three times, "if I were between Musa and Al-Khidhr, I would have informed them that my knowledge exceeds theirs, and I would have taught them things they didn't know. They (Musa and Al-Khidhr) have been blessed with the knowledge of the past, but not the future. However, we inherited from the Prophet the knowledge of everything until the Day of Judgement."[24]

Let us assume that this tradition is authentic and that its narrator, Ibraheem Bin Is'haq Al-Ahmar, was trustworthy. The following two facts explain what seems to be contradictory, in this tradition, to Imam Ja'afar's other statements. First, the infallible leaders did not show off their knowledge on a regular basis. Second, they frequently practiced precautionary dissimulation (Taqiyya). Need less of in dependent assurance, Imam Ja'afar inquired whether or not there was a spy because he took into consideration the level of faith of his companions at the time. On a different occasion, Imam Ja'afar said, "I know what's in heaven and earth. I know what's in paradise and hell-fire, and I know the past and the future." Noticing the startled looks of his audience, Imam Ja'afar immediately added, "I learned all of this from the Holy Book. Allah, the Exalted, says *the Holy Book has a description and explanation of everything (16:89).*"[25]

The infallible leaders accurately assessed their companions and the time period in which they lived. Thus, when his audience seemed perplexed, Imam Ja'afar added to his original statement what was more convincing and pleasing to their ears. He also acknowledged that Al-Khidhr and Musa knew the past. Nevertheless, Imam Ja'afar didn't deny Al-Khidhr's special knowledge of the boy's future, because Allah informed Al-Khidhr of it for a particular reason, and a specific benefit, pertinent to that time period.

Some traditions confirm that if the infallible leader (Imam) wanted to know something, Allah would inform him of it.[26] This, by no means, implies that their knowledge is confined to a time frame. In contrast, the infallible leaders, in these traditions, asserted their superior knowledge, and their ability to utilize the special power Allah had instilled in them at birth, to verify hidden realities whenever they deemed necessary. Only three traditions describe the knowledge of the infallible leaders as conditional or time bound. Al-Majlisi, in his *Mar'aat Al-Uqoul,* rejected all of them because of their weak channel of transmission or because the narrators were totally unknown.

We conclude that Allah blessed the appointed leaders with the power to know universal events, secrets and intricate details about all creatures throughout the world. This should not be beyond belief, especially when we realize how generous Allah is, and how receptive their pure souls are. He grants what He wills to whomever He wills. The infallible leaders mentioned this blessing openly, and added that their hearts are always in need of the continuous flow of the Divine's special blessing, otherwise their knowledge would dry up.

We should submit to these facts and realities. Looking at the whole picture from a different angle would definitely help rid any lingering doubts. In addition to being Divinely purified, the infallible leaders devoted their lives to Allah, and their astounding dedication in serving Him earned them this special bounty. Keeping in mind that they have been selected and entrusted to deliver or preserve the Divine revelations obliterates the difficulty of believing that the infallible leaders possessed unrivaled and superior knowledge. Prominent scholars, such as Al-Sheykh Al-Mufeed in his *Maqalaat (P.77)*, Al-Majlisi in *Mar'aat Al-Uqoul (V.1, P.187)*, and Al-Ashtyani in his *Hashiya (V.2, P.60)* or commentary on Sheykh Al-Ansari's work, have expressed a similar opinion.

Allah says, *"Say no one knows the unseen in heavens and in earth except Allah (27:65)."* The Almighty also says, *"He, who knows the unseen, does not inform anyone of it (72:26)."* Commenting on these verses in his Al-Fatawa Al-Hadeetha (P.222), Bin Hijr Al-Haythami wrote:

> "These verses do not negate that the prophets and the guardians (Awliya') know the unseen, because Allah is the source of their special knowledge. This branch of knowledge is completely different than the one that is entirely His. Allah's Knowledge, an attribute with which He praised Himself, is eternal and invariable. Allah never shares His eternal attributes with anyone. The Prophets and the guardians know from Allah some details of the unseen. Only a stubborn person rejects this conclusion, because it by no means implies that they share with Him the branch of knowledge that is entirely and eternally His. This is what Al-Nawawi stated in his work."

Bin Hijr Al-Haythami clearly illustrated his belief that the guardians knew the unseen. Nonetheless, he disagreed with the followers of the Prophet's household (Shi'a), who contend that the infallible leaders (Imams) know the unseen, including the future, until the Day of Judgement. Bin Hijr believed that only Allah has this kind of knowledge, but He allows His guardians to know some of it. In our point of view, Bin Hijr's conclusion on the guardians' knowledge of the unseen was very restrictive. Allah's generosity in granting this knowledge and the receptivity of the pure souls of the Prophet and his household (Imams) are the key issues in defining the unseen and the infallible leaders' knowledge of it.

The infallible leaders' devotion to Allah placed their pure souls in a perfect position to receive this special bounty. Imam Ja'afar asserted that this special bounty enabled them to verify the realities of all events of the past, present and future. We reiterate that there is a kind of Knowledge that belongs in its entirety to Allah and that He does not share His Exclusive Knowledge with any of His creatures. Moreover, no human can attain this Knowledge, even if he reached the position of utmost perfection.

Al-Naysabouri endorsed Bin Hijr's view of the unseen. In his commentary on the Qur'an, Al-Naysabouri wrote: "The guardians are excluded from the blessing of knowing the unseen, either because Allah is not generous to the believer, or because the latter is not worthy of receiving such a blessing. Both of these reasons are far from reality because Allah's most significant blessing is guiding the believer to the straight path, and all other blessings, including the knowledge of the unseen, are definitely less significant."[27]

Commenting on the knowledge of the unseen, Bin Abi Al-Hadeed wrote:

> "We do not deny the fact that some people know the unseen and that they receive it all from The Exalted. He enables them to know as He provides perfect conditions for them to receive such knowledge... In this verse, *No soul knows what will happen to it tomorrow (31:34)*, and Allah does not negate the Prophet's knowledge of capturing Mecca or fighting the traitors, the transgressors and the apostates. The verse denies a person's ability to know future events on his own, but doesn't negate this special knowledge if Allah is its source. Therefore, it is highly possible that Allah informed His Messenger of future events."[28]

THE VERSE OF SELF-DESTRUCTION

Based on our previous discussion, it is certain that the infallible leaders (Imams) knew the exact time of their martyrdom and the people who would murder them. The knowledge they inherited from their grandfather, the Seal of All Messengers, in addition to the power of enlightenment Allah had instilled in their hearts, enabled them to learn about all events including their own martyrdom.

In the Holy Book, Allah clearly forbids any risky behavior that would result in self-destruction. Islam legislated that it is a duty to protect life, and to refrain from intentionally exposing one-self to any danger. Preserving life is a priority, and only a justifiable cause, such as self-defense or fighting on the way of Allah (Jihad), supersedes this priority. The infallible leaders propagated and implemented the Divine codes, and it is inconceivable that they aided in ending their own lives. Therefore, their determination to be martyred should never be misconstrued as an intention of self-destruction.

The fighters on the way of Allah (Mujahideen) knew that combating the enemies could cost them their lives, nonetheless, they obeyed the Divine instructions and fought. It is worth mentioning that many of these fighters were anxious to embrace martyrdom. Furthermore, a large number of the Prophets sacrificed their Holy lives while delivering the Divine revelations. Allah says, *"Repent to your Creator by killing yourselves (2:54)."* This verse of the Qur'an demonstrates the importance of self-sacrifice in the process of implementing the Divine orders. It also explains that a group of Israelis (Bani Israel) killed themselves in the process of worshipping Allah and submitting to His orders.[29]

Quoting the Qur'an in banning self-destruction is often used out of context. This prohibition is stated as part of a whole verse, in which Allah informs the believers of their duties upon facing any aggression in a sacred month. Allah, the Exalted, says, *"The sacred month for the sacred month, and for breaking the rules there is a law of retaliation, Then whoever initiates aggression against you, retaliate, And be pious, for Allah is with the pious. Spend on the way of Allah, and do not aid the destruction of yourselves, and do good, for Allah is certainly on the side of the good doers (2:194-195)."* Allah instructed the Muslims, when short of weaponry and supplies, to avoid combat against the infidels during the sacred months.[30] It is clear that Allah strictly confined this ban. Therefore, one should not conclude that it could be applicable to every personal situation. This prohibition lies within a frame of certain situations, and under special conditions in which preserving life remains a priority. However, when there is an urgent cause, like preserving the right path and defending the very existence of Islam, this ban becomes inapplicable.

Allah, in His Holy Book, repeatedly emphasized the importance of self-sacrifice and also praised those who fought and lost their lives while supporting the Divine Message. The Omnipotent says, *"Allah has bought the souls and possessions of the believers for the price of paradise; they fight on the way of Allah; they slay and get slain (9:111)."* He also says, *"Do not consider those who are slain on the way of Allah to be dead;*

they are alive enjoying the bounties of their Lord (3:169)." He also says, *"Some sacrifice their lives seeking the pleasure of Allah (2:207)."* In one of his invaluable teachings, the Prophet said that the best martyr was Hamza Bin Abd Al-Muttalib, or an advocate of justice who gets slaughtered for confronting an oppressor.[31]

Expounding further on the importance of self-sacrifice, Mohammed Bin Al-Hasan Al-Sheybani commended a fighter's solo attack against thousands. He stated, "It is not suicidal when a person solely attacks an army, because such action frightens the enemies and injects chaos into their ranks. Achieving these two goals gives the Muslims a major advantage on the battlefield."[32] In agreement with Al-Sheybani's statement, Bin Al-Arabi Al-Maliki, in his *Ahkam (V.1, P.49)*, wrote:

> "Some scholars allowed this solo attack against a whole army because the attacker seeks martyrdom in his action. Such an act is not prohibited and should not be construed as self-destructive. In contrast, this solo action pleases Allah according to the following verse. *Some sacrifice their lives seeking the pleasure of Allah (2:207)*. Moreover, this solo attack encourages other Muslims who watch one of them single handedly attacking thousands."

Allah assigned the infallible leaders of the Community to preserve the Seal of the Divine Messages, and singled them out with special rules in their affairs to fulfill this important mission. Their proximity to Allah, and the reasons behind these special rules, are incomprehensible to us. The infallible leaders exhausted their efforts and resources to preserve their grandfather's message. In order to fulfill their Divinely assigned duty, they sacrificed their lives, spent all their money and gave up their comfort and sanctity on the way of Allah, the Exalted.

Some infallible leaders spent many years in prison or exile. Others were dislocated and endured hardship and verbal abuse until they were martyred. The infallible leaders learned from their grandfather, Prophet Mohammed, that their suffering was a crucial component in preserving the Divine Message, and protecting it from the danger of alteration. In formed of their role and its importance, some were instructed to persevere quietly, while others were commanded to rise up militarily or to ingest poison. Despite the difference in their roles, they implemented the Divine orders and submitted to Allah's

Will, for He knows best the proper time and place in which He implements His ordinances.

Whether rising up against the tyrants or ingesting poisoned food, the infallible leaders knew the outcome of their action. They knew with certainty the murderer, the tool used, the day and the hour of their martyrdom. They obediently submitted to the Divine Will and sacrificed their lives to implement their Lord's command. An exemplary model of dedication in pleasing their Lord, the infallible leaders gladly embraced the path of self-sacrifice as well as other aspects of their Lord's recommendations and prohibitions. They gave up their precious lives unconditionally. They trusted the Wisdom of their Lord, who says, *"He is never questioned, but humans will be questioned (21:23)."* A true submission of this fashion lies in sharp contrast with a conditional one, in which a person inquires about the causes and the benefits sought from the required action. Renowned scholars agree with our definitions of self-sacrifice and self-destruction, and the distinction between the two as far as the lives of the infallible members of the Prophet's family (Ahl Al-Bayt) are concerned. Other writers, due to their ill understanding of the subject matter, relied on their imagination and their conclusion was far from reality.

The infallible leaders said that whenever they sensed that their enemies were about to murder them, or whenever they wanted a break from the hardship of imprisonment, they would supplicate to Allah and complain to their grandfather, Prophet Mohammed. Certain that their ordained Martyrdom was not due, they sought help from Allah and His Messenger to divert the harm coming their way. Imam Al-Baqir said that if the Household Members (Ahl Al-Bayt) were distressed because an evil ruler intended to hurt them, they would say, "You! Who was before anything; You! Who controls everything; bestow your blessings and praise upon Mohammed and his household and grant me my wish."[33]

When Al-Mansoor, the Abbassid tyrant, finalized his plan to murder Imam Al-Sadiq, the latter asked Allah for protection. Allah, the Exalted, granted Imam Al-Sadiq his wish. Moreover, Al-Mansoor, from then on, stood up and hugged Imam al Sadiq anytime he saw him. Al-Mansoor said that he abandoned his plan because in his dream, he saw the Prophet stretching his arms and frowning in his face. The Prophet warned Al-Mansoor in the dream against hurting

Imam Al-Sadiq. Al-Mansoor was thus compelled to express his unequivocal reverence to the sixth infallible leader. He, kindly and respectfully, sent Imam Al-Sadiq back to his grandfather's city, Medina.[34]

Imam Musa Bin Ja'afar suffered a long period of imprisonment under extremely harsh conditions. He finally recited the following supplication, asking Allah to help him out of prison: "You! Who helps the tree grow out in between water and dirt; You! Who makes milk come out in between feces and blood; You! Who creates infants between the uterus and the womb; You! Who creates fire between metal and rocks; You! Who extracts the soul between the chest and guts, save me from Harun."[35] Allah answered Imam Musa's supplication and saved him from the painful shackles and the dark prison. In an encounter between the two, Harun Al-Rasheed offered Imam Musa dates, some of which were poisoned. Imam Musa ate the non-poisoned ones and threw the poisoned ones to Al-Rasheed's dog. In doing so, Imam Musa conveyed his knowledge of Al-Rasheed's evil scheme. The dog's death was a polite message to Al-Rasheed that the time of Imam Musa's martyrdom hadn't come.[36] On a different occasion, Al-Rasheed offered Imam Musa poisoned dates. Imam Musa lifted his hands towards the sky and said, "My Lord! You know that had I eaten the poisoned dates before, I would have aided in killing myself." Imam Musa ingested the poisoned dates this time because his ordained martyrdom was due.[37]

When Imam Al-Hadi was sick, he ordered Abu Hashim Al-Ja'afary to send someone to Al-Husayn's shrine to supplicate for his recovery. He told Abu Hashim, "Allah, the Exalted, loves to hear supplications in that place."[38] In his request, Imam Al-Hadi demonstrated that matters and infliction should be handled promptly and dealt with by normal means. He also emphasized the importance of supplicating to Allah during disasters and hardships. This importance was the reason why Al-Rabee', Al-Mansoor's top advisor, kept Imam Al-Sadiq's supplication and hid it like a treasure. Al-Rabee' did so once he realized that the supplication had an enormous impact on Al-Mansoor, such that the latter reversed his policy and venerated Al-Sadiq instead of killing him.[39]

Imam Al-Hasan, in addition to using some soil from his grandfather's grave, applied what experts and physicians prescribed to treat his illness.[40] He knew at the time of treatment that his illness was not terminal. However, he demonstrated to others that any illness should be treated by normal and known means. When the time of his Martyrdom was due, Al-Hasan was about to break his fast at the end of a very hot day. His wife, Ja'ada Bint Al-Asha'ath, handed him a cup of poisoned milk.[41]

Imam Al-Hasan gazed deeply into the sky and said, "To Allah we belong and to Him we shall return. I thank Allah for my reunion with Mohammed, the Master of All Messengers, my father the Master of All Vicegerents, my mother the Lady of All Women, my uncle Ja'afar who is flying in paradise, and my uncle Hamza the Master of Martyrs."[42] He then drank the milk and told the trembling Ja'ada, "He (Mu'awiya) lured you and disgraced you. I ask Allah to destroy you and to destroy him."[43]

Imam Al-Ridha informed his companions that Al-Ma'moon would murder him, and that they should remain patiently quiet until the murder occurred.[44] Years after murdering Imam Al-Ridha, Al-Ma'moon requested from Imam Al-Jawad to come to Baghdad. Isma'il Bin Mehran, Imam Al-Jawad's companion, became extremely worried. Al-Jawad told him, "There will be no harm on this trip and I shall return safely." Before his second trip to Baghdad to see Al-Ma'moon, Imam Al-Jawad told Isma'il Bin Mehran, "My martyrdom is due this time." He then informed Isma'il that his son, Al-Hadi, would be the next infallible leader (Imam) of the Community (Ummah).[45] Umm Al-Fadhl, Al-Ma'moon's daughter, handed her husband, Imam Al-Jawad, a poisoned towel. Submitting to Allah's Will, Imam Al-Jawad used the towel and told his wife, "I ask Allah to inflict an untreatable illness upon you." She later suffered from a severe illness in the private parts of her body.

There is also a consensus amongst all scholars that Imam Ali foretold his own martyrdom, and that Bin Muljam would murder him. When Bin Muljam was pledging allegiance, Imam Ali pointed towards him and addressed the attendants, "If you are interested, look at this man. He will definitely murder me." Some people asked Imam Ali, "Why don't you kill him?" He exclaimed, "It is amazing! How could you ask me to kill the person who will kill me?"[46] In his response, Imam Ali emphasized that Bin Muljam would murder him, and that the matter had been Divinely ordained and finalized.

Imam Al-Sadiq explained the infallible leaders' submission to the Divine Will when he told Uqbah Al-Assdi, "If the infallible leaders (Imams) insist on asking Allah to destroy the tyrants, the Exalted would easily grant them their wish. However, we unconditionally submit to Allah's Will."[47]

Conclusion

We can fairly claim that the previous discussion, and the solid proofs we presented in it, have unveiled the truth, and that an intelligent reader would doubtlessly agree that the infallible leaders knew all of the ordained events ahead of time. They knew all of the conspiracies against them, but lived in total submission to the Divine Will. The source of their comprehensive knowledge was the Founder of the universe, their grandfather and the Divine Book revealed to him. They knew that martyrdom begets immortal honor and earns them Allah's utmost blessings. Totally submissive to the Will of their Lord, they sacrificed their precious lives for practical benefits that are beyond human understanding. Only Allah fully knows the benefits of their self-sacrifice, and it is not obligatory upon us to detect them. The subject matter is analogous to all matters in jurisprudence; we are supposed to unconditionally abide by Allah's codes without burdening ourselves with pursuing the knowledge of the harms and benefits embedded in each one of His recommendations or prohibitions.

Some of the infallible leaders rose up, or spoke up, while others remained quiet and avoided involvement in public and political affairs. Whatever the path was, authentic traditions assert that they implemented the special instructions Allah conveyed to them through His entrusted Messenger. Some, despite their belief in the infallible leaders' comprehensive knowledge, deliberately ignored these traditions. In fact, the infallible leaders were informed of all events, big or small, and were aware of all details until their death. Confirming their superior knowledge, Imam Al-Baqir said, "I am amazed that some people adhere to our path, consider us the infallible leaders and believe that obeying us is obeying the Prophet, but yet, for a weakness in their faith, revoke their belief and demean us. These people also ridicule the faithful who truly know us and submit to our leadership. How dare they think that Allah will keep the knowledge of the unseen away from us after He appoints us as leaders and selects us to be the source of guidance to people?"

Humran asked Al-Baqir, "The son of Allah's Messenger! How do you explain the uprising of Imam Ali, Al-Hasan and Al-Husayn, and the harm they endured from the tyrants until they were killed or defeated?" Imam Al-Baqir replied, "Listen up Humran! Allah, the Exalted, ordained the affairs of the infallible leaders and gave them the choice to accept before He finalized the ordinances. Imam Ali, Al-Hasan and Al-Husayn were informed and instructed ahead of time by Allah's Messenger to rise up. Similarly, other infallible leaders remained quiet. Had they wanted to fend off the evil of their enemies, they would have persisted in asking Allah to destroy all the tyrants, and Allah would have granted them their wish faster than the blink of an eye. Their suffering was not due to committing sins or mischief, but due to an eternal blessing and honor the Exalted wanted them to attain. Oh Humran! Do not let others confuse you."[48]

This tradition sheds a bright light on the special attributes with which Allah favored the entrusted guardians over all humans. The Divine Wisdom in Al-Baqir's words leads us to conclude the following:

1. The infallible leaders' knowledge was comprehensive. They knew the scope and details of all events, and no information was withheld from them.
2. Suffering oppression at the hands of their contemporary tyrants generated tremendous benefits that are known only to Allah.
3. Their strife and waging war against their enemies, and thus their martyrdom, were on the way of Allah. On the other hand, their silence against the oppressors, coupled with their intent to self-sacrifice, reflect their total submission in implementing their Lord's special instructions. They, as with all humans who select a path in life, willfully embraced this path and were not forced onto it.
4. They submitted to Allah's final ordinance and abstained from asking Him to change it. They gladly accepted it, because Allah's utmost blessings and the associated high position are attainable only by embracing the most honorable

form of death, martyrdom.

The following tradition further explains the infallible leaders' submission to Allah. Someone asked Imam Al-Ridha, "How could Imam Ali subject himself to death, when he knew the murderer and the exact time of the murder?" Imam Al-Ridha replied, "It is true that Imam Ali knew, however, he chose to implement the Divine ordinance on that night."[49] The traditions we mentioned in this section clearly indicate that the infallible leaders' intent to be martyred was a crucial factor in completing their Divine assignment, and in fulfilling their special mission. Allah blessed the infallible leaders with comprehensive knowledge, including that of their fate. Their determination to sacrifice their Holy lives should never be misconstrued as self-destructive. Prominent Shi'a scholars have stated an opinion similar to ours.

Sheykh Al-Mufeed, in his Al-Massai'l Al-A'kbariyya (Answers to Some Questions), wrote:

> "It is fair to say that the infallible leader knows the scope of events, and their associated details. Allah granted him this knowledge. Moreover, we cannot rule out that Imam Ali's perseverance in his Martyrdom was a form of worship by which he attained Allah's blessings. Through his submission, Imam Ali acquired what no one would ever turn down. Imam Ali did not aid in ending his own life, and his inaction was by no means self-destructive. It is utter nonsense to believe otherwise. Some object to this because they look at this matter from a different angle. Also, we cannot rule out that Al-Husayn knew how to obtain water; and it may have been a yard away from him if he dug for it, however, not digging for water is by no means considered self-destructive. His decision might have been a form of submission to his Lord after he was denied natural access to water. Al-Hasan knew the outcome of his truce with Mu'awiya, and we have authentic traditions attesting to this fact. He, knowing the evil schemes of his enemy, signed the truce, and in doing so Al-Hasan delayed his martyrdom and spared the lives of his companions. Moreover, Al-Hasan spared his life and the lives of his family members. He also protected his grandfather's Community

from greater corruption than that which the truce invoked. Al-Hasan was quite aware of these ramifications, but more significant than anything else, the truce was a form of worship and submission to his Lord."

Explaining the infallible leaders' submission to Allah and the distinction between self-sacrifice and self-destruction, Sheykh Yusuf Al-Bahrani wrote:

"They accepted their martyrdom, whether by sword or poison, and the painful abuse from their oppressive enemies, knowing that they could have avoided it all. They knew that enduring pain and suffering pleased Allah, and generated spiritual proximity to Him. They willfully chose this path. Nonetheless, their choice was not the form of self-destruction that is prohibited in the Holy Qur'an. In contrast, the infallible leaders implemented their Lord's ordinance, and their goal in doing so was to please Him. When they sensed that their lives were in danger before the ordained time of their martyrdom, they supplicated to Allah and simultaneously utilized natural means to protect themselves. They, peace be upon them, knew of all of the events and ordinances pertaining to their Holy lives, and gracefully submitted to what the Dominant and Omnipotent chose for them."[50]

When asked about Imam Ali's subjecting himself to death, Al-Allama Al-Hilli replied: "He might have been informed that night of the time and place of his Martyrdom, and his responsibility might have been different than ours. He might have felt duty bound to sacrifice his life. Imam Ali's situation is analogous to that of a man who fights on the way of Allah knowing that the outcome might be an end to his life."[51] Allamah Al-Majlisi, Al-Muhaqqiq Al-Karaki and Al-Hasan Bin Sulayman Al-Hilli expressed similar views.

Notes & References

---

1. Al-Muhtadhar (P.165) & Mukhtassar Al-Basa'ir (P.125)
2. Basa'ir Al-Darajat (P.128)

3. Mukhtassar Al-Basa'ir (P.101)
4. Al-Muhtadhar (P.20)
5. Al-Bihar (V.12, P.29)
6. Usul Al-Kafi (V.1, P.185)
7. Mukhtassar Al-Basa'ir (P.63)
8. Al-Bihar (V.15, P.74)
9. Al-Bihar (V.12, P.22)
10. Ilm Al-Yaqeen (P.86), I'lal Al-Shar'ai (P.14)
11. Al-Bihar (V.11, P.216)
12. Al-Seera Al-Halabiyya (V.l, P.294)
13. Al-Rawdh Al-Anif (V.l, P.154)
14. Uyun Al-Athar (V.l, P.90)
15. Al-Khasa'is Al-Kubra (V.2, P.193)
16. Sharh Al-Mawahib Al-Laduniyya (V.1, P.221)
17. Sharh I'tiqadat Al-Sadouq (P.211)
18. Al-Inayat Al-Radhawiyya (P.51)
19. Majma' Al-Anhur (V.1, P.320)
20. Bassa'ir Al-Darajat (Ps. 57&62); Usul Al-Kafi (V.l, P.186)
21. Manaqib Bin Shahr Ashoub (V.2, P.274); Al-Bihar (V.11, P.70)
22. Al-Bihar (V.11, P.72)
23. Sharh Al-Shafa (V.3, P.150)
24. Usul Al-Kafi (V.1, P.189)
25. Usul Al-Kafi (V.1, P.190)
26. Usul Al-Kafi (V.1, P.187)
27. Al-Nur Al-Safir (P.85)
28. Sharh Al-Nahj (V. l, P.427 & V.2, P.362)
29. See Commentaries on the Quran for more details
30. There are four sacred months in the Islamic or Lunar calendar: Rajab, Thil Qi'da, Thil Hijja & Muharram (the translator).
31. Ahkam Al-Quran (V.l, P.309)
32. Ahkam Al-Quran (V.1, P.309)
33. Muhaj Al-Da'awat (P.365)
34. Muhaj Al-Da'awat (P.299)
35. Amali Al-Sadouq (P.227)
36. Uyun Akhbar Al-Ridha (P.57)
37. Mar'at Al-Uqoul (V.1, P.188); Rawdhat Al-Wa'itheen (P.185)
38. Kamel Al-Ziyarat (P.223)
39. Muhaj Al-Da'awat
40. Kamel Al-Baha'ie (P.453-456) (available only in persian)
41. Al-Khara'ij (P.22)
42. Al-Bihar (V.10, P.133)
43. Al-Irshad & Al-Khara'ij
44. Imam Al-Ridha (P.45)

45. Al-Irshad & A'lam Al-Wara (P.205)
46. Basa'ir Al-Darajat (P.34) & Risalat Bin Badroun (P.156)
47. Usul Al-Kafi (the infallible leaders' knowledge) & Al-Khara'ij (P.143)
48. Usu.l Al-Kafi (V.1 , P.190); Basa'ir Al-Darajat (P.33) & Al-Khara'ij (P.143)
49. Usul Al-Kafi (V.l, P.188)
50. Al-Durra Al-Najafiyya (P.85)
51. Mar'at Al-Uqul (V. l, P.189) & Al-Bihar (V.9, P.663)

AL-HUSAYN'S KNOWLEDGE OF HIS OWN MARTYRDOM

Life is important but faith, Divine revelations and living truthfully are all the more so. Sometimes a person sacrifices his life in order to protect his beliefs and to help others maintain a clear vision of the truth. Imam Husayn, in his incredible stance to defend faith, embraced an ideal self-sacrifice that kept the torch of righteousness visible for decades and centuries. The Umayyad tyrants flagrantly violated the codes of the Divine Message. Al-Husayn's Holy uprising exposed to his contemporaries, and the coming generations, the crimes of these oppressors. Al-Husayn rose up and sacrificed all he had to defend and preserve Prophet Mohammed's Message. Humans learned from Al-Husayn that liberating the oppressed, and firmly protecting the principles of faith, require a major sacrifice.

A Muslim fighter solely attacked thousands to inspire his comrades and to encourage them to hold steadfast against their enemies. Al-Sheybani, as we mentioned previously, praised the action of such a faithful fighter. More faithful than anyone at the time, Imam Husayn attacked thousands of transgressors and sacrificed his Holy life as well as the precious lives of his family members and companions. Despite his knowledge that the women of the Prophet's household would become subject to theft and captivity, Al-Husayn was adamantly determined to fulfill his mission. The Umayyads tried to distort the true Message of Islam that the entrusted Messenger delivered. Al-Husayn's Holy uprising undermined their attempts, exposed their evil schemes, and became a role model for the righteous in their struggle against injustice. Al-Husayn undoubtedly defeated the criminals who attacked him and violated Allah's sanctities. The Prophet's grandson completed his mission and undeniably achieved his goal, and in doing so, he was ultimately victorious.

Some people believe that Imam Husayn expected the Kufans to support his uprising, and that he was disappointed when they turned against him. It amazes me that a person can believe such nonsense. Even if we compromise our belief of his knowledge of the unseen, we can never ignore the fact that Al-Husayn learned the events awaiting him from his father and grandfather. Al-Husayn was certain that he and his supporters, including the men in his family, would be slaughtered in Karbala after being deprived of water. When Umm Salama expressed her worries at his departure from Medina, Al-Husayn informed her that he was marching towards martyrdom. Prophet Mohammed, the most truthful being, had already told Umm Salama that Al-Husayn would be martyred thirsty in the land of Karbala.

Imam Husayn told Umm Salama, "I know the day and the hour in which I'll be killed. I also know which of my family and companions will be killed with me. Do you think that you know what I don't? There is no escape from death. If not today, I will leave tomorrow." He also told his brother, Umar Al-Tara, "My father told me that my grave will be relatively close to his. Do you think that you know what I don't?" He told his other brother, Mohammed Bin Al-Hanafiyya, "Allah ordained to see me martyred, and the women in my family captured." Al-Husayn told Bin Al-Zubayr, "If I were in the deepest cave under the ground, they would come after me to kill me." He told Abdullah Bin Ja'afar, "I saw the Prophet in my dream. He ordered me to do what I am doing." In the meadows of Al-A'qaba, he told everyone in his caravan, "I shall definitely be martyred. I saw in my dream many dogs, fiercest of which was a spotted one, ripping through my flesh." When Amr Bin Luwathan asked him to choose a destination other than Kufa, until he was further assured of the Kufans' support, Imam Husayn replied, "It is a good idea, but Allah's ordinances can never be averted. They will never give up their hunt until they kill me."

There are other traditions in which Imam Husayn expressed that his promised martyrdom in Karbala was a certainty. He stated this in Medina, Mecca and on his way to Kufa, and you'll read all of it later in this book. His speech in Mecca, shortly before he left to Iraq, leaves no doubt that Imam Husayn knew the outcome of his uprising. He said, "The starving wild wolves of the desert, in a land between Nawawees and Karbala, will rip through my joints to fill their empty bellies and satisfy their hunger. There is no aversion to what has already been written in the Divine Tablet." His answer to those who asked him to wait, or to change his destination, proves that Imam Husayn was aware of the malevolent intention of the Kufans, and the outcome of his uprising. His main goal was to implement what was Divinely ordained and to simultaneously provide a venue of guidance to the people who had gone astray. His calls for help and support before and during the battle were timeless.

Imam Husayn selectively informed people of the outcome of his uprising. He didn't indulge those who urged him to avoid Kufa. He was also aware that some people could handle the knowledge of the unseen, and some couldn't, so he conversed with each one accordingly. He answered questions with all consideration given to the time and place, and by sorting out people on the basis of their tolerance. The knowledge of the Prophet's household is, as Imam Al-Sadiq stated, "Extremely difficult to handle. Only a Messenger, a great angel, or a believer whose faith Allah had vigorously tested can handle it."[1]

Notes & References

---

1. Usul Al-Kafi (V.1, P.467) (the translator)

AL-HUSAYN'S VICTORY

Al-Husayn's uncompromising stance reminded the Community that the position of leadership belongs to no one but the Prophet's household. The Prophet's grandson was certain that his uprising, and subsequent martyrdom, would ultimately be crowned with victory. His success in preserving his grandfather's Message and undermining the evil schemes of his enemies was a major component of this victory. Al-Husayn alluded to this victory in his letter to Bani Hashim: "Whichever of you joins us will be martyred, and those who don't will never achieve victory."[1] The word "victory" in the above letter described the outcome of the Holy uprising. Al-Husayn foretold that his self-sacrifice would destroy the pillars of corruption, restore the purity of the Message, and preserve justice and true monotheism. Moreover, he demonstrated to the Community that it is a duty to combat wrongdoing and transgression.

As soon as he arrived to Medina, Imam Zayn Al-Abideen elucidated the true meaning of this victory. Ibraheem Bin Talha asked him, "Who was the victorious party?" Zayn Al-Abideen replied, "When prayer time is due, make the major call to prayer (Athaan), and then the minor call (Iqama), and you'll know who was victorious."[2] In his answer, Zayn Al-Abideen highlighted the real cause of Al-Husayn's self-sacrifice on one hand, and the failure of Yazeed's evil plan on the other. Zaynab, the Honorable, expounded on this victory when she told Yazeed, "Scheme all you want, and work as hard as you can. By Allah! You shall never reduce our significance, eradicate our revelations, nor tarnish our impeccable image. You shall never be absolved from your shameful sins."

Like his father, Yazeed exhausted all means possible in his unsuccessful attempts to veil the Divine light of guidance. Throughout his life, Mu'awiya tried very hard to annul the portion of the call to the five daily prayers that states, "I testify that Mohammed is the Messenger of Allah." This blasphemous attempt is only a glimpse of

Mu'awiya's evil schemes against the Prophet of Islam, whose Message uprooted idolatry. Yazeed's enmity towards the Prophet's household was indescribable. He was inculcated with his father's hatred and viciousness. Mu'awiya and his son unsuccessfully tried to undermine the Prophet's teachings. They schemed against the Prophet, despite knowing that praising him and his household is an integral part of the Muslims' mandatory prayers. It suffices to mention that prayers, in which Muslims do not praise the Prophet's household, are incomplete and thus definitely unaccepted.[3]

An insightful look into Al-Husayn's Holy uprising unveils that martyrdom in Karbala ranks higher than that in Badr, even though the latter marked the first Islamic victory. This is a fact because, in addition to the Prophet's promise of an imminent victory, Muslims fought the Battle of Badr under the Prophet's supervision with three-thousand of Allah's angels supporting them. The Prophet's companions faced the tyrants of Quraysh in Badr with guaranteed security and assured victory. The scene of Karbala, where the Umayyads employed all kind of dirty tactics against the Prophet's grandson and his company, lies in sharp contrast to that of Badr. Bin Sa'ad's army enforced a tight siege around Al-Husayn's camp, denying everyone in it access to water. The women and children in Al-Husayn's camp constantly cried and moaned from thirst. Al-Husayn and his soldiers endured unspeakable hardships. These agonizing conditions, in addition to being cut off from the rest of the world, never deterred the true followers of righteousness from bravely facing their cruel enemy. They fought fearlessly and shook the foundation of the Umayyads' reign of terror. Soon after Ashura, the family of Harb (Abu Sufyan) was wiped off of the face of the earth.

The Battle of Karbala was an Islamic victory against the resurgence of pre-Islamic ignorance. Veiling themselves and their entourage from the light of Prophethood and true monotheism, the Umayyads exhausted all means at their disposal to keep the Muslim Community (Ummah) in total darkness. The position of leadership was not the main goal of Imam Husayn's uprising, and had this been the case, the Prophet's grandson would have sought different venues to achieve this goal. In contrast, He, at a very early stage of his uprising, foretold that he and all the men in his company would be martyred, and that the women would subsequently suffer the hardship of captivity and exile.

Al-Husayn informed his companions of the outcome, and gave everyone permission to leave. At this stage, a large number of his followers were driven by greed and their goal was purely materialistic. These people eventually left him, and only the ones who were later martyred with him stayed. These select few were incredibly loyal to him, and never cowered throughout the Holy uprising. They were extremely determined to achieve the most noble of all goals. Imam Husayn informed them of the difficulties awaiting them, and relieved them from the pledge of allegiance they had given him. Their collective answer was, "We thank Allah, who honored us with martyrdom at your side. If we were guaranteed immortality in this life, we would still prefer to rise up with you rather than staying alive." Sensing his followers' determination in defending the Divine revelations, Al-Husayn underscored their devotion in his response. After he heard their answer, he told them, "I've never heard of any company, family members or relatives more loyal than mine."[4]

Lacking in vision and intellect, some narrators and historians blemished the true image of Al-Husayn's companions. They, describing Al-Husayn's soldiers, wrote: "As conditions during the battle deteriorated, they quivered and became pale from fear, except Imam Husayn, whose face became much more radiant."[5] Failing to find any lapse in Al-Husayn's perfect character, these writers inked their hate and tainted the outstanding image of his companions. These wicked writers intentionally blurred these beautiful images of history. An intelligent reader would definitely realize that the picture was totally different than this false depiction.

More amazing was Zajr Bin Qays Al-Ja'afi's description of the Battle. This man told Yazeed, "As we surrounded them, they ran away from us as pigeons run away from falcons."[6] Zajr's description was a total lie, because many people who witnessed the Battle of Karbala described the situation differently. Al-Husayn's companions fought with unprecedented devotion. Their bravery and determination in defending their faith exceeded that of Imam Ali's companions in the Battle of Siffeen. Their fearlessness and stunning courage in Karbala was, for a long time, the main topic of discussion in every social gathering throughout Kufa. Zajr lied through his teeth, either because he was still in shock from the overwhelming scenes of the

Battle, or because he consciously distorted the facts to appease the drunken Yazeed. The fact is that, in addition to the screams of the orphans and women, the bravery of Al-Husayn and his soldiers gripped Kufa for a long time.

Amr Bin Al-Hajjaj, one of Al-Husayn's bitter enemies, described the incredible bravery of these righteous men. Provoking his comrades to fight fiercely, Amr screamed, "Do you know what you're up against? You're fighting the bravest of all men; men with certainty in their faith and strong determination to self-sacrifice. If you were to fight them face to face, they would annihilate our army. Stone them to death."[7] Shaming a soldier of Bin Sa'ad, a man commented, "You're doomed to have killed the Prophet's family." The soldier responded, "Had you been there, you would have done what we did. A group of men wielding their swords attacked us. They, as brave as lions, destroyed our army from all directions. They were fearless and determined to be martyred. They turned down every offer of security or money. Nothing could have stopped them from taking over the government except martyrdom. Had we been lax in dealing with them, they would have annihilated our army. You're doomed to think that we could have done it differently."[8]

Ka'ab Bin Jaber's words further attested to their remarkable bravery. Condemning her husband for killing Burayr, Ka'ab's wife told him, "You helped the enemies of Fatima's son, and killed The Teacher of Qur'an (Burayr's nickname). You've committed a heinous crime. I shall never talk to you again." He poetically responded, "I have never seen anyone like them throughout my life. They're the bravest of all men. Their steadfastness and perseverance in the battlefield were astonishing."[9] Now, let's ask these wicked historians: Who was trembling from fear in the battlefield? Is it Zuhayr Bin Al-Qayn or Bin A'usaja? Is it Abu Thumama Al-Sa'idi or Sa'iid Al-Hanafi? Is it Bin Shabeeb Al-Shakeri or John? The firm stance of Al-Husayn's companions, coupled with their assertive statements, prove beyond any reasonable doubt that they were incredibly fearless of the outcome. Therefore, the story that they "quivered and became pale from fear" is entirely absurd.

Zuhayr put his hand on Imam Husayn's knee and asked a permission to fight. Zuhayr said, "You're the guidance, and by you we were guided. Today I shall meet your grandfather, the Prophet."

Bin A'usaja consumed his last breath urging Habeeb Bin Muthahir to spare no effort in protecting and supporting Imam Husayn. Despite the pain and suffering he endured on the way of Allah, Abu Thumama Al-Sa'idi was determined to perform his prayers promptly. Sa'iid Al-Hanafi in his turn shielded Al-Husayn during prayers with his own body. Countless arrows landed on Sa'iid, and as he fell down he asked Imam Husayn, "The son of Allah's Messenger! Did I perform well?" Bin Shabeeb Al-Shakeri took off his war vest to attract the enemies towards him. He did this at a time when brave men usually maintain their war vest to avoid being hurt. John was free to leave because Al-Husayn had already relieved him from the duty of fighting. John fell on his leader's feet, kissed them and said, "I'm a humble servant from Africa, and I know nothing about my ancestors. Please allow the breeze of paradise to beautify my scent; honor me with a sense of belonging to a heavenly lineage. By Allah! I shall never leave you. Instead, I shall fight until my blood gets mixed with yours." Imam Al-Baqir said, "Sharp weapons did not inflict any pain on my grandfather's companions."[10]

It has become clear that the determination and passionate pursuit of the Prophet's company obliterated the pain and suffering of Al-Husayn's companions. The path of a loving heart towards his beloved is painless, and it is not an exaggeration to say that the hearts of these dedicated soldiers felt nothing but love. It is evident that these select few were relentless in their cause. Their main objective was to please Allah's Messenger. Their love and determination rendered their wounds painless. Attesting to this fact, historians narrated that Katheer, the famous poet, was sharpening his arrows in his tent when A'zza walked in. Her presence staggered him. He cut his fingers and bled without feeling any pain.[11] In another story a beautiful woman entered an alley in Medina. A man stared at her and followed her. Meanwhile, protruding glass in a wall cut his face open. When the woman disappeared, he noticed blood dripping on his chest and clothes. He told the Prophet the whole story and Allah subsequently revealed to His Messenger, *'Instruct the believers to lower their gaze. (24:30)'*[12] The Prophet said, "When a person is martyred on the way of Allah, the pain of his wounds feels like a little pinch."[13]

Rushayd Al-Hajari's martyrdom is another example of the martyr's painless wounds. Rushayd said that Imam Ali, in the presence of other companions, offered him some dates. He told Imam Ali that the dates were delicious. Imam Ali told Rushayd, "The vile man, Bin Ziyad, would ask you to renounce your adherence to me or he would cut off your limbs and crucify you on the trunk of the palm tree from which you just ate." Rushayd asked Imam Ali, "Will I end up in paradise after all this?" Imam Ali replied, "You'll be my companion in this life and in the next." Rushayd told Imam Ali, "I'll never renounce my adherence to you." Rushayd watered that palm tree every day, and often commented, "I water you to grow for me." Soon after becoming the governor of Kufa, Bin Ziyad asked Rushayd to tell him things he heard from Imam Ali. Rushayd said, "My friend told me that you'll ask me to renounce my adherence to him, but I'll refuse, and you will cut off my arms, my legs and my tongue thereof." Bin Ziyad said, "I shall prove your friend wrong." Bin Ziyad ordered Rushayd's, legs and arms cut off and then taken to his family. As people gathered around Rushayd, he began, in addition to praising the Prophet's household, foretelling future events he had learned from Imam Ali. He yelled to people around him, "Ask me before they cut off my tongue." A man rushed to Bin Ziyad and told him that Rushayd was speaking about future events. Bin Ziyad immediately ordered Rushayd's tongue cut off. Rushayd died that same night, and his body was crucified[14] at the doorstep of Amr Bin Hurayth.[15] Shortly before Rushayd died, his daughter, Qanwa, asked him about his pain. He said, "Daughter! I only feel like I am being crowded."[16] Rushayd occasionally informed people of certain future events relevant to their lives. He had learned the knowledge of fates and disasters[17] from Imam Ali, who nicknamed him Rashid (guide).[18]

These vivid examples demonstrate that being absorbed in loving the Divine enables the devout to envision the bounties of paradise, and to overcome any pain. The Holy Qur'an asserts that the overwhelming power of love effectively annuls pain. Allah describes how Yusuf's staggering beauty totally overwhelmed the women. They cut their hands as soon as they saw him. Allah says in the Qur'an, *"When they saw him, they praised him as they cut their hands. They said, Exalted is our Lord, this is not a human. This is a noble angel (12:30)."* If these women didn't feel the pain of their wounds, then it is fair to conclude that Al-Husayn's companions, who are the core of the universe, didn't feel any pain because their souls were preoccupied with their love of Allah. The honorable goal of pleasing their Lord electrified their existence, and charged their hearts with formidable loyalty to the Master of All Martyrs. They didn't feel the swords and arrows because their passion annihilated their senses, and because their souls were fully absorbed in a climactic vision of the Divine Beauty.

Notes & References

---

1. Kamel Al-Ziyara (P.75)
2. Amali Al-Sheikh Al-Tussi (P.66)
3. Al-Sawa'iq Al-Muhriqa (P.87) & Kashf Al-Ghumma (Al-Sha'rani), (V.1, P.194)
4. Al-Kamel (V.4, P.24)
5. Nafs Al-Mahmoum (P.135) & Al-Bihar (V.2, P.134 & V.10, P.167); both narrated it from Ma'ani Al-Akhbar.
6. Al-Aqd Al-Fareed (V.2, P.313)
7. Tareekh Al-Tabari (V.6, P.247)
8 Sharh Al-Nahj (V.l, P.307)
9. Tareekh Al-Tabari (V.6, P.247)
10. Al-Khara'ij (P.138)
11. Al-Aghani (V.2, P.37)
12. Tafseer Al-Burhan (V.3, P.731)
13. Kanz Al-Ummal (V.2, P.278)
14. Rijal Al-Kashshi (P.51)
15. Mizan Al-I'tidal (V.2, P.339) & Lissan Al-Mizan (V.2, P.461)
16. Rijal Al-Kashshi (P.51) & Amali Bin Al-Sheikh Al-Tussi (P.103)
17. Al-Bihar (V.11, P.246)
18. Amali Bin Al-Sheikh Al-Tussi (P.104)

AL-HUSAYN WITH HIS COMPANIONS

INTRODUCTION

According to Islamic jurisprudence, it is a duty upon every Muslim to rise up and confront corruption and oppression. The infallible leader usually resorts to peaceful means in addressing arising problems. He urges his adversaries to repent and to seek the Lord's judgement to resolve any dispute. The duty of the Muslim Community (Ummah) is to obey the infallible leader and to defend justice. It is crucial to know that the Divinely appointed guide (Imam) is a manifestation of the Divine justice. Allah, the Exalted, instructed the believers to seek justice in their disputes. He, in His Holy Book, says, *"If two groups of the believers fight, try to reconcile between them, however if one oppresses the other, then you fight against the oppressor until it complies with Allah's commands (49:9)."*

During his reign (Khilafa), Imam Ali rose up to defend faith, and simultaneously warn the Community against ignorance. It was a duty upon all Muslims at that time to obey his orders, because he was the legitimate leader. There is a consensus amongst Muslims over the legitimacy of the selection process by which Imam Ali became the leader (Khaleefa). Moreover, all Muslims ruled that Ali rightfully fought his wars against the insurgents. Conforming to authentic traditions and relying on common sense, prominent scholars eloquently discussed and assessed that time period.

Abu Haneefa said, "Ali rightfully fought against his enemies. If we were to ignore Ali's conduct, no one would know how to guide the Muslims. There is no doubt that Ali rightfully fought Talha and Al-Zubayr after they betrayed him. Ali was the most knowledgeable of all Muslims. He implemented justice in the Battle of the Camel, and enforced the right path (Sunnah) in fighting the oppressors."[1] In agreement with his teacher, Abu Haneefa's student, Mohammed Bin Al-Hasan Al-Sheybani (d. 187 A.H. = 803 C.E.) said, "Mu'awiya was undoubtedly the oppressor and the transgressor in his war against Ali. If the latter didn't fight the former, we would have never learned to battle the oppressors."[2] Sufyan Al-Thawri said, "Ali rightfully fought the insurgents."[3] Al-Shafi'e said, "It is better not to discuss the Battle of Siffeen, however, Ali rightfully fought the insurgents."[4]

In his *Ahkam Al-Qur'an (V.3, P.492)*, Abu Bakr Al-Razi Al-Jassas (d.370 A.H. = 981 C.E.) wrote:

> "No one disagrees that Ali rightfully fought the oppressors. Many of the Prophet's companions, some of whom fought in Badr, joined Ali's army. There is no doubt that these men were very faithful."

In his *Al-Awassim*, Al-Qadhi Abu Bakr Bin Al-Arabi (d. 546 A.H. = 1151 C.E.) wrote:

> "Ali was the legitimate leader. People selected him and he, worried that the Divine codes would be distorted and the message of Islam would be altered, could not turn them down. Ali was indeed the fittest for the position of leadership. He accepted the position in order to protect the Muslim Community from more chaos and instability, which would have led to more bloodshed. When the people of Al-Sham asked Ali to turn over the killers of Othman, he told them to accept him as a leader first, and then ask for the killers. Ali was wise and just, for had he complied, the tribes of the alleged perpetrators would have formed a third party and waged a war to defend their members. Ali waited to establish his leadership over the masses before setting a trial to implement justice. The leader of the Community (Ummah) has the right to delay a trial in order to avoid controversy and division. Therefore, the people who turned against Ali were oppressors, and it was a duty to fight them until they complied with Allah's codes. Ali rightfully waged war against the people of Al-Sham because they never accepted his legitimate leadership. Also, he rightfully fought the battles of the Camel and Al-Nahrawan against those who betrayed him.' Peacefully requesting from Ali to consider their demands would have been the right thing to do. Having failed to do so, they became oppressors and Allah, the Exalted, orders us to fight them. *Fight the oppressors until they comply with Allah's commands (49:9)."*

Mu'awiya was annoyed with Sa'ad Bin Abi Waqqas for not siding with him against Ali.[5] In response, Sa'ad expressed his regret for not fighting the oppressors, meaning Mu'awiya and his followers.[6] After praising Imam Ali in his *Tamheed (P.229)*, Abu Bakr Mohammed Al-Baqlani (d. 403 A.H. = 1013 C.E.) wrote:

> "Counting only some of these unrivalled merits, Ali was the most qualified for the position of leadership. His truthfulness compelled the foremost of the Migrants and the Supporters (Al-Muhajireen and Al-Ansar) to select him as a leader three days after Othman's death. Ali declined, but they insisted because he was the most knowledgeable, the best of his time and the fittest for the position. They appealed to him to protect the Muslim Community and preserve the sanctity of Medina. They pledged allegiance to him before the arrival of Talha and Al-Zubayr. Like the rest of the Community, both men willingly pledged allegiance to Ali. Had they not pledged allegiance, they would have sinned. Their argument, later on, that they were compelled to accept him, does not diminish the legitimacy of Ali's leadership, because people had already selected Ali, and Talha and Al-Zubayr accepted him under no pressure. Also, both were wrong to ask Ali to execute Othman's killers, because their request entailed that Ali should kill many people for the murder of one individual. Their request was totally unreasonable. Imam Ali's vision might have been different than theirs, and even if he thought that executing many people for an individual's murder was acceptable, he could have changed his mind, and he had the right to do so. Also, if we suppose that Ali was to execute the killers of Othman, he would not have done so without a request from Othman's sons in a trial in which a valid proof against the alleged murderers must be presented. This process could be performed only if disruption and chaos could be avoided, however, the situation was still turbulent because of Othman's death. Ali may have deliberately delayed the trial to a suitable time to maintain order, and thus better serve the Community and protect it from further instability."

Mohammed Bin Abdullah, known as Al-Hakim Al-Naysabouri (d.405 A. H = 1015 C.E.) stated, "There is a consensus in the authentic traditions over the legitimacy of Imam Ali's leadership." He then narrated that Khuzayma Bin Thabit (one of the Prophet's companions) stood up next to the pulpit and documented the event in his poetry. Khuzayma said, "We accepted Ali as a leader to spare ourselves division. We found him the best leader since he is the most knowledgeable in the Qur'an and the Prophet's traditions (Sunnah). He is the best of Quraysh and he is full of goodness and righteousness."[7] In his commentary on Al-Naysabouri's *Al-Mustadrak,* Al-Thahabi quoted this narration but did not elaborate on it.

Al-Hakim Al-Naysabouri narrated that on his deathbed, Abdullah Bin Omar Bin Al-Khattab said, "Whenever I remember this verse, *fight the oppressors until they comply with Allah's commands (49:9)*, I regret not fighting the oppressors as Allah ordered me to do."[8] Al-Hakim also narrated that Mohammed Bin Is'haq Bin Khuzayma said, "Our teachers believed that whoever fought against Ali Bin Abi Talib was an oppressor. This was also the opinion of Bin Idrees."[9]

Abu Mansoor Al-Baghdadi (d.429 A.H. = 1038 C.E.) stated, "There is a consensus amongst the truthful over the legitimacy of Imam Ali's leadership after Othman was killed. Ali was absolutely correct in his conduct. Moreover, he rightfully fought both the Battle of the Camel, and against Mu'awiya's army in Siffeen."[10]

In his *Muhaththab (V.2, P.234),* Abu Is'haq Ibraheem Bin Ali Al-Sheerazi Al-Fayrouzabadi (d.476 A.H. = 1083 C.E.) wrote:

> "If a group of Muslims revolts against its leader, tries to oust him, disobeys his orders or abstains from fulfilling its commitments, his duty is to fight this group because Allah, the Exalted, orders us to fight the oppressors. Abu Bakr fought a group of Muslims for refusing to pay alms. Ali fought the people of Al-Basra in the Battle of the Camel, Mu'awiya in Siffeen and the apostates in Al-Nahrawan. Ali rightfully fought them because he was the righteous leader, and people should have honored their pledge of allegiance to him. No matter what their reasons were, defying Ali was unjustifiable."

In his *Irshaad (P.433),* Imam Al-Haramayn Al-Juwayni (d.478 A.H. = 1085 C.E.) stated:

"Ali was the righteous leader at the time and his adversaries were oppressors."

In his *Badae'a Al-Sanae'a (V.7, P.140)*, Ala'a Al-Deen Al-Kassani Al-Hanafi (d.587 A.H. = 1191 C.E.) wrote:

> "The Prophet foretold that Ali shall fight to implement the interpretation the way Allah's Messenger fought to deliver the revelations. Ali, our master, confirmed this prophecy when he and the Prophet's companions fought the apostates in Al-Nahrawan. Ali's war against the apostates was over the interpretation of the Holy Book. The Prophet's struggle to deliver the Message is analogous to Ali's in upholding its true interpretation. The Prophet's words have thus confirmed the legitimacy of Ali's leadership. The Prophet rightfully waged wars to deliver the Message, and so did Ali to maintain the true interpretations of its codes. Every able Muslim man at that time should have joined Ali's army because it is a duty to support the leader in enforcing the codes of the Divine law. Abu Haneefa said that a person should stay neutral when there is a confrontation between two Muslim groups. He ruled neutrality in the absence of the legitimate leader, but when there is one, all Muslims should obey his orders."

In his *Sharh Saheeh Muslim (V.10, Ps. 336 & 338)*, Yahya Bin Sharaf Al-Nawawi Al-Sharie (d.677 A.H. = 1278 C.E.) wrote:

> "Ali rightfully waged his wars. Most of the Prophet's companions and their junior compatriots, as well as all Muslim scholars, upheld the duty to rise up against the corrupt and support the righteous party, because Allah orders us to fight the oppressor. This is correct beyond any doubt."

In his *Fat'h Al-Qadeer (V.5, P.461)*, Bin Hammam Al-Hanafi (d.681 A.H. = 1282 C.E.) wrote:

> "Ali rightfully fought in the Battle of the Camel and in Siffeen, where Mu'awiya's soldiers killed Ammar Bin Yasser. The Prophet foretold that the oppressors would kill Ammar. This is a clear indication that Mu'awiya and his soldiers were oppressors. In his *Al-Istee'ab*, Abu Amr narrated that A'isha regretted her stance against Ali, and later told Abdullah Bin Umar that he should have stopped her from going to Basra. Abdullah told her that he couldn't

have, because Bin Al-Zubayr had a strong influence over her. She regretfully exclaimed that if Bin Umar had stopped her, she wouldn't have gone."

In his *Fatawa (V.2, P.251)*, Bin Taymiyya (d.728 A.H = 1328 C.E.) wrote:

"When Othman was killed, the Muslims selected Ameer Al-Mu'mineen, Ali Bin Abi Talib, as their leader because he was the fittest and the best at the time. However, chaos and unrest in the Community escalated into division and hostility amongst its members. The leader and the foremost members of the Community couldn't restore order. The situation led to the rising of the apostates who fought Ameer Al-Mu'mineen Ali and his followers. Ali implemented the commands of Allah and His Messenger, and killed them off. The Prophet foretold that the righteous party would kill off the apostates. Ali and his followers killed them off, and we conclude from the Prophet's words that Ali and his followers were righteous, and Mu'awiya and his followers were not."

In his *Fatawa (V.4, P.224)*, Bin Taymiyya also wrote:

"Shi'as believe that Mu'awiya was no match to Ali, and it was ridiculous for the former to compete for the position of leadership while the latter was still alive. In addition to being supremely virtuous, Ali was elite in his faith, very knowledgeable and very brave. After Othman's death, Ali was the only active living person from the council (appointed by Umar), because Sa'ad Bin Abi Waqqas (the other living member of the council) abstained from participating in public affairs."

In his *Nassb Al-Raya (V.4, P.69)*, Al-Zaylai (d. 762 A.H.= 1361 C.E.) wrote:

"Ali was righteous throughout his leadership, and the Prophet's statement that the oppressive party would kill Ammar Bin Yasser confirms this fact. Mu'awiya's soldiers did kill Ammar. There is a consensus that Ali rightfully fought Talha, Al-Zubayr, A'isha and their followers in the Battle of the Camel, and Mu'awiya and his soldiers in the Battle of Siffeen. When Ali became the leader, Mu'awiya defiantly vowed not to accept or comply with him, nor to ever pledge allegiance to the rightful leader."

In his *Badae'a Al-Fawa'id (V.3, P.208)*, Bin Qayyim Al-Jawziyya (d.751 A.H.= 1350 C.E) wrote:

"Ali was the foremost and the best of all Muslims at the time, and no one was more qualified than him to lead the Community."

In his *Al-Furu' (V.3, Ps. 542 & 543)*, Abu Abdullah Bin Mohammed Bin Muflih Al-Hanbali (d. 763 A.H. = 1362 C.E.) wrote:

"Ali was more righteous than Mu'awiya, and any sensible person would conclude that Ali rightfully fought the oppressors. However, some thought that remaining neutral would have been wise. Bin Hubayra, explaining Abi Bakra's neutrality, said that it was wise to remain neutral during the tumultuous events that led to Othman's murder, but defying Ali was absolutely unjustifiable. Sa'ad, Bin Umar, Osama, Mohammed Bin Muslima, Masruq and Al-Ahnaf regretted their deliberate abstention from supporting Ali. Bin Umar, on his deathbed, said that he deeply regretted his intentional absence from Ali's army. It is also authentically narrated that Masruq and others expressed similar regret before they died."

In his *Fat'h Al-Bari (V.12, P.244)*, Bin Hijr Al-Asqalani (d. 852 A.H. = 1449 C.E.) wrote:

"Imam Ali Bin Abi Talib was righteous and correct in fighting the insurgents who waged war against him in the Battle of the Camel, Siffeen and other battles."

In his *Umdat Al-Qari (V.11, P.346)*, Mahmoud Al-A'yni (d. 855 A.H. = 1451 C.E.) wrote:

"All Muslims agree that Ali and his followers were on the right path. Ali was the most qualified for the position of leadership, and the best man on the face of the earth at that time."

In his *Tuhfat Al-Muhtaj (V.4, Ps 110 & 112)*, Bin Hijr Al-Haythami (d.974 A.H. = 1567 C.E.) wrote:

"Ali's adversaries in the Battles of the Camel and Siffeen

accused him of being an accomplice to Othman's murder. Ali was definitely innocent, and no such act could ever be attributed to him... There was a consensus amongst the Prophet's companions on fighting the oppressors. Following Ali's footsteps, the leader must entrust an intelligent believer to peacefully attempt to resolve the nagging dispute. Ali, a perfect role model to all of us, sent Bin Abbass to talk sense into the minds of the apostates before the battle of Al-Nahrawan. As a result, many of them abandoned their wrongdoing and rejoined Ali's army."

(The dialogue between Bin Abbass and the apostates can be found in the section that lists the merits of Imam Ali of *Khasa'is Al-Nassau's.*)

In his *Sharh Al-Shafa (V.3, P.166)*, Al-Shahab Al-Khafaji (d.1100 A.H. = 1689 C.E.) wrote:

"The Prophet foretold that the oppressive party would kill Ammar. He was on Ali's side in Siffeen, and Mu'awiya's soldiers killed him. Thus it has become clear that Ali was the legitimate leader, and Mu'awiya was wrong in his conduct. People are considered oppressors when they unjustifiably revolt against their legitimate leader. It is also narrated that the Prophet said that Sumayya's son is always on the right path. Ammar, Sumayya's son, was on Ali's side. Therefore, we believe that Ali, may Allah's blessings be upon his face, is on the right path and correct in refusing to arrest the murderers of Othman."

Al-Shawkani (d. 1255 A.H = 1839 C.E.) narrated through Abu Sa'iid that the Prophet said, "My Community (Ummah) shall divide into two groups, between which an apostate third group will emerge. This third group will be killed off by the righteous of the first two groups." Al-Shawkani then commented, "This narration clearly indicates that Ali and his followers were on the right path, while Mu'awiya and his followers were astray."[11]

In his commentary on the Qur'an, Abu Al-Thana Al-Alloussi stated that some Hanbalis firmly believe in fighting the oppressors because Ali set aside the fight against infidels (Jihad), and dedicated the time of his leadership to fight the oppressors. Al-Alloussi explained that the Hanbalis concluded from Ali's conduct that fighting the oppressors is more important than fighting the infidels. Al-Alloussi then mentioned Bin Umar's regret for not fighting on Ali's side against the oppressors, but did not elaborate on it.[12]

In his *Al-Islam Wa Al-Hadhara Al-Arabiyya (V.2, P.380)*, Mohammed Kard Ali wrote:

> "No one objects to Ali's innocence in the murder of Othman. A large number of people from different tribes were involved in murdering Othman. Ali knew that it wasn't feasible to arrest all or some of the killers, even if he knew who they were, especially since the tribes of these men were supporting him. The murder occurred against his wish, but he saw no benefit in becoming an adversary of the tribes that supported him. Ali publicly offered the Umayyads his willingness to bring fifty men from Bani Hashim to testify under oath that he was neither an accomplice in the murder, nor an active rebel against Othman."

These opinions of Sunni scholars confirm the legitimacy of Ali's leadership and that his adversaries were the oppressors. These scholars emphasized that Ali rightfully fought the insurgents to enforce justice. For this reason the Prophet's devout companions and their junior compatriots, including Uwayss Al-Qarani, chose to be on Ali's side. An infantryman in Ali's army, Uwayss was martyred in the Battle of Siffeen.[13]

Abdullah Bin Amr Bin Al-A'as repeatedly expressed his regret for not fighting the oppressors in compliance with Allah's order. He narrated from the Prophet that Ammar would be killed by the oppressive party, and was convinced that Mu'awiya was the oppressor in fighting against Imam Ali. When asked why he wasn't on Ali's side in the Battle of Siffeen, he answered, "I wasn't because the Prophet told me to obey my father, and I did."[14] Bin Amr deliberately circumvented the real meaning of the Prophet's words. His statement was completely deceptive and averse of the truth. His answer was utter nonsense, and such a dumb excuse will bear no fruit for him on the Day of Judgement. How could anyone think that Islamic jurisprudence mandates parental obedience if it entails committing sins and evading Islamic duties? It suffices to state that obeying the legitimate leader, to whom a pledge of allegiance had been given, is a duty upon every Muslim. It is also a duty upon every member of the Community to comply with his leader's commands.

Submission to the infallible leader surpasses that to the parents. Allah, the Exalted, emphasized this when he revealed *"If they (the parents) urge you to consider a partner for Me, then do not obey them (29:8)."* This verse clearly indicates that disobeying Allah, His Messenger and the infallible leader, to whom a person had pledged allegiance, falls under the umbrella of considering a partner for Allah (Shirk). It is worth mentioning that A'isha performed full prayers while she was travelling to Basra because she was aware that short prayers (Qasr) were meant for the travelers who heed the Divine codes during their travel.[15]

The Divine Message instructs the leader of the Muslim Community to reason with his adversaries, and to remind them of Allah's continuous blessings upon them, despite their violation of His codes. The leader must also remind them that Holy book and the Prophet, in his preaching, sternly warned them against investing their time for this mortal life, because it reaps them total loss in the next. The leader's hope in doing so is to guide them to the true path. Imam Ali implemented this Islamic code and reasoned with his adversaries before the onset of each battle. Moreover, he urged his companions not to violate any code of Islamic jurisprudence, one of which was initiating aggression against their enemies. He strictly enforced these codes to prove beyond any doubt that his adversaries were the oppressors. Imam Ali's enemies were the oppressors indeed. They refused to reason and initiated military aggression against him.[16]

Imam Ali, peace be upon him and his infallible sons, sincerely advised his enemies in Basra, Siffeen and Al-Nahrawan, and employed every possible venue to resolve each conflict peacefully. He exhausted all forms of reasoning, leaving no credible excuse for any of his adversaries on the Day of Judgement. His sincere words guided many people to the true path, but many ignored his advice and succumbed to aberration.

AL-HUSAYN ON THE DAY OF ASHURA

Al-Husayn followed the same path of reasoning on the day of Ashura. He didn't initiate any military action, despite being provoked by the large, well-equipped army of his enemies. He sought peaceful venues to resolve the conflict, but the transgressors reciprocated with cruelty. Despite being aware of the Prophet's strict instructions that no human should be denied access to food and water, Bin Sa'ad's army denied Al-Husayn, his family members and companions the water of the Euphrates.

In his first encounter, Al-Husayn reasoned with his adversaries, reminding them that they shall reap in the next life what they sow in this mortal one. In his second address, he reminded them of his kinship to Allah's Messenger and of his grandfather's testimony that "Al-Hasan and Al-Husayn are the Masters of Youth in heaven." Aware that the Prophet *never spoke out of his own desire (53:3)*, the so-called Muslims should have honored the Prophet's testimony, and reflected on it to distinguish between right and wrong. In the third, Imam Husayn proposed to comply with their demands if they could prove that he was indebted to them in money or blood. In the fourth, he crowned himself with a copy of the Qur'an, walked towards them and urged them to accept the judgement of Allah's Holy Book.

Al-Husayn's words fell on deaf ears. Having exhausted peaceful venues, he realized that his enemies were firmly determined to breach the Divine codes and betray Allah's Messenger. At this point, he changed his approach, and reminded the crowd of the bravery and dignity he had inherited from his father. Al-Husayn said, "This man, vicious like his father, is pushing for war or humiliation, and we will never be humiliated. Allah, His Messenger, and the believers do not approve of humiliation. Pure wombs bore our honorable and dignified souls, and we shall never obey the vile in lieu of a blessed martyrdom. My family and I shall fight, despite our small number and lack of supporters."

Al-Husayn's tactics embodied the codes of the Divine Message, and its firm order to proselytize the true path on one hand, and to rise up and seal the door of aberration on the other. According to Islamic jurisprudence, fighting on the way of Allah (Jihad) is a duty upon every Muslim. Boys, the handicapped, old men, women and the adolescent, whose parents disallow him, are optionally relieved from this duty. However, scenes from Ashura overruled all options. Al-Husayn's Holy uprising contained embedded secrets and benefits that are beyond our limited intellect. Al-Husayn learned them all from his father and grandfather.

Al-Husayn did not introduce new codes for warfare. His uprising was rather a Divine lesson engraved in the Divine Tablet on the Day of Creation; confined in its implementation to a specific place at a specific time. Jabra'eel learned it and delivered it to the most beloved of Allah's creatures, who in turn deposited it in the heart of the Master of All Martyrs. Furthermore, Allah blessed His representative on earth at the time, Abu Abdullah Al-Husayn, with the privilege of a special vision and higher comprehension. Human intellect falls short in its attempt to fully ascertain the miracles and the enormous spiritual benefit of the bloody scenes on that day.

The Martyr of Kufa, Muslim Bin Aqeel, adhered to Al-Husayn's path and values. Muslim's exceptional knowledge, dedication, and devotion earned him the position of representing Imam Husayn in Kufa. Muslim Bin Aqeel was thirsty to the extent that jurisprudence would have allowed him to ingest filth (Najasa). Resolutely loyal to Allah and His Messenger, Muslim refused to compromise. He and Al-Abbass Bin Ali graduated from the school of infallibility with highest honors, and thus became role models for piety.

Thousands of Al-Husayn's enemies formed a barrier to prevent Al-Abbass from reaching the Euphrates. Like Muslim Bin Aqeel, Al-Abbass single handedly expelled them. Abu Al-Fadhl fought his way into the water of the Euphrates, but didn't taste any of it. Imam Husayn, the women of the Prophet's household and Fatima's children were extremely thirsty, and Al-Abbass' main goal was to bring them water. He realized that quenching his thirst would delay his delivery. Al-Abbass was unwilling to compromise even a minute in his mission. Al-Abbass was inculcated with the virtue of selflessness from his father Ali, and his two infallible brothers, about whom the Prophet said, "They are infallible leaders whether in war or peace."[17] Abu Al-Fadhl Al-Abbass was martyred before completing his mission.

Al-Husayn rose up with a small number of supporters. Old men, children, nursing infants and women formed the majority in his company. Al-Husayn was fully aware that the Umayyads' goal was to kill off all of his children, and thus uproot the Prophet's family. He was also certain that these transgressors would stop at nothing to achieve their goal. Imam Husayn's insightful tactics, the goals of which are beyond our understanding, exposed to all generations the evil schemes and the unprecedented cruelty of the contemporary tyrants. It is worth repeating that Yazeed's Umayyad forefathers, including Mu'awiya, never believed in the Divine Message, but reluctantly accepted it only to spare their lives. Al-Husayn laid out an immaculate plan and meticulously executed it. His self-sacrifice and the voices of the women of his family rendered his enemies sleepless. Al-Husayn's tactics reaped the desired dividend, for the tyrants' shamelessness and cruelty in Karbala became the main topic of discussions throughout the Community (Ummah).

Relief of Duty

Imam Husayn's words and actions were universal. His precious words, in urging his family and companions to leave, reflect the depth of his wisdom. Al-Husayn relieved everyone in his company from their duty, and absolved them from the pledge of allegiance they had given him. Historians narrated that in the evening preceding the tenth of Muharram, Al-Husayn gathered his family and companions and told them, "I've never heard of companions or family members more loyal than mine. I ask Allah to reward all of you for being here. I believe that tomorrow is *the day*, and I don't mind if you leave. I am relieving all of you from your commitment to me. Take cover in the darkness tonight, and let each one of my companions accompany a man from my family and leave. These people are after me, and once they kill me, they won't go after any of you."[18]

The Prophet's grandson articulated his sharp foresight towards his goal. These golden words proved beyond doubt that Al-Husayn's family and companions were the core of the universe. They were indeed, as Imam Ali described them, "The Masters of All Martyrs, surpassed by no one."[19] Their sincerity and determination towards self-sacrifice engraved on an eternal tablet a timeless lesson of devotion. They favored a dignified death over a life of humiliation under a tyrannical government. Their goal was to either uproot oppression, or to attain the immortal pleasure of martyrdom.

Had Imam Husayn not given his companions an explicit permission to leave, people wouldn't have known the level of their superior knowledge and certitude. Moreover, people wouldn't have realized the insurmountable devotion and sincerity with which they defended their principles and achieved their noble goal. Allah tests people even though He knows the past, the future and the details of all hidden things. Allah knew how submissive Prophet Ibraheem was, but still ordered him to slaughter his son, Isma'il. Allah ordained to further test Ibraheem's submission for a reason beyond our understanding. Imam Husayn employed a similar tactic, and tested his companions' intentions. He, in doing so, conveyed to all people the level of purity and devotion of his companions and family members. The result of this test depicted to all of us these men's irreversible determination to please Allah and His Messenger.

A man's words coupled with his actions are indicative of his sincerity and dedication in obeying and pleasing the Lord. Historians ignored many pious men and women who spared no effort in supporting and protecting the Divine revelations and this, unfortunately, was the case with Al-Husayn's companions and family members. History books, devoid of elaboration on these martyrs' devotion, mentioned only two things; their response to Imam Husayn when he urged them to leave, and the subsequent bloody battle in Karbala. The statements of these men and women on that night reflected a glimpse of their deep faith and the superior knowledge that Allah had instilled in their hearts. Al-Husayn stoked the flames of passion in his soldiers' hearts to transmit bright rays of guidance to all humans.

Muslim Bin Ausaja, for instance, is absent from history books except for a brief description of his bravery in the Battle of Azerbijan. Shibth Bin Rib'ie, one of his enemies in Karbala, said that Bin Ausaja killed six infidels before the onset of that battle. This incident embodied Muslim's astounding loyalty to the Prophet's successors. His faith and devotion never diminished with the lapse of time. Bin Ausaja told Imam Husayn, "How dare we leave you? What would our excuse be when Allah asks us about our loyalty to you? By Allah! I shall never leave you, but instead I intend to break my spear in their chests, and fight with my sword for as long as I can wield it. If I have no weapon, I shall stone them until I die with you." Bin Ausaja's response clearly indicates that he was a man of principles. His main goal in life was to please Allah and His Messenger at any cost; he endured tremendous hardship to achieve it. He lived up to his words and fought very bravely until he was badly wounded. He, lying on the hot sand and choking on his blood, consumed his last breath urging Habeeb Bin Muthahir to defend Imam Husayn. His will to Habeeb was to spare no effort in supporting Al-Husayn. He died advocating the principles and values he had upheld throughout his life.

Sa'iid Bin Abdullah Al-Hanafi spoke after Muslim. Sa'iid expressed his unequivocal loyalty to Al-Husayn. He told Imam Husayn, "By Allah! We will never leave you. Allah knows that our loyalty to you is an extension of that to His Messenger. By Allah! If I were to be killed, and then resurrected, and then burnt to ashes a countless number of times; I would never leave, but instead, I am determined to die defending you. How could I leave when I know that it is only one death, after which comes eternal joy?" Sa'iid bravely shielded Imam Husayn during the noon prayers on Ashura. As soon as Al-Husayn finished his prayers, the badly wounded Sa'iid fell to the ground and asked the Master of Martyrs to evaluate his performance. Al-Husayn assured him that his efforts had pleased the Exalted, and that he was bound to reunite with the Prophet in eternal joy. As Sa'iid finished his statement, Zuhayr Bin Al-Qayn Al-Bajli told Imam Husayn, "By Allah! It is my pleasure to be killed and crucified thousands of times while defending you and your family." In this brief statement, Zuhayr articulated an eternal lesson of devotion in defending the path of righteousness while upholding its principles.

Some people perform good deeds for the sole purpose of accruing rewards for the Day of Judgement. Others, who have certitude in their faith, have a deeper cause and a higher goal. They heed the Divine codes because Allah is worthy of their submission. Zuhayr's words and actions in defending the infallible leader placed him in the second category. Zuhayr was extremely faithful. He fulfilled the sacred duty of defending people whom the Prophet deeply loved. He also sought nothing in return for fighting the transgressors. Completely aware of the strong bond between Al-Husayn and the Prophet, Zuhayr's goal in defending his infallible leader was to defend Allah's Messenger. Mainstream history books only mentioned Zuhayr's loyalty to Othman and his hatred towards the Prophet's grandson. His words in Karbala, however, depict a clear image of his love and loyalty to the infallible leaders who were Divinely appointed to preserve the Holy Message.

The Prophet described the special bond between himself and

Al-Husayn. He said, "Husayn is from me, and I'm from Husayn."[20] It is utter nonsense to think that, in this statement, the Prophet meant to inform the Community of his blood relation to Al-Husayn. The kinship between Al-Husayn and the Prophet was, and still is, obvious to everyone. The most eloquent human (Prophet Mohammed) would never redundantly state the obvious. In these words, the Prophet emphasized a higher dimension in the special bond between himself and Al-Husayn. He explicitly conveyed to his Community that his grandson's uprising against the evil oppressors would reinforce the foundation of Islam and restore its ideals. Imam Husayn rose up to preserve the Divine revelations as his grandfather did to deliver them. The Prophet immaculately articulated this reality. Al-Husayn's uprising successfully obliterated the innovations that the transgressors falsely attributed to the right path. Al-Husayn's self-sacrifice effectively inspired its contemporaries, as well as the coming generations, to confront any criminal who ruthlessly attempts to alter the Divine codes.

A'abiss Bin Abi Shabeeb Al-Shakeri expressed his love and loyalty to the Prophet's household twice. The first was in Kufa, where he expressed his irreversible determination to defend the infallible leader at any cost. He, in the presence of thousands of Kufans, pledged allegiance and then told Muslim Bin Aqeel, "I can neither foresee what these people would do, nor assure you of their loyalty. However, I can tell you about what I intend to do. By Allah! I shall flock to you and fight your enemy. I shall use my sword to defend all of you (Ahl Al-Bayt), seeking in all of this Allah's pleasure."[21]

The beginning of his statement proves that A'abiss was aware that the Kufans were deceptive hypocrites. They initially pledged allegiance to Muslim Bin Aqeel but were easily swayed by their desire to live, and ignored their pledge. By nightfall, Muslim Bin Aqeel ended up alone; not a single person from the thousands who had pledged allegiance to him remained to help show him the way in the narrow alleys of Kufa. Expressing his devotion and sincerity in defending the locus of beings at the time, A'abiss told Imam Husayn in Karbala, "I love you more than anything on the face of this planet. I shall defend you with my soul, and if I could do more I would."[22] Nafi' Bin Hilal told Imam Husayn, "We are neither afraid of the outcome, nor resentful of returning to our Lord. We are adamant about loving whom you love and condemning your enemies." The rest of Al-Husayn's companions expressed a similar level of commitment.

When Imam Husayn gave his family members permission to leave, they collectively exclaimed, "Why would we leave? To outlive you! We ask Allah to never show us that day." Al-Husayn looked at Bani Aqeel and said, "Losing Muslim was hard enough on you. I allow you to leave." They immediately and restlessly expressed their unshakable determination to defend Allah's Message and the Divinely appointed leader. They said, "What would we tell people then? How could we tell them that we abandoned our master and infallible leader? How could we tell people that we deserted our cousins, whose fathers are the best of all human beings, without fighting along their side? We shall never leave, but instead we shall sacrifice our possessions, our families and our lives fighting on your side in this life, to be with you in the next. Life is worthless without you."

It is important to know that Al-Husayn's family, relatives and companions expressed such strong determination to self-sacrifice when they were totally besieged and banned from even a drink of water. Their difficult situation clearly indicates that they had no affinity to life; otherwise they would have taken advantage of the permission to leave and, unlike the people who never supported this uprising, they would have been exonerated on the Day of Judgement. However, their pure souls had already been Divinely infused with faith and certitude. Their main goal in life was to enforce righteousness and obliterate transgression. They rejected any alternative to their noble goal.

In the midst of all this, Mohammed Bin Basheer Al-Hadhrami was informed that his son had been captured in the province of Al-Rayy. Reacting to the bad news, Basheer vented, "I ask Allah to account for me and for him. I hate to live without him." Imam Husayn heard him and gave him permission to leave, so he could work on his son's release. Al-Husayn's words provoked Al-Hadhrami to passionately articulate his absolute determination to self-sacrifice in defending the infallible leader. Basheer replied, "Oh Abu Abdullah! Even if beasts rip through my flesh, I would never leave you. "Basheer's devotion is an example of how submission to Allah and His messenger beget a solid faith, transporting the true believer into the realm of righteousness and ultimate grace. If

Al-Hadhrami's beliefs were superficial, he would have legitimately used the permission to leave as an excuse in this life and in the next.

Al-Husayn didn't want any of his companions to remain only because they were ashamed to leave. The honorable Husayn relieved John, Abu Tharr's servant, from his duties. The Prophet's grandson knew very well the high level of perseverance and faith in John's heart. Nonetheless, he wanted John to articulate another lesson of devotion in supporting the right path against evil. Al-Husayn said, "John! You joined us to earn your living. You are free to leave." Fearing that he might not be fit enough to attain the eternal joy, John tearfully replied, "How could I share your meals in good times and desert you in hardship? I'm a humble servant from Africa, and I know nothing about my ancestors. Please allow the breeze of paradise to beautify my scent; honor me with a sense of belonging to a heavenly lineage. By Allah! I shall never leave you. Instead, I shall fight until my blood gets mixed with yours."[23] Al-Husayn deliberately initiated this dialogue to transmit to all generations John's sincerity, strength of faith and determination to self-sacrifice. The echo of John's words taught the believers that perseverance generates success, and comfort succeeds hardship.

Conclusion

Jurisprudence and intellect equate protecting the infallible leader to protecting the Prophet. A person should never abandon the infallible leader and abstain from supporting him against his enemies, and it is a duty to fend off any aggression against the locus of beings. A believer must sacrifice his life and possessions to defend the infallible leader. The latter, in turn, must make a call to others to support and defend him. However, he is entitled to relieve his supporters from their duty when he is certain that no efforts can preserve his Holy life. Imam Husayn knew what was awaiting him at the hands of his enemies. It was an irrevocable ordinance; a promise bound to be fulfilled. He foretold the outcome of his uprising during his conversation with Umm Salama. He told her, "If I don't rise up today, I will tomorrow, and if not, I will the next day. No one can escape from death. Do you think that you know what I don't?"

Al-Husayn saw no reason in compelling others to defend

him. On the other hand, people who fit in any of the following categories will not be exonerated on the Day of Judgement for abandoning the infallible leader:

1. Those who didn't learn that it was a duty to defend the infallible leader.
2. Those who witnessed the siege in which the Divinely appointed guardian was cut off from the rest of the world, and prevented from getting a drink of water, but still abstained from defending him.
3. Those who witnessed Al-Husayn's condition, but cowered away fearing that the worst was yet to come.

In contrast, those who leave after acquiring his permission will be aquatinted on the Day of Judgement, since the infallible leader is Divinely inspired and has the right to dismiss his soldiers. Those who leave after receiving his permission would not be in breach of the Divine codes. The infallible leader's decisions are based on facts and realities. Therefore, his decision to dismiss his supporters should never be perceived as self-destructive. There would be no blame on the dismissed soldiers as long as they do not witness the battle in which the infallible leader is calling for support. However, even after their dismissal, if they see and hear the infallible leader calling for support, they have to rush and defend him or they will be punished on the Day of Judgement for their inaction.

Al-Husayn's dialogue with Ubaydallah Bin Al-Hurr Al-Ja'afi confirms our conclusion. After Al-Ja'afi's refusal to join the uprising, Imam Husayn told him, "I advise you to flee to some place where you do not see the battle, or hear our voices and calls for support. Those who see the battle or hear our voices, but do not defend us will definitely end up in hellfire." This clearly indicates that those who heard Al-Husayn, but did not defend him, will not be exonerated, while those who were dismissed, and couldn't hear his calls, would be.

Al-Dhahhak Bin Abdullah Al-Mashriqi will not be exonerated on the Day of Judgement because he saw and heard Imam Husayn during the battle. Before the battle, this man told Imam Husayn, "I'll fight for as long as there are other supporters around you, but when there is none, I'll leave." Imam Husayn agreed. Seeing the horses of his comrades being killed, Al-Mashriqi hid his horse and fought on foot. As soon as he saw Imam Husayn alone in the battlefield, Al-Mashriqi said, "I want to honor the condition." Imam Husayn replied, "You're free to go if you can make it to safety." Al-Mashriqi rode his horse out of the tent and fled through the enemy lines. Fifteen men chased him and captured him on a bank of the Euphrates. Three out of the fifteen identified him as their cousin and successfully convinced their comrades to release him.[24]

Driven by his desire to live, Al-Mashriqi was determined to leave. Imam Husayn knew that it was useless to ask Al-Mashriqi to stay and get killed. Therefore, Al–Husayn's response, "You're free to go" will not be an excuse for this man on the Day of Judgement because, as mentioned previously, Allah will definitely condemn to hellfire all of those who heard the infallible leader's calls, but did not defend him. Al-Mashriqi heard the calls and should have defended Al-Husayn until the last breath.

Notes & References

1. Manaqib Abu Haneefa (V.2, Ps.83 & 84)
2. Al-Jawahir Al-Mudhee'a (V.2, P.26)
3. Hulyat Al-Awliya' (V.7, P.31)
4. Adab Al-Shafi'ie wa Manaqibuhu (P.314)
5. Al-Kamel (V.3, P.74)
6. Ahkam Al-Quran (V.2, Ps. 224 & 225)
7. Al-Mustadrak (V.3, P.115)
8. Al-Mustadrak (V.2, P.463)
9. Ma'rifat Ulum Al-Hadeeth (P.84)
10. Usul Al-Deen (Ps. 286 thru 292)
11. Nayl Al-Awtar (V.7, P.138)
12. Ruh Al-Ma'ani (V.26, P.151)
13. Umdat Al-Qari (V.11, P.346)
14. Umdat Al-Qari (V.11, P.346)
15. Nayl Al-Awtar (V.3, P.179)
16. Nahj Al-Balagha (V.3, P.304)
17. Kashf Al-Ghumma (Al-Arbali), (P.159)
18. Tareekh Al-Tabari (V.6, P.238); Al-Kamel (V.4, P.24) & Al-Bidaya (V.8, P.178)
19. Kamel Al-Ziyarat (Ps. 970 & 999)

20. Kamel Al-Ziyarat (P.53); Manaqib Al-Husayn (Al-Tarmathi); Al-Mustadrak (V.3, P.177); Tahtheeb Tareekh Dimashq (V.4, P.314); Majma' Al-Zawa'id (V.9, P.181); Al-Sawa'iq Al-Muhriqa (P.115); Al-Adab Al-Mufrad & Kanz Al-Ummal (V.7, P.107)
21. Tareekh Al-Tabari (V.6, P.199)
22. Tareekh Al-Tabari (V.6, P.254)
23. Al-Luhuf (P.61)
24. Tareekh Al-Tabari (V.6, P.255)

AL-HUSAYN IS THE PRESERVER OF FAITH

Al-Husayn's Holy uprising implemented the last and most radiant chapter of the final revelations. It demonstrated to the masses how to distinguish between right and wrong, and how to identify each party's adherents. It has been said that Islam was founded by Mohammed, and preserved by Al-Husayn. This is true indeed. Al-Husayn's infallible descendants focused on this Holy uprising to push their reform agenda and promulgate the true teachings of Islam. Their goal in reminding people of the atrocities that the Prophet's household endured was to maintain the true message of their grandfather.

The infallible leaders urged the Community to support this cause and organize gatherings (Majalis) to inform the masses of the oppression, hardship, pain and suffering inflicted upon the Martyr of Reform, his family members and companions. The infallible leaders were certain that the details of their grandfather's plight (Al-Husayn) would imbue passion in the hearts of people. The listeners in these gatherings would learn that Al-Husayn sought no material gain in his uprising, and that leadership was a Divine right he legitimately inherited from his grandfather and father. The audience would also learn that Al-Husayn was the rightful leader who could not tolerate tyranny, and that his enemies and their successors falsely proclaimed themselves as leaders. The infallible leaders aimed, through these gatherings, to convey to people that Al-Husayn and his infallible sons were a manifestation of justice and righteousness. The infallible leaders hoped that, once convinced, the audience would embrace the true path. Strongly urging their followers to organize such events, the infallible leaders aimed at preparing a fertile ground for the seeds of true Islam.

The oppressive regimes of the Umayyads and Abbassids confined the infallible leaders to their homes and banned the believers from seeing and meeting the Prophet's infallible descendants. Furthermore, the tyrants murdered en masse the followers of the Prophet's household. Al-Mansoor and Harun Al-Rasheed, for instance, mercilessly murdered Fatima's descendants and built palaces over the victims' remains.[1] During these tumultuous periods, the infallible leaders favored solitude over rebellion against the transgressors. The oppressors enforced a tight siege around the infallible leaders and prosecuted the followers of Prophet's household. The devout believers endured unspeakable torment and horror during their leaders' forced isolation.

Al-Husayn's infallible descendants focused on the greater struggle (Al-Jihad Al-Akbar). They instructed their followers to sponsor emotional gatherings and tearfully remind[2] the audience of the sacrilegious violations that the criminals committed against the Prophet's household in Karbala. They emphasized the bounties and rewards the believers accrue in these gatherings. They also asserted that these organized mourning events are a strong factor in strengthening the bond of faith and unity among their followers; the very same unity for which Imam Ali and his two infallible sons sacrificed their precious lives.

The Prophet's household employed many tactics to attract people to these gatherings (Majalis). They, particularly and generally, delineated the strong correlation between these gatherings and maintaining the pure path. Imam Al-Baqir said, "May Allah's mercy be upon a person meeting with another to remember us, for the third would be an angel asking Allah to forgive all of their sins. Whenever two persons meet to remember us, Allah shows them off to His angels. Whenever you meet, remember us because the reminders in such gatherings do maintain our cause. People who remember us and invite others to do so are ranked the best after us."

Imam Al-Sadiq asked Al-Fudhayl Bin Yassar, "Do you meet and talk?" Al-Fudhayl answered, "Yes." Imam Al-Sadiq said, "I love these gatherings. The hearts of those who maintain our cause will not die when other hearts do." The infallible leaders aimed to teach the Community that Allah ranked the Prophet's household very high, and blessed them with unrivaled merits including the power of infallibility. They employed every possible means to inform the Community that they are the rightful and Divinely appointed leaders, and that the tyrants had usurped their right.

These gatherings, whether in homes or streets, and the associated oral presentations, whether in the form of mourning, wailing or chest beating, have definitely contributed positively to proselytizing the path of righteousness. Imam Al-Baqir said that Allah will combine the rewards of two million mandatory pilgrimages (Hajj), two million minor pilgrimages (Umra), and two million battles on the side of the Prophet and the infallible leaders, and give it to the believer who gathers with others to weep on Al-Husayn on the day of Ashura.[3] Describing the immeasurable intensity of their bereavement on Al-Husayn, Imam Al-Sadiq said that Fatima's daughters beat their faces and chests, and the believers should do similarly.[4]

Poetry and oral narration depict to audiences of all classes, even children, clear images of the tragic events in Karbala. Books and literature can never rival the astounding effect of oral narration. The latter is definitely more effective in emotionally stirring the audience, strengthening their beliefs and further nourishing the bond between them and their infallible leaders. Some Shi'a organize acting events like plays and public displays to simulate the painful tragedy of Karbala. More than anywhere else, this is common amongst the Shi'a of India.[5]

In addition to expressing their unconditional love towards their followers, the infallible leaders articulated their appreciation to the believers' efforts in organizing these gatherings. They often asserted the effectiveness of such organized events in maintaining the cause of the Prophet's household. Full understanding of the significance of these gatherings might be beyond most people's reach, and some attend only to accrue rewards for the next life. However, an insightful look into the infallible leaders' words and actions unveils their deep objective in praising these organized events on one hand, and the depth of their exceptional knowledge and kindness in urging their followers to attend them on the other.

Notes & References

1. Uyun Akhbar Al-Ridha (P.62)

2. Qurb Al-Isnad (P.26) & Kamel Al-Ziyarat (P.100)
3. Kamel Al-Ziyarat (P.174)
4. Al-Tahtheeb (V.2, P.283)
5. Al-Habl Al-Mateen newspaper (issue 27 of its 17th year)

WEEPING ON AL-HUSAYN

Authentic traditions urge the believers to shed tears for Al-Husayn's suffering. Narrated traditions, from all channels, describe in great detail the tremendous benefit of weeping on Al-Husayn. It is narrated that the reward of an atom's load of tears may put out hellfire. A person weeps for his or her own suffering, or for the loss of a dear one, and in the process the weeper would instinctively condemn the criminals who caused their sufferings. Fully aware of this human instinct, the infallible leaders urged people to weep on Al-Husayn because the process simultaneously condemns his oppressive enemies. The infallible leaders strongly encouraged the Community of believers to weep on Al-Husayn, in order to shield itself from the abominable propaganda of its enemies.

One must remember, and remind others, of Al-Husayn's plight. Such reminders invoke feelings of resentment towards the brutal tyrants, and subsequently lead the believers to condemn the enemies of Allah and the enemies of His Messenger. This explains why Imam Husayn said, "I am the Martyr of Tears, a true believer would weep whenever he (or she) remembers me."[1] A believer's emotional attachment to Al-Husayn, and adherence to his path, compel him (or her) to react and weep whenever he (or she) remembers the atrocities committed against the Prophet's household.

In his statement, Imam Husayn introduced a vital benefit of his martyrdom. Al-Husayn's self-sacrifice preserved the purity of the Divine revelations, and people exponentially attain rewards for their tearful reaction to his martyrdom. Tears are a derivative of an emotional reaction. A tender-hearted believer would definitely conclude that Al-Husayn rose up to destroy the distortion and alteration that the oppressors, who usurped leader ship from the rightful leaders, falsely attributed to the Islamic path of guidance. Al-Husayn's statement emphasized the strong relation between his martyrdom and people's tearful reaction to it, because the pain of this tragedy is eternal, and the agony is immortal. Imam Husayn's contentment and perseverance in Karbala mesmerized the angels. Believers love Al-Husayn dearly and shed tears on him. Shedding more tears further nourishes this love. For this reason, Al-Husayn correlated tears to his own martyrdom. He clearly highlighted the emotional aspect of his uprising when he said, "I am the Martyr of Tears."

Adding the most popular attribute or performance to someone's name was commonly used amongst the Arabs before and after Islam. Arabs, for instance, called the tribe of Madhar "Red Madhar," and the tribe of Rabee'a "Rabee'a with Horses." They called Zayd Bin Musa Bin Ja'afar "Zayd of Fire," the sons of Bin Abi Ma'eet "the sons of hellfire," and Ja'ada "The Murderer of Husbands." "Red" was added to Madhar's tribe, because their war banner was always red, and the men of Rabee'a tribe stressed their bravery by frequently riding their "Horses." Zayd, the son of Imam Musa Bin Ja'afar, set the palaces of the Abbassids on "Fire" in the city of Basra. Before his execution, Uqba Bin Abi Ma'eet asked the Prophet, "Who will take care of my sons?" The Prophet replied "Hellfire." Ja'ada Bint Al-Asha'ath gave her husband, Imam Al-Hasan, a cup of poisoned milk and "Murdered" him. The tribes and people in these examples have definitely done in their lives more than what has been described, but Arabs selected their most famous action, and added it to their names. Imam Husayn's statement "I am the Martyr of Tears," and Imam Al-Sadiq's oath "By my father, the Martyr of Tears" are linguistically compatible with the previous discussion because of the strong correlation between Al-Husayn's martyrdom and its power to invoke tears.

Mock Weeping (Tabaki)

The infallible leaders aimed at preserving the memories of Karbala for generations to come. Their goal was to maintain the intensity of these events, and in order to achieve it, they encouraged those who could not weep to feign weeping and vent their grief. Imam Al-Sadiq said, "Whoever feigns weeping secures a place in paradise."[2] This tradition is a spiritual prescription for those who cannot weep but emotionally react to the pain and suffering of the Prophet's household.

In another authentic narration, the Prophet recited on a group of his supporters in Medina the last few verses from Surat Al-Zumar, beginning with *"when the nonbelievers are driven to hell fire... (39:71-75)"* to the end of it. Everyone wept except one young man, who said, "I couldn't shed tears, but I feigned weeping." The Prophet commented, "Whoever feigns weeping shall end up in paradise."[3] Jareer narrated that the Prophet said, "I shall recite Surat Al-Takathur (102) before you, and whoever weeps or feigns weeping will end up in paradise."[4] Moreover, Abu Tharr narrated from the Prophet, "Shed tears if you can, and if you can't, stimulate your hearts with a touch of sadness, and feign weeping, because a hard hearted person is distant from Allah."[5]

These traditions prove that mock weeping is as good an expression of sadness as genuine weeping. Some weep, or feign, because the sins they committed in this life might cause them suffering and chastisement in the next. If genuinely remorseful, mock weeping usually pushes a true servant of Allah away from sins onto the straight path. Weeping, or mock weeping, on the other hand, for the suffering of the Prophet's household begets animosity towards their brutal enemies.

In agreement to what has been discussed, Sheykh Mohammed Abdu, in his *Tafseer Al-Manar (V.8, P.301)*, wrote:

> "Mock weeping is the actual act of forcing oneself to weep without the intention of showing off."

In his *Ta'reefat (P.48)*, Al-Shareef Al-Jarjani wrote:

> "Impersonating, or pretending to possess a certain quality is often condemned because it involves acting. However, the Prophet urged his sincere followers to feign weeping when they could not shed tears. The Prophet urged the devout, and not the heedless, to do so."

The crimes and hostilities against the Prophet's household equally touch the hearts of the weeper and the mock-weeper, and the emotional reaction compels both to condemn the tyrants who oppressed the Prophet's household and usurped the Divine rights of the infallible leaders.

Those who still equate mock weeping to showing off ought to carefully assess the eloquent words of the Prophet and his infallible descendants. A person has to implement the teachings of the Prophet's household before he or she acquires the ability to understand the depth of their instructions. The infallible leaders endured the excruciating pain of abuse throughout their lives. The treacherous path they treaded to preserve their grandfather's Message, and the abuse they endured from their enemies in the process, effectively stimulate the hearts of the believers. Utilizing this aspect of their Holy lives, they employed accurate guiding instructions to attract the masses in order to convey that the Divinely allocated position of leadership was an exclusive right of the Prophet's household. Imam Al-Baqir paid some women eight hundred Dirhams to mourn and wail on Al-Husayn in Mina during pilgrimage (Hajj).[6] He selected Mina over Arafat and the Ka'aba for two reasons. First, pilgrims are usually busy in their worship and supplication in Arafat and at the Ka'aba. Secondly, the duration of stay in these two places is too short. On the other hand, pilgrims, from all over the world, stay in Mina for three days, and hold festive gatherings to greet and congratulate one another. Al-Baqir knew that wailing would definitely provoke the pilgrims to inquire about the reasons behind the tears in these festive days. The pilgrims would inquire about Al-Husayn's uprising and its cause, on one hand, and about the oppressors who fought him and usurped his rights on the other.

Al-Baqir offered the inquisitive minds a chance to discover the true path. It is indeed true that the Light of the Divine is always visible and can never be extinguished. Playing the role of an information network, the pilgrims would definitely transmit to their communities the things they witnessed during their pilgrimage. Therefore, people who didn't travel to Medina, the residence of the infallible leader at that time, could not justify their ignorance of the Divinely appointed guardians, and their strife against Allah's enemies to preserve the true Message.

Al-Baqir tactfully avoided Mecca and Medina because women in the two Holy cities can only mourn and wail behind closed doors, a domain inaccessible to the public, especially men. Mourning indoors hinders the impact of these rituals because Imam Al-Baqir's goal was to attract public attention. Some claim that such mourning rituals violate women's modesty. This baseless claim can be easily dismissed because it was the infallible leader who ordered the women to publicly wail on Al-Husayn. Moreover, Al-Kulayni narrated that a wise and a brilliant woman called Umm Khalid visited Imam Ja'afar Al-Sadiq while Abu Baseer happened to be there. Imam Al-Sadiq offered the woman an empty seat on his couch and asked Abu Baseer, "Would you like to listen to her?" She spoke wisely with an astonishing eloquence.[7] Had it been a violation of women's modesty, Imam Al-Sadiq would not have allowed Abu Baseer to listen to her.

In another tradition, Imam Al-Sadiq told Hammad Al-Kufi, "I heard that some Kufans visit Imam Husayn's grave in the middle of Sha'aban. Some of them recite and narrate... Meanwhile some women mourn and wail." Hammad said, "I witnessed some of this." Imam Al-Sadiq said, "I thank Allah, who enabled some of our followers to visit, praise and tearfully commemorate us."[8] It was absolutely clear to Imam Al-Sadiq that men could hear women's voices in Al-Husayn's shrine, however he did not object to it. In contrast, the scene pleased him such that he asked Allah to bestow his mercy upon the participants in these gatherings.

No tradition prohibits a woman from speaking in public. Some traditions, however, forbid a strange man (non-mahram) from conversing with a woman, or spending the night in the same house alone with her. This prohibition was legislated to prevent potential physical attraction or sexual arousal. Based on this, Al-Allamma Al-Hilli, in his *Tahreer*, stated that a blind man should not listen to a woman's voice. He explained that a woman's voice is an integral part of her beauty, and that it shouldn't be heard in public. However, Al-Hilli never stated a clear-cut edict prohibiting women from speaking in public. The author of *Al-Jawahir*, the most popular compilation of Shia traditions on jurisprudence, challenged Al-Hilli's opinion and proved beyond doubt that women publicly conversed with the infallible leaders, and that Fatima and her daughters spoke in public and addressed crowds on many occasions.

Shafi'es are split over this matter, but in general, Sunni jurisprudence allows women to speak in public. According to *Fiqh Al-Mathahib Al-Arba'a* (Jurisprudence of the Four Sects) (V.1, P.167), it is not immodest for women to speak in public because the Prophet's companions conversed with his wives to learn about Islamic Jurisprudence. In his *Nayl Al-Ma'arib* (V.2, P.127), Al-Sheybani Al-Hanbali stated that is not immodest for women to speak in public, but it is forbidden for men to tune in for pleasure. In his *Kaff Al-Ra'aa* (V.1, P.27), Bin Hijr stated a similar opinion. In his *Al-Bahr Al-Ra'iq* (V.1, P.270), Bin Nujaym Al-Hanafi detailed the rules for women's conduct, and stated that they are prohibited from speaking in public and in his *Al-Ashbaah Wa Al-Natha'ir* (P. 200), he stated that hermaphrodites are also prohibited. In his *Furu'* (V.3, P.12), Bin Muflih Al-Hanbali stated that a woman is not prohibited from speaking in the presence of a male stranger. In his *Tarh Al-Tathreeb* (V.1, P.250), Zayn Al-Deen Al-Iraqi quoted Bin Abd Al-Barr and confirmed that Shafi'es believe it is not immodest if a woman's voice is heard in public. In his *Commentary on Majmou'* (V.7, P.249), Al-Nawawi quoted Al-Darimi and Al-Qadhi Abu Al-Tayyib, and stated that it is not immodest if a woman's voice is heard in public. In his *Nayl Al-Awtar* (V.4, P.274), Al-Shawkani stated similarly.

Notes & References

1. Kamel Al-Ziyarat (P.108)
2. Amali Al-Sadouq (P.86)
3. Kanz Al-Ummal (V.1, P.147)
4. Kanz Al-Ummal (V. 1, P.148)
5. Al-Lu'lu' wa Al-Marjan (P.47)
6. Al-Tahtheeb (V.2, P.108) & Al-Muntaha (V.2, P.112)
7. Al-Wassa'il (V.3, P.25)
8. Kamel Al-Ziyarat (P.325)

Prostrating on Clay from Karbala

Al-Husayn's Holy uprising reinforced the righteous codes of Mohammed's Message in people's minds, and kept the torch on the path of guidance eternally lit. The infallible leaders expounded on the exceptional significance of this uprising, and instructed their followers to prostrate on clay from Karbala (Turba Hussayniyya) in their five daily prayers. They utilized the clay of Karbala as a visual aid, hoping that their followers would constantly remember Al-Husayn's uprising and plight. Prostrating on clay from Karbala reminds the worshippers of the noble cause for which Al-Husayn and his followers sacrificed their lives. The infallible leaders employed this method of reminder to ensure that their followers would always remember the atrocities committed against Allah's sincere servants. It is stated in *Kamil Al-Ziyarat* (P.270), that the clay of Karbala has been mixed with the blood of The Oppressed and his followers, who, as Imam Ali described them, are the insurmountable foremost of the Community.

Touching the clay of Karbala with their foreheads on a daily basis, the followers of the Prophet's household are bound to experience tenderness in their hearts, shed tears, detest the oppressive murderers, and condemn oppression. Prostrating on clay from Karbala, engraves in the worshippers' minds that Al-Husayn and his companions sacrificed their possessions and lives to protect the Divine codes on one hand, and to uproot tyranny on the other. To further reinforce the importance of this Holy uprising in peoples' minds and hearts, the infallible leaders also urged their followers to make beads from the clay of Karbala. Some, ignorant of the wisdom behind these practices, accuse us of deviation and innovation. These people unleashed such venomous accusations due to their ill understanding of the authentic tradition in which the Prophet said, "Earth has been made as a pure medium of prostration for me." The followers of the Prophet's household prostrate on a dried mixture of clay and water to implement the Prophet's instruction in this authentic tradition.

LEGISLATING THE VISITATION RITUAL (ZIYARA)

Seasonal trips to visit Allah's sincere servants have been encouraged because the visited represent true faith and the light of guidance to it. In addition to meeting one another, Al-Husayn's visitors from around the world crowd in his shrine to express their attachment to him, and their gratitude to his efforts in maintaining the pure path to the Lord of the Worlds. The visitors usually convey to the infallible subject of their visitation their high regard and admiration of his principles and action s. Visiting Karbala increases the believers' attachment to Imam Husayn, and stimulates them to learn more about him, his uprising, and the heinous crimes committed against him. In addition to the enormous spiritual benefit, people who sincerely visit Al-Husayn's shrine experience tenderness in their hearts. The visit also strengthens the bond of brotherhood among the believers, a deed that Allah encourages. Allah says, *"The believers are indeed brothers (49:10)."* During their trip, and while gathering around the grave, the visitors help each other and also discuss important issues relevant to their faith. In doing so, the believers further nourish the existing bond of brotherhood amongst themselves.

The infallible leaders embodied the purity of Islam and became the medium of Allah's miracles. Their devotion and proximity to the Exalted are indescribable. Visiting them invokes tremendous blessings and rewards. This visitation ritual is spiritually uplifting. The believer who sincerely performs this ritual would sense and develop a stronger inclination to the life of guidance and reform. The infallible leaders were the most truthful of all beings. Their astounding dedication in serving their Lord earned them a remarkable status. Seasonal trips to the Holy Shrines, with the intention of pleasing Allah, reinforce these realities in the visitors' minds and hearts. This is the general goal in visiting the infallible leaders. However, Al-Husayn's infallible descendants emphatically urged their followers to visit the Master of Martyrs on different occasions throughout the year. The Umayyads, vanished long ago from the face of the earth, had subtly inserted an ideology of atheism amongst the masses to undermine the purity of the Divine Message. The infallible leaders were completely aware that the Umayyads' dirty tactics would influence the coming generations. In order to combat and expose the tyrants' deliberate distortion of the true Message, the Divinely appointed guardians urged their followers to frequently visit Al-Husayn.

The infallible leaders sacrificed their Holy lives to protect the true Message of their grandfather, Prophet Mohammed. They employed all possible means to defend the Divine revelations from any distortion or alteration. Fully aware that the tragedy of Karbala would touch the hearts, the infallible leaders instructed their followers to focus on Al-Husayn's uprising to constantly remind the whole Community that the position of leadership had been usurped from its rightful inheritors. They legislated this visitation ritual to ensure that their followers would always be alert that oppression is a potential threat to any community, at any given time. They urged the believers to flock to Al-Husayn's shrine on many occasions throughout the year, hoping that the spirit of activism would permanently mature in the believers. The infallible leaders wanted their followers to be fully ready to support righteousness and condemn oppression. Dignity and honor compel any person to condemn atrocities against human beings, let alone the family of the greatest Prophet. The infallible leaders intended to provoke their followers to resent and dread the Umayyad tyrants, who brutally slaughtered the infants and dislocated the women of the Prophet's household. The emotional reaction to these crimes leads the victims' sympathizers to conclude that these criminals have deviated far from the path of Islam. This conclusion, Imam Husayn's main goal in his uprising, has an unparalleled positive impact on people's faith. Having suffered more than the rest of the infallible leaders, Imam Husayn became the strongest weapon of his infallible descendants against their contemporary enemies, in particular, and against all oppressors in general. For this reason, they urged their followers to visit Imam Husayn, weep on him, and at times hold ceremonies to commemorate him. The infallible leaders emphasized that the believers who remember Al-Husayn, and live by his principles and emulate his path, would be honored in the next life.

Imam Al-Sadiq expounded on the depth and significance of the visitation rituals. Al-Sadiq emanated bright rays of guidance, and instilled in the hearts of the devout great comfort. Mu'awiya Bin Wahab narrated that Imam Al-Sadiq prostrated and supplicated:

> "Our Lord! I call upon You! You blessed us with dignity, promised us the position of intercession, favored us with guardianship, granted us the knowledge of the past and the future, and made us attractive to people's hearts. Forgive me, my brothers, and the visitors of Al-Husayn's grave who spent their money and exhausted their bodies consoling us to please You, and to please Your Messenger. They, in doing so, obeyed us and angered our enemy, and their goal is to please You. Reward them with Your Grace, protect them day and night, and provide for the families and the children they left behind. Befriend them and protect them from the evil of tyrants, humans and demons.
>
> Give them the best of what they hoped for in their travel, and the best reward for favoring us over their children, families and relatives.
>
> My Lord! Our enemies belittle them for visiting us, but they defied the pressure, opposed our enemies, and were never deterred from visiting us.
>
> My Lord! Bestow Your Mercy upon the faces that get baked under the blazing sun.
>
> Bestow Your Mercy upon the cheeks that rub against Al-Husayn's grave.
>
> Bestow Your Mercy upon the tearful eyes that console us.
>
> Bestow Your Mercy upon the broken hearts that feel for us.
>
> Bestow Your Mercy upon those who weep on us.
>
> My Lord! I trust in You to protect these souls and bodies until you feed them from The Pond on the Day of Great Thirst."

Mu'awiya Bin Wahab was completely stunned at the amount of blessings that Al-Husayn's visitors attain. Noticing looks of shock on Bin Wahab's face, Imam Al-Sadiq added, "The inhabitants of heavens who supplicate for the well-being of Al-Husayn's visitors outnumber those on planet earth."[1]

The depth and beauty of this supplication is clearly visible to those who abide by the path of the Prophet's household. The empathy and selflessness of the infallible leaders is a source of spiritual nourishment to their followers. Imam Al-Sadiq's supplication confirms that the weeping and wailing of men and women, whether in houses, streets or the Holy shrines, for the suffering of the infallible members of the Prophet's household, generate infinite spiritual benefit in this life, and unparalleled comfort in the next.

Rubbing the cheeks against the Holy grave adds to these benefits. It is recommended to do this on any grave, and not only Al-Husayn's. In *Al-Tahtheeb* (V.1 P.200), Al-Sheykh Al-Tussi narrated that Mohammed Bin Abdullah Al-Himyari said, "I asked The Scholar (Imam Mahdi) about visiting the graves. He replied that it is not permissible to prostrate during the mandatory or recommended prayers on any grave. However, the visitor can rub his right cheek on any grave since it is highly recommended to do so on the graves of the infallible leaders."

Notes & References

---

1. Kamel Al-Ziyarat (P.116) & Thawab Al-A'maal (P.54)

The Infallible Leaders' Selflessness (Eethaar)

The previously mentioned supplication informs us that the infallible leaders approve of any expenditure in keeping their cause alive. They are pleased that their followers favor them over their own families, children and relatives, and spend their money and energy on mourning or festive gatherings to remember their infallible leaders. Selflessness (Eethaar) is to favor others, financially or emotionally, over oneself. The ethics of Islam, the path to eternal happiness, strongly urge the believer to be selfless. The Community is always indebted to the infallible leaders because, in addition to being the best guide to the best life, they exhausted themselves in maintaining the true path, and at times gladly chose martyrdom to keep the torch of guidance immortally lit. A derivative of generosity and ideal values, selflessness is a great quality which Allah praises in his Holy Book. Allah praises His selfless servants, regardless to whether the receiving party deserves this selflessness. The Exalted says, *"They, even though needy, favor others over themselves (59:9)."* The infallible leaders, Allah's most virtuous servants, are the medium of Divine blessings and the fortress of true faith. Therefore, it is quite remarkable to be selfless, and more so when selflessness maintains their cause.

Imam Musa Bin Ja'afar sacrificed his life to shield his followers from imminent wrath. Imam Musa said, "Allah's wrath was to fall upon our followers, but He allowed me to sacrifice my life to defend them, and I did."[1] Al-Majlisi stated that the followers of the Prophet's household invoked wrath upon themselves because they abandoned the practice of precautionary dissimulation (Taqiyya). Moreover, Imam Al-Sajjad told Umm Farwa, "I numerously ask Allah every day to forgive the sins of our followers. I do so because we persevere, and they do too, but we possess special knowledge while they don't."[2] Out of deep love, the infallible leaders ask Allah day and night to bestow His Mercy upon their followers. They become happy for their followers' happiness, and sad for their sadness. The relation between the infallible leaders and their followers resembles that of a firm tree and its leaves. Imam Mahdi, may Allah hasten his return, recited the following supplication:

> "My Lord! Our followers have been created from the rays of our light and from the remains of the clay from which You created us. They have committed many sins. They rely on their love and attachment to us to acquire Your forgiveness. It pleases us if You forgive their private sins. But for the sins in which they hurt one another, we ask You to take away from our rightfully allocated possessions to settle their claims against one another, and to reconcile amongst them. Make paradise their destination, and spare them hellfire and the wrath that You ordained to inflict upon our enemies."[3]

Having learned this, it is reasonable to believe that the infallible leaders' astounding selflessness is compelling enough a reason for the devout believer to utilize every possible means to console them; to favor them over himself, his family and all of his possessions. Imam Ja'afar Al-Sadiq used the plural throughout his supplication to assert that the believer ought to honor the memories of all of the infallible leaders, and favor all of them over himself, to attain rewards. Al-Sadiq asked Allah to bless the selfless believers who regard all matters that pertain to all of the infallible leaders above anything else. In his supplication he used "favoring us" instead of favoring him (meaning Al-Husayn), to emphasize to their followers that they should be selfless in commemorating and honoring all of the infallible leaders.

Maintaining the rituals of visiting Al-Husayn's grave must undeniably be the main focus and top priority of this selflessness. Visiting Karbala is more significant because it reminds the visitor of the Holy uprising, in which the honorable Husayn and his devout followers embodied righteousness and defended justice, while the evil Yazeed and his cruel soldiers treaded the path of transgression and oppression. As a result, the believers would be heavily inclined to embrace the former and condemn the latter. Affirming this goal of visiting Al-Husayn, Al-Sadiq, in his previously mentioned supplication, said, "My Lord! Our enemies belittle them for visiting us, but they defied the pressure, opposed our enemies, and were never deterred from visiting us." One of Imam Al-Sadiq's goals in this supplication is to encourage the believers to organize mourning rituals, maintain the Holy shrines, and propagate the Divine principles. In doing so, the followers of the Prophet's household would indeed console their infallible leaders. Al-Sadiq also alluded that Allah is Watchful of the abusive enemies who constantly attempt to undermine the believers' efforts to please Him, and to please His infallible appointees. Moreover, this supplication elucidates that the enemies' sarcasm, and the hardships incurred on the believers in the process would never blur the image of the truth, nor hinder the perpetuity of the righteous rituals.

History tells that the Jews in Medina ridiculed the call to the five daily prayers (Athaan), and so did the idolaters of Mecca with prostration (Sujud). The believers, however, never succumbed to the pressure nor relinquished their practices. In brief, the enemies' conspiracies never deter true Muslims from embracing the straight path and practicing its associated rituals. The ridicule and sarcasm of the non-believers should never dissuade Al-Husayn's visitors from gathering around his grave to conduct mourning rituals. Describing those people who are condescending, and sometimes abusive, to the believers, Imam Ja'afar Al-Sadiq said, "By Allah! They're mistaken, deprived of Allah's blessings and totally distant from Mohammed."

Thareeh Al-Muharibi told Imam Al-Sadiq, "My sons and relatives ridicule me when I talk about the rewards of visiting Imam Husayn." Al-Sadiq said, "Ignore what people say and be with us."[4] Also, as we mentioned previously, Imam Al-Sadiq told Hammad Al-Kufi, "I heard that some Kufans visit Al-Husayn's grave in the middle of Sha'aban. Some of them recite Qur'an while others praise, and, at the same time, some women mourn and wail on Al-Husayn." Hammad said, "I witnessed some of this." Imam Al-Sadiq said, "I thank Allah for blessing us with followers who visit, praise and mourn us, despite the mockery and sarcasm of our enemies."[5]

Totally foreign to the path of the Prophet's household, some ridicule the visitation and mourning rituals. The believers must always keep in mind that such utter ignorance would never diminish the enormous benefit of these rituals. The believers would eventually sense the positive impact of these rituals in this life, and certainly reap the associated rewards in the next. Allah's Messenger once told the Commander of the Faithful (Imam Ali), "Some scummy people will shame the visitors of your graves the way an adulteress is shamed. Those (scummy people) are the evil of my Community (Ummah), and I ask Allah to deprive them of my intercession on the Day of Judgement."[6]

Notes & References

1. Usul Al-Kafi (V. 1, P.189)
2. Uyun Al-Mu'jizaat (P.76)
3. Jannat Al-Ma'wa (P.281)
4. Kamel Al-Ziyarat (P.143)
5. Mazar Al-Bihar (P.124) & Kamel Al-Ziyarat (P.325)
6. Farhat Al-Ghariyy (P.31)

Commemorating the Prophet's Household in Poetry

No matter how great, a person's significance tends to fade away with the lapse of time. Arabs employed poetry to define and immortalize their commendable heroes. Poetry was the Arabs' powerful tool that preserved a person's merits and achievements. Poetry in early Arab societies played the role of an information network, equal in reporting events to our modern day media. Poetry was passed on from parents to children, and from one community to another. Arabic literature, mostly in poetic form, documented major events of the early Arab communities. In their poetry, early Arabs depicted their wars and the details of battles of the period before and after Islam. Du'bul Al-Khuza'ie, a very famous poet, said, "The poet dies, but poetry, and the person praised in it, never do." Urwa Bin Uthayna, another famous poet, said, "People fear that I might revile them in my poetry, but I never do. An individual's reputation is defined by his action. Ink on paper is immortal."[1]

The lives of the Prophet's household delineated true faith and reform. We apply to our lives what we learn from theirs. The Prophet's household endured unspeakable pain. They were content to suffer in order to preserve the Divine Message. They urged the believers to focus on this aspect of the infallible leaders' Holy lives in order to propagate the unrivaled significance of the Prophet's household. The Divinely appointed guardians often stated that the efforts of their followers in enlightening others shall successfully keep the infallible leaders' cause alive. Moreover, they emphasized that Allah bestows His Mercy upon those who remember and remind others of the Prophet's household, and maintain their cause.

The infallible leaders, in many authentic traditions, articulated that commemorating them in poetry is one of the best venues of proximity to Allah. In one tradition, they said that Allah builds a house in paradise for person who commemorates them in his poetry.

In another tradition, they said that the Holy Spirit protects the poet who commemorates them. In a third, they said that Allah builds the poet a city in paradise, where he visits with Allah's most honorable angels and messengers.[2]

After listening to his poetry, Imam Al-Baqir told Al-Kumayt, "The Holy Spirit shall protect you."[3] The same poet met Imam Al-Sadiq in Mina and asked his permission to recite poetry. Al-Sadiq disapproved of reciting poetry in the Holy days of the pilgrimage season (Hajj). Aware that the mandatory utterance in these Holy days includes commemorating the infallible leaders, Al-Kumayt said, "My poetry commemorates you." Al-Sadiq was pleased. He called upon his family members to gather while Al-Kumayt began reciting his poetry. All the attendants wept, meanwhile, Imam Al-Sadiq raised his hands and said, "My Lord! Forgive all of Al-Kumayt's sins; the past, the future, the public and the private ones, and give him from Your bounties until he is pleased."[4]

Imam Al-Jawad allowed Abdullah Bin Assalt to commemorate him and his father, Imam Al-Ridha, in poetry. Furthermore, Abu Talib wrote poetry commemorating Imam Al-Ridha, and sent it to Imam Al-Jawad. The latter kept it and wrote him back: "Well done! I ask Allah to reward you for it."[5]

Once, Imam Al-Sadiq gathered his wife, Umm Farwa, and his children, and told Sufyan Bin Mus'ab, "Recite poetry commemorating Al-Husayn." Sufyan started, "Farwa! Shed your tears." Umm Farwa and the women in Al-Sadiq's house wept loudly. People in Medina flocked to Imam Al-Sadiq's door to see what happened. In order to cover up the reason of their weeping, Imam Al-Sadiq showed them a little boy who had passed out, and said, "They're weeping for the little boy."[6] This story is a perfect example of how precautionary dissimulation (Taqiyya) can be practiced. Imam Al-Sadiq did mention the "boy," and many boys from the Prophet's household passed out on the day of Ashura. Al-Sadiq may have meant Abdullah, Imam Husayn's nursing infant, or Abdullah, Imam Al-Hasan's young son, who was slaughtered on Imam Husayn's chest. It is also possible that he meant Mohammed Bin Abu Sa'iid Bin Aqeel Bin Abu Talib, who was a little boy in Al-Husayn's camp in Karbala. The infallible leaders instructed their followers to strictly practice precautionary dissimulation, but never discouraged poets from publicly commemorating the Prophet's household. In contrast, they condoned such public presentations, and frequently reminded the poets of the associated rewards they would accrue in supporting the cause of the Prophet's household.

Ja'afar Bin Affan was a famous poet, and a devout follower of the Prophet's household.[7] Imam Al-Sadiq asked him, "You are good at commemorating Al-Husayn in your poetry, aren't you?" Bin Affan answered, "Yes." Al-Sadiq requested to hear some. Ja'afar recited, while Imam Al-Sadiq wept until his tears soaked his bear d. He told Bin Affan, "Allah's greatest angels have heard your poetry, and wept on Al-Husayn as we did. Allah has guaranteed you paradise." Imam Al-Sadiq then said, "Allah has guaranteed paradise for any poet who stimulates people to weep, while tearfully commemorating Al-Husayn."[8] A poet who commemorates the infallible leaders is considered a propagator of the true path, and earns in this life unimaginable rewards for the next. Allah guarantees the poet who supports righteousness and reform, and simultaneously condemns oppression and its adherents, the immortal pleasure of paradise.

Poetry was the most powerful media tool at the time. The infallible leaders employed it to propagate a true understanding of the Divinely ordained position of leadership. They financially compensated the poets, such as Du'bul Al-Khuza'ie and Al-Kumayt, for enduring a great deal of abuse from their enemies. They encouraged the poets to publicly commemorate them in order to provide an opportunity to people of all classes to learn about the true leaders, who devoted their lives to preserve the Divine Message. Poetry was the most effective tool of transmitting the true path to the coming generations, and a very strong weapon in combating the distortion and confusion that the oppressors injected in the community.

The blessed efforts of these faithful advocates have definitely contributed in promulgating the true path. Devoted followers of the Prophet's household, such as Hijr Bin Udayy, Amr Bin Al-Hamaq, Maytham Al-Tammar and many others, sacrificed their lives to defend the Divine Message. Their self-sacrifice taught their successor's impeccable lesson of loyalty to Allah and His Messenger. Their firm stance in defending the Divine codes enabled the faithful to distinguish between the path of righteousness of the Prophet's household, and the path of transgression and oppression of their enemies. Allah says, *"Who is worthy of being followed, the one who guides to the truth, or the one who needs guidance? How shall you judge? (10:35)."*

Notes & References

1. Al-Muwashshah (Ps. 280 & 281)
2. Uyun Akhbar Al-Ridha (P.5)
3. Rijal Al-Kashshi (P.136)
4. Al-Aghani (V.15, P.118) & Ma'ahid Al-Tansees (V.2, P.27)
5. Rijal Al-Kashshi (P. 350)
6. Rawdhat Al-Kafi (tradition 263)
7. Al-Aghani (V.7, P.8)
8. Rijal Al-Kashshi (P.187)

The Predicament of Exposing the Family

Certain that he and his companions would be martyred, Imam Husayn carefully planned the scope of his uprising. The Prophet's grandson realized the necessity of assigning a competent and a brave spokesperson who could, after Al-Husayn's martyrdom, transmit to the masses the core ideology of the Holy uprising. The responsibility of this spokesperson was also to condemn Yazeed and Bin Ziyad for their dreadful crimes against the Prophet's household on one hand, and to combat the innovations that these tyrants falsely attributed to the Divine Message on the other. Imam Husayn was aware that the religious scholars feared the ruling party, and as a result, they had become complacent to its oppressive measures. The incident in which Bin Ziyad ordered his thugs to brutally murder Bin Afeef Al-Azdi attests to such complacency.

Imam Husayn was confident that the Prophet's daughters were incredibly faithful, and that they would persevere and endure the cruelty of their enemies. He trusted their ability to confront the tyrants, expose their transgression, and in form the confused masses that the Martyr of the Straight Path rose up to preserve the message of his grandfather. Despite their grievances and suffering, the Prophet's daughters played their intricate roles, and defended the codes and principles of the Divine Message with the utmost dignity. Seeming unaffected by captivity, exile, the sarcasm of her enemies, the wailing of women, weeping of children and moaning of Ali Bin Al-Husayn, the honorable daughter of the Commander of the Faithful rose up and spoke. These conditions, in addition to her severe thirst and the scene of the bloody bodies under the blazing sun, were enough to render any human distraught and speechless. However, the strong faith and tranquility of Ali's daughter prevailed. She eloquently expressed her thoughts; her words fell on her enemies like thunder.

Nostalgic for her brothers' protection, Zaynab rose up alone to confront her evil enemy, Bin Ziyad, who had ordered the martyrs' heads carried on spears and placed facing the Prophets' daughters. She ridiculed the murderer in front of the masses. Reminding the attendants of her father's bravery and eloquence, she pointed to the martyrs' heads and said to Bin Ziyad, "These embraced the martyrdom that their Lord ordained. Allah shall surely try you in front of them. You'll lose then and learn who is indeed victorious. You! Marjana's son! May you be dead soon."

Zaynab detailed the atrocities and crimes of Bin Ziyad and his soldiers. Her composure and wit in the main square of Kufa stunned the weeping masses. She, describing the murderers, said, "Murdering the Prophet's son, the core of the Message and the Master of Youth in Heaven is a heinous crime, for which they will never be forgiven. Their efforts are worthless, their actions are fruitless, and they are in total loss. They have angered Allah and invoked His wrath to fall upon them in the next life. They do not know that the chastisement Allah prepared for them is greater than that which is being described."

Fatima Bint Al-Husayn spoke after Zaynab. Her words astonished and silenced the crowd. Her tranquil, yet firm, composure awakened the Kufans, who wept hysterically once they realized the gravity of their crime. They pleaded with her, "You, the daughter of the purified! You have broken our hearts. Please stop." Umm Kulthoum, Imam Ali's daughter, spoke right after Fatima. Umm Kulthoum reiterated the heinous crimes and reminded the crowd of the enormity of their dreadful violation. The Kufans wailed and screamed. Some said that this tearful scene was unprecedented.[1]

The tribal codes of protection had somehow become suspended, and one can only imagine how intimidating it must have been for anyone to object or condemn the actions of Yazeed and Bin Ziyad. Except Imam Ali's brave daughters, everyone was tongue tied and terrified. Some say it is inappropriate for women to address a crowd in a public forum. We agree to this if women intentionally expose themselves to show off, or if their cause is a worldly matter. However, when necessary, and if the cause is religious, the codes of Islam urge women to defend the Divine Message, and inform the masses of what has been falsely attributed to it. Allah exempted women from fighting and physically confronting the enemies, instructing them to look after their households. This is the general ruling, since the responsibility of physically defending religion is mandated for men. However, when preserving the Message depends on their action, women must rise up against the enemy and fulfill their duty in defending their faith. This is the reason that compelled the Lady of All Times, (Fatima Al-Zahra), to rise up and defend the Divine definition of the position of leadership, and the fact that the legitimate leader must be Divinely selected. She eloquently addressed the Muslims in the Prophet's mosque in Medina because the legitimate leader, the Master of All Successors, (Imam Ali), had been Divinely instructed to remain silent.

Al-Husayn's enemies broke the tribal codes of protection, and violated all the cultural norms. However, the Prophet had already foretold that the enemies, despite their unprecedented cruelty, would not shame or disgrace the women after they slaughtered Al-Husayn in Karbala. Imam Husayn's final statement to the women in his family attests to this. He told them, "Wear your garments, get ready to face difficulties, but be certain that Allah shall guard and protect you. He shall save you from the evil schemes of your enemy, and shall convert the outcome to your favor. Allah shall chastise your enemy and reward you for your pain with all kinds of blessings and bounties. Do not be doubtful of this, and do not say what undermines your elite status."

We haven't mentioned in this discussion that the Master of All Martyrs was the Divinely appointed leader at the time. Therefore, he, in addition to being infallible in his actions and words, knew the details of all events, the past and the future. His assessment of things emerged from his impeccable knowledge, and the Divine blessing of infallibility instilled in him. Al-Husayn's implementation of righteousness was a derivative of the Divine wisdom. We should avoid questioning Al-Husayn's actions, and unconditionally submit that he was ultimately truthful in his words and deeds. Our intellect falls too short from fully understanding the reason and impact of certain actions. However, we can employ it to submit to Allah's Will, because at the end, the Exalted will only judge us for heeding His commandments and prohibitions, and not for our ability to analyze and discover the rationale behind them.

Notes & References

1. Read the speeches in full under "Events After Al-Husayn's Martyrdom"

The Uprisings of Ali's Descendants

This Holy uprising was ultimately victorious. Al-Husayn became an exemplary model for reform-seekers in general, and the active followers of the Prophet's household in particular. Political activists and reform advocates, some of whom were not loyal to the Prophet's household, selected the infallible leaders' right of leadership as an icon of their reform agenda to recruit the masses. Supporting the cause of the infallible leaders, and deposing the existing oppressive regime, formed the driving force of all the uprisings subsequent to Ashura. Before Al-Husayn's uprising, Muslims believed that it would be self-destructive to rise up against the oppressors, who mercilessly smothered any opposition to their rule. The Master of Youth in Heaven injected a spirit of activism into the Community, and paved the way to a true understanding of combating tyranny, even when the process requires self-sacrifice.

Al-Husayn rose up and implemented this fundamental code of the Divine Message. His resounding victory lies in the fact that he successfully demonstrated to the believers that in the absence of an alternative, it is a religious duty to confront falsehood and rise up militarily against the tyrants to uproot oppression. When righteousness is a genuine ingredient, an uprising would ultimately achieve victory. The righteous soldiers, or their successors on the path, would eventually reap the fruits of their struggle. An insightful look into history proves the validity of this conclusion. There were many uprisings against the Umayyad tyrants after Al-Husayn's martyrdom. Al-Mukhtar rose up against them; the cause of his uprising was to avenge the Prophet's household. Zayd Bin Ali Bin Al-Husayn and his son Yahya rose up, and their cause was to restore the Divinely appointed position of leadership to their contemporary infallible leader from the Prophets household. Moreover, many Hashimites publicly condemned their contemporary tyrants, and rose up to combat corruption and seal the door of transgression.

Some of the infallible leaders practiced precautionary dissimulation and disassociated themselves from the contemporary uprisings. They distanced themselves from all opposition movements because the tyrants at the time mercilessly murdered any opponent to their oppressive regime. It is crucial to always keep in mind that Allah appointed the infallible leaders to guide people to the true path and simultaneously uproot oppression and confront its advocates. This guiding role, in addition to their teachings, indicates their subtle approval of the bloody uprisings against the tyrants who usurped the position of leadership that the infallible leaders rightfully inherited from their grandfather. These uprisings, and the cause behind them, became a dominant discussion amongst the Muslims. As a result, the Community learned that the position of leadership is a Divine right of Allah's honorable Messenger, and his infallible successors. The ideology of these uprisings resonated through the social strata of the Community. Consequently, Muslims fully realized that the legitimate leader (Khaleefa or Imam) must be an infallible member of the Prophet's household. The fact that the Prophet named and appointed his successors became basic common knowledge, to the extent that ignorance could no longer be justified.

It is important to know that some rebels exploited the cause of the Prophet's household and used it to attract the naive. Bin Al-Zubayr, for instance, publicly praised Al-Husayn, and condemned the atrocities in Karbala. However, soon after he ruled, he retracted his sympathy and bluntly expressed his enmity towards the Prophet's household. He deliberately abstained from praising or even mentioning the Prophet in his sermons for forty Fridays. When some objected to his blatant violation of the Friday sermon, Bin Al-Zubayr said, "His household members are corrupt, and if I mention him, they will become proud and happy. I do not like to make them happy."[1]

Mu'awiya Bin Abu Sufyan, a forerunner in publicly expressing his enmity towards the Prophet and his household, had definitely influenced Bin Al-Zubayr's aberration. It is narrated that when the caller to the five daily prayers was giving his testimony that Mohammed is the Messenger of Allah, Mu'awiya said, "The name of Hashim's brother (Prophet Mohammed) is mentioned five times every day. All of my efforts are so far fruitless. Damn you! By Allah! I shall not rest until I bury this name."[2] Al-Ma'moun heard this story and became furious. He ordered the speakers to curse Mu'awiya on every pulpit. Al-Ma'moun's new policy caused an uproar and chaos throughout the Muslim community. His advisors persuasively convinced him to rescind his order.[3]

At the early stages of their revolution against the Umayyads, the Abbassids utilized every possible means to express their heartfelt sympathy for the suffering of the Prophet's household, but once they prevailed, they reversed course, and mercilessly persecuted the Prophet's descendants. Musa Bin Isa, the Abbassid leader who killed Zayd Bin Ali Bin Al-Husayn in Fakh, said, "If the Prophet competes with us over the position of leadership, we would strike his face with our swords."[4] These faithless rebels, and their like, had no integrity or dignity, and the benefit of their revolution was confined to deposing a tyrant of their own caliber.

Notes & References

1. Maqatil Al-Talibiyyeen (P.165)
2. Sharh Al-Nahj (V.2, P.537)
3. Murnj Al-Thahab (V.2, P.343)
4. Maqatil Al-Talibiyyeen (P.158)

PART II:

THE STORY OF KARBALA

The Prophet, peace be upon him and his household, said:
"The murder of Al-Husayn instilled in the believers' hearts a burning sensation that will never cool down." (Mustadrak Al-Wasa'il, V.2, P.217

Yazeed After Mu'awiya

Mu'awiya died in Damascus in the middle of Rajab in 60 A.H. (680 C.E.). Yazeed was in the city of Hawran. Al-Dhahhak Bin Qays arranged the funeral, and spoke to the crowd from the pulpit. He praised Allah and said, "Mu'awiya was the Arabs' fortress, their protector and leader. Allah made him the people's king, employed him to seal the door of rivalry, and blessed him with territorial expansion. He has died and we are about to lay him in his grave, where he'll be with his deeds until the Day of Judgement. Everyone is welcome to attend the funeral." Al-Dhahhak then performed the funeral prayers and buried him in Bab Al-Sagheer cemetery. After the burial, he wrote to Yazeed asking him to hasten his return, so people could renew their pledge of allegiance to him as the new king.[1] He attached to the letter two lines of poetry that read, "Abu Sufyan's son passed on, and you're in charge of us. You are our hope after him, so maintain his way and the straight path."[2]

Bereaved at the news of his father's demise, Yazeed immediately left Hawran towards Al-Sham. He arrived to Damascus three days after Mu'awiya's burial. Al-Dhahhak arranged a red carpet welcome, and then took him to his father's grave. After he prayed on it, Yazeed entered the city and addressed the crowd from the pulpit. He said, "Oh People! Mu'awiya was one of Allah's blessed servants. He is better than his successors and lesser in rank than his predecessors. I shall not praise him for his dedication to Allah, because He knows him best. The Merciful can forgive him, but He might also chastise him. I am in charge now. I neither regret my action, nor do I apologize for my wrongdoing; after all, Allah does what He wills. Mu'awiya sent you across the ocean on boats to fight the enemy, and ordered you to spend the harsh winter at the border of Byzantium. I shall annul these policies. He also paid you three times a year, and I shall pay you all of it at once."[3]

Silence prevailed and no one extended any condolences to

Yazeed until Abdullah Bin Hammam Al-Salouli broke the ice. He looked at Yazeed and said, "You, the commander of the faithful! May Allah console your heart, grant you bounties and help you govern people. Your loss is great but the blessings you have been given are greater. Thank Allah for what you've been given and persevere in your loss. You've lost Allah's representative but you've been granted His representation. Mu'awiya has died, so may Allah bless him with joy. You've become the chief in command and I ask Him to guide you in all of your affairs."[4] After Al-Salouli, a man from the tribe of Thaqeef greeted Yazeed and said, "You, the commander of the faithful! You lost the best of all fathers but you have been blessed with all sorts of bounties. Persevere in your loss and thank Allah for His generosity, because no bereaved has been blessed like you."

People lined up to extend their condolences and to congratulate him at the same time. Yazeed said, "We are the supporters of faith and righteousness. You, people of Al-Sham! You should be glad that you've been the hosts of goodness. There shall be a fierce battle between the people of Iraq and me. I dreamt three nights ago that a rushing river of blood separates me from them, and that no matter how hard I tried, I couldn't cross it but Obeydallah Bin Ziyad did." The crowd collectively chanted, "Take us wherever you want. The people of Iraq still remember our sharp swords in Siffeen." Yazeed thanked them and gave them a great deal of money for their show of support.

Yazeed wrote to all of his governors to inform them of his father's death and to endorse their posts. Sarjoun, Yazeed's advisor, convinced him to appoint Obeydallah Bin Ziyad as the new governor of Iraq. Yazeed did so reluctantly. He then wrote to Al-Waleed Bin Utbah, the governor of Medina: "Allah blessed His servant Mu'awiya with dignity and victory, but He took his soul to either enjoy the bounties and mercy, or to suffer the chastisement of the next life. He lived and died according to what has been ordained. In his will, Mu'awiya urged me to be cautious in dealing with Abu Turab's (Imam Ali) family because they are savvy with bloodshed. Waleed! You must know that the members of Abu Sufyan's family are the supporters of righteousness and the enforcers of justice. Allah, the Exalted, shall undoubtedly guide and aid them to avenge the oppressed Othman. Ask the people of Medina to pledge allegiance to me as soon as you read this letter." Yazeed wrote a small note and attached it to the letter. The attachment read: "Be extremely harsh with Al-Husayn, Abdullah Bin Umar, Abdurrahman Bin Abu Bakr and Abdullah Bin Al-Zubayr. Shall any of these men refuse to pledge allegiance, kill him and send me his head"[5]

Al-Waleed sent Abdurrahman Bin Amr Bin Othman Bin Affan at midnight to invite Al-Husayn and Bin Al-Zubayr to the governor's house.[6] The messenger found them both in the Prophet's mosque. Bin Al-Zubayr was extremely worried, because governors normally manage all of their affairs in broad daylight.[7] However, the Divinely appointed guardian, Al-Husayn, informed Bin Al-Zubayr of Mu'awiya's death, and that Al-Waleed wanted them to pledge allegiance to Yazeed. Al-Husayn told Bin Al-Zubayr that he had learned about this in a vision, in which he saw that Mu'awiya's house was on fire, and that his pulpit was turned upside down.[8] Sensing that Al-Husayn had already decided to see the governor late that night, Bin Al-Zubayr advised him against it. Bin Al-Zubayr warned the Prophet's grandson against the danger of a potential ambush. In his response, Al-Husayn asserted his ability to fend off any aggression.[9] Al-Husayn held his grandfather's cane and marched towards the governor's house. Thirty armed men from his relatives, servants and followers accompanied him.[10] Al-Husayn instructed them to wait by the door, and to storm into the house as soon as they heard him raising his voice.[11]

As Al-Husayn sat down, Al-Waleed announced Mu'awiya's death and asked the Prophet's grandson to pledge allegiance to Yazeed. Al-Husayn answered, "I would never pledge allegiance privately. Call us along with the rest of the people, so it will be a collective affair.[12] Al-Waleed was convinced but Marwan interjected, "If he leaves without pledging allegiance now, your second chance will be only after a bloody battle. Detain him until he pledges allegiance, and execute him if he doesn't." Al-Husayn told Marwan, "You, the son of Al-Zarqa'![13] Do you think that you or he can kill me? You are a liar and a transgressor.[14] Imam Al-Husayn then looked at Al-Waleed and said, "You, the governor! We are the members of the Prophet's household, the core of this Message, the congregational medium of angels. Allah started (creation) with us, and shall seal it all with us. Yazeed is a shameless transgressor, an alcoholic and a murderer. A man of my rank can never pledge allegiance to someone like him. Let us all wait till tomorrow morning and look into which of us is rightfully fit for the position of leadership."[15] Al-Waleed responded harshly, and a loud argument ensued during which nineteen of Al-Husayn's armed companions forced their way into the governor's house, and escorted the Prophet's grandson back to his home.[16]

Marwan told Al-Waleed, "You've turned me down. By Allah! He will never allow you a second chance." Al-Waleed answered, "Marwan! Scold someone else. How dare you ask me to jeopardize my faith? Shall I kill Al-Husayn for refusing to pledge allegiance? By Allah! The person who spills Al-Husayn's blood is a loser who shall suffer severe chastisement and enjoy none of Allah's mercy on the Day of Judgement."[17] Asma' Bint Abdurrahamn Bin Al-Harith Bin Hisham, Al-Waleed's wife, was disappointed with her husband for being so harsh with Al-Husayn. Trying to justify his conduct, Al-Waleed told her that Al-Husayn initiated the verbal abuse. She said, "Even if he initiated, how could you insult him or insult his father?" Al-Waleed said, "I shall never do it again."[18]

Al-Husayn visited his grandfather's grave later that night. As he hovered over the Prophet's grave, a bright light emanated from it.[19] Al-Husayn said, "Oh Messenger of Allah! I greet you with peace. I am Al-Husayn, your grandson; the son of your daughter Fatima. I am your grandson, whom you appointed to lead your community. Oh Prophet of Allah, be my witness! They turned away from me and mistreated me. This is my complaint to you until our reunion." Al-Husayn prayed by the Prophet's grave for the rest of that night until the morning.[20]

Al-Waleed sent someone to spy on Al-Husayn. The spy couldn't locate him, and thought that he had already left Medina. Al-Waleed thanked Allah for sparing him further confrontation with Al-Husayn. That morning Marwan met Al-Husayn and said, "Pledging allegiance to Yazeed contributes positively to your faith and improves your life." Al-Husayn said, "Islam is in great danger if the Community accepts the leadership of someone like Yazeed. I heard my grandfather, Allah's Messenger, say that it is forbidden for any member of Abu Sufyan's family to become a leader. My grandfather also ordered the Muslims to kill Mu'awiya if they ever saw him on the Prophet's pulpit. The people of Medina saw him on the pulpit, but didn't kill him. As a result, Allah punished them and empowered Yazeed, the transgressor, over them."[21] Al-Husayn and Marwan talked for a long time, until the latter walked away angrily.[22]

Al-Husayn visited his grandfather's grave the following night. He prayed for a while, and then recited the following supplication; "My Lord! This is the grave of your Prophet Mohammed, and I am his grandson. You know what I am about to face. My Lord! I love righteousness and condemn falsehood. I ask You, the Source of Dignity and Generosity, by this grave and its occupant, to choose for me what pleases You and Your Messenger." Al-Husayn then wept. Shortly before sunrise, Al-Husayn rested his head on the Prophet's grave and fell asleep. He dreamt that his grandfather, accompanied by angels, hugged him, kissed him between his eyes, and said, "Dear Husayn! I see that soon a gang from my community will slaughter you thirsty on the sandy plains of Karbala. They wish to obtain my intercession on the Day of Judgement, but I shall ask Allah to never grant them their wish. Dear Husayn! Your father, mother and your brother are here with me, and they miss you." Al-Husayn wept and asked his grandfather to take him into the grave with him. Urging his grandson to move on with his assigned mission, in order to earn more bounties from the Divine for the Day of Judgement, the Prophet told Al-Husayn, "You must be martyred to earn Allah's utmost rewards. You, your father, your uncle (Ja'afar) and your father's uncle (Hamza) shall be together on the Day of Judgement until all of you enter paradise." Al-Husayn woke up and narrated the dream to his family. They were overcome by sadness and wept for a long time.[23] They sensed the proximity of the tragic events that Allah's Messenger had foretold. Fearing to lose the Prophet's extended light of guidance, Al-Husayn's relatives pleaded with him to either comply with Yazeed's demands or to depart from Medina to a safer place.

Notes & References

---

1. Al-Bidaya (V.8, P.143)
2. Maqtal Al-Khawarizmi (V.1, P.178)
3. Al-Bidaya (V.8, P.143)

4. Al-Bayan wa Al-Tabyeen (V.2, P.109); Al-A'qd Al-Fareed (V.2, P.309)
5. Maqtal Al-Khawarizmi (V.l, P.178-180)
6. Tareekh Dimashq (V.4, P.327)
7. Tareekh Al-Tabari (V.6, P.189)
8. Mutheer Al-Ahzaan (P.10)
9. Al-Kamel (V.4, P.6)
10. Al-Luhuf
11. Maqtal Al-Khawarizmi (V.l, P.183)
12. Tareekh Al-Tabari (V.6, P.189)
13. In Tathkirat Al-Khawas and in Al-Kamel, Marwan's grandmother, Al-Zarqa', was a prostitute.
14. Tareekh Al-Tabari, Al-Kamel, Al-Irshaad, A'alam Al-Wara
15. Mutheer Al-Ahzaan
16. Manaqib Bin Shahr Ashoub (V.2, P.208)
17. Tareekh Al-Tabari (V.6, P.19) & Al-Luhuf (P.13)
18. Tareekh Dimashq (V.4, P.328)
19. Amali Al-Sadouq (P.93)
20. Maqtal Al-Awalim (P.54) & Al-Bihar (V.10, P.172)
21. Al-Luhuf (P.13) & Mutheer Al-Ahzaan (P.10)
22. Maqtal Al-Khawarzrni (V. l, P.185)
23. Maqtal Al-Awalim (P.54)

People Fearing for Al-Husayn

Omar Al-Atraf

Omar Al-Atraf, Imam Ali's son, told Al-Husayn, "Al-Hasan narrated from his father, the Commander of the Faithful, that you shall be killed. It is better if you pledge allegiance. "Al-Husayn replied, "My father told me that Allah's Messenger informed him of his martyrdom, and of mine, and that his grave will be close to mine. Do you think that you know what I don't? I shall never compromise my faith. Fatima shall complain to her father about his community hurting her family. Those who hurt her family shall never enter paradise."[1] Omar Bin Ali Bin Abu Talib joined Al-Mukhtar when the latter rose up in Kufa. Al-Mukhtar asked him, "Did Mohammed Bin Al-Hanafiyya come with you?" Omar said, "No." Al-Mukhtar dismissed him and ordered him to leave. Omar left and joined Mus'ab. He fought on Mus'ab's side (against Al-Mukhtar) and was killed in battle.[2]

Bin Al-Hanafiyya

Mohammed Bin Al-Hanafiyya told Imam Husayn, "Brother! You, of all people, are the most beloved and the dearest person to my heart. I sincerely advise you to flee to a safe place, where you can avoid pledging allegiance to Yazeed. Write to people asking them to pledge allegiance to you, and be grateful to your Lord if they do, but it is never an admonishment to your faith or intellect if they don't. However, I am worried that you might go to a place where people split into two groups, one for you and another against you, and a bloody battle ensues in which you would be murdered. If this happens, the best member of this Community, the son of the best father and mother, will be killed, and as a result, your family will be devastated." Al-Husayn asked his brother, "Where should I go?" Bin

Al-Hanafiyya replied, "Go to Mecca. If you don't feel safe there, take to the desert or the mountains and keep moving from one town to another until you have a clear picture of what people intend to do. You will have leverage when you step back and assess the situation ahead of time, rather than living the chaos of being chased around."[3] Al-Husayn replied, "Brother! Even if there is no shelter or a resting place on the face of earth, I shall never pledge allegiance to Yazeed Bin Mu'awiya." Mohammed wept interrupting Imam Husayn. Al-Husayn continued, "My Brother! I ask Allah to reward you for your sincere advice. You are correct indeed, because I intend to go to Mecca. My brothers, my nephews and followers have expressed their trust in my leadership and unconditional submission to my plan. We shall depart soon. I recommend that you stay in Medina to inform me of all developments."

After conversing with his brother, Imam Husayn entered the Prophet's Mosque saying, "I am neither afraid of fighting Yazeed, nor of death. The ordained is inevitable." Abu Sa'iid Al-Miqbari heard him and concluded that Al-Husayn was up to major action.[4]

UMM SALAMA

Umm Salama said, "Your departure to Iraq shall devastate me, because I heard your grandfather, Allah's Messenger, say that you will be murdered in Iraq in a place called Karbala. The Prophet gave me a bottle containing your soil." Al-Husayn said, "Mother! I know that I shall be unjustly slaughtered. Allah has ordained that my wives and family members become dislocated, and my children slaughtered or captured. They shall appeal for support, but will get none." Umm Salama exclaimed, "Amazing! Where do you intend to go if you know you'll be slaughtered?" Al-Husayn replied, "Mother! If I don't go today, I'll go tomorrow or the next day. Death is inevitable. I know the day and the hour in which I'll be slaughtered. I know my burial place as I know you, and I see it as I see you. Would you like to see it along with the burial place of my companions?" She requested from him to see it. He showed her the burial place of his companions, gave her some of the soil, and told her to keep it in a bottle.[5] He also told her that the soil in the bottle would turn into blood once he was murdered. Umm Salama saw both bottles bubbling with blood in the afternoon on the day of Ashura.[6]

The Women of Bani Hashim

Grief-stricken, the women of Bani Hashim wept for Al-Husayn's departure. Al-Husayn pleaded with them to heed the instructions of Allah and His Messenger, and to maintain the secrecy of his planned action. They collectively replied, "How could we not weep? Your departure reminds us of losing Allah's Messenger, Ali, Fatima, Al-Hasan, Zaynab and Umm Kulthoum (the Prophet's daughters). By Allah! We beg you to stay. We ask Allah to take our souls and spare yours. You are the dearest to the most pious who have already died." An aunt of his told him that she heard a voice say, "A man from Bani Hashim shall be martyred in Al-Taff. His martyrdom will invoke humiliation upon Quraysh."[7] Al-Husayn consoled her and explained to her that the matter was irrevocable, and that the ordained must be implemented.

Abdullah Bin Omar

Abdullah Bin Omar insisted that Al-Husayn stay in Medina. Al-Husayn declined, and said, "Abdullah! Allah ordained that this life is worthless. It is extremely so, such that the head of Yahya Bin Zakariyya was given as a gift to an adulterer from Bani Israel. Similarly, my head shall be taken as a gift to an adulterer from the Umayyads. Don't you know that Bani Israel killed seventy Prophets every day, but went about doing business as if they had done nothing? Allah did not rush their punishment, but later He avenged His Prophets and destroyed the murderers. He is The Most Capable Avenger."[8] Realizing that Al-Husayn was adamant about leaving Medina, Bin Omar concluded that the Prophet's grandson was determined to combat evil, and uproot the wrongdoing that the transgressors falsely attributed to the Divine Message. Having failed in his persuasion, Bin Omar asked Imam Husayn to allow him to kiss the part of his body the Prophet had frequently kissed. Al-Husayn uncovered his stomach. Abdullah Bin Omar kissed it three times and wept.[9] Al-Husayn told Bin Omar, "Abu Abdurrahman! Be pious and do not abstain from supporting me."[10]

THE WILL

Al-Husayn wrote his will shortly before he left Medina. It read: "In the name of Allah, the most Gracious and the most Merciful. This is Al-Husayn's will to his brother Mohammed Bin Al-Hanafiyya. Al-Husayn testifies that there is no God but Allah, who has no partners and that Mohammed is His Servant and His Messenger, who delivered the message of righteousness. Al-Husayn also testifies that paradise is real, hellfire is real, the Hour is imminent and that Allah shall definitely resurrect the dead. I am not rising up for wealth, nor to corrupt and oppress. I am rising up seeking reform in the community of my grandfather. I intend to enforce righteousness and forbid wrongdoing. I am on the path of my grandfather and father, Ali Bin Abi Talib. Allah, the Source of Righteousness, shall be with those who accept me along with my righteous goal. I shall persevere against those who denounce my mission until Allah judges between us, for He is indeed the Supreme Judge. My brother! This is my will to you. I ask Allah to bless me with success. I rely on Him and to Him I shall return."[11] Al-Husayn folded his will, sealed it and handed it to his brother Mohammed.

Notes & References

1. Al-Luhuf (P.15)
2. Al-Akhbar Al-Tiwaal (P.29)
3. Tareekh Al-Tabari (V.6, P.191) & Al-Kamel (V.4, P.7)
4. Tareekh Al-Tabari (V.6, P.191) & Al-Aghani (V.17, P.68), Maqtal Al-Khawarizmi (V. 1, P.186)
5. Madinat Al-Ma'ajiz (P.244)
6. Maqtal Al-Awalim (P.47)
7. Kamel Al-Ziyara (P.96)
8. Al-Luhuf (P.17), Mutheer Al-Ahzaan (P.11)
9. Amali Al-Sadouq (P.93)
10. Al-Luhuf (P.17)
11. Maqtal Al-Awalim (P.54), Maqtal Al-Khawarizmi (V. 1, P.188)

Departing Medina

Accompanied by his sons, brothers, Al-Hasan's sons and the rest of his family, Al-Husayn left Medina on a Sunday night at the end of the month of Rajab.[1] As he marched Al-Husayn recited, *"So he left the city with fear and caution. He said my Lord! Save me from the oppressors (28:21)."* He took the main road. Some suggested taking side roads as Bin Al-Zubayr did to avoid troubles. Al-Husayn said, "By Allah! I shall stay on this road until Allah ordains what He Wills." He arrived in Mecca on the third of Sha'aban. As he entered the Holy city, he recited, *"And when he turned towards Madyan, he said may my Lord guide me to the right path (28:21)."*[2] He settled in the house of Al-Abbass Bin Abd Al-Muttalib.[3] Meccans, the pilgrims and people from neighboring communities visited him frequently. Bin Al-Zubayr, who often remained by the Ka'aba, also visited him. Since Al-Husayn was more respected and revered, his presence in Mecca delayed Bin Al-Zubayr's agenda. People stopped pledging allegiance to Bin Al-Zubayr as soon as Al-Husayn arrived in Mecca. Al-Husayn visited the grave of his grandmother Khadija, where he prayed and supplicated for a long time.[4]

Notes & References

---

1. Tareekh Al-Tabari (V.6, P.190)
2. Al-Irshaad
3. Tareekh Dimashq (V.4, P.328)
4. Al-Khasa'is Al-Husayniyya (P.35)

In Mecca

In Mecca, Al-Husayn sent a letter to the following community leaders in Al-Basra: Malik Al-Bakri, Al-Ahnaf Bin Qays, Al-Munthir Bin Al-Jaroud, Mas'oud Bin Amr, Qays Bin Al-Haytham and Amr Bin Obeyd Bin Mu'ammar. Al-Husayn wrote: "Greetings! Allah selected Mohammed amongst all of His creatures, blessed him with Prophethood, entrusted him with His Message, and then took him after he delivered the entrustment and taught it to people. We are his family, closest of kin to him, the successors who inherited him and the rightful personnel to fulfill his vacant position. People usurped this right of ours and we, fearing division and loving unity, endured their abuse. However, we knew that the position of leadership was our Divinely ordained right and not theirs. I have sent you my messenger with my letter inviting you to Allah's book and the path of His Messenger. The Prophet's teachings are being undermined and innovation has been revived. Shall you comply with me, you'll be guided to the right path."

He sent this letter with a person called Sulayman. Bin Ziyad was the son in law of Al-Munther Bin Al-Jaroud. Al-Munther was afraid that Sulayman was Bin Ziyad's undercover agent, so he turned him over to his son in law. Bin Ziyad crucified Sulayman (Al-Husayn's messenger) on the day he left from Basra to Kufa. Bin Ziyad rushed to Kufa to arrive before Al-Husayn.[1] Al-Ahnaf wrote Al-Husayn back: *"Persevere. Allah's promise shall come true and do not let the condescending attitude of the nonbelievers affect you (30:60)."*[2]

Yazeed Bin Mas'oud gathered Bani Tameem, Bani Hanthala and Bani Sa'ad and asked them, "What do you think of me and how do you view me?" They answered, "By Allah! You are our leader, the source of our pride, the backbone of our community and the most honorable of us." Bin Mas'oud said, "I gathered you to consult with you on an important issue, and to ask you to aid me in it." They said, "By Allah! We are your sincere advisors and we unconditionally trust your judgement and accept your decision. Speak up, we are all ears." He continued, "Mu'awiya died and none of us will miss him. The door of tyranny has been broken, and the pillars of oppression have been weakened. He selected his son to succeed him. He schemed to maintain control after his death, but he failed miserably. Yazeed, an alcoholic and an evil transgressor, is now proclaiming to be the leader of the Muslims without their consent. He is ignorant, ill-tempered and devoid of righteousness. By Allah! Fighting against him is more significant than fighting against idolaters. The most honorable, the most knowledgeable and the wisest in the Community, Al-Husayn Bin Ali, the son of Allah's Messenger, is still amongst us. He is the most qualified leader because he is older, experienced, kind to the young, generous with the old and closest of kin to the Prophet. He is the true leader, with whom Allah ordered us to align ourselves. Do not veil yourselves from the light of righteousness, and do not indulge in more aberration. Sakhr Bin Qays led you astray in the Battle of the Camel, and now is the time to restore your honor and support the son of Allah's Messenger. By Allah! You shall invoke humiliation upon yourselves if you abstain from supporting Al-Husayn. I have worn my war vest and prepared myself for battle. Death is inevitable, and none of you can escape from it. Let me hear a positive response, may Allah bestow His mercy upon all of you."

Bani Hanthala answered, "Abu Khalid! We are your spears and your soldiers. We are ready to kill your enemies and achieve victory. By Allah! We shall venture with you and endure every hardship alongside with you. We shall support you with our swords and protect you with our bodies, if you like." Bani Tameem responded, "Abu Khalid! We are your brothers and allies. We are never pleased when you are angry, and we shall never stay behind if you leave. We shall submit to your orders. Call us anytime you please." Bani Sa'ad said, "Abu Khalid! We hate to oppose and disobey you. We obeyed Sakhr Bin Qays, and remained neutral in the Battle of the Camel. We are grateful because his decision preserved our dignity. Give us some time to think it over before we get back to you." Bin Mas'oud told Bani Sa'ad, "If you do not comply, you shall be stifled under sharp swords and Allah shall not spare you the ugly circumstances of your inaction."

Bin Mas'oud wrote back to Al-Husayn: "Greetings! I received

your letter and understood what you assigned me to do. You urged me to accept your leadership and to support you, so I could reap the associated rewards. I also understood that Allah never leaves the earth without a representative who guides people to safety. You are the infallible leader over His creatures, and His entrustment on earth. You have grown on the Mohammedan tree. He is the trunk and you, his household members, are the branches. May you have a happy and safe arrival; I have recruited all of Bani Tameem. They will flock in submission to you, the way thirsty camels flock to water. I have also recruited others." Al-Husayn read Bin Mas'oud's letter, and said, "May Allah dignify you, protect you from any fear and quench your thirst on the Day of Calamity." When Bin Mas'oud was about to leave Basra, he was informed that Al-Husayn had been martyred. He was devastated for missing the opportunity of martyrdom and eternal joy.[3]

Maria's house was a congregational place for the followers of the Prophet's household in Basra. It is narrated that, while at Maria's house, Yazeed Bin Nabeet asked Abdullah and Obeydallah, two of his ten sons, to travel with him and join Al-Husayn. Some of his friends commented, "We are worried that Bin Ziyad's soldiers will capture you." He said, "I am leaving no matter what. Let them capture me if they can!" He immediately left with his two sons and his servant Amer. Sayf Bin Malik and Al-Adham Bin Umayya traveled with them.[4] They joined Al-Husayn in Mecca and were all martyred before him in Karbala.

The Letters from the Kufans

While in Mecca, Al-Husayn received many letters from the Kufans, urging him to come to Kufa. They stated that they had no leader, and that they hadn't participated in any congregational prayer behind Al-Nu'man Bin Basheer, the Umayyad governor. Letters poured from Kufa; on one day Al-Husayn received six hundred letters. Kufans sent a total of twelve thousand letters, in which they begged Al-Husayn to come and be their leader. Al-Husayn was yet to respond. The last letter came from Shibth Bin Ribi'e, Hajjar Bin Abjar, Yazeed Bin Al-Harith, Uzra Bin Qays, Amr Bin Al-Hajjaj and Mohammed Bin Umayr. It read: "People are waiting for you and have chosen none but you. You, the Prophet's son! Hurry up and harvest the ripe fruits. Please come over any time you want, and you'll have brave soldiers ready for your command."[5]

AL-HUSAYN'S RESPONSE

Al-Husayn collected the letters in two huge bags. He replied to all with one letter, and sent it with Hani Bin Hani Al-Subayi'e and Sa'iid Bin Abdullah Al-Hanafi, who were the last mail carriers from Kufa to him. Al-Husayn wrote: "In the name of Allah, the most Beneficent and the most Merciful, from Al-Husayn Bin Ali to all the believers and the Muslims. Greetings! Hani and Sa'iid were the last of your messengers to hand me your letters. I fully understand the context of your letters in which you stated that you have no leader, and in which you urged me to come over and guide you to the right path. I have sent you my cousin, who is the confidant of my household, and whom I endear like my real brother. I ordered him to report your situation and other relevant affairs to me. Once he informs me that your community leaders and the masses in your area are united on what I read in your letters I, Allah willing, shall make it over soon. The true leader rules by the Holy Book, enforces justice, lives righteously and steadfastly upholds the Divine codes. Greetings!"[6] He gave this letter to Muslim Bin Aqeel, and told him, "I am sending you to the Kufans and Allah shall ordain for you what pleases Him. I hope that you and I will earn the rank of martyrs. Go on accompanied by Allah's blessings and help. Once you arrive to Kufa, stay with a very trustworthy person."[7]

Notes & References

1. Tareekh Al-Tabari (V.6, P.200)
2. Mutheer Al-Ahzaan (P.13)
3. Mutheer Al-Ahzaau (P.13) & Al-Luhuf (P.21)
4. Thakheerat Al-Darayn (P.224)
5. Maqtal Al-Khawarizmi (V.1, P.193), Mutheer Al-Ahzaan (P.11)
6. Tareekh Al-Tabari (V.6, P.198) & Al-Akhbar Al-Tiwaal (P.238)
7. Maqtal Al-Khawarizmi (V.1, P.196)

THE MARTYR OF KUFA

MUSLIM'S TRIP

He sent Qays Bin Mus'her Al-Saydawi, Amara Bin Abdullah Al-Salouli and Abdurrahman Bin Abdullah Al-Azdi with Muslim. Al-Husayn urged his cousin to maintain his piety, carefully assess the situation, and write him back quickly if he saw a firm unity amongst the Kufans.[1] Muslim left Mecca in the middle of the Holy month of Ramadhan.[2] He stopped in Medina, prayed in the Prophet's mosque, and bid farewell to his family,[3] He hired two guides from the tribe of Qays to navigate him to Kufa. The guides lost their way, and became extremely thirsty and exhausted. They suggested to Muslim to move onward. The guides said, "This track looks familiar. Stay on it. Hopefully, you might make it." Unable to carry the two guides, Muslim left them behind and continued his trip. The two guides died from dehydration.[4]

Muslim was neither certain that he was on the right track, nor did he know how close the next oasis was. The guides weren't even able to ride, whether alone or behind anyone, and had Muslim and his other companions stayed to nurse them, they all would have perished in the dead heat. Therefore, it was a duty upon Muslim to march onwards in order to save his own life and the lives of his other companions. Muslim and his companions barely made it to the main road where they found water. He hired a man from that area and sent a letter to Al-Husayn. In his letter, Muslim listed the death of the two guides, the hardships of the trip, the name of the place where he was, and asked Al-Husayn for further instructions. The man delivered the letter, and returned from Mecca with another in which Al-Husayn urged Muslim to rush to Kufa. Muslim left immediately.[5]

Muslim entered Kufa on the fifth of Shawwal. He stayed in the house of Al-Mukhtar Bin Abi Obeyd Al-Thaqafi.[6] Al-Mukhtar was a faithful man and an honorable leader of his community. He was brave and extremely firm in his stance against the enemies of the Prophet's household. He was wise, very experienced in the culture of war, tactful and creative in the battlefield. He was a devout follower of the Prophet's household. He lived according to the high moral values he had learned from them, and supported their cause privately and publicly.

THE PLEDGE OF ALLEGIANCE

The followers of the Prophet's household flocked to Al-Mukhtar's house to welcome Muslim. He was pleased to see the cheerful crowd and hear their expression of support and submission to him. He read them Al-Husayn's letter out loud. As soon as he finished reading, A'abiss Bin Shabeeb Al-Shakeri stood up and said, "I can neither foresee what people will do, nor assure you of their loyalty. However, I can tell you about what I intend to do. By Allah! I shall rush to you and fight your enemy once you make the call. I shall use my sword to defend all of you (Ahl Al-Bayt) seeking in all of this Allah's pleasure." Habeeb Bin Muthahir looked at A'abiss and said, "You've eloquently expressed your determination and, by Allah, my intent is exactly like yours." Sa'iid Bin Abdullah Al-Hanafi spoke, expressing a similar commitment.[7]

A total of eighteen thousand people pledged allegiance to Muslim in Al-Mukhtar's house.[8] Other historians, such as Bin Shahr Ashoub, say the number was twenty five thousand. Al-Sha'abi stated that the number reached forty thousand. Muslim sent A'abiss to deliver the following letter to Al-Husayn: "My messenger is truthful. Eighteen thousand people pledged allegiance to me in Kufa. Expedite your arrival after you read my letter."[9] The Kufans wrote Al-Husayn a letter, and attached it to Muslim's. They wrote: "You, the son of Allah's Messenger! Hurry up! There are a hundred thousand armed men in Kufa waiting for your command. Don't delay your arrival!"[10] These developments and events occurred twenty-seven days prior to Muslim's martyrdom.[11]

Loyal to the Umayyads, some Kufans like Omar Bin Sa'ad Bin Abu Waqqas, Abdullah Bin Muslim Bin Rabee'a Al-Hadhrami and Amara Bin Uqba Bin Abi Ma'eet were extremely disturbed by the unfolding events. They wrote Yazeed informing him that the Kufans pledged allegiance to Muslim Bin Aqeel upon his arrival, and that the appointed governor, Al-Nu'man Bin Basheer, was weak and totally helpless.[12] Yazeed consulted with his intimate friend and advisor Sarjoon. The latter immediately suggested appointing Obeydallah Bin Ziyad as a new governor of Kufa. Yazeed condemned the choice, and justified that the proposed candidate was incompetent. Sarjoon said, "If Mu'awiya were alive to select him, would you have accepted it?" Yazeed said, "Yes." Sarjoon immediately pulled out a letter and showed Yazeed that, before his death, Mu'awiya had already chosen Obeydallah Bin Ziyad for this job. Sarjoon told Yazeed, "I hid this letter from you because I knew that you despise Obeydallah Bin Ziyad." Yazeed sacked Bin Basheer and replaced him with Bin Ziyad. Yazeed wrote Bin Basheer the following letter: "We regard you very highly. In fact, you are honorable and deserve being raised above the clouds. Sometimes an honorable man unfairly becomes a reject, and the reject is honored."[13] Yazeed ordered Bin Ziyad to rush to Kufa and arrest, excommunicate or kill Muslim Bin Aqeel.[14]

Bin Ziyad, with five hundred men in his company, left Al-Basra towards Kufa immediately. Muslim Bin Amr Al-Bahili, Al-Munthir Bin Al-Jaroud, Abdullah Bin Al-Harith Bin Nawfal accompanied him. Bin Ziyad rode nonstop leaving behind some of his companions who fell off their horses. Shareek Bin Al-A'war and Abdullah Bin Al-Harith fell off, and hoped he would wait for them, but he didn't. His servant Mehran also fell off his horse in Al-Qadissiyya, but instead of waiting for him, Bin Ziyad told him to hang on, if he could, and collect a hefty reward in Kufa. Mehran expressed his inability to continue. Bin Ziyad left him behind and continued. Bin Ziyad disguised himself with a Yamani cloak under a black turban. People addressed him as the son of Allah's Messenger in their greetings. He maintained his silence until he entered Kufa from its side facing Al-Najaf.[15]

Deceived by his disguise, the Kufans collectively cheered him. They greeted him, "The son of Allah's Messenger! We welcome you." The scene of the cheerful crowd agitated Bin Ziyad. He continued riding until he arrived to the governor's palace. Al-Nu'man Bin Basheer refused to open the door and screamed from the balcony, "The son of Allah's Messenger! I shall not turn this entrustment over to you." Bin Ziyad said, "Open up. You have had a long night!" A man recognized his voice and told the crowd, "By the Lord of the Ka'aba! This is Bin Ziyad."[16] The crowd immediately dispersed. The next morning Bin Ziyad summoned the people to the main mosque of Kufa, and sternly warned them. He said, "If any one hosts an adversary of the commander of the faithful (Yazeed), and does not turn him in to us, the host will be crucified on his own doorstep."[17]

Muslim's Reaction

Muslim was informed of Bin Ziyad's warning and sensed a change of attitude in people. Worried of being ambushed, Muslim switched his residence from Al-Mukhtar's house to that of Hani Bin Urwa Al-Mithhaji. Hani was a devout follower of the Prophet's household,[18] an honorable leader of the Murad community[19] and renowned teacher of the Holy Book.[20] His authority stretched over thirty thousand men in Kufa. He fought on Imam Ali's side in the Three Battles,[21] and was one of his closest companions. He met the Prophet and was honored to have become his companion (Sahabiyy). He was a little over ninety years of age when he was martyred.[22]

Shareek Bin Abdullah Al-A'awar Al-Harithi Al-Hamadani Al-Basri was also one of Imam Ali's devout followers in Al-Basra,[23] and fought alongside Ammar Bin Yasser in the Battle of Siffeen.[24] Shareek, Hani's intimate friend, stayed with Muslim Bin Aqeel in Hani's house. Shareek was honorable and faithful such that Obeydallah Bin Ziyad had once appointed him on Mu'awiya's behalf to be the governor of Karman.[25] Shareek became extremely ill in Hani's house, and was certain that Bin Ziyad would eventually come to check on him. Shareek told Muslim, "Your goal and the goal of your followers is Bin Ziyad's death. So hide in the closet and kill him as soon as he sits next to me. I'll secure the rest of Kufa for you."[26]

Meanwhile, someone announced Bin Ziyad's arrival. Muslim hid in the closet while Shareek anxiously waited for him to act. Muslim's inaction made Shareek antsy. He took his turban off of his head, and put it on the ground, and then back on his head. He did this many times while he chanted, "Greet Salma! Why don't you greet her? I am thirsty. Please give me a drink of water even if it kills me. If you are afraid of Salma's watchful eyes now, you shall suffer more from her in the future." Shareek repeated this chant numerously while he glanced at the closet. He finally screamed, "Feed me water even if it kills me."[27] Obeydallah Bin Ziyad looked at Hani and said, "Illness has rendered your cousin senile." Hani said, "Shareek has been hallucinating and speaking jargon since he became ill."[28]

When Bin Ziyad left, Shareek asked Muslim, "Why didn't you kill him?" Muslim said, "Two reasons. The first is Ali's narration from the Prophet that ambush is inverse to faith; a true believer should never ambush anyone.[29] The second is Hani's wife. She held onto me and wept. She asked me by Allah not do this in her house." Hani said, "Poor woman! She inadvertently killed me and killed herself and she trapped herself in what she tried to avoid."[30] Shareek died three days later, and was buried in Al-Thawiyya. Bin Ziyad performed the funeral prayers on him. Later on, Bin Ziyad discovered that Shareek planned to assassinate him. He angrily said, "By Allah! I shall never pray on the funeral of any Iraqi, and had Ziyad's grave been somewhere else, I would have exhumed Shareek's body."[31]

The followers of the Prophet's household secretly met Muslim in Hani's house and urged one another to maintain the secrecy of their meetings. Bin Ziyad was unaware of these activities, but anxious to discover Muslim's hiding place. He gave his servant Mi'qal three thousand Dinars and instructed him to feign allegiance to the Prophet's household in order to meet Muslim. Mi'qal entered the main mosque of Kufa, where Muslim Bin Ausaja happened to be praying. Mi'qal approached Bin Ausaja and told him that he was a man from Syria, and that he loved the Prophet's household. He also told Bin Ausaja that he would like to deliver three thousand Dinars to Al-Husayn's messenger. Bin Ausaja was impressed with Mi'qal and took him to hand the money to Muslim Bin Aqeel. Mi'qal paid the money and pledged allegiance to Muslim.[32] The latter handed the money over to Abu Thumama Al-Sa'idi. Muslim had assigned Abu Thumama, one of the bravest men in Kufa, to purchase arms and weapons. Mi'qal spent his days with and around Muslim, and at night he reported all of Muslim's movements to Bin Ziyad.[33]

HANI'S REACTION

Bin Ziyad, certain that Muslim was staying in Hani's house, asked Asma' Bin Kharija, Mohammed Bin Al-Ash'ath and Amr Bin

Al-Hajjaj about Hani, and his puzzling absence from public. They told Bin Ziyad that Hani had been sick. Bin Ziyad was not convinced with their response, because his spies had informed him that Hani sat at his doorstep every night. Bin Ziyad ordered the three men to go to Hani and tell him that the governor missed him, and would like to see him. They walked to Hani's and insisted that he go visit Bin Ziyad. Hani rode his mule and went to the governor's palace. As soon as he saw Hani, Bin Ziyad said, "Here comes the traitor." Bin Ziyad looked at Shurayh Al-Qadhi and said, "I am compassionate with him, but he wants to kill me. He is a man from Murad!"

Bin Ziyad looked at Hani and said, "You are hosting and arming Muslim." Hani denied the accusations, and a loud argument between the two ensued. Bin Ziyad called Mi'qal to testify. At this point, it became clear to Hani that Bin Ziyad had an inside informant. He looked at Bin Ziyad and said, "I am indebted to your father, and I would like to reward him. I advise you to take your family and relatives, and flee to a safe and sound place, because a person more qualified than you and Yazeed has arrived to govern."[34] Bin Ziyad said, "Amazing! You are so blunt about it too."[35] Bin Ziyad resumed, "By Allah! You are never leaving this place until you turn him (Muslim) over to me." Hani replied, "By Allah! If he is under my foot, I'll never lift it." Bin Ziyad reviled Hani, and threatened to kill him. Thinking that his tribe, Murad, would protect him, Hani said, "You'll get yourself in trouble if you kill me." Bin Ziyad brutally struck Hani's face with the sword, breaking his nose and scattering the flesh of his forehead and cheeks onto his beard, and then imprisoned him.[36]

Amr Bin Al-Hajjaj, Hani's brother in law, was informed that Hani had been killed. Amr recruited the tribe of Mithhaj and besieged the governor's palace. Bin Ziyad ordered Shurayh Al-Qadhi to assure Amr and his tribesmen that Hani was still alive. Shurayh narrated, "Once Hani saw me, he appealed to the Muslims to come and rescue him. Had Rameed Bin Bakr Al-Ahmari, one of Bin Ziyad's police, not been hovering over me, I would have transmitted Hani's words to his tribesmen. Instead, I told them that Hani was still alive." Amr Bin Al-Hajjaj thanked Allah and dispersed with his tribesmen.[37]

Muslim's Uprising

Muslim became extremely worried after he learned that Hani was captured. He ordered Abdullah Bin Hazem to call upon all of his followers ahead of the set schedule. Four thousand armed soldiers chanting the slogan of Muslims in the Battle of Badr, "Mansoor! Kill," filled the neighborhood. Muslim appointed Obeydallah Bin Amr Al-Kindi to lead Kinda and Rabee'a tribes. Muslim ordered Amr to lead the horsemen and march forward. He appointed Muslim Bin Ausaja Al-Assdi to lead the communities of Mithhaj and Assad and all the infantry. He appointed Abu Thumama Al-Sa'idi to lead the communities of Tameem and Hamadhan and Al-Abbass Bin Ja'ada Al-Jadali to lead the soldiers who were from Medina. Muslim's army marched towards the governor's palace where Bin Ziyad helplessly hid behind locked gates. There were only thirty soldiers and twenty Umayyad supporters inside the palace. However, the hypocritical nature of the Kufans surfaced in the ranks of Muslim's army, and the number of his soldiers dwindled down from four thousand to three hundred.[38] Al-Ahnaf Bin Qays had once described the Kufans as "politically promiscuous."[39] His description was indeed accurate.

People in the governor's palace screamed, "You Kufans! Be pious and do not wage war against the people of Al-Sham; you know how tough and brave they are." Kufans began talking their brothers and cousins out of their commitment. Wives nagged their husbands to come home. As a result, the majority of the remaining three hundred soldiers in Muslim's army sneaked out[40] Muslim led the evening prayers in the main mosque of Kufa with thirty men behind him. After that he left towards Kinda neighborhood with only three men.[41] Soon enough he had no one to navigate him to the main road. Muslim was unfamiliar with area and didn't know which direction to take. He got off of his horse and walked quietly in the narrow alleys of Kufa.[42]

As people abandoned Muslim, and the boisterous crowd dispersed, Bin Ziyad became suspicious of the mysterious calm. He ordered his soldiers to look out from the balconies and try to see what was happening in and around the main mosque. Bin Ziyad's thugs lit canes and lanterns and threw them in to the mosque, but dead calm prevailed. They concluded that the mosque was empty and informed

Bin Ziyad.

Bin Ziyad immediately summoned all Kufans to the main mosque. As the mosque filled up, he stood on the pulpit and said, "You know that Muslim Bin Aqeel had led the insurgency and caused divisions. We condemn anyone who hosts him, and we shall reward the person who captures him. You, the servants of Allah! Be pious, loyal to your original pledge of allegiance and do not invoke a wrath upon yourselves." Bin Ziyad ordered Al-Hossayn Bin Numayr Al-Tameemi, his police chief, to search for Muslim Bin Aqeel in every corner of Kufa. Bin Ziyad threatened to kill his police chief if Muslim escaped the city.[43] Bin Numayr put guards on every intersection and arrested two community leaders, Abdul A'ala Bin Yazeed Al-Kalbi and Amara Bin Salkhab Al-Azdi. Bin Numayr executed both of them for supporting Muslim's uprising. He also imprisoned many revered and influential Kufan figures, such as Al-Isbagh Bin Nabata and Al-Harith Al-A'awar Al-Hamadhani.

Imprisoning Al-Mukhtar

Al-Mukhtar was in his village Al-Khatwaniyya during Muslim's uprising.[44] He marched with his followers under a green banner, and along his side marched Abdullah Bin Al-Harith carrying a red one. Al-Mukhtar erected his banner on the door of Amr Bin Hurayth and said, "I marched to protect Amr."[45] Al-Mukhtar and Bin Al-Harith learned that Hani and Muslim had been executed, and were advised to remain neutral and thus safe in Amr's house. Amr testified in front of Bin Ziyad that Al-Mukhtar and Abdullah Bin Al-Harith were innocent and did not support Muslim Bin Aqeel. Bin Ziyad cursed Al-Mukhtar and struck his face with a cane poking his eye.[46] Bin Ziyad detained both men until after he murdered Al-Husayn.[47] Bin Ziyad ordered Mohammed Bin Al-Ash'ath, Shibth Bin Rib'ie, Al-Qa'qa' Bin Shawr Al-Thahli, Hajjar Bin Abjar, Shimr Bin Thil Jawshan and Amr Bin Hurayth to lure people into safety and to discourage them from rising up against the Umayyads.[48] As a result, some Kufans became fearful and others became greedy. They all swallowed the bait and the seemingly sincere and righteous soldiers, who were anxious to uproot evil, completely vanished.

Muslim in Tawaa's House

Muslim walked in the alleys of Kufa until he ended up in Kinda neighborhood, around the homes of Bani Jibilla. He stood on the doorstep of a woman called Tawaa, who was a former concubine of Al-Asha'ath Bin Qays. She, after Al-Asha'ath freed her, married Ussayd Al-Hadhrami and bore Bilal for him. Like the vast majority of Kufans, her son was swayed towards the Umayyads. Tawaa was waiting for her son at her front door.

Muslim asked Tawaa for water, she gave him some. He told her that he had no family or friends in this town, and that he is Muslim Bin Aqeel. He explained to her that his family had the unique privilege of interceding for the believers on the Day of Judgement, and asked her to host him. She hosted him in a house adjacent to her son's. She offered him food and checked on him sporadically. Her son sensed something unusual, and asked her about her frequent stops next door. After he swore and promised to tell no one, Tawaa finally gave in to her son's persistence, and told him the whole story.

Early next morning, Bilal (Tawaa's son) informed Bin Ziyad of Muslim's place. Bin Ziyad sent seventy soldiers under Bin Al-Ash'ath to arrest Muslim. Muslim heard the approaching horses and was certain that they were coming after him.[49] He rushed his morning supplication and quickly wore his war vest. He then told Tawaa, "You've done a good enough job and secured your share of intercession from Allah's Messenger. I saw my uncle, the Commander of the Faithful, in my dream last night. He told me that I'll be reunited with him tomorrow.[50] As Muslim was about to step out, Bin Al-Ash'ath and his soldiers stormed into Tawaa's house. Muslim repelled the attackers and forced them out of the house twice. He fought as he chanted, "Death is inevitable. Do as you wish now for, you shall all die. I shall persevere on what Allah has ordained. The Divine ordinances are definitely implemented." Muslim was remarkably strong and brave. He threw men high up in the air,[51] and killed forty-one of the attackers.[52]

Bin Al-Asha'ath sent to Bin Ziyad requesting troop reinforcement. The latter sent the messenger back to scold the former for his shameful performance. Bin Al-Asha'ath sent the messenger again, and told Bin Ziyad, "Do you think that you assigned me to arrest a shopkeeper in Kufa or a coward from Al-Heera? You have dispatched me against a sharp sword from the swords of Mohammed Bin Abdullah (Prophet Mohammed)." Bin Ziyad sent reinforcements.[53] A fierce battle ensued. Bakeer Bin Humran Al-Ahmari struck Muslim's face with the sword, cutting off his upper lip and splitting open the lower one. Muslim fatally struck him back, once on the head, and another on the shoulder.[54]

Meanwhile, some soldiers had already climbed up onto the roof and began throwing flames and rocks at Muslim. Bin Aqeel fought back chanting, "I may despise death, but I have sworn to die free."[55] At this point, the badly wounded Muslim became exhausted from heavy bleeding. He leaned against the wall of Tawaa's house to rest. Arrows and rocks fell on him like rain. Muslim yelled, "How dare you stone me like an infidel? I am from the Prophet's family! How dare you disrespect Allah's Messenger and hurt his family?" Bin Al-Asha'ath told Muslim, "Your action is self-destructive; stop resisting and I guarantee your safety." Muslim replied, "As long as I have energy to fight, you will never arrest me. By Allah! I would never surrender." Muslim attacked Bin Al-Asha'ath, but the latter ran away. Thirsty and exhausted, Muslim was completely surrounded. A man stabbed him in the back. Muslim fell onto the ground and was captured.[56] It was also narrated that they dug a pit and covered it with dirt. Muslim was captured after he fell in it.[57] Muslim choked on his tears when they snatched his sword away. Amr Bin Obeydallah Al-Salmi was amazed to see Muslim weep.

Muslim Facing Bin Ziyad

They took Muslim to Bin Ziyad. Muslim saw a cool jug of water at the door of the palace and asked for a drink. Muslim Bin Amr Al-Bahili told him, "You shall taste the stinking, boiling water of hellfire before you taste this." Muslim Bin Aqeel asked, "Who are you?" Al-Bahili answered, "I am an adherent to the righteousness you condemned, and a supporter of the leader you betrayed." Bin Aqeel said, "May you be destroyed! You are heartless and merciless. You are Bin Bahila! You belong in hellfire." Muslim Bin Aqeel then sat down and leaned against the wall of the governor's palace.[58] Amara Bin Uqbah Bin Abi Ma'eet sent his servant Qays to give Muslim Bin

Aqeel a drink of water. Muslim tried to drink twice, but each time blood from his mouth poured into the cup. A piece of his lip fell into the cup in his third attempt, so he set the cup aside and said, "Had this water been ordained for me, I would have had some of it by now."

One of Bin Ziyad's guards escorted Muslim Bin Aqeel into the palace. Muslim did not greet anyone. The guard said, "Greet your commander." Muslim replied, "Shut your mouth! He is not my commander."[59] It was also narrated that Muslim said, "Greetings to the followers of guidance who fear the outcome of death and obey the High and Divine." Bin Ziyad laughed and said, "You are dead whether you greet or not."[60] Muslim answered, "It is not surprising if you kill me. A man, more evil than you, has already killed a man more righteous than me. Moreover, your cruelty and wickedness define you as a ruthless murderer." Bin Ziyad said, "You have revolted against your leader, divided the Muslims and bred corruption." Muslim replied, "You are a liar! Mu'awiya and his son, Yazeed, divided the Muslims, and your father bred corruption. I ask Allah to grant me martyrdom on the hands of His most evil creatures."[61]

Muslim requested to state his will to someone he knew. Bin Ziyad allowed him. Muslim looked at the attendants and chose Omar Bin Sa'ad. Muslim told Omar, "We are relatives, and I would like you to do something for me, but I want it to remain private." Omar Bin Sa'ad refused to listen to Muslim but Bin Ziyad intervened and told Bin Sa'ad, "Fulfill your cousin's wish." Muslim and Bin Sa'ad stepped away and stood in a place where Bin Ziyad could see them. Muslim asked Omar to pay off his accrued debt since his arrival to Kufa. The amount, including the prices of his sword and war vest, was six hundred Dirhams. He also asked Bin Sa'ad to retrieve his body from Bin Ziyad and bury it, and then write to Al-Husayn to inform him of the latest events. Omar Bin Sa'ad immediately transmitted the contents of Muslim's will to Bin Ziyad. The latter said, "The honorable would never betray, but sometimes a man is compelled to trust a traitor."[62] Bin Ziyad looked at Muslim and said, "Son of Aqeel, You amaze me! You came to a united community and divided it." Muslim said, "No, I did not do that. People of this town claimed that your father was a tyrant who spilled their blood and executed their leaders. We came to restore justice and rule by the Divine Book." Bin Ziyad said, "What made this matter any of your business? Weren't we just?" Muslim replied, "Allah knows that you are dishonest and that you murder others just out of enmity, anger and suspicion." Bin Ziyad reviled Muslim, Ali, Aqeel and Al-Husayn.[63] Muslim said, "These dirty words suit you and your father. You are an enemy of Allah. Do what you wish."[64]

Bin Ziyad ordered a man from Al-Sham to behead Muslim on the roof of the palace, and to throw the head and the body down to the ground. Muslim began praising Allah as the man drove him to the roof[65] Muslim then said, "My Lord! These people invited us. They then betrayed us and accused us of lying. Be the Judge between us and them. "Muslim then turned towards Medina and greeted Al-Husayn.[66] The man pushed Muslim to the side of the roof facing the shoe market. He decapitated Muslim and threw the body and the head down to the ground.[67] The man from Al-Sham came down terrified. Bin Ziyad asked him, "What's wrong?" The man said, "When I killed him, I saw an angry and a horrible looking man standing next to me. The scene terrified me." Bin Ziyad said, "You are just hallucinating."[68]

After Muslim's martyrdom, Hani was shackled and dragged to the sheep market. He screamed out loud, "Mithhaj! Where is my Mithhaj?" Realizing that no one was around to rescue him, Hani forcefully freed his arms and said, "Is there a knife, rock or even a bone for a man to defend himself?" They pinned him down and asked him to stretch his neck. He said, "I can never be generous with it, and I would never assist you to murder me." Rasheed, one of Bin Ziyad's servants, ineffectively struck him with the sword. The uninjured Hani said, "To the Lord we shall return. My Lord! To your Mercy and Paradise." Rasheed struck him again and killed him.

Bin Ziyad ordered the decapitated bodies of Hani and Muslim dragged through the markets[69] and then crucified upside down in Al-Kanasa.[70] He sent their heads to Yazeed, who in turn hung them up above one of the main roads in Damascus.[71]

Bin Ziyad wrote to Yazeed the following letter: "I thank Allah who restored the rights of the commander of the faithful, and protected him from his enemies. I would like to inform the blessed commander of the faithful that Muslim Bin Aqeel was staying in the house of Hani Bin Urwa Al-Muradi. I employed secret agents and schemed until Allah helped me extract and kill both of them. I have sent you their heads with two of my obedient and trustworthy soldiers, Hani Bin Abi Hayya and Al-Zubayr Bin Al-Arwah. The commander of the faithful can ask them whatever he wants. They are honest, knowledgeable and pious. Greetings."

Yazeed wrote Bin Ziyad back: "You have done what I like. You have done your job with remarkable bravery and steadfastness. You have done extremely well. You have upheld the standards and lived up to my expectations. I conversed with your messengers, and found them as you mentioned, wise and pious. Reward both of them on my behalf. I heard that Al-Husayn Bin Ali has left towards Iraq. Deploy your reconnaissance and police, and try people on suspicion.[72] Your time and place have compelled you to confront Al-Husayn. You should be up to this task, or else you will return a slave instead of remaining free.[73] Fight him or bring him to me."[74]

Notes & References

1. Al-Irshaad
2. Muruj Al-Thahab (V.2, P.86)
3. Tareekh Al-Tabari (V.6, P.198)
4. Al-Akhbar Al-Tiwaal (P.232)
5. Al-Irshaad
6. Tareekh Al-Tabari (V.6, P.199)
7. Tareekh Al-Tabari (V.6, P.199)
8. Tareekh Al-Tabari (V.6, P.211), Tathkirat Al-Khawass (P.138)
9. Tareekh Al-Tabari (V.6, P.210)
10. Al-Bihar (V.10, P.185)
11. Tareekh Al-Tabari (V.6, P.224)
12. Tareekh Al-Tabari (V.6, P.201)
13. Ansaab Al-Ashraaf (V.4, P.82)
14. Tareekh Al-Tabari (V.6, P.199)
15. Mutheer Al-Ahzaan
16. Tareekh Al-Tabari (V.6, P.201)
17. Al-Irshaad
18. Al-Kamel (V.4, P.10)
19. Al-Akhbar Al-Tiwaal (P.235)
20. Al-Aghani (V.14, P.95)

21. Thakheerat Al-Darayn (P. 278)
22. Al-Issaba (V.3, P.616)
23. Mutheer Al-Ahzaan (P.14)
24. Tareekh Al-Tabari (V.6, P.203)
25. Al-Nujum Al-Zahira (V. l, P.153) & Al-Kamel (V.3, P.206)
26. Mutheer Al-Ahzaan (P.14)
27. Riyadh Al-Massa'ib (P.60) & Tareekh Al-Tabari (V. 6, P.204)
28. Mutheer Al-Ahzaan (P.14)
29. Al-Kamel (V.4, P.11) & Tareekh Al-Tabari (V.6, P.240)
30. Mutheer Al-Ahzaan (P.14)
31. Tareekh Al-Tabari (V.6, P.202)
32. Al-Akhbar Al-Tiwaal (P.237)
33. Al-Irshaad
34. Muruj Al-Thahab (V.2, P.88)
35. Al-Mustaqsa (V.1, P.15)
36. Mutheer Al-Ahzaan
37. Tareekh Al-Tabari (V.6, P.206)
38. Tareekh Al-Tabari (V.6, P.207)
39. Ansaab Al-Ashraaf (V.5, P.338)
40. Tareekh Al-Tabari (V.6, P.208)
41. Al-Akhbar Al-Tiwaal (P.240)
42. Al-Luhuf (P.29)
43. Tareekh Al-Tabari (V.6, P.209 & 210)
44. Ansaab Al-Ashraaf (V.5, P.214)
45. Tareekh Al-Tabari (V.6, P.215)
46. Al-Ma'arif (P.253)
47. Ansaab Al-Ashraaf (V.5, P.215)
48. Al-Kamel (V.4, P.12
49. Tareekh Al-Tabari (V.6, P.210)
50. Nafs Al-Mahmoum (P.56)
51. Nafs Al-Mahmoum (P.57)
52. Manaqib Bin Shahr Ashoub (V.2, P.212)
53. Al-Muntakhab (P.299)
54. Maqtal Al-Khawarizmi (V.l, P.210)
55. Al-Luhuf (P.30)
56. Manaqib Bin Shahr Ashoub (V.2, P.212) & Maqtal Al-Khawarizmi (V.l, P.209 & 210)
57. Al-Muntakhab (P.299)
58. Al-Irshaad
59. Al-Luhuf (P.30) & Tareekh Al-Tabari (V.6, P.212)
60. Al-Muntakhab (P.300)
61. Mutheer Al-Ahzaan (P.17) & Maqtal Al-Khawarizmi (V. l, P. 211)
62. Al-Irshaad & Tareekh Al-Tabari (V.6, P.212)

63. Al-Kamel (V.4, P.14) & Tareekh Al-Tabari (V.6, P.213)
64. Al-Luhuf (P.31)
65. Tareekh Al-Tabari (V.6, P.213)
66. Asrar Al-Shahada (P.259)
67. Mutheer Al-Ahzaan (P.18)
68. Maqtal Al-Khawarizmi (V.1, P.312)
69. Al-Muntakhab (P.301)
70. Manaqib Bin Shahr Ashoub (V.2, P.212) & Maqtal Al-Khawarizmi (V.1, P. 215)
71. Tareekh Abu Al-Fida (V.1, P.190) & Al-Bidaya (V.8, P.157)
72. Tareekh Al-Tabari (V.6, P.214)
73. Maqtal Al-Awalim (P.66) & Tareekh Dimashq (V.4, P. 332)
74. Maqtal Al-Khawarizmi (V. 1, P. 215)

AL-HUSAYN DEPARTING TO IRAQ

Yazeed appointed Amr Bin Sa'iid Bin Al-A'as to be in full charge of the pilgrimage season, and instructed him to kill Al-Husayn anywhere he found him.[1] Informed of this scheme, the Prophet's grandson performed the rituals of the minor pilgrimage (Umra), instead of the major one (Hajj), and prepared to leave Mecca. Unwilling to compromise the sanctity of the Holy House, Al-Husayn planned to avoid being hurt in Mecca at any cost.[2]

AL-HUSAYN'S SPEECH IN MECCA

Shortly before his departure, Al-Husayn addressed the Meccans and the pilgrims. He said:

> "Praise is due to Allah. What He ordains happens. All power comes from Allah, and I ask Him to bestow His blessings upon His Messenger. Death is the inescapable destiny of all humans, and I am as anxious to see my ancestors as Yaqoub was to see Yusuf. I shall embrace death in the fashion chosen for me. I can foresee my flesh being torn and eaten by the wolves of the desert in a place between Naynawa and Karbala. There is no escape from what has been written in the Divine Tablet. What pleases us, the Prophet's household, pleases Allah. We persevere with what He ordained, and He rewards us for it. The family of Allah's Messenger is bound to reunite with him. The Prophet shall be pleased to see his promise fulfilled, and his family next to him in a divinely protected place. I am inviting those who are loyal to us, and determined to joyously return to Allah, to join us. Allah willing, I am leaving tomorrow morning."[3]

Al-Husayn left Mecca on the eighth of Thil Hijja. His family and followers from Hijaz, Basra and Kufa who joined him in Mecca left with him. He gave each individual in his caravan ten Dinars and a camel to ride.[4]

ATTEMPTS AT CONVINCING AL-HUSAYN TO STAY

Worried that the Kufans might change their minds and betray Al-Husayn, some of his relatives asked him to delay his trip. Al-Husayn was very careful in articulating his answers because not all of the people around him were receptive to the fact that he already knew the outcome of his trip. The level of faith and receptivity of the people, who conversed with Al-Husayn, varied significantly. Fully aware of this, the Prophet's grandson engaged each one accordingly.

He told Bin Al-Zubayr, "My father told me that a person will be killed in Mecca, and, as a result, the sanctity of the Holy House will be violated. I do not want to be this person. Being killed a yard away from Allah's sanctuary is better than being killed in it. By Allah! If I go under the ground, they'll hunt me down to kill me. They shall abuse me the way the Jews abused their Sabbath." When Bin Al-Zubayr walked away, Al-Husayn told the attendants, "My departure from Hijaz is his most favorite thing. He knows that people rank me higher than him, so he likes me to leave to enjoy people's exclusive attention.[1]

Mohammed Bin Al-Hanafiyya told Al-Husayn on the eve of his departure, "You know that the Kufans betrayed your father, and your brother. I am afraid that they would do that to you too. Stay here! You are the most honorable and the most dignified figure in this sanctuary." Al-Husayn replied, "I am afraid that Yazeed Bin Mu'awiya will murder me in Allah's sanctuary, and that I would become the reason that the sanctity of this Holy House is violated." Bin Al-Hanafiyya suggested that Al-Husayn change his destination to Yemen, or anywhere other than Kufa. Al-Husayn promised to look into his brother's suggestion. Al-Husayn departed shortly before dawn on that night. Bin Al-Hanafiyya held the bit of Al-Husayn's camel, and said, "Didn't you promise to consider my suggestion?" Al-Husayn replied, "Yes, but right after you left, Allah's Messenger came to me. He ordered me to depart and said that Allah has ordained to see me murdered." Bin Al-Hanafiyya wept and wondered why Al-Husayn would take his family with him. Al-Husayn explained, "Allah, The Exalted, has ordained for the women to become captives."[2]

Abdullah Bin Ja'afar Al-Tayyar had sent a letter to Al-Husayn with his sons, Awn and Mohammed. He wrote in it: "I ask you by Allah to change your plan when you read my letter. I am very worried that you, and the rest of your family, might be killed. Shall this happen, darkness will prevail, for you are the banner of guidance, and the hope of the believers. Please wait! I shall arrive to Mecca soon. Greetings."

Abdullah acquired an official document from Amr Bin Sa'iid Bin Al-A'as, Yazeed's appointed governor on Mecca, in which he guaranteed Al-Husayn's safety. Abdullah Bin Ja'afar and Yahya Bin Sa'iid Bin Al-A'as delivered the document to Al-Husayn. Bin Ja'afar tried his best to influence Al-Husayn to change his plan, but the Prophet's grandson declined to give in. Al-Husayn told Bin Ja'afar that Allah's Messenger appeared to him in a dream and ordered him to do what must be irrevocably done. Bin Ja'afar inquired about the dream. Al-Husayn replied, "I have not mentioned it to anyone, and I never will until I return to my Exalted Lord."[3]

Bin Abbass told Al-Husayn, "Cousin! I try to persevere but I cannot. I am afraid you will be murdered. Do not go to Iraq because its people are disloyal. Stay here. You are the undisputed master of Hijaz. If the people of Iraq want you, as they claim, let them get rid of their governor, who happens to be their real enemy, before you go there. If you insist on leaving, then go to Yemen. It is wide, well-fortified and your father has a large number of followers in it. Over there, you can write to people and send them messengers. You can then achieve your desired goal without being harmed." Al-Husayn replied, "Cousin! I know that you are sincere in your advice, but I am determined to leave." Bin Abbass said, "Do not take the women and children with you. I'm afraid that they would be traumatized seeing you murdered." Al-Husayn replied, "By Allah! They (Kufans) will never leave me alone until they kill me, and once they do, Allah shall allow the tyrants to smother them and treat them like scum."[4]

FACTS BEHIND THE DEPARTURE

These encounters reveal that the people who hoped that

Al-Husayn would delay his trip to Iraq lacked vision and foresight. Al-Husayn was fully aware of the Kufans' hypocrisy and disloyalty, however, he honored his promise after they appeared to be united, obedient and loyal to him. At this point, Kufans were still seemingly supportive of Al-Husayn, and anxiously awaiting his arrival. Kufans persisted in asking him to guide them, rescue them from the tyrants, and lead them to what pleases the Lord of the Worlds. The infallible leader, whose duty was to guide humans, could not have overlooked their request. Had Al-Husayn ignored their pleas, people would have been critical of his inaction. The infallible leader is, and must always be, above leaving himself open to criticism or blame. Moreover, the countries that Bin Abbass and others suggested as alternative destinations were not very safe. The atrocities that Bisr Bin Artat committed in Yemen proved that its inhabitants were incapable of defending themselves, and thus very weak to resist aggression.

In agreement with our discussion, Al-Sheykh Al-Shoshtari, may Allah be pleased with him, wrote in his *Khassa'is:*

> "Al-Husayn had two responsibilities: 1, a factual one and 2, an apparent one. The factual responsibility compelled him to sacrifice his life and, with advanced knowledge of the outcome, expose his family and children to captivity and slaughter. The Umayyad tyrants believed that they were on the right path, and Ali and his children were not. The Umayyads introduced and emphasized the cursing of Ali as an integral part of Friday prayers. It was narrated that a speaker forgot to curse Ali in a Friday sermon but later, while traveling, remembered and made it up. The Umayyads built a mosque for the sole purpose of cursing Ali and called it the Mosque of Utterance. Had Al-Husayn pledged allegiance to Yazeed and accepted him as a leader, people would have thought that the Prophet's grandson condoned the Umayyads as legitimate and righteous rulers. In contrast, Al-Husayn fought them and risked his Holy life, and the lives of his family members, to demonstrate to his contemporaries and the coming generations that he was the legitimate and righteous leader, and those who oppressed him were faithless transgressors.
>
> The apparent responsibility is embedded in Al-Husayn's tremendous efforts to protect himself and his children at

any cost. Nonetheless, the siege around him was suffocating. Yazeed ordered his governor in Medina to kill Al-Husayn. As a result, the Prophet's grandson fled to Mecca. Al-Husayn should have been totally secure in the sanctuary of the Holy House (Mecca), but the Umayyads were determined to arrest him and murder him, even if he was hanging onto the cover of the Ka'aba. Al-Husayn compromised his pilgrimage plan and left Mecca towards Kufa. He did so because the Kufans bad sent him numerous letters in which they pledged allegiance to him, and urged him to liberate them from the Umayyads' evil reign. After such a display of loyalty and commitment from Kufans, Al-Husayn was compelled to assume his Divinely assigned responsibility of guiding them, and that was why he complied with their request. Al-Husayn fulfilled his mission, and therefore, the Kufans will have no excuse on the Day of Judgement for reversing the course of their action. Had Al-Husayn refused to go to Kufa, people, on the Day of Judgement, could claim that they tried but be declined. On the other band, Al-Husayn would not have been safe anywhere else. In his response to his brother, Bin Al-Hanafiyya, be underscored the false sense of safety in his relatives' suggestions. Justifying his departure to his brother, Al-Husayn said that even if he hid underground, they would relentlessly hunt him down until they murdered him. Moreover, in his dialogue with Abi Hirra Al-Assadi, Al-Husayn said that he persevered when the Umayyads cursed him and confiscated his possessions, so he decided to move on because they were after him to spill his blood."

The Meccans were saddened by Al-Husayn's departure. They begged him to stay. Al-Husayn, quoting the man from the tribe of Aws (a large tribe in Medina that supported the Prophet in his wars against the idolaters), said, "I shall go because it is never shameful to fight and die as a Muslim while defending the right path. My soul longs being with pious men, and is anxious to fight against transgressors and criminals." Al-Husayn then recited, *"And Allah's command is an ordained matter. (33:38)"*[5]

Notes & References

1. Al-Muntakhab (P.304)
2. Mutheer Al-Ahzaan (P.89) & Tareekh Al-Tabari (V.6, P.177)
3. Al-Luhuf (P.33) & Mutheer Al-Ahzaan (P.20)
4. Nafs Al-Mahmoum (P.91)
1. Al-Kamel (V.4, P.16)
2. Al-Bihar (V.10, P.184)
3. Tareekh Al-Tabari (V.6, P.219); Al-Kamel (V.4, P.17) & Al-Bidaya (V.6, P.163)
4. Al-Kamel (V.4, P.16)
5. Tathkirat Al-Khawass (P.304)

AL-HUSAYN'S JOURNEY

AL-TAN'EEM

Al-Husayn left Mecca and passed through Al-Tan'eem[1] where he came across a caravan loaded with precious goods sent by the governor of Yemen, Baheer Bin Yassar, to Yazeed Bin Mu'awiya in Damascus. Al-Husayn confiscated the goods and told the owners of the camels, "Whoever likes to go with us to Iraq will be financially compensated and cared for. Those who don't want to join us will be paid for the distance they have traveled."[2] Some joined him and some didn't. Al-Husayn was the infallible leader at the time. The Supreme appointed him to be the guardian over all of His creatures. The goods that Al-Husayn took were rightfully his. Yazeed and his father illegally seized the possessions of Al-Husayn as well as those of the majority of the Muslims. Al-Husayn's followers had been complaining to him about poverty and shortages of supplies. The infallible leader had the right to claim possession of what originally belonged to the Muslims in order to replenish the supplies of his followers. In fact, because of his ordained martyrdom, the Master of Martyrs fell short from reclaiming all the assets that the oppressors had usurped from the community of Allah's Messenger. Nonetheless, Al-Husayn restored things of more significance. The Umayyad tyrants tarnished the true concept of leadership, and usurped the position from its rightful personnel. Al-Husayn's self-sacrifice annulled the perpetuity of the evil scheme of the Umayyads, and shattered their deliberate distortion of the true Message.

AL-SSIFAAH

Al-Husayn met Al-Farazdaq Bin Ghalib, the infamous Arab poet, in Al-Ssifaah and asked him about Kufans. Al-Farazdaq replied, "Their hearts are attached to you but their swords support the Umayyads and the ordained comes from heaven." Abu Abdullah said, "You're absolutely correct. Allah ordains and does what He wills. He ordains various matters everyday. We thank Allah for His bounties if He ordains what we hope, and if not, the person whose intention is righteousness and his path is piety should never feel discontented." Al-Farzdaq asked Al-Husayn about some jurisprudence related matters and then left.[3]

It was also narrated that Al-Farazdaq left Basra towards Mecca to perform the minor pilgrimage (Umra). On his way there, he saw a boot camp in the open meadows. He inquired about it and was told that it was the army of Al-Husayn Bin Ali. Al-Farazdaq thought that he should convey his respect to Allah's Messenger. He walked over and greeted Al-Husayn. The Prophet's grandson asked him, "Who are you?" He replied, "I am Al-Farzdaq Bin Ghalib." Al-Husayn commented, "You're too brief in introducing yourself." Al-Farazdaq said, "You could more brief if you like, for you are the grandson of Allah's Messenger."[4]

THAAT I'RQ

Undeterred by difficulties, Abu Abdullah marched onwards. He met Bishr Bin Ghalib in Thaat I'rq. Al-Husayn asked him about the Kufans. Bishr replied, "Their swords are on the Umayyads' side, but their hearts are on yours." Al-Husayn said, "You're correct indeed."[5] Al-Riyashi quoted the following from a man who met Al-Husayn on his way to Kufa. The man said that after he performed pilgrimage, he was traveling alone and saw some tents. He walked over and inquired about them. He was told that these tents belong to Al-Husayn Bin Ali and Bin Fatima. The man moved closer, and saw Al-Husayn sitting in front of a tent reading a letter. He looked at Al-Husayn and said, "You are the grandson of Allah's Messenger, and I endear you more than I endear my father and mother. What brought you to this dry and unsafe part of the world?" Al-Husayn replied, "They (Umayyads) are after me, and these letters are from the Kufans who will eventually murder me. Once they do it, and violate all the Divine codes, Allah shall empower the tyrants to murder and dispose of them like rejects."[6]

AL-HAAJIR

Upon his arrival to Al-Haajir, Al-Husayn wrote back to the Kufans and sent the letter with Qays Bin Mas'har Al-Saydawi. He wrote in it: "Greetings! Muslim Bin Aqeel sent a letter informing me of your unity in supporting us. I asked Allah to bless us and grandly reward you. I left Mecca towards Kufa on Tuesday the eighth of Thil Hijja. As my messenger arrives, I urge you to maintain your unity. I shall arrive in the next few days."

BA'ADH AL-UYOUN

He marched on from Al-Haajir. Whenever he stopped at an oasis, the Arabs around it joined him.[7] He met Abdullah Bin Mutee' Al-Adawi at one oasis. After learning that Al-Husayn was traveling to Iraq, Abdullah said, "The son of Allah's Messenger! Remember that the sanctity of Islam will be violated. I ask you by Allah to preserve the sanctity of the Arabs. By Allah! If you intend to reclaim your rightful leadership from the Umayyads, they will murder you, and if they do, they will never fear anyone after you." Al-Husayn was undeterred by Al-Adawi's comments. The Prophet's grandson was adamant about continuing his journey.[8]

AL-KHUZAYMIYYA

He stayed in Al-Khuzaymiyya for a day and a night. Early that morning, his sister Zaynab told him that she heard a voice chanting, "I call upon the eye to be ready to weep on the martyrs. A group of people are riding to fulfill a promise, and embrace their death." Al-Husayn said, "Sister! The ordained shall definitely be implemented."

ZUROUD

Al-Husayn camped in Zuroud, and close to him camped Zuhayr Bin Al-Qayn. The latter was neither a supporter of the Prophet's household, nor did he like to camp close to Al-Husayn. However, Zuhayr was compelled to rest next to the only oasis in that area. As Zuhayr was feasting with his companions, a messenger came inviting him to see Al-Husayn. Zuhayr declined to go, but his wife Dalham Bint Amr urged him to accept the invitation, and persuaded him to go and listen to what the Prophet's grandson had to say. Soon after he left, Zuhayr returned very cheerful. He collected his belongings to join the Master of Youth in Heaven. Zuhayr told his wife, "I care for your well-being and I do not like you to be hurt because of me. Please, return to your family." He also told his companions, "I shall never see you again unless you decide to support the Messenger's grandson." He then told them what he heard from Salman Al-Farisi when the Muslims triumphed in Balanjar. Zuhayr said that the Muslims were ecstatic on that day because the amount of war gains was incredibly large. Seeing how festive and cheerful we were, Salman said, "If you live long enough, you should definitely be more festive and cheerful on the day you see the Master of Youth of the Prophet's household, and fight on his side. I am departing but I trust in Allah to guard all of you."[9] Zuhayr's wife told him, "Allah has blessed you, and I ask you to remember me on the Day of Judgement when you see Al-Husayn's grandfather."[10]

In Zuroud, Al-Husayn was informed that Muslim Bin Aqeel and Hani Bin Urwa were martyred. He numerously asked Allah to bestow His mercy upon both of them, and frequently uttered, "To Allah we belong and to Him we shall return." Al-Husayn wept along with the Hashimites. Women in the caravan wept loudly for the loss of Muslim. The scene was tearful and emotional.[11] Abdullah Bin Saleem and Al-Munthir Bin Al-Misha'al, both from Bani Assad, told Al-Husayn, "We ask you by Allah to choose another destination, because you have no supporters at all in Kufa." Aqeel's family heard them, and immediately responded, "We are determined to avenge Muslim or taste what he had tasted." Al-Husayn looked at his cousins, and said, "Life is worthless without them (Muslim and Hani)."[12]

AL-THA'ALABIYYA

In Al-Tha'alabiyya, a man asked Al-Husayn about the meaning of the following verse of the Holy Book: *"We, one day, shall call each group of people with its leader (17:71)."* Al-Husayn replied, "A leader guided his followers to the true path and they complied, while another lead his followers astray and they also complied. The first group is in paradise while the other is in hellfire. This is what Allah meant when He said *a group will be in paradise and another will be in hellfire. (42:7)*"[13] A Kufan met Al-Husayn in Al-Tha'alabiyya. The Prophet's grandson told the Kufan, "Had I met you in Medina, I would have shown you Jabra'eel's prints and the marks he left in our house upon delivering the Divine revelations to my grandfather. You Kufan! We are the masters of all the knowledge. It is inconceivable that they know and we don't!"[14]

Bajeer, a resident of Al-Tha'alabiyya, was a young child when Al-Husayn passed by them. Bajeer narrated that his brother told Al-Husayn, "I see that you only have a few people around you." Al-Husayn pointed with his whip to a large bag and replied, "This is full of letters."[15]

AL-SHUQUQ

In Al-Shuquq, Al-Husayn asked a man coming from Kufa about the situation in Iraq. The man said that they are all united against him. Al-Husayn said, "Allah is the Supreme Commander, and He does what He wills. The Exalted has a different ordinance every day." He then said, "If life is precious, Allah's bounties are more so. If possessions are to be abandoned, how could a person remain greedy? Since wealth is Divinely allocated, then it is wise to be less eager to accrue profits. And since our bodies are destined to perish, then martyrdom is the noblest way to die. Members of the Prophet Mohammed's family! I bid all of you farewell, because soon I shall depart away from you."[16]

ZUBALAH

In Zubalah, he was informed that Abdullah Bin Yaqtar was martyred. Al-Husayn had sent Abdullah to deliver a letter to Muslim. Al-Hossayn Bin Numayr arrested him in Al-Qadissiyya and turned him over to Obeydallah Bin Ziyad. The latter ordered Abdullah to curse Al-Husayn and his father from the pulpit. Abdullah looked at the Kufans and said, "People! I am the messenger of Al-Husayn Bin Fatima. I advise you to protect him and support him against Marjana's son (Bin Ziyad)." Obeydallah ordered him thrown from the roof of the palace. Abdullah's bones were crushed but he was still breathing. A man called Abdul Malik Bin Omayr Al-Lakhmi rushed over and slaughtered him. After being shunned for his cruelty, Bin Omayr said, "I wanted to end his suffering." It was also narrated that a tall man, who resembled Bin Omayr, slaughtered Bin Yaqtar.

Al-Husayn informed his followers of Abdullah Bin Yaqtar's martyrdom, and absolved all of them from their pledge. Many people left. The only ones who stayed were those who had joined him in Mecca. A large number of poor nomads joined Al-Husayn after he left Mecca. These opportunists thought that Al-Husayn would arrive to a red carpet welcome in Kufa. The Prophet's grandson was direct in informing his company of the upcoming hardships. Moreover, he was certain that once he relieved all of his followers from their commitment, only the sincere ones, who were determined to self-sacrifice, would stay.[17]

BATN AL-AQABA

Al-Husayn marched from Zubalah and camped in Batn Al-Aqaba where told his companions, "I foresee myself murdered; I saw in my dream that dogs, fiercest of which was a spotted one, were ripping through my flesh."[18] Amr Bin Luwathan reminded Al-Husayn of the Kufans' treachery and disloyalty and suggested to him returning to Medina. Al-Husayn said, "I am aware of this option, but Allah's command can never be overridden."[19] He then said, "They will never leave me alone until they murder me, and once they do it, Allah will belittle them with humiliation until they become the lowest of all communities."[20]

SHARAAF

He marched from Batu Al-Aqaba and camped in Sharaaf. After midnight, Al-Husayn ordered the men to load more water than they normally did. Noon of the next day, one of his companions chanted "Allah is the Greatest." Al-Husayn asked, "What's the matter?" The man said, "I saw palm trees." People in the caravan stated that palm trees did not grow in that area, and what he saw were the spearheads and the ears of horses. Al-Husayn said, "I see spears and horses too." He asked his companions if there was a decent location in the area to shelter them. They said, "There is Thu Hussm on the left of us. You will find it suitable." Al-Husayn marched towards it and camped there.

Al-Hurr Al-Riyahi arrived with one thousand soldiers. Bin Ziyad had sent to either escort Al-Husayn to Kufa, or to prevent him from returning to Medina. Al-Hurr and his soldiers stood facing Al-Husayn in the dead heat of noontime.[21] Having noticed that Al-Hurr and his soldiers were extremely thirsty, Al-Husayn ordered his companions to give them water and offer some to their horses. Al-Husayn's companions filled up many containers from which Al-Hurr, his soldiers and their horses drank until they were full.[22] Extremely thirsty and exhausted, Ali Bin Al-Ta'aan Al-Muharibi, one of Al-Hurr's soldiers, arrived late. Al-Husayn told Ali, "Lower your ride." Ali didn't understand because he was not familiar with the dialect of Al-Hijaz. Al-Husayn said, "Lower your camel." Ali tried to drink, but water spilled all over the place. Al-Husayn said, "Hold the jug tightly." Ali was so disoriented, he did not know what to do. Al-Husayn walked over, helped him drink, and gave the rest of the water to Ali's horse.

Knowing how precious a drop of water is in the open desert, this encounter reflected Al-Husayn's incredible kindness, even to his adversaries. Al-Husayn was certain that soon he and his companions would be banned from a drink of water, however, generosity was but one of the many genuine moral values he was inculcated with by his grandfather and father. Shortly after that, Al-Husayn spoke to them. He, after praising Allah, said, "Allah: The Exalted likes to hear me justify my action and you should too. I came to you because I of the numerous letters you have sent me in which you urged me to come to you. You wrote that you have no leader, and that Allah will guide you by me. If you intend to honor your promise, then appease me with your pledge and commitment. And if you happen to resent my presence, then let me return to the place from which I came."

Silence prevailed. Al-Hajjaj Bin Masruoq Al-Ja'afi made the call for noon prayers. Al-Husayn told Al-Hurr, "Would you like to lead your companions?" Al-Hurr replied, "No. All of us will pray behind you." Al-Husayn led the prayers. After he finished, he faced the crowd and praised Allah and His Messenger, and then said, "People!

Your piety and knowledge of the righteous individuals please Allah. We, the members of Mohammed's household, are the rightful leaders, and those who rule with oppression and tyranny are usurpers. However, if you dislike us or intend to ignore our significance, or have changed your minds from the time you sent me your letters, I will leave." Al-Hurr exclaimed, "I do not know anything about the letters you keep mentioning." Al-Husayn ordered Uqbah Bin Sam'aan to pull out two bags full of these letters. Al-Hurr said, "I did not write you any letter. I was ordered that once I see you, I should not leave you alone until I bring you to Bin Ziyad in Kufa." Al-Husayn said, "Death is closer to you than your goal." He then ordered the women and his companions to move onwards.

Al-Hurr blocked Al-Husayn's caravan from moving towards Medina. Al-Husayn said, "May your mother weep on you! What do you want from us?" Al-Hurr replied, "If any Arab, no matter who he is, was in your situation, and challenged me as you did, I would have reciprocated. But, by Allah, I can only praise and speak highly of your mother. Direct your caravan to a road that takes you neither to Medina nor to Kufa, until I write to Bin Ziyad. I ask Allah to guide me to goodness and spare me from inflicting any harm on you." He then said to Al-Husayn, "By Allah! I advise you to change your plan. I am certain that if you fight, you'll be killed." Al-Husayn replied, "Are you scaring me with death? I am aware that you (Kufans) will murder me. I shall reiterate what the man from the tribe of Aws said to his cousin before joining the Prophet's army. I shall go because it is never shameful to fight and die as a Muslim while defending the right path. My soul longs being with pious men, and is anxious to fight against transgressors and criminals. If I live I will not regret my actions, and if I die no one will shame me because the true shame is to live smothered and humiliated." Al-Hurr stepped aside after he heard this. Al-Husayn marched with his companions on one side of the road, while Al-Hurr and his soldiers marched on the other.[23]

AL-BAYDHA

In Al-Baydha, Al-Husayn addressed Al-Hurr's army. After praising Allah, the Prophet's grandson reminded them that Allah's Messenger said, "If an oppressive ruler violates the Divine codes, breaches the path of Allah's Messenger, and rules the people with evil and tyranny; the person who sees all this and does not act for reform or request any change, then Allah will justly herd the complacent along with such a tyrant on the Day of Judgement." Al-Husayn continued: "These people (Umayyads) have obeyed Satan and disobeyed the Omnipotent. They spread corruption, broke the codes, embezzled the wealth of Muslims, allowed what has been for bidden, and forbade what has been allowed. It is my rightful duty to seek reform. I received your letters in which you pledged not to abandon or betray me. If you honor your pledge, you would be guided. I am Al-Husayn, Ali's son and the son of Fatima, the daughter of Allah's Messenger. I am one of you, and my family would be with yours. Accept me as your role model. However, it would not surprise me if you ignore your commitment and revoke your pledge of allegiance to me, because, by Allah, you have already betrayed my father, my brother and my cousin Muslim. You are totally disloyal and I will not be deceived by your false promises. You are missing a very rewarding opportunity. Nonetheless, whoever revokes his pledge hurts only himself. Allah shall definitely aid me in my mission without you. Peace, mercy, and blessings be upon all of you."[24]

AL-RAHEEMA

Abu Haram was a Kufan. He met Al-Husayn in Al-Raheema and asked him, "Why did you leave your grandfather's sanctuary?" Al-Husayn replied, "Abu Haram! I persevered when the Umayyads cursed me and confiscated my possessions, but now they are after me to kill me. By Allah! They will murder me, and as a result, Allah shall deal them a comprehensive wrath, and empower a tyrant to humiliate them until they suffer like the people of Sab'a who were the subjects of a female tyrant taxing their wealth and spilling their blood."[25]

AL-QADISIYYA

Bin Ziyad had ordered his soldiers to guard the roads between Al-Qadisiyya and Khafan all the way to Al-Qatqatana. Al-Husayn sent a letter to the Kufans with Qays Bin Mus'her Al-Saydawi. Al-Hossayn Bin Numayr Al-Tameemi arrested Qays in

Al-Qadisiyya. Immediately after his arrest, Qays destroyed Al-Husayn's letter in his possession. The guards took him to Bin Ziyad. The latter asked him, "Why did you destroy the letter?" Qays answered, "To prevent you from reading it." Bin Ziyad persistently pressured him to divulge its contents, but Qays firmly refused. Bin Ziyad then told Qays, "Curse Al-Husayn, his father, and brother from the pulpit, or I will chop you up into pieces." Qays stood up on the pulpit. After he praised Allah and His Messenger, he numerously asked Allah to bestow His Mercy upon the Commander of the Faithful (Imam Ali) and his two infallible sons, Al-Hasan and Al-Husayn. He then cursed Obeydallah Bin Ziyad, his father (Ziyad Bin Abeeh), and all of the Umayyads. He then said, "People! I am Al-Husayn's messenger. I urge you to rush and join him in the assigned location." Bin Ziyad ordered Qays thrown from the roof of the palace. Qays' bones were crushed upon landing.[26] Noticing that Qays was still breathing, a man rushed over and slaughtered him. The man's comrades shunned him for his cruelty. He justified, "I killed him to end his suffering."[27]

AL-UTHAYB

Amr Bin Khalid Al-Saydawi, his servant Sa'ad, Majma' Bin Abdullah Al-Mithhaji and their guide Al-Turummah Bin Uday Al-Ta'ie rode their horses from Kufa, and met Al-Husayn in Uthayb Al-Hijanaat. Expecting to meet Nafi' Bin Hilal in this location, these four men brought an extra horse with them. The guide was chanting, "My camel! Don't be annoyed that I am rushing you. Ride fast to meet the best of all riders, whom Allah selected to guide people to the best path. I ask Allah to bless him with a long life." Al-Husayn heard the chant and said, "By Allah! I trust that, whether we are victorious or martyred, Allah ordains nothing but goodness." Al-Husayn asked them about the latest. They said, "Community leaders have been bought out with hefty bribes, and the masses are sympathetic to you, but active soldiers against you." They also informed him that Qays Bin Mus'her Al-Saydawi was martyred. Al-Husayn said, *"Some have been martyred and some are waiting and both are ranked similarly (33:23). My Lord! Make paradise their destination and ours. Bless them with us in a settlement under your Mercy so we can enjoy Your bounties."*

Al-Turummah told him, "Upon my departure from Kufa, I saw people assembling in the meadows behind the City. I inquired about them they told me that men are being recruited and dispatched to fight Al-Husayn. By Allah! None of them would support you, and I beg you to avoid going there. What I saw was large enough an army against you. Come with us to our mountain Aja. We used it as a fortress to defend ourselves from our enemies. By Allah! Within ten days you will recruit a large army from the tribe of Tay'. I guarantee you twenty thousand obedient soldiers from Tay', with whom you can complete your mission." Al-Husayn commended him and his tribe's stance, and said, "There is a commitment and a promise between us and these people. I cannot turn away from them until I see the outcome of this whole affair." Al-Turummah asked Al-Husayn's permission to deliver the goods to his family, and promised to rush back. His friends stayed with Al-Husayn. Al-Turummah delivered the goods and rushed back. As he arrived to Uthayb Al-Hijanat, he learned that Al-Husayn has been martyred, so he rode back home.[28]

QASR BANI MAQATIL

Al-Husayn moved onwards from Uthayb Al-Hijanaat and camped in Qasr Bani Maqatil. In this location, he saw a spear next to a horse in front of a tent. Al-Husayn inquired, and someone told him that it was Obeydallah Bin Al-Hurr Al-Ja'afi. He sent Al-Hajjaj Bin Masrouq Al-Ja'afi to Bin Al-Hurr. The latter asked the former, "What is it?" Al-Hajjaj replied, "The best gift, and an utmost blessing if you accept. Al-Husayn is inviting you to join him. If you fight on his side, you will be greatly rewarded, and if you are killed, you will be a martyr." Bin Al-Hurr said, "By Allah! I left Kufa because his followers had turned him down, and because I saw a large army marching to fight against him. I thus concluded that he would be murdered and I cannot do much for him. I neither like him to see me, nor do I like to see him."[29] Al-Hajjaj transmitted to Al-Husayn Bin Al-Hurr's words. Al-Husayn, accompanied by some of his family members and companions, went to see Bin Al-Hurr. The latter narrated, "I have never seen anyone more beautiful and pleasing to the eye than Al-Husayn. I have never been more sympathetic to anyone than I was to him, especially when I saw him walking with young boys around him. I looked at his beautiful black beard, and asked whether it was natural or a dye. He replied that his hair had turned gray too soon, so I concluded it was a dye."[30]

Al-Husayn praised Allah as he sat down. He then said to Bin Al-Hurr, "Your townsmen sent me letters to inform me of their unity and determination to support me, and asked me to come to them. Nonetheless, it seems that this is no longer the case.[31] You have committed so many sins. Would you like to repent and erase them?" Bin Al-Hurr asked, "Son of Allah's Messenger! How could I do that?" Al-Husayn said, "Support the son of the Prophet's daughter, and fight on his side."[32] Bin Al-Hurr said, "By Allah! I know that joining you begets the joy of the next life, but I cannot contribute much to your cause, especially now that you have no supporters at all in Kufa. By Allah! Excuse me from this burden; I do not like to die. I, on the other hand, have the fastest horse in the area. Take it, it is yours." Al-Husayn said, "Since you are totally self-centered, we are needless of you or your horse.[33] I shall never seek support from transgressors.[34] I advise you, as you advised me. Try not to hear or see the battle, because whoever hears our calls and does not support us, Allah shall throw him in hellfire."[35]

It is narrated that Bin Al-Hurr regretted missing the opportunity of supporting Al-Husayn. Later in life, he expressed his regret for not joining the grandson of Allah's Messenger.[36]

In this location, Amr Bin Qays Al-Mashrifi and his cousin met Al-Husayn. The Prophet's grandson asked them, "Are you here to join me?" They said, "We have a lot of children. We are also afraid that the goods in our possession will be lost, since we are not sure of the outcome." He said, "Move on so you would not hear or see us, because whoever does, and abstains from supporting us, Allah shall definitely throw him in hellfire."[37]

THE VILLAGES OF AL-TAFF

Al-Husayn ordered his companions at the end of that night to load up water, and leave Qasr Bani Maqatil. As they moved, his companions heard him repeatedly uttering, "To Allah we belong and to Him we shall return, and all praise is due to the Lord of the Worlds." Ali Al-Akbar asked his father about the reason behind the utterance.

Al-Husayn said, "I nodded my head and saw a person on a horse. The rider was saying that people are marching while death is approaching them. I concluded that we are very close to death." Ali Al-Akbar exclaimed, "May Allah protect you from any harm! Aren't we on the right path?" Al-Husayn replied, "By the Lord to Whom all people shall return! We are definitely so." Ali Al-Akbar said, "Father! Nothing else matters, as long as we die righteously." Al-Husayn said, "May Allah reward you with the most any son can be rewarded with for supporting his father."[38]

Al-Husayn marched on until he arrived to Naynawa, where an armed rider approached them. Everyone stopped and waited. Bin Ziyad had sent this man to deliver a letter to Al-Hurr. The letter read, "Harass Al-Husayn as soon as you read this letter, and force him to camp in the open desert where there is no shelter or water." Al-Hurr read the letter to Al-Husayn. The latter told the former, "Let us camp in Naynawa or Al-Ghadhiriyyat or Shufya." Al-Hurr said, "I cannot, because this messenger is a spy on me."[39] Zuhayr Bin Al-Qayn interjected, "Son of Allah's Messenger! Fighting this group is easier than fighting their reinforcement. By Allah! If we wait, we shall have to combat a very large army." Al-Husayn said, "I never initiate fighting." Zuhayr said, "There is a fortified village on the Euphrates, totally surrounded by water except one side of it." Al-Husayn asked, "What is it called?" Zuhayr replied, "Al-Iqr." Al-Husayn said, "I seek refuge in Allah from the bad outcome (Iqr)."

Al-Husayn looked at Al-Hurr and said, "Let us move onwards a little." They all marched until they arrived to a land called Karbala. Al-Hurr and his soldiers formed a wall in front of Al-Husayn, preventing him from moving farther. Al-Hurr's soldiers justified, "This place is close enough to the Euphrates." It has also been narrated that as they were marching, Al-Husayn's horse stopped just as the Prophet's camel stopped in Al-Hudaybiya.[40] At that point, Al-Husayn asked about the name of the land. Zuhayr said, "March on, and hesitate none until Allah allows a relief. This land is called Al-Taff." Al-Husayn asked, "Does it have another name?" Zuhayr replied, "It is known as Karbala." Al-Husayn tearfully commented, "My Lord! I seek refuge in You from any disaster and hardship (Karb Wa Bala')."[41] Here is our destination. This is the place in which we will be slaughtered and buried. This is what my grandfather, Allah's Messenger, told me."[42]

KARBALA

Al-Husayn arrived to Karbala on the 2nd of Muharram in 61 A.H. (681 C.E.)[43] He gathered his sons, brothers and the rest of his family, looked at them and wept. He then said, "My Lord! We are the family of Your Messenger Mohammed. We have been dislocated, harassed and exiled from our grandfather's sanctuary. The Umayyads have abused us. My Lord! Restore our rights and bless us with victory over the oppressors." Al-Husayn then looked at his companions and said, "People are but slaves of this materialistic life, and their faith is a lip service to earn their living. Once they face hardships, they immediately abandon their faith."[44] He then praised Allah and His Messenger, and said, "You can see how things have turned. Life has changed to the worst, and its goodness has totally vanished. It now resembles an empty bucket of water or dried up grass, on a pile of garbage upon which animals graze. You could see that righteousness has been abandoned, and evil has become dominant. At a time like this, a true believer should desire returning to Allah, for I see death as the onset of joy, and life with oppressors is nothing but misery."[45]

Zuhayr said, "The son of Allah's Messenger! We heard you. Even if we were guaranteed immortality, we would still prefer rising up with you than living." Burayr said, "Allah has indeed blessed us with your company. We are pleased to die defending you and, consequently, earn your grandfather's intercession on the Day of Judgement."[46] Nafi' Bin Hilal said, "You know that your grandfather neither forced himself into people's hearts nor did he enjoy their full compliance. Some people promised to support him, but instead they betrayed him. These people were total hypocrites. They used sweet words in his presence, but expressed their enmity behind his back, until Allah took him. Your father's life was analogous to your grandfather's. Only some supported him in his wars against Al-Nakitheen (traitors), Al-Qasiteen (transgressors) and Al-Mariqeen (apostates), until he returned to his Merciful Lord. Today, your situation is similar to theirs. Nonetheless, the person who revokes his pledge and ignores his commitment will only harm himself. Allah shall definitely spare us the company of such a traitor. You, on the other hand, are our blessed guide! Lead us whichever direction you want, for, by Allah! We are neither afraid to embrace what Allah ordains, nor disdainful of returning to our Lord. We, with unshakable certitude, are vehemently determined to befriend your friends, and to combat your enemies."[47]

Al-Husayn purchased the land from the inhabitants of Naynawa and Al-Ghadhiriyya for sixty thousand Dirhams. He gave them the money as a charity (Sadaqa) on the condition that they escort the visitors of Karbala to his grave, and that they host them for three days. Al-Husayn's sanctuary, or the land he purchased, was originally sixteen square miles. This blessed piece of land had become a property of his, his children and their followers. Adversaries of the Prophet's household were to be denied access to it at all times. Imam Ja'afar Al-Sadiq said, "They (the inhabitants of Naynawa and Al-Ghadhiriyya) did not honor this condition."[48] Al-Husayn camped in Karbala and immediately sent a letter to Mohammed Bin Al-Hanafiyya and the Hashimites. Al-Husayn wrote: "It seems like this life never was, while the next had always been. Greetings."[49]

Notes & References

1. A road junction four miles away from Mecca, Mu'jam Al-Buldan (V.2, P.416)
2. Tareekh Al-Tabari (V.6, P.218), Maqtal Al-Khawarizmi (V. I, P.220); Al-Bidaya (V.8, P.166); Mutheer Al-Ahzaan (P.21) & Al-Irshaad
3. Tareekh Al-Tabari (V.6, P.218); Al-Kamel (V.4, P.16) & Al-Irshaad
4. Anwaar Al-Rabee' (P.703)
5. Mutheer Al-Ahzaan (P.21)
6. Al-Bidaya (V.8, P.169)
7. Al-Bidaya (V.8, P.168)
8. Al-Irshaad
9. Al-Irshaad; Rawdhat Al-Wa'itheen (P.153); Muntheer Al-Ahzaan (P.23); Maqtal Al-Khawarizmi (V. l, P.225); Al-Kamel (V.4, P.17)
10. Tareekh Al-Tabari (V.6, P.224); Maqtal Al-Khawarizmi (V. l, P.222)
11. Mutheer Al-Ahzaan (P.23); Al-Luhuf (P.40)
12. Al-Luhuf (P.41)
13. Amali Al-Sadouq (P.93)
14. Basa'ir Al-Darajat (P.3)
15. Sayr A'laam Al-Nubala' (V.3, P.205)
16. Maqtal Al-Khawarizmi (V.1, P.223)

17. Tareekh Al-Tabari (V.6, P.226)
18. Kamel Al-Ziyaraat (P.75)
19. Tareekh Al-Tabari (V.6, P.226)
20. Al-Irshaad; Nafs Al-Mahmoum (P.98)
21. Maqtal Al-Khawarizmi (V.l, P.230)
22. Tareekh Al-Tabari (V.6, P.226)
23. Al-Irshaad
24. Tareekh Al-Tabari (V.6, P.229); Al-Kamel (V.4, P.21)
25. Maqtal Al-Khawarizmi (V.l, P.226); Amali Al-Sadouq (P.93)
26. Al-Irshaad; Al-Bidaya (V.8, P.118); A'alaam Al-Wara (P.136)
27. Al-Irshaad
28. Tareekh Al-Tabari (V.6, P.230)
29. Al-Akhbaar Al-Tiwaal (P.246)
30. Ansaab Al-Ashraaf (V.5, P.291); Khuzanat Al-Adab (V. l, P.298)
31. Nafs Al-Mahmoum (P.104)
32. Asraar Al-Shahada (P.233)
33. Al-Akhbar Al-Tiwaal (P.249)
34. Amali Al-Sadouq (P.94)
35. Khuzanat Al-Adab (V.l, P.298)
36. Maqtal Al-Khawarizmi (V.l, P.228); Al-Akhbar Al-Tiwaal (P.258)
37. Iqaab Al-A'maal (P.35); Rijaal Al-Kashshi (P.74)
38. Tareekh Al-Tabari (V.6, P.231)
39. Al-Irshaad
40. Al-Muntakhab (P.308)
41. Al-Bihar (V.10, P.188)
42. Al-Luhuf (P.43)
43. Tareekh Al-Tabari (V.6, P.233); Al-Kamel (V.4, P.20); Al-Irshaad
44. Al-Bihar (V.10, P.198); Maqtal Al-Khawarizmi (V.l, P.237)
45. Al-Luhuf (P.44); Tareekh Dimashq (V.4, P.333); Al-A'qd Al-Fareed (V.2, P.213); Hilyat Al-Awliya' (V.3, P.39)
46. Al-Luhuf (P.44)
47. Maqtal Al-Awalim (P.76)
48. Al-Luhuf (P.44)
49. Kamel Al-Ziyaraat (P.75)

AL-HUSAYN AND BIN ZIYAD

Al-Hurr informed Bin Ziyad that Al-Husayn had settled in Karbala. Bin Ziyad wrote to Al-Husayn: "Husayn! I learned that you have camped in Karbala. The commander of the faithful, Yazeed, ordered that I should neither rest nor enjoy a meal before I kill you, unless you submit to us as your leaders. Greetings!" Al-Husayn tossed the letter after he read it, and said, "Damned are the people who anger the Creator to please a creature." The messenger asked him to write a response. Al-Husayn said, "I will not respond to him, because he has already invoked the wrath of the next life upon himself." The messenger transmitted Al-Husayn's words to Bin Ziyad. The latter became furious and ordered Omar Bin Sa'ad, who was leading four thousand soldiers towards Dastaba, to redirect his army to Karbala.[1] Bin Ziyad had issued an official document in which he appointed Bin Sa'ad to govern the provinces of Al-Rayy, Dastaba and Al-Daylam.[2] Bin Sa'ad was conspicuously reluctant to fight Al-Husayn. Bin Ziyad ordered him to relinquish the official document in his possession immediately. Succumbing to the mounting pressure, Bin Sa'ad requested a grace period of that night to think about the matter.

Bin Sa'ad consulted his relatives and intimate friends. They strongly advised him against fighting Al-Husayn. His nephew, Hamza Bin Al-Mugheera Bin Shu'ba, said, "By Allah! If you fight Al-Husayn, you would disgrace your ancestors and sin against your Lord. By Allah! Losing your life, your money and all the wealth on this planet is better than returning to Allah with Al-Husayn's blood on your hands."[3] Bin Sa'ad told his nephew, "Allah willing, I'll consider what you said." He spent that night pondering and his nephew heard him chant, "How could I ignore Al-Rayy and I desire to govern it? How could I dishonor myself and murder Husayn? If I kill him, I'll end up in hellfire. But I am wholeheartedly in favor of governing Al-Rayy." In the morning He told Bin Ziyad, "People know that you have instructed me to go to Dastaba. Let me continue my mission and send someone else to fight Al-Husayn." Bin Ziyad replied, "I am about to discharge you from your position. Do what I say, or relinquish the document." Bin Sa'ad gave in to Bin Ziyad's persistence, and said, "I shall do it."[4] He led his four thousand soldiers, and joined Al-Hurr. Bin Sa'ad ordered Uzra Bin Qays Al-Ahmasi to meet Al-Husayn, and ask him about the reason that had brought him there. Uzra and other community leaders were ashamed to meet Al-Husayn, because they were among those who wrote him letters begging him to come to Kufa.

Katheer Bin Abdullah Al-Sha'abi, known to be shameless and pugnacious, said, "I'll meet him, and if you want me to kill him, I will." Bin Sa'ad said, "No. Just ask him why he came here." Katheer rode towards Al-Husayn's camp. Abu Thumama Al-Sa'idi intercepted him, and said you have to leave your sword outside before you can see Al-Husayn." Katheer arrogantly refused, and left. Bin Sa'ad then sent Qurra Bin Qays Al-Hanthali to ask Al-Husayn why he had come. After listening to Qurra, Al-Husayn replied, "People in your area wrote to me urging me to come to Kufa. If you resent my presence, I can leave." Bin Sa'ad heard Al-Husayn's response, and wrote it in a letter and sent it to Bin Ziyad. Bin Ziyad wrote Bin Sa'ad back: "Ask Al-Husayn and his companions to pledge allegiance to Yazeed. Once they do, we'll see what to do next."[5]

Notes & References

---

1. Al-Bihar (V.10, P.198); Maqtal Al-Awalim (P.76)
2. Tareekh Al-Tabari (V.6, P.232)
3. Al-Akhbar Al-Tiwaal (P.251)
4. Al-Kamel (V.4, P.22)
5. Tareekh Al-Tabari (V.6, P.233 & 234)

Bin Ziyad's Speech

Bin Ziyad summoned the Kufans to the great mosque of the city and addressed them. He said,

> "You have always had a soft spot in your hearts for Abu Sufyan's family. Here we are with the commander of the faithful, Yazeed, who is pious, honorable, generous, and rewards appropriately. Under his leadership, people are secure and safe as they were during his father's time. Mu'awiya's son, Yazeed, is so generous. He doubled your allocated share of money, ordered me to dispense it immediately, and to recruit you to fight his enemy, Al-Husayn. Listen to him and comply."

Bin Ziyad paid each person the assigned amount of money and marched to his boot camp in Al-Nakheela. He ordered Al-Hossayn Bin Numayr Al-Tameemi, Hajjar Bin Abjar, Shimr Bin Thil Jawshan and Shibth Bin Ribi'e to join and assist Omar Bin Sa'ad. Shibth claimed to be sick and declined to go.[1] Bin Ziyad wrote him: "My private-eye told me that you are pretending to be sick. I am afraid that you are a hypocrite with two faces, loyal to us in our presence but scheming against us behind our back. If you are still loyal to us, hurry and join us." Shibth joined the Umayyad army after dark. He didn't want Bin Ziyad to see him in broad daylight, and thus discover that he lied in claiming to be ill. From then on, Shibth fully complied with all of Bin Ziyad's orders.

Bin Ziyad's objective was to deny the followers of the Prophet's household inside Kufa the opportunity to join Al-Husayn. He appointed Zajr Bin Qays Al-Ja'afi in command of five hundred armed soldiers, and instructed him to guard the main road of Kufa. Bin Ziyad ordered Zajr to intercept anyone trying to leave the city. Zajr saw Amer Bin Abi Salama Bin Abdullah Bin Arar Al-Dalaani on the main road, and told him, "I know where you're going. Go back." Amer immediately attacked the army and stormed through their lines to the other side. Zajr's soldiers were afraid to chase him. He rode nonstop until he joined Al-Husayn. Amer fought on Al-Husayn's side and was martyred with him. It is worth mentioning that Amer was a devout believer and a dedicated solider in Imam Ali's army in the Three Battles (Al-Jamal, Siffeen, and Al-Nahrawan).[2]

Notes & References

1. Al-Akhbar Al-Tiwaal (P.253)
2. Al-Ikleel (V.10, P.87 & 101)

The Kufans' View of Al-Husayn

Completely aware that Al-Husayn was the Master of Youth in Heaven, and the endeared grandson of the Holy Messenger, Kufans were extremely reluctant to fight against him. The Prophet and Imam Ali had already conveyed to the Community the unrivaled merits of Al-Husayn and Al-Hasan. Moreover, the memories of the severe drought in Kufa were still afresh in the Kufans' minds. People, on the verge of facing a deadly famine, flocked to their leader (Imam Ali) for a solution. During the difficult days of this natural disaster, Kufans learned and experienced the bliss and significance of Al-Husayn. Imam Ali asked Al-Husayn to lead a special prayer (Salat Al-Istisqa') to end the drought. Allah answered the Holy branch of light of the Mohammedan tree, and rain fell until grass grew everywhere in Kufa. Also, Al-Husayn was the leader who controlled the banks of the Euphrates during the Battle of Siffeen, and allowed the thirsty and exhausted Muslims equal access to water.[1] Furthermore, the story of giving water to Al-Hurr, his soldiers and their horses in the dry desert was still resonating throughout Kufa. Experiencing or knowing these merits of Al-Husayn did not deter the Kufans from attacking him. The desire-driven Kufans were weak in their hearts. They succumbed to their infatuation with this mortal life, and eventually became aggressive oppressors. Otherwise, they could not have had the audacity to fight Al-Husayn.

In fact, many Kufans deserted Bin Sa'ad's army and sneaked out of Karbala. At some point, Bin Sa'ad's large army dwindled significantly. Once informed, Bin Ziyad ordered Suwayd Bin Abdurrahman Al-Minqari and a group of soldiers to ride through the neighborhoods of Kufa, and call its people to join the fight against Al-Husayn. Bin Ziyad also ordered them to arrest the objectors. It happened that a man from Syria traveled to Kufa to collect his inheritance. This man was inadvertently arrested upon his arrival. Bin Ziyad charged the man with treason and immediately executed him.

Terrified of Bin Ziyad's cruelty, the Kufans rushed out and joined the Umayyad army.[2]

THE ARMIES

Al-Shimr led four thousand. Yazeed Bin Al-Rikaab led two thousand. Al-Hossayn Bin Numayr Al-Tameemi led four thousand. Shibth Bin Ribi'e led one thousand. Ka'ab Bin Talha led three thousand. Hajjar Bin Abjar led one thousand. Madhayir Bin Raheena Al-Mazini led three thousand. Nasr Bin Harsha led two thousand soldiers. These leaders marched with their soldiers to Karbala. By the sixth of Muharram, Bin Sa'ad had twenty thousand soldiers under his command. Bin Ziyad dispatched more soldiers until the number reached thirty thousand soldiers.

Imam Al-Sadiq narrated that Al-Husayn wept on Al-Hasan's bedside shortly before the latter died. Al-Hasan asked, "Abu Abdullah! Why are you weeping?" Al-Husayn replied, "I weep for what they did to you." Al-Hasan said, "I have been poisoned, and I shall be martyred, but my day is no match to yours. Abu Abdullah! I can foresee thirty thousand men claiming to be Muslims from the community of our grandfather, but uniting to spill your blood. They will murder you, violate your sanctity, capture your women and children, and rob your possessions. Once this happens, the wrath will befall the Umayyads. The sky will rain ashes and blood. All the creatures, even the beasts in the wilderness and the whales in the oceans, will weep on you."[3]

Bin Ziyad wrote Bin Sa'ad: "You have more soldiers and horses than you can possibly need. Act now. The details of your moves are reported to me by daybreak and nightfall." Bin Ziyad urged Bin Sa'ad to ignite the battle on the sixth of Muharram.[4] Bin Sa'ad ordered his troops to control the Euphrates and deny Al-Husayn access to it. Al-Husayn's companions, having no access to water, became extremely thirsty. Al-Husayn held an axe behind the women's tent and walked nineteen steps towards Mecca. He dug until pure water sprayed out and everyone in his camp drank from it. Shortly after, the spring disappeared and was never seen again.

Bin Ziyad wrote Bin Sa'ad: "I heard that Al-Husayn is digging up wells, and that he and his companions are drinking enough water.

Once you read this letter, tighten the siege around them, and utilize all means possible to prevent them from digging." Bin Sa'ad immediately sent Amr Bin Al-Hajjaj with five hundred soldiers to control the banks of the Euphrates.[5] This happened three days prior to Al-Husayn's martyrdom.[6]

Notes & References

1. Maqtal Al-Awalim (P.15 & 45)
2. Al-Akhbar Al-Tiwaal (P.253)
3. Amali Al-Sadouq (P.71)
4. Tathallum Al-Zahra' (P.101)
5. Nafs Al-Mahmoum (P.116); Maqtal Al-Awalim (P.78), Maqtal Al-Khawarizmi (V.1, P.244)
6. Tareekh Al-Tabari (V.6, P.234); Al-Kamel (V.4, P.22); Al-Irshaad

The Seventh of Muharram

By the seventh of Muharram, the siege around Al-Husayn and his followers had become incredibly tight. Having been denied access to the Euphrates, they ran out of water. Thirst exhausted Al-Husayn's companions and family members. Women in Al-Husayn's camp wept as the children constantly grunted and moaned from severe thirst. Al-Husayn, the men of his family, and their companions painfully watched the suffering of the women and children. The scene rendered the brave and protective soldiers of Al-Husayn restless, because bringing water entailed facing hundreds of well-armed enemies. Meanwhile, Al-Abbass (The Cup Bearer) could no longer tolerate the situation. Al-Husayn selected his brother, Al-Abbass, for the difficult mission of providing water for the women and children. He also ordered twenty infantries to carry twenty jugs and accompany Al-Abbass. The men, under the command of Al-Abbass (The Lion Heart of Mohammed's household), marched fearlessly towards the Euphrates under night cover. Nafi' Bin Hilal Al-Jamali carried the banner and moved towards the water. Amr Bin Al-Hajjaj screamed, "Who is it?" Nafi' replied, "We came to drink the water that you denied us." Amr said, "Drink and enjoy but don't take any to Al-Husayn." Nafi' said, "By Allah! I shall not taste a drop of it whilst Al-Husayn, his family and companions are thirsty."

Nafi' screamed to his comrades, "Fill up the jugs!" Amr Bin Al-Hajjaj and his soldiers attacked. Al-Husayn's companions broke off into two groups, one fighting and another filling up water. Abu Fadhl Al-Abbass, known to have inherited bravery from his father, Haydar (Imam Ali), single handedly provided enough protection for everyone to fill up and pull out. They made it back under the watchful eyes of their enemies. Amr Bin Al-Hajjaj and his soldiers cowered from even thinking to chase Al-Abbass and his soldiers. The bravery and the heroic performance of Abu Al-Fadhl Al-Abbass stunned the enemies, and spread fear in their ranks. The women and the innocent children quenched their severe thirst.[1] Nonetheless, one should keep in mind that there were over hundred and fifty people in Al-Husayn's camp. Others narrated that there were close to two hundred people. This amount of water was barely enough for only one use. Soon after, the women and children became thirsty again. We complain of these circumstances, and of such hardships, to Allah and His Messenger.

Bin Sa'ad's Arrogance

Al-Husayn sent Amr Bin Qartha Al-Ansari to Bin Sa'ad to arrange a night meeting between the two halfway between the two camps. Each led twenty soldiers and went to the assigned place. Al-Husayn ordered everyone to stay behind except his brother, Al-Abbass, and his son Ali Al-Akbar. Bin Sa'ad did the same, and only his son Hafas and his servant remained with him. Al-Husayn said, "Bin Sa'ad! How dare you fight me? Aren't you afraid of Allah, to Whom you shall return? You know who my father is! Why don't you join us and quit being with them, for such a move would assure you proximity to Allah?" Bin Sa'ad replied, "I am afraid that my house will be demolished." Al-Husayn said, "I will rebuild it for you." Bin Sa'ad said, "I am afraid that my property will be confiscated." Al-Husayn said, "I will replace it with a more valuable one from the money I left in Al-Hijaz."[2] Al-Husayn owned a huge farm called Al-Bughaybigha. Mu'awiya unsuccessfully tried to purchase it from the Prophet's grandson for one million Dinars. It is narrated that Al-Husayn offered Bin Sa'ad Al-Bughaybigha.[3]

The latter said, "I left my children in Kufa and I am afraid that Bin Ziyad would kill them." Certain that it was hopeless to convince Bin Sa'ad, Al-Husayn stood and said, "You are doomed! Allah shall ordain you slaughtered on your bed, and shall never forgive you on the Day of Resurrection. By Allah! I hope that you eat very little food in Iraq (your days in Iraq are numbered)." Bin Sa'ad sarcastically replied, "Wheat is sufficient."[4]

Losing the privilege to govern Al-Rayy was the beginning of the downward spiral in Bin Sa'ad's life. After the Battle of Karbala, Bin Ziyad ordered Bin Sa'ad to relinquish the official document in which the former appointed the latter to govern the Persian province.

Bin Sa'ad initially claimed to have lost it, but finally told the persistent Bin Ziyad, "I gave it to the old folks of Quraysh to read, hoping that they may pardon me for killing Al-Husayn. By Allah! I sincerely advised you against fighting Al-Husayn." Othman Bin Ziyad, Obeydallah's brother, commented, "He is correct indeed! I wish that Al-Husayn was never murdered. Instead, I wish that Ziyad's sons were enslaved and shackled until the Day of Judgement."[5]

When Al-Mukhtar rose up in Kufa, he assured Bin Sa'ad safety. However, Al-Mukhtar hired women to weep on Al-Husayn in front of Bin Sa'ad's house. This attracted the Kufans' attention and reminded them that the owner of this house had murdered Al-Husayn. Bin Sa'ad became extremely annoyed at this scene and requested from Al-Mukhtar to dismiss the women, or relocate them. Al-Mukhtar responded, "Doesn't Al-Husayn deserve to be mourned?" Also, when the Kufans nominated Bin Sa'ad to temporarily govern them after the death of Yazeed Bin Mu'awiya, women from the tribes of Rabee'a and Ramadan flocked to the main mosque, wailing and screaming. They collectively complained, "How could Bin Sa'ad become our governor after he murdered Al-Husayn?" The Kufans wept and cancelled the nomination.[6]

BIN SA'AD'S FABRICATION

Foolishly attempting to restore order, and preserve the well-being of the Community, Bin Sa'ad fabricated a compromise and falsely attributed it to Al-Husayn. Bin Sa'ad wrote to Bin Ziyad: "Greetings! Allah had mended the rift, united the dividing parties, and preserved the well-being of the Community. Al-Husayn had agreed to return, or move and live safely enjoying his rights and fulfilling his duties like any Muslim, or meet with the commander of the faithful, Yazeed, to reconcile the differences between the two of them. This initiative shall definitely please you and better serve the Community."[7]

Al-Husayn taught the masses ideal lessons of perseverance in hardships, and demonstrated the necessity of self-sacrifice in defending values and principles. It is inconceivable that the Prophet's grandson would contradict any of his previous statements, or submit to his contemporary tyrants, Bin Ziyad and Yazeed. How could anyone believe Bin Sa'ad's fabrication after learning what Al-Husayn articulated at the early stages of his Holy uprising? The Prophet's grandson told his brother Omar Al-Atraf, "By Allah! I shall never humiliate myself." And told his other brother, Bin Al-Hanafiyya, "Even if it causes me to become homeless, I shall never pledge allegiance to Yazeed." He also told Zurara Bin Saleh, "I am certain that I'll be murdered along with my companions. My son Ali (Zayn Al-Abideen) will be the only survivor," and told Ja'afar Bin Sulayman Al-Dhabi'e, "They will never leave me alone until they murder me."

Al-Husayn's last statement in Karbala proves beyond doubt that he never compromised his stance against the oppressors. On the day of Ashura, Al-Husayn said, "This man, vicious like his father, is pushing for war or humiliation, and we will never be humiliated. Allah, His Messenger, and the believers do not approve of humiliation. Pure wombs bore our honorable and dignified souls, and we shall never obey the vile in lieu of a blessed martyrdom." Al-Husayn's firm stance was further confirmed in the following narration. Uqbah Bin Sam'aan (Al-Rabaab's servant) said, "I accompanied Al-Husayn from Medina to Mecca, and then to Iraq, and I remained with him until he was martyred. I heard everything he said, and contrary to what people claim, he never agreed to reconcile with Yazeed or move to a safe place. He never suggested any of this, whether in Medina, Mecca, on the road, in Iraq, or in his camp in Karbala. However, I did hear him say that they should let him go somewhere else on this wide earth."[8]

AL-SHIMR'S TYRANNY

Bin Ziyad read Bin Sa'ad's letter, and commented, "This is a message from a sincere advisor who cares about the well-being of his townsmen." Bin Ziyad was about to write back, but Al-Shimr interjected, "How could you accept this after Al-Husayn has already settled in your jurisdiction? By Allah! If he leaves without pledging allegiance to you, he will become more powerful and you will become weak and helpless."

Persuaded by Al-Shimr, Bin Ziyad wrote Bin Sa'ad the following: "Greetings! I didn't send you to reconcile with Al-Husayn, nor to negotiate with him, guarantee him safety, or to intercede for him. If Al-Husayn and his companions obey my orders, send them to me alive. If they refuse, fight them, kill them all off, and mutilate their bodies, because they deserve it. After you kill Husayn, let the horses stomp upon his back and chest. I do not think it makes a difference after his death. However, I have vowed to do this to him after I kill him, and I would like to honor my vow. We shall reward you once you implement our orders. Shall you refuse, step aside and let Shimr Bin Thil Jawshan assume full leadership of the army thereof."[9]

Al-Shimr delivered the letter to Bin Sa'ad. The latter looked at the former and said, "Damn you! May Allah send a wrath upon you for bringing this ugly message! I know that you convinced him to reject my offer. You spoiled my peace plan. By Allah! Al-Husayn would never surrender; his father's bravery and dignity are instilled in his soul." Al-Shimr asked Bin Sa'ad, "What is your plan now? Will you implement the governor's orders? If not, let me assume the leadership of the army." Bin Sa'ad replied, "I shall remain the commander and deprive you of such an honor. Be the leader of the infantry."[10]

INVITATION TO SAFETY

Al-Shimr screamed aloud, "Where are our nephews? Where are Al-Abbass and his brothers?"[11] No one answered him. Al-Husayn said, "Answer him even if he is a transgressor." They responded, "What is it? What do you want?" Al-Shimr said, "You are my sister's sons, and I assure your safety. Obey Yazeed, the commander of the faithful, instead of losing your lives with Al-Husayn." Al-Abbass replied, "May Allah curse you, and curse your safety proposal! You are granting us safety and excluding the grandson of Allah's Messenger. How dare you ask us to obey vicious individuals (Yazeed and Bin Ziyad) who, like their fathers, deserve the wrath of hellfire?"[12] Al-Shimr had to be extremely vicious and arrogant to believe that he could lure a protective hero into humiliation and aberration. He mistakenly wished that Abu Al-Fadhl Al-Abbass would abandon the light in favor of darkness, or replace the banner of Prophethood with that of Maysoon's son (Yazeed).

As Al-Abbass returned to the camp, Zuhayr Bin Al-Qayn asked him, "Would you like to hear what I heard?" Al-Abbass answered, "Yes." Zuhayr narrated, "When your father wanted to get married, he asked his brother Aqeel, who was an expert in Arab genealogy, to select a wife whose fathers and grandfathers were known to be incredibly brave. Your father told Aqeel that he wanted a woman to bear him a brave son who would support Al-Husayn in Karbala. Your father raised you for this day. Do not spare any effort in supporting your brother and protecting your sisters." Al-Abbass exclaimed, "You are trying to charge me up! By Allah! I shall boggle your mind."[13] Al-Abbass fearlessly attacked the enemies, crushing all that stood in his way. This dialogue, and the subsequent show of force, occurred while Al-Abbass was delivering water to Al-Husayn's children. It is important to note that this scene depicted only a glimpse of Al-Abbass' strength and bravery. Abu Al-Fadhl was, at the time, more focused on delivering the water than engaging the enemies.

The Tribe of Banu Assad

Banu Assad, Habeeb's tribesmen, happened to be camping close by. Habeeb Bin Muthahir asked Al-Husayn's permission to go and talk to them. Habeeb introduced himself and asked them to support the son of the Prophet's daughter. Habeeb told his tribesmen that joining Al-Husayn begets the ultimate honor in this life and in the next. Ninety men complied. A spy informed Bin Sa'ad of their plan. The latter immediately dispatched Al-Azraq with four hundred soldiers to prevent Banu Assad from joining Al-Husayn. A fierce battle ensued in which a group of men from Banu Assad were killed while the rest, fearing another ambush from Bin Sa'ad's soldiers, returned home. Habeeb informed Al-Husayn of the outcome. Al-Husayn said, "There is no power and strength except that of Allah, the Great."[14]

Notes & References

1. Maqtal Mohammed Bin Abi Talib
2. Maqtal Al-Awalim (P.78)
3. Tathallum Al-Zahra' (P. 103)
4. Tathallum Al-Zahra' (P. 103); Maqtal Al-Khawarizmi (V.1, P.245)
5. Tareekh Al-Tabari (V.6, P.368)

6. Muruj Al-Thahab (V.2, P.105)
7. Al-It'haaf Bihubb Al-Ashraaf (P.15); Tahtheeb Al-Tahtheeb (V.2, P.253)
8. Tareekh Al-Tabari (V.6, P.235)
9. Al-Kamel (V.4, P.23)
10. Tareekh Al-Tabari (V.6, P.236)
11. Umm Al-Baneen and Al-Shimr were from the same tribe and distant relatives, Jamharat Ansaab Al-Arab (Ps. 261-265)
12. Mutheer Al-Ahzaan (P.28)
13. Asraar Al-Shahada (P.387)
14. Maqtal Al-Khawarizmi (V.1, P.243)

The Ninth of Muharram

On the evening of Thursday, the ninth of Muharram, Bin Sa'ad ordered his troops to initiate the offense. Al-Husayn was sitting in front of his tent. He dozed off and saw Allah's Messenger telling him, "Soon you will be with us." Zaynab heard the loud noise of the attacking soldiers, and told Al-Husayn, "The enemy is approaching us." Al-Husayn told his brother Al-Abbass, "Your presence equates mine! Go and ask what brought them here?"[1] Al-Abbass rode along with twenty soldiers, including Zuhayr and Habeeb, towards the advancing enemies. Bin Sa'ad's troops told Al-Abbass, "Our commander ordered us to attack you right now, unless you surrender and accept his conditions."

Al-Abbass rode back to inform Al-Husayn, while the rest remained to advise their adversaries. Habeeb Bin Muthahir said, "By Allah! On the Day of Judgement, Allah shall condemn the people who murder the descendants and family members of His Messenger. Allah shall also condemn the people who murder His devout servants; the locals of this area who sincerely worshipped Him in it." Uzra Bin Qays interjected, "You are too self-righteous." Zuhayr said, "Uzra! Allah had guided him to righteousness. Uzra! Accept my advice and fear Allah. Uzra! Do not aid the transgressors in murdering the pure members of the Prophet's household." Uzra said, "Zuhayr! You never liked these people, in fact, you were opposed to them." Zuhayr replied, "Doesn't my stance now tell you that I am one of them? By Allah! I never wrote to him, nor sent him a messenger, nor did I ever promise him my support. Our paths crossed, and when I saw him, I remembered Allah's Messenger and his proximity to him. I also learned the evil intent of his enemies, so I decided to join him, support him, and risk my life to protect his. All of you, on the other hand, have betrayed Allah's Messenger."

Al-Husayn told Al-Abbass, "Go back and request a grace period until tomorrow, so we may pray, supplicate and ask our Lord to forgive us. Allah knows that I love to praise him, recite His Book, supplicate, and ask His forgiveness." Al-Abbass delivered the message. Bin Sa'ad consulted with his associates. Astonished with Bin Sa'ad's reluctance to grant Al-Husayn such a short grace period, Amr Bin Al-Hajjaj interjected, "Praise is due to Allah! You should honor their request, even if they were idolaters." Qays Bin Al-Ash'ath added, "Grant them their wish. They will definitely fight you tomorrow." Bin Sa'ad said, "I am not so sure that they would. By Allah! If I were certain that they would fight tomorrow, I wouldn't delay the battle." He sent someone to tell Al-Husayn, "We have granted you a grace period till tomorrow. If you decide to surrender, we'll escort you to Bin Ziyad, otherwise it is an all-out war."[2]

TRUE FREEDOM OF THE SOULS

Al-Husayn gathered his companions on the eve of his martyrdom, and said,

> "I praise Allah the best He can be praised, and thank Him for difficult and good times. Allah! I thank You; You blessed us with Prophethood, taught us the Qur'an, granted us a special knowledge of your Divine Message, gave us the senses to hear, see and understand, and protected us from idolatry. I do not know of any companions more loyal than mine, or family members more righteous and genuine than mine. I ask Allah to reward all of you for being with me.[3] My grandfather, Allah's Messenger, informed me that I would be trapped and martyred in a part of Iraq called A'moura and Karbala. The time of his prophecy is very close.[4] I believe that tomorrow is the day. I absolve you all from your responsibility, and relieve you all from your commitment to me. The darkness of tonight has already hovered. Utilize it as a cover and disperse. I suggest that each of my companions accompany a man from my family. I ask Allah to reward all of you. Go back to your homes. These people are after me, and once they kill me, they wouldn't go after any of you."

Al-Husayn's brothers, sons, nephews and the sons of Abdullah Bin Ja'afar said, "Shall we leave to outlive you? We ask Allah that we never see that day." This was mainly Al-Abbass' response. The rest of Bani Hashim responded similarly.

Al-Husayn then looked at Banu Aqeel, and said, "Losing Muslim (Bin Aqeel) was hard enough on you. You can leave. I relieve you from your commitment to me." They answered, "What would we tell the critics then? It would be quite shameful to say that we abandoned our leader and master. It would be embarrassing to say that we deserted our cousins, who happened to be the sons of our best uncles, without defending them, or without even knowing the outcome of their battle. By Allah! We shall never leave, but instead, we shall sacrifice our lives, money and families to stay and defend you. Life is worthless without you."[5] Muslim Bin Ausaja said, "How could we abandon you? What would our excuse be when Allah asks us about our loyalty to you? By Allah! I am not leaving until I break my spear in their chests, and strike them with my sword for as long as I can wield it. If I become unarmed, I shall throw rocks at them until I am martyred with you." Sa'iid Bin Abdullah Al-Hanafi said, "By Allah! We shall never abandon you. In contrast, we shall stay to prove our loyalty to Allah's Messenger. We would like Allah to witness how much we revere His Messenger. By Allah! If I were to be killed and then live and then numerously get burned into ashes, I am never leaving you. How could I choose otherwise, and I know it is on death, after which comes eternal joy?" Zuhayr Bin Al-Qayn said, "By Allah! I wish to be killed, and then live, and then killed numerously in the process of defending you and your family members." Similarly, the rest of his companions expressed their irreversible commitment to him. Al-Husayn asked Allah to reward them for their firm stance.[6] In the meantime, Mohammed Bin Basheer Al-Hadhrami was informed that his son had been captured as a prisoner of war in the province of Al-Rayy. He said, "I wish I was dead before I heard of his captivity." Al-Husayn told him, "I absolve you from your pledge to me. Go and work on freeing your son." Bin Basheer said, "By Allah! I will never do that. I would never leave you, even if wild beasts rip through my flesh." Al-Husayn said, "Give your other son these five expensive fabrics so he can free his brother." The fabrics were worth one thousand Dinars.[7]

Certain of his followers' loyalty to him and determination to self-sacrifice, Al-Husayn informed them of what had been irrevocably ordained. He said, "All of us, without exception, will be killed tomorrow. Al-Qassim and my nursing son Abdullah will be killed too. Only my son Ali, Zayn Al-Abideen, will survive because Allah had ordained to extend my family through him. He is the father of eight infallible leaders."[8] Al-Husayn's companions collectively answered, "We thank Allah, for He guided us to support you, and honored us with martyrdom on your side. The son of Allah's Messenger! How could we not be pleased to be with you in this life and enjoy your company in the next?" Al-Husayn supplicated for their well-being, and unveiled before their eyes the bliss and eternal pleasure Allah had prepared for them in paradise.[9]

Absorbing this reality should not be difficult at all, especially when we keep in mind that the Almighty had blessed the infallible leader with such a capability. Authentic traditions confirm this. It is narrated that the magicians initially supported the Pharaoh against Musa, but after they witnessed the miracles, they immediately switched over to Musa's side. As the Pharoah of Egypt ordered their execution, Musa unveiled to them their positions in paradise.[10]

Imam Mohammed Al-Baqir narrated that Al-Husayn told his companions the following, "Be glad to have earned paradise! By Allah! We shall remain there after our martyrdom until the last infallible leader rises up. He shall destroy the oppressors and avenge the oppressed. Allah shall then resurrect us to witness the tyrants shackled, chained and chastised." Imam Al-Baqir said that someone asked Al-Husayn, "Who from your family will rise up?" Al-Husayn answered, "The seventh descendant of my grandson, Mohammed Bin Ali Al-Baqir. His name is Al-Hujja Bin Al-Hasan Bin Ali, Bin Mohammed, Bin Ali, Bin Musa, Bin Ja'afar, Bin Mohammed, Bin Ali, my son. He is the one who, after a long occultation, will enforce justice and restore order on earth. He shall do so after a long period of tyranny and oppression."[11]

THE EVE OF ASHURA

The Eve of Ashura was undeniably the most difficult night on the Prophet's family. The Umayyad army surrounded Al-Husayn's camp and enforced a tight siege around it. Al-Husayn and everyone in his company were banned from all natural resources. Women wept in distress as their children screamed for water. The difficulties and hardships of that night were the onset of the imminent danger and the disastrous outcome. One can only wonder whether this situation had affected the honorable men of Bani Hashim and their dignified companions. Or whether this scene had shaken their determination to fight and simultaneously look after their families. Contrary to what most people believe, the lions from the family of Abdul Muttalib and their select companions were serene, determined, and pleased with the luxury and blessing awaiting them. The difficult situation rendered them cheerful, optimistic, and more energetic. Burayr Bin Khudayr joked with Abdurrahman Al-Ansari. The latter said, "This is not an appropriate time for joking!" Burayr said, "People know that I, young and old, was never into mischief. However, I am optimistic with the outcome. By Allah! Battling those is what separates us from the eternal joy of paradise. I wish they attack us now."[12] Habeeb Bin Muthahir was extremely cheerful. Yazeed Bin Al-Hasseen Al-Hamadani told him, "It is not appropriate to be cheerful at a time like this." Habeeb answered, "When could there be better time than this to rejoice? We shall embrace the beautiful maidens of paradise soon after the battle."[13]

The scene of Al-Husayn's camp resembled that of a beehive. Some were busy praying and supplicating while others were preparing themselves and their weapons for the battle. Abdullah Bin Al-Dhahhak Al-Mashriqi narrated that a group of soldiers from Bin Sa'ad's army passed by Al-Husayn's as Al-Husayn was reciting, *the non-believers should not think that Our Respite is a good sign. It is a period in which they increase their sins, for which they will be severely chastised. Allah will not leave the believers in the situation you are in until He sorts out the wicked from the pious (3:178-179)*. One of these soldiers heard Al-Husayn, and said, "We are the pious against you after the sorting process." Burayr told him, "You are a transgressor! How could you be considered pious? Switch over to our side and repent from your dreadful sins. By Allah! We are the pious and you are the wicked." The man sarcastically replied, "I shall testify in favor of your statement."[14] It is narrated that Al-Husayn's companions spent a great portion of that night worshipping Allah. The scene of devotion and submission in Al-Husayn's camp, on the eve of Ashura, attracted thirty-two men from Bin Sa'ad's army to switch over.[15]

Ali Bin Al-Husayn narrated that his father prepared his

sword, and said, "Span of time between sunrise and sunset is a disloyal friend. A man is killed for his stance, and time is never content with an alternative. It is the ordinance of the Omnipotent. Every living creature is bound to die." Zayn Al-Abideen continued, "I heard my father repeat this two or three times. I knew what he meant, and choked on my tears. I concluded that the disaster was imminent. I remained silent. My aunt Zaynab heard him and immediately went to him weeping." Zaynab told Al-Husayn, "I wish I had been long dead. Today is equivalent to the day in which my mother Fatima, my father Ali, my brother Al-Hasan died. You are their successor and all that is left."[16] Al-Husayn consoled her, and asked her to persevere. He also told her, "Sister! Rely on Allah so He would ease your grief. The inhabitants of earth and heaven are all bound to die. Everything shall die, except the Exalted. Allah's Messenger is a perfect role model to me and to all Muslims." Zaynab replied, "It breaks my heart and is very difficult for me, because I feel that you are rushing your death."[17]

Umm Kulthoum and the rest of the women wept. They also moaned, "We weep on Mohammed! We weep on Ali! We weep on our mother (Fatima)! We weep on Al-Husayn. Husayn! We are in total loss after you." Al-Husayn said, "Sister (Zaynab), Umm Kulthoum! Fatima! Rabaab! Listen up. Once I am murdered, do not mourn immodestly or vent inappropriately."[18] Al-Husayn assigned his sister, Zaynab to disperse religious edicts. He instructed her to learn them from his son Ali and teach them to their followers. Al-Husayn tactfully instructed his sister to practice precautionary dissimulation (Taqiyya) in order to provide a shield of safety around Imam Zayn Al-Abideen.

The following narration attests that an infallible leader can take such a measure to protect his successor. Ahmad Bin Ibraheem narrated, "I visited Hakeema the daughter of Mohammed Bin Ali Al-Ridha, and the sister of Ali Al-Hadi in Al-Medina in 282 A.H. (895 C.E.). I spoke to her while she stood behind a curtain. I asked her about her faith and her leader. She said that her leader was the son of Al-Hasan. I asked whether she sees him or not. She replied that she doesn't see him but she learns from the woman he entrusted with this responsibility; just as Al-Husayn Bin Ali Bin Abi Talib entrusted Zaynab to be the spokesperson of Ali Bin Al-Husayn." Elucidating the delicate situation further, Hakeema explained, "Zayn Al-Abideen's knowledge was tactfully attributed to his aunt. Zaynab assumed this responsibility in order to protect Ali Bin Al-Husayn, the infallible leader at the time."[19]

On the eve of Ashura, Al-Husayn ordered his companions to bring the tents closer together, and to excavate a trench behind them. He also ordered to fill the trench with wood, and instructed his soldiers to light it as soon as the battle begins. Al-Husayn planned to limit the course of attacks on his camp to one direction, and thus confine all combat into one zone.[20] Al-Husayn walked out of his camp in the middle of the night to survey the surrounding hills. Nafi' Bin Hilal Al-Jamali followed him. Al-Husayn asked him, "What brought you out?" Nafi' replied, "Son of Allah's Messenger! I am worried that you are walking too close to that tyrant's boot camp." Al-Husayn said, "I was trying to assess whether the enemies can utilize these hills and meadows to ambush us during the battle." Holding Nafi's hand, Al-Husayn walked back towards his camp saying, "This is it. This is it. By Allah! It is an irrevocable promise." He then told Nafi', "Why don't you use the darkness of tonight as a cover, and flee to safety?" Nafi' immediately fell on Al-Husayn's feet. He kissed them, and said, "I am doomed if I leave! My sword and horse are prepared to fight thousands. By Allah, who blessed us with your company! I shall never leave until I fully utilize them in battle."

Al-Husayn entered Zaynab's tent. While waiting outside, Nafi' heard Zaynab asking her brother, "Are you sure of your companions' determination? I am afraid they will abandon you at the crucial moment." Al-Husayn replied, "I tested them, and found them all strong and brave. They are comfortable to be martyred with me the way a nursing infant is comfortable on his mother's breast." Nafi' said, "I wept when I heard the dialogue, and immediately informed Habeeb Bin Muthahir." Habeeb said, "By Allah! Had we not been waiting for his orders, I would have fought tonight." Nafi said, "Al-Husayn is in Zaynab's tent right now, and I believe the rest of the women are awake and have concerns similar to Zaynab's. Why don't you call upon our comrades, so we all reassert our irreversible intention before the women? This way, we could assure them and soothe their hearts."

Habeeb stood up and yelled, "I call upon the protective men

and the fearless lions!" Men rushed out of their tents like roaring lions. Intending to call only upon the companion, Habeeb asked Bani Hashim to return to their tents and rest. He then looked at the rest of his comrades, and told them what Nafi' heard and witnessed. They collectively responded, "By Allah, who blessed us with this honorable situation! If we weren't waiting for his orders, we would have attacked the enemies now. We assure you of our determination, and we hope that you are pleased with it." Habeeb commended their stance and said, "Let us all console the women and convey our firm determination to them." Habeeb walked with his comrades towards Zaynab's tent and loudly yelled, "I call upon the women of the Prophet's family! Your soldiers have pledged to sheathe their swords in the necks of your enemies, and to bury spears in the chests of those who intend to harm you." The women of the Prophet's household wept and said, "You pious men! Protect the daughters of Allah's Messenger and the honor able daughters of the Commander of the Faithful (Imam Ali)." Everyone wept and the scene was intensely emotional.[21]

Shortly before the dawn of that night, Al-Husayn dozed off briefly. As he woke up, he told his companions that he saw dogs, fiercest of which was spotted one, ripping his flesh, and that the person who would kill him is leprous. He also said that he saw Allah's Messenger with a group of his companions telling him, "You are the Martyr of this Community (Ummah). The inhabitants of heavens and their superiors are anxiously awaiting your arrival. You shall break your fast with me tonight. Hurry and do not hesitate, for an angel has descended from heaven to collect your blood in a green bottle."[22]

Notes & References

1. Tareekh Al-Tabari (V.6, P.137); Rawdhat Al-Wa'itheen (P.157); Al-Bidaya (V.8, P.176); Al-Irshaad
2. Tareekh Al-Tabari (V.6, P.337)
3. Tareekh Al-Tabari (V.6, P.238 & 239); Al-Kamel (V.4, P.34)
4. Ithbaat Al-Raja'a
5. Tareekh Al-Tabari (V.6, P.238); Al-Kamel (V.4, P.24); A'laam Al-Wara (P.141); Sayr A'laam Al-Nubala' (V.3' P.202); Al-Irshaad

6. Tareekh Al-Tabari (V.6, P.239); Al-Irshaad
7. Al-Luhuf (P.53)
8. Asraar Al-Shahada (P.389)
9. Nafs Al-Mahmoum (P.122)
10. Akhbar Al-Zamaan (P.247)
11. Ithbaat Al-Raja'a
12. Tareekh Al-Tabari (V.6, P.241)
13. Rijaal Al-Kashshi (P.53)
14. Tareekh Al-Tabari (V.6, P.240)
15. Sayr A'laam Al-Nubala' (V.3, P.210), Tareekh Al-Ya'aqoubi (V.2, P.217)
16. Tareekh Al-Tabari (V.6, P.240); Al-Kamel (V.4, P.24); Maqtal Al-Khawarizmi (V.1, P.238); Maqatil Al-Talibiyyeen (P.45)
17. Al-Luhuf (P.54)
18. Al-Irshaad
19. Ikmaal Al-Deen (P.275)
20. Tareekh Al-Tabari (V.6, P.240)
21. Al-Dam'a Al-Sakiba (P.325)
22. Nafs Al-Mahmoum (P.125

PART III:

THE DAY OF ASHURA

"I see death as a joy and life with the oppressors as a complete misery."

—*Al-Husayn ibn Ali ibn Abu Talib*

The Tenth of Muharram (Ashura)

This day passed leaving behind it tremendous grief for the Prophet's household. The crimes committed on this day broke so many hearts. The tears of the bereaved mixed with the blood of their loved and lost ones. One can imagine the wailing and moaning of the dust-covered women and children, who seemed to be aimlessly wondering around. The enormity of the loss is indescribable. The inhabitants of heavens and the beautiful maidens of paradise wept and moaned. The infallible leaders constantly cried and mourned the tragedy of Karbala inflicted horrendous shock and excruciating emotional pain on the Prophet's family. This appalling crime emotionally scarred the survivors in Al-Husayn's camp, and rendered them totally distraught. The Martyr (Al-Husayn) was a manifestation of the Divine Message, and the marvelous jewel on the crown of infallibility. The intense grief felt at his loss was by no means an overreaction. Al-Husayn was the grandson of Allah's Messenger, Fatima's sweetheart, Ali's endeared son, Al-Hasan's brother, and the Divinely appointed leader of all people at the time. Furthermore, Al-Husayn was indeed the medium of blessings and mercy. He was Allah's entrustment, and the Divine scale by which people were tested and sorted.

A person can never overreact to such a loss. One can never weep and mourn enough for losing the medium of Allah's blessings on earth. Members of Mohammed's family lay slaughtered on the hot sands; with their dismembered limbs scattered around, and their chests invisible from the protruding spears and arrows. Envisioning this scene intensifies the grief. One should keep in mind that the enemies of Allah massacred Prophet Mohammed's family after they besieged them for a long period of time, and deprived them of that which animals were freely allowed to acquire water. The Prophet was completely bereaved, and mourned for the loss of his grandson. A true believer should console the Prophet and mourn along with him.[1] Mohammed's true followers should hold mourning sessions, and urge one another to weep on the Master of all Martyrs. The followers of the Prophet's household should commemorate Al-Husayn on Ashura of every year, and extend condolences to one another for his Martyrdom. Imam Al-Baqir articulated the format of extending condolences. He instructed the believers to say, "We ask Allah to reward all of us for our bereavement on Al-Husayn. We also ask Him to enable us to avenge him under the banner of his son, The Guided (Al-Mahdi) of the Prophet's household."[2]

Abdullah Bin Sannan visited Imam Al-Sadiq on the tenth of Muharram (Ashura). The sixth infallible leader was sad and pale as his tears rolled down his cheeks like white pearls. Abdullah asked, "The son of Allah's Messenger! Why are you crying?" Imam Al-Sadiq exclaimed, "Aren't you aware that today marks Al-Husayn's martyrdom?" Al-Sadiq ordered Abdullah to unbutton his shirt, uncover his arms and look as bereaved as possible. He also instructed him to fast half a day, and break it with a drink of water in the afternoon; the time of climactic grief for the Prophet's household. Imam Al-Sadiq continued, "Had Allah's Messenger been alive, condolences should have been extended to him."[3] Imam Musa Al-Kathim was never seen smiling on the first ten days of Muharram. He was in grief throughout the ten days, but looked intensely bereaved and sad on the tenth. Imam Al-Ridha said, "People should always weep on Al-Husayn. His day rendered our eyes continuously tearful. His suffering on the plains of Karbala scarred our hearts." The twelfth infallible leader from the Prophet's household, may Allah hasten his return, visited (Ziyara Al-Nahiya) Al-Husayn, and said, "I shall mourn you day and night, and on you my eyes shall shed blood instead of tears." We in our turn, after learning this, ought to break our joyful routine, wear the cloak of grief, uphold the Divine rituals, and mourn the Thirsty Martyr on the tenth of every Muharram.

AL-HUSAYN ON THE DAY OF ASHURA

Al-Husayn led his companions in the congregational morning prayers on the day of Ashura. He then stood up, praised Allah and said, "Allah, the Exalted, had ordained that you and I will be slaughtered today, so I urge you to persevere and fight bravely."[4] Al-Husayn lined up his soldiers. They were eighty-two infantry and horsemen all together. He appointed Zuhayr Bin Al-Qayn to lead the companions on the right wing, and Habeeb Bin Muthahir to lead on the left, while he and his family remained in the middle.[5] He gave his banner to his brother, Al-Abbass,[6] because he was the bravest, most protective of the family, most experienced, closest of his kin and the most qualified for this responsibility.

Omar Bin Sa'ad marched with over thirty thousand soldiers towards Al-Husayn's camp. The leadership of Bin Sa'ad's army was divided as follows. Abdullah Bin Zuhayr Bin Saleem Al-Azdi led the soldiers of Medina, Abdurrahman Bin Abi Sabra Al-Hanafi led the tribes of Mithhaj and Assad, Qays Bin Al-Asha'ath led the tribes of Rabee'a and Kinda, and Al-Hurr Bin Yazeed Al-Riyahi led the tribes of Tameem and Ramadan. Eventually, all of them participated in the battle against Al-Husayn, except Al-Hurr. Omar Bin Sa'ad appointed Amr Bin Al-Hajjaj Al-Zubaydi to lead the right flank, Shimr Bin Thil Jawshan to lead the left, Uzra Bin Qays Al-Ahmasi to lead the horsemen, Shibth Bin Rib'ie to lead the infantry, and gave the banner of the army to his servant, Thuwayd.[7] Bin Sa'ad's soldiers roamed around Al-Husayn's tents. They were dumbfounded by the raging fire in the trench behind the camp. Al-Shimr screamed, "Husayn! Are you rushing the chastisement of the Day of Judgement upon yourself?" Al-Husayn inquired, "Who is this? It sounds like Shimr Bin Thil Jawshan!" Someone said, "Yes it is." Al-Husayn said, "You are a loser, and hellfire surely is your destination." Muslim Bin Ausaja aimed with his bow at Al-Shimr to shoot him, but Al-Husayn stopped him and said, "I despise initiating war."[8]

AL-HUSAYN'S SUPPLICATION

Watching the large army of his enemies marching towards him like a rushing river, Al-Husayn raised his arms and supplicated. He said, "My Lord! When distressed, I trust in You. You are my hope in every hardship, and I count on You to help through any troubling ordeal. I have always lamented to You about stressful situations that weaken the heart and cause any person to feel helpless. I complain to You about the joy of our enemies, and the lack of our supporters. You have always helped me out, and I always sought no one but You, because You are the source of all blessings and the recipient of all love."[9]

AL-HUSAYN'S FIRST SPEECH

Al-Husayn rode his horse towards his enemies, and spoke loudly such that everyone could hear him. He said,

> "You people! Hold your horses and listen to my words. It is my duty to advise you, and explain to you why I came here. Assess my words justly and listen carefully to my explanation. Doing so will contribute to your well-being. If you believe me, you will conclude that that your enmity towards me can never be justified. However, if you decide to be unjust and thus disagree with me then *unite with your associates on your scheme and do not worry over your decision and do not respite me (10:71). My Guardian is Allah, Who revealed the Book, and He indeed is the Guardian of the righteous (7:196)."*

The women in his camp wept when they heard his words. He told his brother Al-Abbass and his son Ali Al-Akbar, "Go and calm them down. By Allah! Soon they will weep plenty." As the women calmed down, Al-Husayn resumed speaking with unrivaled eloquence.[10] He numerously praised Allah and asked-Him to bestow His blessings upon Mohammed, the angels and all the prophets. He then said,

> "You, Allah's servants! Be pious and heed Allah's admonishment. This life is mortal. Had immortality been granted to anyone, the prophets, due to their contentment with the ordained, would have earned such a privilege. Nonetheless, Allah ordained the new of this vanishing life to become old, its glamour to deplete and its pleasure to end. Dwelling is a transit station, and homeland is a temporary fortress. Load up! Piety is your best load. Be pious in order to succeed.[11]

> People! Allah ordained for people to live through the ups and downs of this mortal life. This life deceives the foolish, and lures the loser. Do not allow it to deceive you, because your desire and greed in it reap you great disappointment. I see that you united on a scheme that angered

Allah. Your transgressions shall invoke Allah's wrath upon you and deprive you of His Generosity. You are the worst servants of the best Lord, because you claim your submission to Him, and believe that Mohammed is His Messenger, and at the same time, you march towards his beloved family to murder them. You are doomed for what you intend to do. Satan has controlled your minds and rendered you forgetful of Allah the Great. You are condemned in your evil scheme. We all belong to Allah, and to Him we shall return. You people have become apostates after adhering to faith, *so may the wrath befall the oppressors (23:41).*[12]

People! Learn who I am. Judge for yourselves, and assess if it is permissible for you to murder me and violate my sanctity. Aren't I the grandson of your Prophet and the son of his successor and cousin, who was the first believer in the Divine Revelations? Isn't Hamza, the Master of Martyrs, my father's uncle? Isn't Ja'afar Al-Tayyar my uncle? Weren't you informed that the Prophet pointed at my brother and me, and said that these two are the Masters of Youth in Heaven? You should trust me and believe these facts, because I always speak the truth. I am truthful because I know that Allah despises and severely punishes liars. However, if you are doubtful of what just said, there are people with whom you can verify the truth of my statements! Ask Jaber Bin Abdullah Al-Ansari, Abu Sa'iid Al-Khadari, Sahl Bin Sa'ad Al-Sa'idi, Zayd Bin Arqam or Anas Bin Malik. These men should confirm to you that they heard the Prophet saying this to me and to my brother. Isn't this a good enough reason to stop you from spilling my blood?"

Al-Shimr interjected, "He (Al-Husayn) worships Allah conditionally, and utters nonsense." Habeeb answered Al-Shimr, "By Allah! You are so disloyal to Allah. I bear witness that your veiled heart can never understand what Al-Husayn said." The Prophet's grandson continued,

> "You might be doubtful of what I stated, but are you doubtful that I am your Prophet's grandson? By Allah! I am the only grandson of a prophet on the face of the earth. Damn you! Are you after me for murdering anyone,

stealing any money or committing any crime?"

No one answered him. He then called, "You! Shibth Bin Rib'ie, Hajjar Bin Abjar, Qays Bin Al-Ash'ath and Zayd Bin Al-Harith! Didn't you write me urging me to come here? Didn't you write that the time is perfect, and that I will arrive to soldiers ready for my command?" They answered, "No, we did not." He said, "Allah is worthy of all praise. By Allah! You did." Al-Husayn then commented, "If you happen to dislike me now, then let me leave and go somewhere else on this earth." Qays Bin Al-Ash'ath said, "Why don't you accept your cousins' leadership? They will treat you well and never harm you." Al-Husayn answered him, "You are just like your brother! Do you want the Hashimites to charge you with more than the blood of Muslim Bin Aqeel? No. By Allah! I shall never surrender and humiliate myself, nor shall I cower away. You, the servants of Allah! I seek refuge in our Lord from your evil. *I seek refuge in our Lord from every arrogant person who disbelieves in the Day of Judgement (40:27).*" Al-Husayn stepped down off of his horse and asked Uqbah Bin Sam'aan to tie it.[13]

BLISS AND GUIDANCE

Bin Sa'ad's army marched onwards towards Al-Husayn's camp. Abdullah Bin Hawza Al-Tameemi screamed, "Where is Al-Husayn?" He repeated his question until Al-Husayn's companions replied, "This is Al-Husayn. What do you want from him?" He yelled, "Husayn! You are bound to hellfire." Al-Husayn replied, "You are a liar. I shall return to a Forgiving, Generous, Absolute and a Merciful Lord. Who are you?" He answered, "I am Bin Hawza." Al-Husayn lifted his arms, exposing the flesh of his biceps, and said, "Oh Allah! Drag him into fire." Bin Hawza became enraged and charged his horse towards Al-Husayn, losing his balance in the process. His body hung on one side of the horse, while his foot remained stuck on the other. The horse ran around, cutting off his leg, while the rest of his body was still hanging sideways on the saddle. The horse smashed him into rocks and trees, and finally threw him into the raging fire of the trench behind Al-Husayn's camp.[14]

Al-Husayn prostrated in gratitude, and thanked Allah for immediately answering his supplication. Al-Husayn then loudly said,

"Allah! We are the household members and descendants of Your Messenger, and closest of kin to him. Destroy those who oppressed us and usurped our rights, for You are Close and Attentive." Mohammed Bin Al-Ash'ath sarcastically asked Al-Husayn, "What kinship is there between you and Prophet Mohammed?" Al-Husayn said, "Oh Allah! Mohammed Bin Al-Ash'ath denies my kinship to Prophet Mohammed. Oh Allah! Allow me to see a wrath befall him soon." Allah answered Al-Husayn's supplication. Mohammed Bin Al-Asha'ath went to a secluded area to empty his bowels. A scorpion fatally stung him. He died smeared with his waste,[15] and with his genitals exposed.[16]

Masrouq Bin Wa'il Al-Hadhrami narrated, "I rode my horse to the forefront of the battlefield, hoping to carry Al-Husayn's head to Bin Ziyad and collect a huge reward. When I saw what happened to Bin Hawza, I realized that Allah blessed the members of this household with special sanctity and ranked them high. I consciously left the scene, because I was convinced that if I fought them, I would definitely end up in hellfire."[17]

The Speech of Zuhayr Bin Al-Qayn

Fully armed, Zuhayr Bin Al-Qayn rode his horse to address Bin Sa'ad's army. He said:

> "You, Kufans! I sternly warn you against a wrath from Allah. It is a duty upon every Muslim to advise his Muslim brother, and until now we have not fought, so we are still brothers in faith. We, at this point, still owe you advice, but once the battle begins, ties will be cut and your community becomes an adversary of ours. Allah is testing all of us to see how well we revere the family of His Messenger, Mohammed. We invite you to support the Prophet's household. We also urge you to abandon the tyrants, Yazeed and Obeydallah Bin Ziyad, because you will see nothing but the cruelty of their reign. They shall poke your eyes, cut off your limbs, mutilate you and crucify you on palm trees. Moreover, they shall murder your leaders and the devout worshippers as they murdered Hijr Bin Udayy and his companions, Hani Bin Urwa and other devout Muslims."

The crowd cursed Zuhayr and simultaneously praised Bin Ziyad and prayed for his well-being. They also told Zuhayr, "We are committed to kill your friend (Al-Husayn) and his company, or take them as captives to Obeydallah Bin Ziyad." Zuhayr continued:

> "Fatima's children are more worthy of your love and support than Sumayya's. If you refrain from supporting them (Fatima's children), I ask you by Allah not to murder them. Let the man (Al-Husayn) confront Yazeed, for the latter would be pleased with your compliance even if you do not murder Al-Husayn."

Al-Shimr shot an arrow towards Zuhayr and said, "Shut up! May Allah shut your mouth! You have annoyed us with your long speech." Zuhayr told Al-Shimr, "You are a loser! I was not talking to you because you are like an animal. I don't think you are capable of reciting even two verses from the Holy Book. However, anticipate the wrath and great chastisement to befall you on the Day of Judgement." Al-Shimr replied, "Allah shall kill you and your friend shortly." Zuhayr said, "Are you scaring me with death? By Allah! Dying with him is better than an immortal life with you all." He then moved closer to the crowd and said, "Servants of Allah! Do not allow this vicious transgressor and his peers to sway you away from true faith. By Allah! Mohammed will never intercede for the people who murder his family, his household, their supporters and the defenders of the Prophet's daughters." A comrade of his yelled, "Al-Husayn asks you to return. He says you have done as good a job advising them as the Believer from the Family of Pharaoh (40:28). However, your words and advice are falling on deaf ears."[18]

BURAYR'S SPEECH

Burayr Bin Khudhayr was a Tabe'ie (the generation junior to the Prophet's companions). He was old and well known for his dedication and devotion to Allah. He was a prominent teacher of the Holy Qur'an in the main mosque of Kufa (Qari'e). He was also honorable and greatly revered in the tribe of Ramadan. After acquiring Al-Husayn's permission to talk, Burayr approached Bin Sa'ad's army and said:

"People! Allah sent Mohammed as a bright light of guidance to His path. Allah sent him in order to deliver the glad tidings and admonish all of us. This is the Euphrates, from which wild dogs and hogs drink, whilst the grandson of Allah's Messenger is denied access to it. Is this your gratitude to Mohammed?"[19]

They said, "You have talked quite a bit. Leave us alone. By Allah! Al-Husayn shall remain thirsty." Burayr inquired, "People! Mohammed's entrustment is amongst you. These are his household members, descendants, relatives, and daughters. Let me know what you intend to do to them." They replied, "We intend to forcefully take them to the governor, Bin Ziyad, and he will decide what to do with them." He resumed:

"Why don't you let them return to the place from which they came? Kufans! You are doomed! Have you forgotten that you asked Allah to be the witness on the letters you have sent, and the pledges you have made? You have invited your Prophet's household and promised to risk your lives protecting them, but once they arrived, you abandoned them in favor of Bin Ziyad, and then denied them the water of the Euphrates. You are so disloyal to your Prophet in doing this to his family. You are the worst community! I ask Allah to deprive you of water on the Day of Judgement."

Some of them responded, "We don't understand what you are saying." He answered, "I thank Allah who verified your real image before my eyes. Oh Allah! I dissociate myself from the actions of these people. Oh Allah! Disrupt their lives with feudalism so You would be angry with them when they return to You." The crowd shot arrows towards Burayr forcing him to retreat.[20]

AL-HUSAYN'S SECOND SPEECH

Al-Husayn crowned himself with the Holy Book and rode his horse towards Bin Sa'ad's army. He stood facing them and said, "People! Let the Holy Book and the path of my grandfather, Allah's Messenger, be the judge between us."[21] He then asked them to acknowledge his significance, and to acknowledge that he was carrying the Prophet's sword, and wearing his turban and war vest. After he heard their acknowledgement, he asked them about the reason of their intent to kill him. They said, "We are implementing the orders of the governor, Obeydallah Bin Ziyad." Al-Husayn said:

> "You are indeed condemned! We responded to your calls, rushed to save you, and in return you waged war against us. You should have waged this war against our enemies. You betrayed us and became submissive to your true enemies, knowing that they were never kind or just to you. You shall reap disasters! You abandoned us and rendered your swords useless. You conceded your bravery and intelligence to cowardice and idiocy. You initially flocked to us like birds and butterflies flock to eat, but soon after ignored your commitment to our cause. You are condemned to have become rejects and slaves of this life. You are condemned to have abandoned the Holy Book and deliberately altered its concepts. You are trying to destroy the pure path. You are condemned to have become transgressors, and representative of Satan. How dare you support these people and desert us? By Allah! Your souls have become contaminated with betrayal and disloyalty. You are like poisonous fruit of a beautiful but evil tree. You have become a ripe fruit for the oppressor to eat. This man, vicious like his father, is pushing for war or humiliation. We will never be humiliated. Allah, His Messenger, and the believers do not approve of it for us. Pure wombs bore our honorable and dignified souls, and we shall never obey a vile man in lieu of a blessed martyrdom. My family and I shall fight, despite our small number and lack of supporters."[22]

Al-Husayn then quoted Farwa Bin Musayk Al-Muradi, "If we defeat them, it is because we have always defeated the enemy. However, if we are defeated, we can never be considered losers. We are not cowards, but it is our ordained death and the onset of their reign. Tell those who are happy with the outcome that they shall face a similar destiny. Once death is done with a group of people, it shall chase another." Al-Husayn then continued:

> "By Allah! You shall live very shortly after this. It has been absolutely ordained that you shall plunge into a downward

spiral, and that your lives shall become turbulent as if you have been placed on an axle. This is a Divine promise. My father learned it from my grandfather and informed me. *Unite with your associates on your scheme and do not worry over your decision and do not respite me, for I rely on Allah, my Lord and your Lord. The destiny of every creature is in His Hand. He is definitely on the Straight Path. (11:56)*"[23]

Al-Husayn then turned his palms towards the sky and supplicated, "Oh Allah! Withhold rainfall from them and make them suffer years of drought similar to those of Prophet Yusuf's. Allow the man from Thaqeef (Al-Mukhtar) to rule them with an iron fist, because they betrayed and forsook us. You are our Lord; on You we rely, and to You we shall return.[24] By Allah! He (Al-Mukhtar) shall avenge me and destroy each one of them. It will be an eye for an eye, and a tooth for a tooth kind of revenge. He shall victoriously avenge me, my family and my followers."[25]

Bin Sa'ad's Aberration

Al-Husayn requested to meet with Bin Sa'ad. The latter was disgruntled at the request, and reluctantly agreed to it. Al-Husayn told him, "Omar! Do you think that after you murder me, the wicked will appoint you to govern the province of Al-Rayy and Jarjan? By Allah! It has been ordained that you shall never enjoy such a privilege. Do whatever you like, because after my death, you shall have no joy in this life and in the next. I foresee little boys in Kufa rolling your head with canes, throwing it around and playing with it like a ball." Omar Bin Sa'ad angrily looked away and left.[26]

Al-Hurr's Repentance

After listening to Al-Husayn's words and calls for support, Al-Hurr asked Bin Sa'ad, "Do you intend to fight this man?" Bin Sa'ad replied, "By Allah! I shall definitely do so. I intend to wage a bloody war in which heads and limbs will fly off." Al-Hurr then asked, "Why don't you consider the alternatives he offered you?" Bin Sa'ad answered, "Had the decision been mine, I would have accepted, but your governor rejected all of his offers." Al-Hurr walked away, and mingled into the crowd. Qurra Bin Qays stood next to Al-Hurr. Al-Hurr asked Qurra, "Did you water your horse today?" Qurra replied, "No." Al-Hurr said, "Don't you want to water it?" Qurra walked away after he realized that Al-Hurr wanted to be alone.

Al-Hurr slowly approached Al-Husayn's camp. Al-Muhajir Bin Aws asked Al-Hurr, "Are you going to attack?" Al-Hurr quivered and remained silent. Puzzled by Al-Hurr's strange behavior, Al-Muhajir exclaimed, "If someone inquires about the bravest Kufan, I would say it is you! What is the matter?" Al-Hurr replied, "I am choosing between paradise and hellfire. By Allah! Even if I am burned alive, I shall choose nothing over paradise." Al-Hurr turned his spear upside down, his shield inside out and rode his horse towards Al-Husayn.[27] Nodding his head down, and bashful for hurting the Prophet's family and trapping them in the open dry desert, he loudly said, "Oh Allah! To you I turn to accept my repentance. I have terrorized Your dedicated servants, and the children of Your Prophet. Abu Abdullah! I repent. Is there a chance that my repentance will be accepted?"

Al-Husayn replied, "Allah shall definitely accept your repentance."[28] Assured of the eternal blessing and joy, Al-Hurr became elated. It also became clear to him that the voice he heard upon leaving Kufa was real. Al-Hurr told Al-Husayn that upon his departure from Kufa, he heard a voice saying, "Hurr! You are guaranteed paradise." Al-Hurr continued, "As I heard that voice, I subconsciously thought that I was doomed; how could I be assured paradise when I was marching to fight the grandson of Allah's Messenger?"[29] Al-Husayn told Al-Hurr, "You are bound to reap goodness and rewards."[30] With a Turkish servant on his side, Al-Hurr joined Al-Husayn.[31]

AL-HURR ADVISES THE KUFANS

After acquiring Al-Husayn's permission to advise the Kufans Al-Hurr loudly said:

> "Kufans! You are miserable fools! You asked him to come, and promised to support him, but instead you abandoned him. And now, you besieged him along with his family and prevented them from travelling to a safe place on this earth. He has become like a helpless prisoner of war

amongst you. You denied him, and his women and children, the rushing water of the Euphrates, from which Jews, Christians and fire worshippers are allowed to drink, and in which wild dogs and hogs are allowed to swim. Look at them! They are suffering a great deal from thirst. You are so disloyal to Mohammed to inflict this pain on his family. I ask Allah to deprive you of water on the Day of Great Thirst."

A group of Bin Sa'ad's soldiers attacked Al-Hurr and shot arrows towards him. Al-Hurr retreated and stood next to Al-Husayn.[32]

Notes & References

1. Al-Khassa'is Al-Kubra (V.2, P.125); A'laam Al-Nubuwwa (P.83)
2. Kamel Al-Ziyaraat (P.175); Musbaah Al-Mutahajjid (P.39)
3. Mazar Bin Al-Mashhadi
4. Kamel Al-Ziyaraat (P.73); Ithbaat Al-Wassiyya (P.139)
5. Maqtal Al-Khawarizmi (V.2, P.4)
6. Tareekh Al-Tabari (V.6, P.241); Tathkirat Al-Khawass (P.143)
7. Tareekh Al-Tabari (V.6, P.241)
8. Tareekh Al-Tabari (V.6, P.242); Al-Irshaad
9. Al-Kamel (V.4, P.25); Tareekh Dimashq (V.4, P.233)
10. Tareekh Al-Tabari (V.6, P.242)
11. Zahr Al-Aadaab (V.1, P.62)
12. Maqtal Mohammed Bin Abu Talib
13. Tareekh Al-Tabari (V.6,, P.243)
14. Al-Kamel (V.4, P.27)
15. Maqtal Al-Khawarizmi{V.1, P.249)
16. Rawdhat Al-Wa'itheen (P.159)
17. Al-Kamel (V.4, P.27)
18. Tareekh Al-Tabari (V.6, P.243)
19. Amali Al-Sadouq (P.96)
20. Maqtal Mohammed Bin Abu Talib
21. Tathkirat Al-Khawass (P.143)
22. Al-Luhuf (P.54)
23. Tareekh Dimashq (V.4, P.334); Maqtal Al-Khawarizmi (V.2, P.7); Al-Luhuf (P.54)
24. Maqtal Al-Khawarizmi (V.2, P.7); Al-Luhuf (P.56)
25. Maqtal Al-Awalim (P.84)
26. Maqtal Al-Awalim (P.84); Tathallum Al-Zahra' (P.110); Maqtal Al-Khawarizmi (V.2, P.8)

27. Tareekh Al-Tabari (V.6, P.244)
28. Al-Luhuf (P.58); Amali Al-Sadouq (P.97); Rawdhat Al-Wa'itheen (P.159).
29. Amali Al-Sadouq (P.93)
30. Mutheer Al-Ahzaan (P.31)
31. Maqtal Al-Khawarizmi (V.2, P.9)
32. Al-Kamel (V.4, P.27)

The Battle of Karbala

The First Attack

Omar Bin Sa'ad walked towards Al-Husayn's camp and shot an arrow. He told his soldiers, "Testify in front of the governor that I shot the first arrow." Bin Sa'ad's soldiers followed suit.[1] Arrows fell like rain, poking every tent in Al-Husayn's camp.[2] Al-Husayn told his companions, "May Allah's Mercy be upon you! Get ready to embrace your inevitable death. These arrows are a message of war from these people." Al-Husayn's soldiers attacked their enemies. A fierce battle ensued in which fifty of Al-Husayn's companions were martyred.[3] After that Yassar and Salem, servants of Ziyad and his son Obeydallah, asked for a duel. Habeeb and Burayr stepped forward to fight, but Al-Husayn stopped them.

Abdullah Bin Omeyr Al-Kalbi, nicknamed Abu Wahab from Bani Aleem, stood up and expressed his willingness to fight. He, with wide shoulders, was tall and very strong. He was also brave, experienced and well respected in his community. Al-Husayn gave him permission, and said, "I believe he is strong enough to defeat his rivals." Yassar and Salem asked Abu Wahab, "Who are you?" After he introduced himself, they condescendingly responded, "You are an underdog. Let Zuhayr, Habeeb or Burayr come out to fight us." Meanwhile, Yassar had walked closer to Abu Wahab.

The latter told the former, "Damn you! You think that I'm not good enough for you!" Abu Wahab attacked Yassar, and fatally struck him with the sword. Salem circled around Abu Wahab and tried to attack him from behind. Al-Husayn's companions screamed to warn Abu Wahab. The latter fearlessly fended off Salem's sword with his left hand, and lost his fingers in the process. Abu Wahab then attacked Salem and killed him. Having killed both men, Abu Wahab proudly walked back towards Al-Husayn.

Meanwhile, Umm Wahab Bint Abdullah Bin Al-Nimr Bin

Qassit, Abu Wahab's wife, picked up a pole, ran towards her husband and told him, "May my parents be sacrificed for your well-being! Fight to defend Mohammed's family." Abu Wahab unsuccessfully tried to send her back to her tent. She firmly held onto his cloak, and said, "I am not leaving until I die with you." Al-Husayn intervened and told her, "I ask Allah to reward you for defending your Prophet's household. Return to your tent. Women are exempt from military combat."[4]

Fighting in Small Groups

When the remainder of Al-Husayn's companions saw that many of their comrades had been martyred, they, two, three and four at a time, asked permission to fight. They bravely stormed onto the battlefield to defend Al-Husayn and his family. Extremely protective of one another, they fought fearlessly. Sayf Bin Al-Harith Bin Saree' and Malik Bin Abid Bin Saree', paternal cousins and maternal brothers, wept before their departure. Al-Husayn asked them, "Why are you weeping when you are about to be eternally joyous?" They answered, "We ask Allah to take our lives in order to protect yours. We are not weeping on ourselves, but on you. We see the siege around you, but we cannot do much about it." Al-Husayn commended their efforts. They fought close to him until they were martyred.[5]

Abdullah and Abdurrahman, the sons of Urwa from the tribe of Ghafar, told Al-Husayn, "We would like to remain close to you." They fought close by until they were martyred.

Amr Bin Khalid Al-Saydawi, his servant Sa'ad, Jaber Bin Al-Harith Al-Salmahi and Majma'a Bin Abdullah Al-Adawi formed a group and attacked the Kufans. They penetrated deep into Bin Sa'ad's army until they became totally surrounded. Al-Husayn sent his brother to rescue the four badly wounded men. Al-Abbass single handedly pulled them out, but on the way back, Bin Sa'ad's army attacked them. Despite their severe wounds, they counter-attacked and fought fiercely. The four men were martyred together in one spot.[6]

Appeal and Subsequent Guidance

Having lost most of his companions in the battle, Al-Husayn

firmly held his Holy beard and said, "The wrath of Allah fell upon the Jews when they claimed He had a son. It fell on the Christians when they made Him a part of the Trinity. It fell on the Magians for worshipping the sun and the moon, instead of Him, and now it is falling upon a group of people uniting to murder their Prophet's grandson. By Allah! I shall never comply with any of their demands. Instead, I shall return to Allah covered with my blood." He then loudly called, "Is there any supporter out there? Is there anyone who could help us, and defend the women of Allah's Messenger?"[7] Women in his camp screamed and wept loudly. Sa'ad Bin Al-Harith and his brother Abu Al-Hutouf, both from Medina, were, until then, soldiers in Bin Sa'ad's army. When they heard Al-Husayn's call for support, and the weeping of his children, they switched sides. They attacked Al-Husayn's enemies and fought until they were martyred.[8]

STEADFASTNESS OF THE RIGHT FLANK

At this point, the number of Al-Husayn's companions had significantly dwindled. They began fighting one at a time, inflicting heavy casualties on their enemies. Amr Bin Al-Hajjaj screamed at his comrades, "Do you know what you are up against? You are fighting heroes of strong certitude in their faith, and men ready to be martyred. As few as they are, they will destroy you all. By Allah! You should stone them in order to kill them." Omar Bin Sa'ad said, "You are correct. Forbid all the soldiers from engaging in duels, because if we keep doing so, they will finish all of us."[9]

Amr Bin Al-Hajjaj attacked the right wing of Al-Husayn's army. Al-Husayn's companions firmly held their positions. They loaded arrows in their bows, and knelt down ready to fire. The horses of the enemies stopped advancing for a minute; once they resumed, Al-Husayn's companions launched their arrows, killing and injuring many of the attacker.[10] Amr Bin Al-Hajjaj repeatedly told his soldiers: "Fight the apostates and the source of disunity." Al-Husayn responded loudly, "Amr! You are damned! How dare you instigate the people against me? Are we apostates while you are a believer? Once our souls depart our bodies, you all shall know who truly deserves hellfire."[11]

Muslim Bin Ausaja

Amr Bin Al-Hajjaj redirected his attack from the side of the Euphrates. A fierce battle ensued, during which Muslim Bin Abdullah Al-Dhababi and Abdullah Bin Khashkara Al-Bajali attacked Muslim Bin Ausaja. Thick dust filled the air over the battleground. The dust settled on Muslim as he lay on the ground. He was badly wounded, but still blinking. Al-Husayn and Habeeb Bin Muthahir walked over to see him. The Prophet's grandson told Muslim, "I ask Allah to include you in His Mercy. *Some passed away while some await, and they are all alike. (33:23)*" Habeeb leaned close to Muslim and said, "I am saddened to lose you! You should be glad that are on your way to paradise." Muslim replied with a faint voice, "I ask Allah to bless you with similar glad tidings." Habeeb said, "If I weren't following you, I would have inquired about your will." Muslim pointed at Al-Husayn and said, "My will is this. Die defending him." Habeeb said, "By the Lord of the Ka'aba! I shall do that." Muslim died while Habeeb and Al-Husayn hovered over him. His maid tearfully and loudly mourned him. She yelled, "Oh! Muslim, Oh! My master, Oh! Bin Ausaja." The soldiers of Bin Al-Hajjaj rejoiced because of Muslim's death. Shibth Bin Rib'ie scolded the cheering men around him and said, "May your mothers weep on you! How could you be happy that Muslim has been killed? His performance when we fought for Azerbaijan was quite commendable. He, single handedly, killed off six idolaters in a skirmish before the onset of the main battle."[12]

The Left Wing

Al-Shimr and his soldiers attacked the left wing of Al-Husayn's army, but the soldiers of the Prophet's grandson firmly held their positions and repelled the attackers. Abdullah Bin Umayr Al-Kalbi, Abu Wahab, killed nineteen horsemen and twelve infantrymen during this attack. Abu Wahab fought until Hani Bin Thabeet Al-Hadhrami cut off his right hand, and Bakr Bin Hayy cut off his leg.[13] He was then captured and executed.[14] His wife, Umm Wahab, sat on his side and leaned over his head. She then wiped the blood off of his face, and said, "I congratulate you for entering paradise. I ask Allah, who granted you paradise, to grant me your company in it." Al-Shimr ordered his servant Rustum to strike her head with a pole. Rustum smashed her head, killing her on the spot. She was the first female martyr amongst Al-Husayn's companions.[15]

The enemies decapitated Abu Wahab, and threw his head over to Al-Husayn's camp. His mother picked it up and wiped the blood off of it. She then grabbed the pole of a tent and attacked the enemies. Al-Husayn sent her back and said, "May Allah's Mercy include you! Return to your tent. You are exempt from combat." As she returned to her tent, she said, "Oh Allah! Do not render me hopeless." Al-Husayn said, "Allah shall never render you hopeless."[16]

Al-Shimr attacked the camp, stabbed Al-Husayn's tent with his spear, and asked for a torch to burn it down on its occupants. The women ran out of the tent screaming. Al-Husayn called him, "You! Bin Thil Jawshan! How dare you try to burn my house down on my family? Allah shall definitely burn you in hellfire." Shibth Bin Rib'ie scolded Al-Shimr and said, "Have you become a specialist in terrorizing women? I have never heard a foul mouth or seen an evil stance like yours." Al-Shimr bashfully left. Zuhayr Bin Al-Qayn, with ten of his comrades, counter-attacked Al-Shimr and his soldiers and forced them away from the tents.[17]

UZRA REQUESTS REINFORCEMENT

Realizing his soldiers' incompetence and failure to achieve anything in each of their attacks, Uzra, the commander of the horsemen in Bin Sa'ad's army, requested troop reinforcement. Bin Sa'ad asked Shibth Bin Rib'ie to lead the reinforcement to Uzra. Shibth told Bin Sa'ad, "I praise Allah! Why would you select the leader of this community when you have others who can do as good a job?" All along, Shibth condemned the idea of waging war against Al-Husayn. Some heard Shibth say, "We fought for five years on the side of Ali Bin Abu Talib and his son against the family of Abu Sufyan. Then we flocked against his other son, the 'best living being on earth, fighting on the side of Mu'awiya's family and the son of Sumayya, the adulteress. There is no more aberration than this. By Allah! Allah shall never bless the people of this land, nor shall He guide them to the true path."[18]

Al-Hossayn Bin Numayr led five hundred archers to reinforce Uzra. Fierce fighting ensued. Al-Husayn's companions inflicted heavy casualties on the attackers. Moreover, they disabled the horses of Uzra's soldiers, and forced them to fight on foot.[19] Unable to penetrate due to the closeness of the tents, Omar Bin Sa'ad ordered his men to encircle the camp and tighten the siege around it. Al-Husayn's companions divided themselves into groups of three and four men, and fought back from the alleys between the tents. They killed off and wounded the looting attackers from close range.

Bin Sa'ad ordered his soldiers to set Al-Husayn's camp on fire. As they did, the women screamed and the children were petrified. Al-Husayn said, "Let them set it on fire. Once they do that, they cannot pass over and reach you." Indeed, and as Al-Husayn said, the raging fire in the camp prevented the enemies from physically hurting the women and children.[20]

ABU AL-SHA'THAA'

Yazeed Bin Ziyad, also known as Abu Al-Sha'thaa' Al-Kindi, was a soldier in Bin Sa'ad's army. Abu Al-Sha'thaa' switched sides right after Al-Husayn's conditions for a truce were turned down. He, a skilled archer, knelt down and shot a hundred arrows before Al-Husayn's watchful eyes. Each time Abu Al-Sha'thaa' fired an arrow, Al-Husayn said, "Allah! Help him hit his target and reward him with paradise." He ran out of arrows and said, "I am certain that I killed five of them."[21] He then attacked the enemies killing nine more before he was martyred.[22]

NOONTIME

Abu Thumama Al-Sa'idi looked at the sun, and realized that it was noontime. He told Al-Husayn, "My soul is ready to depart defending yours. I see the enemies approaching you. By Allah! I intend to be martyred before you, however, I would like to return to Allah after I pray the noon prayers, since its time is already due." Al-Husayn looked at the sky and said, "You remembered the prayers! I ask Allah to count you amongst His devout servants and worshippers. Noon prayers are due indeed. Ask them to halt their attack until we pray." Al-Hossayn Bin Numayr said, "Your prayers will not be accepted."

Habeeb Bin Muthahir

Habeeb Bin Muthahir replied, "You are a jackass! You think it will not be accepted from the Prophet's family, but it will from you!" Al-Hossayn attacked Habeeb. The latter struck Al-Hossayn's horse with the sword. The horse jumped high throwing Al-Hossayn onto the ground but his comrades rescued him and carried him away.[23] Meanwhile, Habeeb attacked the Kufans. Despite his old age, he fought fiercely killing sixty-two men. Badeel Bin Suraym struck Habeeb with a sword, while another man from the tribe of Tameem stabbed him with a spear. Habeeb fell onto the ground, and while trying to stand up, Al-Hossayn struck him with a sword on the head. Habeeb fell again face down onto the ground. The man from Tameem decapitated him. Al-Husayn was totally devastated for losing Habeeb. Expressing his grief, the Prophet's grandson said, "I ask Allah to account for me, and for my protective companions." He also repeatedly uttered, "We all belong to Allah, and to Him we shall return."[24]

Al-Hurr Al-Riyahi

Al-Hurr and Zuhayr Bin Al-Qayn stormed onto the battlefield right after Habeeb's martyrdom. They fought back to back, protecting and rescuing one another. They took turns watching each other's back.[25] They did so for a while until Al-Hurr's horse was badly wounded, and blood heavily dripped over its face. Al-Hurr chanted, "I indulged the neck of my horse, until it became soaked with blood."

Al-Hossayn told Yazeed Bin Sufyan, "You have always wished to kill Al-Hurr. This is your opportunity." Bin Sufyan said, "Yes indeed." Bin Sufyan asked for a duel, but Al-Hurr quickly killed him. Ayyoub Bin Mashrah Al-Kheewani shot Al-Hurr's horse with an arrow and killed it. Wielding his sword, Al-Hurr jumped like a lion off of his falling horse,[26] and fought bravely on his feet, killing over forty men.[27] The infantry of Bin Sa'ad's army attacked Al-Hurr, and killed him. Al-Husayn's companions carried him and placed him next to the martyrs in front of the most protected tent. Each time a martyr was carried over, Al-Husayn said, "A kill equivalent to that of the prophets and their families."[28]

Al-Hurr was still breathing. Al-Husayn hovered over him, gently wiped the blood off of his face, and told him, "You are free, as your mother suitably named you. You are free, in this life and in the next." One of Al-Husayn's companions, or Ali Bin Al-Husayn, or Al-Husayn, commemorated Al-Hurr in the following poem. "The most honorable Hurr (free man) is Al-Hurr of Bani Riyah, who ominously persevered in battle. The most honorable Hurr is the one who embraced the path of self-sacrifice to defend Al-Husayn."[29]

Noon Prayers

Al-Husayn stood up to perform prayers. It is narrated that he led half of his remaining companions in congregational prayers, according to the format of praying under fear (Salat Al-Khawf). Zuhayr Bin Al-Qayn, Sa'iid Bin Abdullah Al-Hanafi, and the rest formed a wall to shield Al-Husayn during prayers.[30] It is also narrated that Al-Husayn and all of his companions prayed individually, according to the format of gesture prayers (Salat Al-Eimaa').[31]

Sa'iid Bin Abdullah Al-Hanafi was badly wounded. He fell onto the ground and said, "Oh Allah! Bestow on them a wrath similar to that of A'ad and Thamud. Convey my greetings to Your Messenger, and inform him of my multiple wounds. I truly sought Your reward in supporting Your Messenger's household."[32]

He then looked at Al-Husayn, and asked, "The son of Allah's Messenger! Did I do well?" Al-Husayn replied, "Yes, you are off to paradise ahead of me."[33] In addition to his multiple stabs and wounds, Sa'iid died with thirteen protruding arrows in his body.[34]

After finishing his prayers, Al-Husayn told his companions, "You, the blessed ones! Paradise, with its flowing rivers and ripe fruits, had opened its doors for you. Allah's Messenger, and the martyrs who were killed on the way of Allah, are also expecting your arrival, and are anxiously waiting to see you. Defend Allah's Message, His Messenger, and the Prophet's family." They collectively responded, "Our souls shall be sacrificed protecting yours, and our blood shall be spilled defending yours. By Allah! They shall never inflict any harm upon you or your family as long as we have a pulse in our bodies."[35]

Disabling the Horses

Bin Sa'ad ordered Amr Bin Sa'iid to lead a group of archers towards Al-Husayn's camp. The archers launched their arrows onto Al-Husayn's companions and disabled all of their horses.[36] The only horseman left in Al-Husayn's camp was Al-Dhahhak Bin Abdullah Al-Mashriqi. This man narrated, "When I saw the horses of my comrades being shot, I hid mine in a tent." Fierce fighting ensued.[37] Before departing the camp towards the battlefield, every companion bid farewell to Al-Husayn. Each one of his soldiers said, "The son of Allah's Messenger! Peace be upon you." Reciprocating each greeting, Al-Husayn said, "And peace be upon you. We shall join you soon." He then recited, *"Some passed away while some await, and they are all alike (33:23)."*[38]

Abu Thumama

Abu Thumama fought until he was badly wounded. Qays Bin Abdullah, a cousin of his in Bin Sa'ad's army, killed him off avenging an old feud between the two.

Zuhayr and Bin Madharib

Salman Bin Madharib Al-Bajali, Zuhayr's cousin, fought until he was martyred. Zuhayr put his hands on Al-Husayn's knee, and asked permission to fight. Zuhayr said, "Lead! You are guided, and you are the banner of guidance. Today I shall be with your grandfather, Al-Hasan, and Ali the dignified. Today I shall be with the honorable man with wings (Ja'afar Al-Tayyar) and the Living Martyr, the Lion of Allah (Hamza)." Al-Husayn replied, "And I am on my way to be with them too."

Zuhayr chanted, "I am Zuhayr, and I am the son of Al-Qayn. I shall fight you with my sword defending Al-Husayn." He attacked the enemies, killing one hundred and twenty men. Katheer Bin Abdullah Al-Sa'abi and Al-Muhajir Bin Aws teamed up against Zuhayr and killed him. Expressing his grief, Al-Husayn stood up and said, "Zuhayr! I ask Allah to bless you. I ask Him to condemn your murderers, the way He condemned others into monkeys and pigs."[39]

AMR BIN QARTHA AL-ANSARI

Amr Bin Qartha Al-Ansari stood in front of Al-Husayn to shield him from the attacking enemies. Amr received the piercing arrows with his chest and face, successfully providing complete protection to Al-Husayn. The badly wounded Amr looked at Al-Husayn and inquired, "The son of Allah's Messenger! Did I do a good job?" Al-Husayn replied, "You sure did. You are off to paradise ahead of me. Convey my greetings to Allah's Messenger, and inform him that I am on my way." Amr died in his spot.[40]

Ali, Amr's brother, a soldier in Bin Sa'ad's army, screamed, "Husayn! You are a liar! You deceived my brother and killed him." Al-Husayn replied, "I did not deceive your brother. Allah guided him and cursed you into aberration." Ali said, "May Allah kill me if I don't kill you." He attacked Al-Husayn, but Nafi' Bin Hilal Al-Jamali intercepted him with a spear and threw him onto the ground. Ali's comrades rescued him and carried him away. He was treated and later recovered from his injury.[41]

NAFI' AL-JAMALI

Nafi' Bin Hilal Al-Jamali had poisoned his arrows and carved his name on them.[42] While firing his arrows, Nafi' chanted, "I launch them poisoned and marked. They are bound to fill the ground. The soul never benefits when it is terrified."[43] He killed twelve men, and wounded many. When his arrows ran out, he unsheathed his sword and fought. They surrounded him and stoned him until they broke his shoulders. Al-Shimr and his comrades captured Nafi', and dragged him to Bin Sa'ad.[44] The latter asked him, "Why did you do this to yourself?" Nafi' replied, "My Lord knows what I intended to do." Seeing the blood dripping all over Nafi's face and beard, a man asked him, "Can't you see what has happened to you?" Nafi' responded, "By Allah! I killed twelve men and wounded many, and I am not at all remorseful. Had both of my shoulders not been broken, you would never have captured me."⁴⁵ As Al-Shimr unsheathed his sword, Nafi' said, "Shimr! By Allah! Had you been a Muslim, you would have realized the enormity of returning to Allah with our blood on your hands. I thank Allah for ending our lives on the hands of His most evil creatures." Al-Shimr maliciously shoved Nafi' down and beheaded him.⁴⁶

WADHIH AND ASLAM

Wadhih, a Turkish servant of Al-Harath Al-Mithhaji, fought and received multiple wounds. He fell down and called Al-Husayn to rescue him. Al-Husayn came to him and hugged him. Wadhih said, "The son of Allah's Messenger put his cheek on mine. This is the ultimate honor." Wadhih died right after.⁴⁷ Similarly, Al-Husayn walked over and hugged his servant, Aslam. Still breathing, Aslam felt honored, and smiled in gratitude before he died.⁴⁸

BURAYR BIN KHUDAYR

Yazeed Bin Mi'qal yelled, "Burayr! How do you feel, about what Allah has done to you?" Burayr answered, "Allah had blessed me with goodness, and cursed you into aberration." Yazeed responded, "You are lying, and you haven't lied before. Do you remember the day we walked in Bani Luwathan's neighborhood? You told me there that Mu'awiya was a transgressor, and Ali Bin Abi Talib was the leader to guidance." Burayr said, "I do remember, and that is my belief still." Yazeed said, "I testify that you have gone astray." Burayr proposed that both men supplicate, asking Allah to curse and destroy the liar. They supplicated for a while and then fought. Burayr struck Yazeed on the head, splitting his skull open, and exposing his brain. Yazeed fell with Burayr's sword still stuck in his head. As Burayr tried to retrieve his sword, Radhiyy Bin Munqith Al-Abdi ambushed him, and grabbed him by the neck. The two men wrestled until Burayr pinned Radhiyy to the ground, and firmly held his chest. Radhiyy called on his comrades to help him. As Ka'ab Bin Jaber Bin Amr Al-Azdi took off to attack Burayr, his friend and comrade, Afeef Bin Zuhayr Bin Abi Al-Akhnas, screamed at him, "This is Burayr, who taught us the Qur'an in the great mosque of Kufa!" Ka'ab ignored

Afeef, and stabbed Burayr in the back. Burayr fell on Radhiyy, and bit off part of his nose. Ka'ab used his spear to push Burayr off of Radhiyy, and then struck Burayr with the sword and killed him. Radhiyy Al-Abdi stood up, dusted his clothes, and told Ka'ab, "I shall never forget the favor that you have done for me."

When Ka'ab returned home, his wife, Al-Nawwar, expressed her disappointment with him. She told him, "You fought against Fatima's son and killed Burayr, the best teacher of Qur'an. You have done an awful thing. By Allah! I shall never talk to you again." Responding to his wife's remarks, Ka'ab said, "I obeyed the governor, Obeydallah and saved Radhiyy's life." Radhiyy heard Ka'ab's words and said, "I wish I had never lived through the curse and shame of fighting against Al-Husayn."[49]

HANTHALA AL-SHABAMI

Hanthala Bin Sa'ad Al-Shabami called, *"People! I fear for you a doomsday similar to that of the parties; a wrath similar to that falling on the people of Nuh, A'ad, Thamud and their successors, for Allah never oppresses his creatures. I fear for you from the Day of the Great Call, in which you try to run away, but nothing can protect you from Allah. There will be no guide for those who are deprived of Allah's guidance. (40:30-33)* People! Do not murder Al-Husayn! If you do, Allah shall definitely chastise you. Transgressors are bound to reap great disappointment."

Commending Hanthala's efforts, Al-Husayn said, "May Allah include you in His Mercy! They have invoked a wrath upon themselves when they rejected your advice, and rose up to murder you after they already murdered your pious comrades." Hanthala said, "Son of Allah's Messenger! You are indeed truthful. Shall we depart to the next life?" Al-Husayn gave him permission to fight. Hanthala fought until he was martyred.[50]

A'ABISS

Shawthab was a faithful man. His house was a congregational place in which the followers of the infallible leaders remembered and praised the Prophet's household. A'abiss walked towards Shawthab, and asked him, "What do you intend to do?" Shawthab answered, "I shall fight alongside with you until I am killed." A'abiss commended Shawthab, and told him, "Go ahead before Al-Husayn, so he would account for you along with other martyrs. This is the day in which we should exhaust all efforts to attain the rewards." Shawthab greeted Al-Husayn, and then fought until he was martyred.

After Shawthab's martyrdom, A'abiss stood in front of Al-Husayn and said, "You are the dearest to my heart on the face of the earth. Had I been able to protect you with anything more than my life, I would have done so. Peace be upon you! I testify that you are my guide and so was your father." Known to be one of the bravest men, A'abiss marched towards the enemies, and yelled, "Is there a man to fight?" No one dared to confront him. Omar Bin Sa'ad screamed, "Stone him." A'abiss immediately took off his vest, threw his shield down, and attacked them. He chased away more than two hundred men. They finally surrounded him and killed him. Hoping to collect a hefty reward, many of his enemies fought over his head. Bin Sa'ad divided the reward amongst them, and said, "None of you can claim the exclusive credit of killing him."[51]

JOHN

John, Abu Tharr's servant, stood in front of Al-Husayn, and asked his permission to fight. The Prophet's grandson said, "John! You came to us to earn a living. You are free to leave." John immediately fell on Al-Husayn's feet, kissed them and said, "How could I eat your meals in peace and desert you in hardship? I'm a humble servant from Africa, and I know nothing about my ancestors. Please allow the breeze of paradise to beautify my scent; honor me with a sense of belonging to a heavenly lineage. By Allah! I shall never leave you. Instead, I shall fight until my blood gets mixed with yours." Al-Husayn gave him permission to fight.[52] John killed twenty-five men before he was martyred. Al-Husayn stood next to his body, and supplicated, "Oh Allah! Honor him, beautify his scent, adjoin him to Mohammed, and bless him with the company of Mohammed's household." People, passing by the spot where John was martyred, could smell a scent more beautiful than musk.[53]

Anass Al-Kahili

Anass Bin Al-Harith Bin Nabeeh Al-Kahili was an old man at the time. He had been honored with the Prophet's companionship (Sahabiyy). He saw and heard Prophet Mohammed, and fought the battles of Badr and Hunayn under his leadership. After he acquired Al-Husayn's permission to fight, Anass wrapped his turban on his waist to straighten his back, and held his eyebrows up under his headband. Al-Husayn looked at him and wept. He then told Anass, "Sheykh (old man)! I ask Allah to reward your efforts." Despite his old age, Anass killed eighteen men before he was martyred.[54]

Amr Bin Janada

Amr Bin Janada Al-Ansari was only eleven years old. Shortly after his father was martyred, he asked Al-Husayn to allow him to fight. Refusing to send this boy to battle, Al-Husayn justified, "This is a boy whose father has been martyred during the first attack. His mother would probably hate to lose her son." The boy replied, "My mother ordered me to fight." Al-Husayn allowed him. Soon after his departure, the boy's head was thrown to the camp. His mother wiped the blood off of it, and fatally struck an enemy with it from close range.[55] She then grabbed a pole or a sword, and attacked the enemies. On her way to the battlefield, she chanted, "I am an old woman. I am weak and helpless. I shall exhaust all of my strength to defend the children of the honorable Fatima." Al-Husayn sent her back to her tent after she wounded two men.[56]

Al-Hajjaj Al-Ja'afi

Al-Hajjaj Bin Masrouq Al-Ja'afi stormed onto the battlefield and fought for a while. Drenched with his own blood, he returned to the camp, stood before Al-Husayn, and said, "Today I shall see your grandfather, the Prophet, and your honorable father, Ali, the man we know as the rightful successor." Al-Husayn replied, "I shall also see them soon after you." Al-Hajjaj returned to the battlefield and fought until he was martyred.[57]

SIWAR

Siwar Bin Abu Himyar, a descendant of Fahm Bin Jabir Bin Abdullah Bin Qadim Al-Fahmi Al-Hamadani, fought fiercely. Badly wounded, Siwar fought until he was captured.[58] Bin Sa'ad ordered his execution, but his tribe successfully interceded for him. He lived for six months before he finally succumbed to his wounds.[59] A portion of the visitation ritual of the Holy site (Ziyara) mentions Siwar's fate. The visitation rituals read, "Greetings to the wounded captive, Siwar Bin Abi Himyar Al-Fahmi Al-Hamadani, and to the badly wounded Omar Bin Abdullah Al-Janda'ie."

SUWAYD

Weakened by his wounds, Suwayd Bin Amr Bin Abu Mutaa' fell to the ground and was presumed dead. When he heard the crowd screaming that Al-Husayn was martyred, he attacked the enemies and fought until he was martyred. He was the last of Al-Husayn's companions to be martyred.

Notes & References

---

1. Al-Khitat Al-Miqreeziyya (V.2, P.287)
2. Maqtal Al-Awalim (P.84)
3. Al-Luhuf (P.56)
4. Tareekh Al-Tabari (V.6, P.245); Al-Kamel (V.4, P.37)
5. Al-Kamel (V.4, P.29)
6. Tareekh Al-Tabari (V.6, P.255)
7. Al-Luhuf (P.57)
8. Al-Hada'iq -Wardiyya
9. Tareekh Al-Tabari (V.6, P.249)
10. Al-Kamel (V.4, P.27)
11. Al-Bidaya (V.8, P.182)
12. Tareekh Al-Tabari (V.6, P.249)
13. Manaqib Bin Shahr Ashoub (V.2, P.217)
14. Maqtal Al-Khawarizmi (V.2, P.13)
15. Tareekh Al-Tabari (V.6, P.251)
16. Tathallum Al-Zahra' (P.113)
17. Tareekh Al-Tabari (V.6, P.251)

18. Tareekh Al-Tabari (V.6, P.251)
19. A'laam Al-Wara (P.145); Al-Kamel (V.4, P.28)
20. Al-Kamel (V.4, P.28); Maqtal Al-Khawarizmi (V.2, P.16)
21. Tareekh Al-Tabari (V.6, P.255)
22. Amali Al-Sadouq (P.97)
23. Maqtal Al-Khawarizmi (V.2, P.17)
24. Tareekh Al-Tabari (V.6, P.251); Al-Kamel (V.4, P.29)
25. Tareekh Al-Tabari (V.6, P.252); Al-Bidaya (V.8, P.183)
26. Tareekh Al-Tabari (V.6, P.248 & 250)
27. Manaqib Bin Shahr Ashoub (V.2, P.217)
28. Tathallum Al-Zahra' (P.118); Al-Bihar (V.10, P.117)
29. Rawdhat Al-Wa'itheen (P.160); Amali Al-Sadouq (P.97)
30. Maqtal Al-Awalim (P.88); Maqtal Al-Khawarizmi (V.2, P.17)
31. Mutheer Al-Ahzaan (P.44)
32. Maqtal Al-Awalim (P.88)
33. Thakheerat Al-Darayn (P.178)
34. Al-Luhuf (P.62)
35. Asraar Al-Shahada (P.175)
36. Mutheer Al-Ahzaan (P.34)
37. Tareekh Al-Tabari (V.6, P.255)
38. Maqtal Al-Awalim (P.85); Maqtal Al-Khawarizmi (V.2, P.25)
39. Tareekh Al-Tabari (V.6, P.253); Maqtal Al-Khawarizmi (V.2, P.20)
40. Maqtal Al-Awalim (P.88)
41. Al-Kamel (V.4, P.27)
42. Tareekh Al-Tabari (V.6, P.252); Al-Kamel (V.4, P.29); Al-Bidaya (V.8, P.184)
43. Maqtal Al-Awalim (P.90)
44. Maqtal Al-Khawarizmi (V.2, P.21)
45. Tareekh Al-Tabari (V.6, P.253)
46. Tareekh Al-Tabari (V.6, P.253); Al-Bidaya (V.8, P.184)
47. Maqtal Al-Awalim (P.91); Ibsaar Al-A'yn (P.85)
48. Thakheerat Al-Darayn (P.366)
49. Tareekh Al-Tabari (V.6, P.248)
50. Tareekh Al-Tabari (V.6, P.254)
51. Tareekh Al-Tabari (V.6, P.254)
52. Mutheer Al-Ahzaan (P.33)
53. Maqtal Al-Awalim (P.88)
54. Thakheerat Al-Darayn (P.208)
55. Manaqib Bin Shahr Ashoub (V.3, P.219); Maqtal Al-Khawarizmi (V.2, P.22)
56. Al-Bihar (V.10, P.198); Maqtal Al-Khawarizmi (V.2, P.22)
57. Al-Bihar (V.10, P.198)
58. Al-Ikleel (V.10, P.103)
59. Al-Hada'iq Al-Wardiyya

The Martyrdom of the Prophet's Household

Ali Al-Akbar

At this point, all of Al-Husayn's companions were martyred. The only soldiers left in his camp were the men of his family. The men of Prophet's household were determined to put up a fierce resistance, and bravely embrace death. They began bidding farewell to one another.[1] Ali Al-Akbar was the first man from Al-Husayn's family to venture out into battle. Al-Akbar was born on the eleventh of Sha'aban 33 A.H. (654 C.E). He was only twenty-seven years of age. He, in addition to his eloquence, was an identical reflection of the Prophet's physical beauty and impeccable moral character. Describing Ali Al-Akbar, a contemporary poet said, "His beauty is unrivaled. He favors nothing in life over his faith. He never abandons righteousness in favor of any wrongdoing. He is the son of Layla, whose forefathers were also honorable."[2] Ali Al-Akbar was a marvelous branch of the Mohammedan tree. He was a medium of bliss and fit to be an infallible leader. Nonetheless, the position of leadership is Divinely ordained, and the names of the incumbents were delivered by Jabra'eel to Allah's Messenger on a heavenly tablet.

It was extremely difficult for the women of the Prophet's household to eyewitness Al-Akbar's departure because his presence assured them security and protection. Besides Al-Husayn, he was the brightest hope in life for his aunts and sisters. His imminent departure meant that the reflection of the Prophet's character was about to be lost. The women in Al-Husayn's camp felt as if the voice of the revelation was receding, and the radiant sun of Prophethood was about to be eclipsed. They hung onto his clothes, and begged him to stay. They told him, "Think of our plight! We cannot withstand being separated from you" Certain that the vicious enemies were determined to spill his father's blood, Ali Al-Akbar was undetermined by the women's plea. He rode Lahiq, Al-Husayn's horse, and asked his father's permission to fight.

Layla, Ali Al-Akbar's mother, was the daughter of Maymouna, who in turn was Abu Sufyan's daughter.[3] An enemy yelled, "Ali! You are related to the commander of the faithful, Yazeed, and we respect this kinship. We can grant you safety if you like." He replied, "My kinship to the Prophet is more worthy of being respected."[4] Ali Al-Akbar introduced his honorable lineage, defined his sacred cause, and simultaneously attacked the enemies. As he charged towards the enemies, he chanted, "I am Ali, the son of Al-Husayn, who is the son of Ali. By the Lord of the Ka'aba! We are the Prophet's closest kin. By Allah! A vile man's son shall never govern us. I shall heavily strike you with my sword and defend my father. I am a descendant of Hashim from Quraysh."[5]

Al-Husayn couldn't help but shed his tears.[6] He screamed at Omar Bin Sa'ad, "What is it with you? I ask Allah to obliterate you for ignoring my kinship to Allah's Messenger, and for killing my family. I ask Allah to enable someone to slaughter you on your bed." Al-Husayn then lifted his Holy beard towards the sky and said, "Oh Allah! Be my witness against these people! The man who just attacked them is the identical reflection of Your Messenger's physical features, moral character and eloquence. We looked at him whenever we missed seeing Your Prophet. Oh Allah! Prevent them the bounties of the earth, divide them, destroy them, erupt feudalism amongst them and never allow the rulers to be pleased with them. They invited us promising their support, but instead waged war on us." Al-Husayn then recited, *"Allah selected Adam, Nuh, the family of Ibraheem and the family of Imran over all people. Descendants who are inter related to one another and Allah is the All Hearing; All Knowing (3:33, 34)."*[7]

Ali Al-Akbar attacked the right and left flanks of Bin Sa'ad's army. He then penetrated into the middle, forcing his enemies to retreat. He killed a total of one hundred and twenty men. Extremely thirsty and exhausted, he rode back to the camp to rest. Ali Al-Akbar mentioned his unbearable thirst to his father.[8] Al-Husayn wept, and said, "You shall see your grandfather soon. He shall feed you a drink from his cup and you shall never be thirsty again." Al-Husayn poured some of his saliva into his son's mouth, and also gave Ali Al-Akbar a ring to suck on.[9]

Having heard the glad tidings of seeing his grandfather, Prophet Mohammed, Al-Akbar cheerfully returned to the battlefield. He, with the same tenacity and determination, attacked his enemies again, injecting havoc and fear in their ranks. The Kufans were totally stunned by Ali Akbar's bravery. His fearlessness and strength, in destroying all that stood in his way, echoed the memorable images of Ali Bin Abi Talib, The Lion of Battlefields. Ali Al-Akbar's sword glittered like thunder, raising the number of its fatal strikes to two hundred.[10] Murra Bin Munqith Al-Abdi said, "By the honor of my Arab ancestors! I shall kill him and devastate his father."[11] He charged his horse, stabbed Al-Akbar in the back with a spear and struck him on the head with a sword. Murra then drove Al-Akbar's horse to Bin Sa'ad's camp where the criminals surrounded Ali Al-Akbar, and chopped him with their swords into pieces.

Ali Al-Akbar yelled, "Abu Abdullah! I greet you with peace! My grandfather had just fed me a sip from his cup. I shall never be thirsty again. He also said that there is a special cup reserved for you."[12] Al-Husayn rushed to the site and leaned over his son. He put his cheek on his son's, and said, "Life is worthless without you. They are so daring in disobeying the Omnipotent, and in violating the sanctity of His Messenger.[13] It is so painful to your father and grandfather that they cannot answer you when you call them, or help you when you ask them."[14] Al-Husayn scooped up Ali's Holy blood, and threw it upwards. None of it fell back to the ground. This, fact is attested to in the visitation ritual (Ziyara) of Al-Akbar. It reads, "May my mother and father be sacrificed for You for being slaughtered without having committed any crime. May my mother and father be sacrificed for You, as your blood rose to Allah's most beloved creature (Mohammed). May my mother and father be sacrificed for You, for being sacrificed in front of your father, who wept over you with a broken heart. His heart ached over You and He raised Your blood with His hands to the heavens and not a single drop from Your blood returned to the earth. Your Father's sorrow over You did not stop after He bid farewell to You"[15]

Al-Husayn ordered his family members to carry Ali Al-Akbar. They lay him in front of the tent that faced the battleground.[16] Looking at the countless stabs and wounds in Ali's bloody and chopped body, the women of the Prophet's household ran towards him weeping and beating their chests. The echo of their loud cries resonated throughout the heavens. The dignified woman of Bani Hashim, Zaynab Bint Fatima Bint Mohammed, led the Hashimite women in mourning Ali Al-Akbar. She fell on him, hugged him, and wept.[17] Ali's presence was an assurance of her safety. He was very protective of her sanctity. His permanent departure sounded the alarm of the oncoming devastation.

Abdullah Bin Muslim

Abdullah Bin Muslim Bin Aqeel Bin Abu Talib, the son of Ruqayya Bint Ali Bin Abu Talib, set out to battle after the martyrdom of Ali Al-Akbar. As he marched towards the enemies, he chanted, "Today I shall see Muslim, my father. Today I shall see the devout believers who died on the Prophet's path." He raided the enemies three times, killing many of them.[18] Yazeed Bin Al-Raqqad Al-Juhani shot him with an arrow. Abdullah tried to intercept it with his hand, but the arrow pierced it, and landed deep into his forehead. Unable to remove the arrow from his head, Abdullah said, "Oh Allah! They betrayed and abused us. Kill them as they killed us."[19] Meanwhile, a man attacked him and stabbed him with a spear in his heart. Abdullah died immediately.[20] Yazeed Bin Al-Raqqad Al-Juhani tried to retrieve his arrow from Abdullah's forehead. He pulled out the wooden shaft, but the metal blade remained in Abdullah's head.[21]

The Raid of Abu Talib's Family

When Abdullah Bin Muslim was martyred, men from Abu Talib's family formed a group, and attacked the enemies. As they set out to fight, Al-Husayn told them, "Cousins! Persevere as you embrace death. You shall never experience a hardship after today."[22] Awn Bin Abdullah Bin Ja'afar al Tayyar, Zaynab's son, his paternal brother Mohammed, Abdurrahman Bin Aqeel, his brother Ja'afar Bin Aqeel and Mohammed Bin Muslim Bin Aqeel, were all martyred. In addition to receiving eighteen, wounds, Al-Hasan Al-Mathna, Imam Al-Hasan's son, lost his right hand in the battle, but was not martyred. Soon after the members of Abu Talib's family were martyred, Abu Bakr, whose real name was Mohammed, the son of the Commander of the Faithful, fought until Zahr Bin Badr Al-Nakh'ie killed him.[23] After Abu Bakr's martyrdom, Abdullah Bin Aqeel stormed onto the battlefield and fought fiercely. He, weakened by multiple wounds, fell down onto the ground. Othman Bin Khalid Al-Tameemi attacked him and killed him.

AL-QASSIM AND HIS BROTHER

Ramlah's son, Abdullah Al-Akbar, also known as Abu Bakr Bin Al-Hasan Bin Ali Bin Abi Talib, fought until he was martyred.[24] His brother Al-Qassim, a young boy who had not reached puberty, ventured out to the battlefield after his brother's martyrdom. Al-Husayn hugged Al-Qassim, and wept. He then gave him permission to fight. Al-Qassim, wearing a buttoned shirt and sandals, wielded his sword and marched towards the enemies. His face radiated like a full moon on a dark night.[25] While fighting, his left sandal slipped off of his foot.[26] Al-Qassim's pride compelled him to disengage while barefoot. The Prophet's great grandson ignored thousands, and fearlessly leaned over to fix his sandal.[27] It is fair to speculate that Al-Qassim might have felt that his sandal was more worthy of his attention than his vicious enemies. Amr Bin Sa'ad Bin Nafeel Al-Azdi charged his horse towards Al-Qassim. Hameed Bin Muslim intercepted Amr and said, "What do you want from this young boy? The men who surrounded him are more than enough." Amr replied, "By Allah! I shall attack him." Amr struck Al-Qassim's head with the sword. The boy fell down and yelled, "My uncle!" Witnessing the cruelty of his merciless enemies, Al-Husayn became enraged. He attacked Bin Sa'ad's army, and struck Amr with the sword. The latter maneuvered to avoid the strike, but Al-Husayn's sword sliced off his arm at the elbow. Amr screamed so loud. His comrades rushed to rescue him, but instead stampeded him to death with their horses.

The dust settled on Al-Husayn hovering over his nephew. Al-Qassim restlessly stomped his feet on the ground. Al-Husayn leaned closer to him, and said, "Damned are your murderers! Your grandfather shall prosecute them on the Day of Judgement." He then said, "It hurts your uncle that when you call him, he doesn't answer you, and that when he does, he can't do much for you. By Allah! We have a large number of enemies, but very few supporters."

Al-Husayn rested his nephew's chest on his and carried him. Al-Qassim's feet dragged on the ground all the way back to the camp. Al-Husayn lay him next to Ali Al-Akbar, and the other martyrs from his family.[28] He then gazed into the sky, and said, "Oh Allah! Account for each one of them (the enemies), prosecute them, and never forgive any of them. My cousins! Persevere. My family members! Persevere. You shall never see a hardship after this day."[29]

AL-ABBASS' BROTHERS

Al-Abbass had three full brothers, Abdullah, Othman and Ja'afar. Seeing casualties in the family rising, Al-Abbass looked at his brothers, and said, "My mother's sons! Fight the enemies and prove your loyalty to Allah and His Messenger." He looked at Abdullah, the oldest of the three, and said, "Brother! Fight, so I can account for you as a martyr."[30] The three fought bravely before their brother's watchful eyes until they were martyred.

AL-ABBASS' MARTYRDOM

At this point, the siege around Al-Husayn's camp was extremely tight. Al-Abbass watched the women wail, and the children constantly cry and moan from thirst around the bereaved infallible leader. Al-Abbass could no longer tolerate the situation, nor could he be patient with the cruel enemies who murdered his comrades and family members. He asked his brother's permission to fight. Al-Abbass was the most valuable asset to Al-Husayn's army for two reasons. First, the enemies feared him and deliberately avoided fighting him. Second, his presence was an assurance of security for the women. The Prophet's daughters felt safe as long as his war banner (Liwa' Al-Hamd) flapped above them. These two reasons contributed to Al-Husayn's reluctance to grant his brother permission to fight. Responding to Al-Abbass' request, Al-Husayn tenderly said, "Brother! You are the carrier of my banner!"[31] Al-Abbass explained, "I cannot withstand these hypocrites any longer! I would like to fight them and avenge." Al-Husayn ordered his brother to bring some water for the children.

Al-Abbas marched toward the enemies. He advised them, and warned them against the wrath of the All-Powerful, but to no avail.

He then called out loud, "You, Omar Bin Sa'ad! This is Al-Husayn, the grandson of Allah's Messenger. You have killed his companions and the men in his family. His women and children are thirsty. Give them some water. They are extremely thirsty. Al-Husayn has been asking you to let him migrate from Al-Hijaz and Iraq to Byzantium or India."

Al-Abbass' words touched the hearts of his adversaries, such that some of them wept. However, Al-Shimr loudly interjected, "You, Abu Turab's son! Had we been in control of all of the water on earth, we still wouldn't give you a drop of it until all of you pledge allegiance to Yazeed."

Al-Abbass returned to the camp and informed Al-Husayn of the enemies' response. As the wailing of women and the screaming of the thirsty children rang in his ears, Al-Abbass carried empty jugs, and rode his horse towards the Euphrates.[32] In an attempt to block his path, four thousand archers surrounded him and rained their arrows on him. Unabated by their numbers, Al-Abbass attacked them, and penetrated through their lines with the banner flapping over his head. Al-Abbass was a role model of bravery and protectiveness. He was inculcated with impeccable moral values and incredible bravery from his father, Ali Bin Abu Talib, the Lion of Battlefields. Al-Abbass' astounding strength astonished his enemies. He, with incredible serenity, chased them away clearing his path into the Euphrates.

Al-Abbass scooped some water to drink. As he was about to sip, he remembered the severe thirst of Al-Husayn and his family members. Abu Al-Fadhl threw the water down[33] and said, "My soul! You have no life without Al-Husayn, and without him you shall never be. My soul! How could you enjoy a cold drink, while Al-Husayn is in grave danger? By Allah! Such an act contradicts faithfulness."[34] He filled up the jug and rode back toward the camp. The enemies blocked his path again. He attacked and killed many of them. As he fought, Abu Al-Fadhl chanted, "Death never scares me when it hovers, and it never deters me from using my sword against others. My soul is dedicated to protect the prophet's grandson. I, Al-Abbass, am carrying the water. I am never fearful in combat." He eventually broke through the enemy lines, and cleared his way back to the camp.

Zayd Bin Al-Raqqad Al-Juhani and Hakeem Bin Al-Tufayl

Al-Sunbussi had hidden behind palm trees. Zayd ambushed Al-Abbass and cut off his right arm. Al-Abbass said, "By Allah! Even if you cut my right arm, I shall always defend my faith. I shall defend the truthful infallible leader, who is the son of the pure and trustworthy Prophet." Al-Abbass paid little attention to losing his right arm, because his main concern was to deliver the water to the women and children in Al-Husayn's camp. Hakeem Bin Al-Tufayl ambushed Al-Abbass, and cut off his left arm.[35] Instantly after, a large number of enemies attacked, and arrows fell on him like rain. An arrow poked the jug, spilling the water in it, while another landed in his chest.[36] Immediately after, a man struck Al-Abbass with a pole on the head, breaking his skull open.

Al-Abbass fell onto the ground and yelled, "Abu Abdullah! I greet you with peace!" Al-Husayn immediately walked over to tend to his brother.[37] One can only imagine how intense this reunion was. One can also ponder whether Al-Husayn rushed in the hope of rescuing Al-Abbass, or whether the supernatural bond of love between the two compelled Al-Husayn to witness the permanent departure of his brother! In Al-Husayn's mind and heart, losing Al-Abbass equaled total devastation. Al-Husayn rushed over, but only to see his brother's Holy and bloody body on the hot sands, completely covered with arrows. Al-Abbass lay speechless and sightless as his brain slowly seeped out of his skull onto the ground. The scene of this reunion was incredibly touching. Al-Husayn was visibly heartbroken and grief-stricken. This tremendous loss took its toll Abu Abdullah's physical strength. Losing Al-Abbass rendered Al-Husayn lonely against his enemies. Expressing his intense bereavement, Al-Husayn said, "I feel like my backbone has been broken. I have become truly helpless."[38]

Al-Husayn deliberately left Al-Abbass in that spot, for a reason that time later revealed. Unlike the other martyrs, Al-Abbass was buried alone. Al-Abbass' burial site has become a shrine to which people flock to visit and supplicate. His shrine has become a blessed medium of Divine miracles, and a congregational place for those who seek proximity to their Lord. The Community has thus become well aware of the high rank and honor with which Allah blessed Al-Abbass. Moreover, the believers have also realized that loving and visiting Al-Abbass are but two powerful means of seeking proximity to Allah, the Exalted. Abu Abdullah, the infallible leader at the time, foresaw the positive physical and spiritual impact of Al-Abbass on the Community. In accordance with the will of the Omnipotent, Al-Husayn left him where he died, so the masses would learn about, and witness, Abu Al-Fadhl's significance in this life and in the next.

Bereaved and heartbroken, Al-Husayn wiped his tears with his sleeve, and returned to his camp. He saw the enemies attacking his camp, so he loudly called, "Is there anyone who can rescue us? Is there anyone who can shelter us? Is there a righteous person who can support us? Is there anyone who can defend us, and spare himself hellfire?"[39] Sukayna walked towards her father, and asked about her uncle. Al-Husayn informed her of his martyrdom. Zaynab overheard Al-Husayn, and immediately screamed, "I mourn for my brother! I mourn for my Abbass! We are in total loss after you!" The rest of the rest of the women wailed. Al-Husayn heavily wept and said, "We are in total loss after you."

Notes & References

1. Maqtal Al-Khawarizmi (V.2, P.26)
2. Maqatil Al-Talibiyyeen (P.32)
3. Al-Issaba (V.4, P.178)
4. Nassab Quraysh (P.57)
5. Al-Irshaad
6. Mutheer Al-Ahzaan (P.35); Al-Irshaad
7. Maqtal Al-Khawarizmi (V.2, P.30)
8. Maqatil Al-Talibiyyeen (P.47); Maqtal Al-Awalim (P.96); Rawdhat Al-Wa'itheen (P.161); Mutheer Al-Ahzaan (P.35); Al-Luhuf (P.64)
9. Maqtal Al-Khawarizmi (V.2, P.31); Maqtal Al-Awalim (P.95)
10. Maqtal Al-Khawarizmi (V.2, P.31)
11. Tareekh Al-Tabari (V.6, P.256); Al-Irshaad
12. Maqtal Al-Khawarizmi (V.2, P.31); Maqtal Al-Awalim (P.95)
13. Tareekh Al-Tabari (V.6, P.265)
14. Maqtal Al-Awalim (P.95)
15. Kamel Al-Ziyarat (P.239)
16. Tareekh Al-Tabari (V.6, P.256); Al-Irshaad; Maqtal Al-Khawarizmi (V.2, P.31)
17. Tareekh Al-Tabari (V'.6, P.256); Maqtal Al-Khawarizmi (V.2, P.31
18. Manaqib Bin Shahr Ashoub (V.2, P.220)
19. Maqatil Al-Talibiyyeen(P.27)

20. Al-Irshaad
21. Tareekh Al-Tabari (V.6, P.179)
22. Tareekh Al-Tabari (V.6, P.256); Maqtal Al-Khawarizmi (V.2, P.78); Al-Luhuf (P.64)
23. Al-Irshaad
24. Tareekh Al-Tabari (V.6, P.269); Maqatil Al-Talibiyyeen(P.34)
25. Tareekh Al-Tabari (V.6, P.256); Maqtal Al-Khawarizmi (V.2, P.27); Al-Irshaad; A'laam Al-Wara (P.146)
26. Tareekh Al-Tabari (V.6, P.256); Maqtal Al-Khawarizmi (V.2, P.27)
27. Thakheerat Al-Darayn (P.152); Ibsaar Al-Ayn (P.37)
28. Tareekh Al-Tabari (V.6, P.257); Al-Bidaya (V.8, P.186); Al-Irshaad
29. Maqtal Al-Khawarizmi (V.2, P.28)
30. Maqatil Al-Talibiyyeen (P.32 & 33)
31. Al-Bihar (V.10, P.251); Maqtal Al-Awalim (P.94)
32. Tathallum Al-Zahra' (P.118)
33. Al-Muntakhab (P.311); Al-Bihar (V.10, P.201)
34. Riyadh Al-Massa'ib (P.311)
35. Manaqib Bin Shahr Ashoub (V.1, P.221)
36. Riyadh Al-Massa'ib (P.315)
37. Al-Muntakhab (P.312); Riyadh Al-Massa'ib (P.315)
38. Al-Bihar (V.10, P.251); Tathallum Al-Zahra' (P.120)
39. Al-Muntakhab (P.312)

The Master of Martyrs in the Battlefield

Al-Abbass was the last active soldier in Al-Husayn's army. After his brother's martyrdom, Al-Husayn was alone against the enemies. Al-Husayn stared at the bloody corpses of his companions and family members, while the moaning and weeping of his women and children constantly rang in his ears. The Prophet's grandson screamed, "Is there anyone who can defend the daughters of Allah's messenger? Is there a monotheist who, out of fearing Allah, would support us? Is there anyone who, seeking Allah's mercy, can rush to rescue us?" Women in the camp wept loudly.[1] Extremely ill, Al-Sajjad dragged his sword and leaned on a cane to stand up. Al-Husayn emphatically told Umm Kulthoum, "Stop him, or Mohammed's descendants will vanish from the face of the earth." She escorted Al-Sajjad back to his mattress.[2]

Al-Husayn asked his children and the women to calm down to bid them farewell. He wore a glittery dark shirt, and a turban with two ends dangling over his shoulders. He also wore the cloak of Allah's Messenger on his shoulders, and wielded the Prophet's sword.[3] He requested unattractive underclothes, because he was certain that he would be robbed after his martyrdom. They offered him an overall, but he rejected it, because it was the dress code of slaves.[4] He finally selected a decent garment, tore it, and wore it under his clothes.[5] He then tore some trousers and wore them. Certain that his clothes would be robbed, Al-Husayn amicably planned to protect his body from exposure.[6]

The Nursing Infant

Al-Husayn requested to bid his nursing infant farewell. Zaynab handed him Al-Rabaab's son, Abdullah. Al-Husayn rested the infant on his lap, kissed him numerously[7] and said, "These people are condemned. Your grandfather, Al-Mustafa shall definitely prosecute them."[8] He then carried him, walked towards the enemies and asked them for some water to quench the infant's thirst. Harmala Bin Kahil Al-Assadi pierced the infant's neck with an arrow, slaughtering him on his father's arms. Al-Husayn scooped the blood with his hand, and threw it towards the sky. Imam Abu Ja'afar Al-Baqir said, "Not a drop of it fell back down."[9] In Ziyarat Al-Nahiya Al-Muqadassa, the twelfth Imam, may Allah hasten his return, said, "May peace be upon the nursing infant, Abdullah, who was savagely slaughtered on his father's lap and, whose blood ascended to heaven. I ask Allah to curse the murderer, Harmala Bin Kahil Al-Assadi, and his comrades."

Al-Husayn said, "Knowing that Allah is watchful eases my suffering.[10] Oh Allah! Consider him no less significant than the baby of Salih's she-camel. My Lord! Grant us the bountiful outcome in lieu of an empirical victory. Avenge us by destroying the oppressors.[11] Reward us in the next life for our suffering in this one.[12] My Lord! You are the Witness on these people, as they murdered the identical reflection (Ali Al-Akbar) of Your Messenger, Mohammed."[13] Al-Husayn heard a voice telling him, "Husayn! Let go of him. He has a wet nurse in paradise."[14] Al-Husayn stepped off of his horse, dug with his sword, buried the blood-covered infant, and performed the funeral prayer on him.[15] It is also narrated that he placed him next to the Holy bodies of his family members.[16]

With no any affinity to this life, Al-Husayn wielded his sword, and ostensibly marched towards Bin Sa'ad's army. He engaged his enemies, killing many of them in duels.[17] He then attacked the right flank, as he chanted, "Death is more tolerable than shame, and shame is more tolerable than hellfire."[18] He then attacked the left flank, as he chanted, "I am Al-Husayn, the son of Ali. I vowed never to surrender. I protect my father's family. I adhere to the Prophet's religion."[19] Abdullah Bin Ammar Bin Yaghouth narrated, "I have never seen a bereaved man who lost all of his boys, kin and companions, braver, stronger or more determined than him (Al-Husayn). Men ran away from him whenever he attacked. No one was able to stop him."[20] Omar Bin Sa'ad screamed at his soldiers, "This is the son of Ali Bin Abu Talib. This is the son of the bravest Arab. Attack him from all directions."

Four thousand arrows were immediately, and at once, fired

on Al-Husayn.[21] At the same time, Bin Sa'ad's troops formed a human barrier between Al-Husayn and his camp. The Prophet's grandson screamed at them, "You! The followers of Abu Sufyan's family! If you are faithless and not afraid of the Day of Resurrection, then be free in this life. Honor your cultural values, if you claim to be real Arabs." Al-Shimr asked, "You, the son of Fatima! What are you trying to say?" Al-Husayn replied, "I am fighting you! Women should never be harmed. Stop your thugs from attacking my women, for as long as I am alive." Al-Shimr replied, "We have granted you that."

The enemies attacked the extremely thirsty infallible leader, and fierce fighting ensued.[22] Amr Bin Al-Hajjaj, with his four thousand soldiers, had been in full control of the banks of the Euphrates. Al-Husayn attacked them, penetrated through their lines, and rode his horse into the rushing river. As the horse reached into the water to drink, Al-Husayn said, "You are thirsty and so am I. I cannot drink until you do." The horse immediately raised its head and stopped drinking, as if it understood Al-Husayn's words. Al-Husayn scooped some water with his hand, and as he was about to sip it, one of the criminals screamed, "How could you enjoy the water while your women are being abused?" Al-Husayn dropped the water before tasting any of it, and instantly rode back to his camp.[23]

THE SECOND FAREWELL

Al-Husayn bid a second farewell to his family. He instructed them to persevere and patiently deal with the disastrous outcome. Al-Husayn told them, "Be ready to embrace hardships. Be certain that Allah will protect, guard, and save you from these evil oppressors. Allah shall reward you with goodness and severely chastise your enemies. Allah shall compensate and bless you with enormous bounties for your suffering. Be doubtless of all this, and do not vent inappropriately."[24]

This was indeed one of the most difficult moments for the Master of Martyrs on that day. These moments were loaded with agony. The women of the Prophet's family realized that the pillar of their existence, the protector of their dignity and honor was set to depart, and never return. Al-Husayn's departure meant that the Prophet's daughters were bound to mourn their loved ones with no one around to console them. His absence meant that no man would be around to protect the Prophet's family from the cruel enemies. The thought of a permanent separation compelled the terrified women, the moaning boys and the screaming girls to huddle around Al-Husayn. The thirsty children requested water; the women hoped for a safe shelter. One can only imagine what Al-Husayn, the protective and the compassionate, thought and how he felt. One can only contemplate the emotional impact of these moments on Al-Husayn, as he foresaw the entrustment of the Allah's Messenger, the dignified and heart-broken women of the Prophet's family on the verge of insurmountable devastation, in the middle of the hot and dry desert.

The scene of the women, after Al-Husayn's martyrdom, was even more touching. They wept and moaned. They helplessly ran to avoid being robbed or beaten. No one was around to protect them. The infallible leader, Zayn Al-Abideen, was extremely ill, and physically too weak at the time to do anything.

During the difficult moments of the second farewell, the honorable Hashimite woman, Zaynab Al-Kubra, gazed at the women and children with pity. Zaynab anticipated witnessing a fracture in the knot of infallibility. She was certain that the extension of Prophethood, the projected radiance of guidance, was about to recede, and that the tree of faith was about to wit her. Al-Husayn once told his nephew, Al-Hasan Al-Mathna, that Sukayna was entirely absorbed in her devotion to Allah. On the day of Ashura Sukayna sat alone, weeping and moaning. Al-Husayn walked over, hovered over her and tried to console her.

Omar Bin Sa'ad told his soldiers, "You're doomed! Attack him while he's busy with his family. By Allah! He shall destroy the whole army once he's free." They attacked him and shot him with arrows, some of which landed in the camp, and poked into the clothes of some women. Completely terrified, the women screamed, and ran into the tent. They stared at Al-Husayn and anxiously waited for his reaction. Al-Husayn, like a roaring lion; fearlessly attacked the enemies. He killed everyone in his path while arrows still fell on him from all directions.

Al-Husayn rode back to the camp, and numerously uttered, "There is no power and strength except that of Allah, the Great."[25] He then asked for water. Al-Shimr said, "You shall never taste it until you go to hellfire." Another man said, "Can't you see the Euphrates full of snakes? You shall never drink from it. Instead, you shall die thirsty." Al-Husayn instantly supplicated, "Oh Allah! Make him die thirsty." Later in life, this man constantly requested water, but spat it soon after he sipped it. He did that until he died from dehydration.[26]

Abu Al-Hutouf Al-Ja'afi shot Al-Husayn with an arrow in the forehead. Abu Abdullah extracted it. With blood dripping all over his face, Al-Husayn supplicated, "Oh Allah! You see the harm that these transgressors are inflicting on me. Oh Allah! Account for each one of them, obliterate them, wipe them off of the face of the earth, and never forgive any of them." Al-Husayn then yelled, "You are an evil community. You are extremely disloyal to Mohammed for doing this to his family. You shall never hesitate murdering anyone after you murder me. By Allah! I hope that Allah blesses me with martyrdom, and avenges me when you least expect it." Al-Hossayn asked, "You, Fatima's son! How would He avenge you?" Al-Husayn replied, "He shall disrupt your lives with feudalism, causing you to murder one another. After that, His wrath will befall you all."[27]

Al-Husayn took a break to recuperate. A man threw a rock, which landed on Al-Husayn's forehead. Blood dripped all over his face. As Al-Husayn grabbed his cloak, to wipe the blood off of his eyes, another man shot him in the chest with a three-headed arrow. Al-Husayn said, "In the name of Allah, by Allah, and on the path of Allah's Messenger." He then raised his head, gazed into the sky and said, "My Lord! You know that they are killing a peerless man. You know that there is no prophet's grandson on the face of this earth besides me."

Al-Husayn pushed the arrow in, and pulled it out from his back. Blood gushed out like an open tap.[28] He put his hand under the wound until it filled with blood. He threw the blood upward and said, "Knowing that Allah is watchful eases my suffering." Not even a drop of that blood fell back to the ground.[29]

He filled his hand again from the same wound, and smeared the blood on his head, face and beard. He then said, "This is how I should be, drenched with my blood, until I return to Allah and see my grandfather, Allah's Messenger. I shall then complain to my grandfather about each one of these criminals."[30]

Heavy bleeding exhausted Al-Husayn. He sat on the ground

and slumped over, with his neck bent. Malik Bin Al-Nissr attacked him, cursed him, and struck his Holy head with the sword. Blood gushed out and soaked Al-Husayn's turban. He told Malik, "You shall never eat or drink with your right hand, and Allah shall herd you with the oppressors." Al-Husayn removed his turban, but left the cap on his head.[31]

Mohammed Bin Abu Sa'iid

Hani Bin Thabeet Al-Hadhrami narrated, "I was one of ten men watching Al-Husayn being killed. I saw a boy from Al-Husayn's family, wearing a garment and a shirt, and holding a pole of some tent with his hand. The boy turned left and right and seemed terrified. A man charged his horse towards the boy, and struck him on the head with the sword, killing him. The man bashfully walked away after his comrades slandered him for murdering a little boy." This boy was Mohammed Bin Abu Sa'iid Bin Aqeel Bin Abu Talib.[32] His mother watched him being murdered. She was completely distraught.[33]

Abdullah Bin Al-Hasan

No longer able to stand up, Al-Husayn sat on the ground. After a brief lull, the enemies surrounded him. Abdullah, Imam Al-Hasan's son, was eleven years old. He saw the enemies approaching his uncle and ran towards him. Zaynab tried to stop the boy, but he slipped away. He reached his uncle while Bahr Bin Ka'ab was swinging his sword to strike Al-Husayn. The boy screamed, "You evil man! How dare you hurt my uncle!" Ka'ab swung his sword towards Al-Husayn, but Abdullah Bin Al-Hasan blocked it and lost his arm. With his arm hanging by the skin, the boy screamed, "Oh my uncle!" He then fell on his uncle's lap. Al-Husayn hugged him and said, "Nephew! Persevere and count on reaping goodness and rewards for your incurred injuries. Allah shall surely reunite you with your righteous fathers." Al-Husayn raised his hands and supplicated, "Oh Allah! Shall they enjoy a brief period of time, divide them up, tear them apart with feudalism, and never allow the rulers to be kind to them. They invited us and pledged to support us, but instead betrayed and waged war on us."[34]

Harmala Bin Kahil shot the boy with an arrow, slaughtering him on his uncle's lap.[35] At this point, Al-Husayn lay still on the ground. Bin Sa'ad's soldiers could have easily killed the Prophet's grandson, but each tribe abhorred being the direct murderer. Each tribe relied on another to do it.[36] Al-Shimr screamed, "Why are you standing still? What are you waiting for? Our spears and arrows have badly wounded the man! Attack him."[37] Zar'aa Bin Shareek pounded Al-Husayn's left shoulder while Al-Hossayn Bin Numayr shot an arrow into his mouth.[38] Another man struck him on his upper shoulder. Sannan Bin Anass stabbed him in his collarbone and in his ribs and then shot an arrow into his neck.[39] After that, Salih Bin Wahab stabbed him in his side.[40]

Hilal Bin Nafi' narrated, "I was relatively close to Al-Husayn shortly before he died. By Allah! He was totally drenched with blood, but his face was more beautiful and radiant than anything I have ever seen. The beauty of his face distracted me from the thought of killing him. As bad as his condition was, he asked for water, but they still refused to give him any." A man told him, "You shall not taste any water. Instead, you shall drink the boiling water of hellfire." Al-Husayn replied, "Me in hellfire? In contrast, I shall reunite with my grandfather, Allah's Messenger, in his permanent residence. I shall be with him on a special seat, reserved for the truthful, under the blessings of The Able King. I shall complain to him about what you did to me." The merciless enemies became outraged after hearing his response.[41]

THE SUPPLICATION

As his condition deteriorated, Al-Husayn gazed into the sky, and supplicated, "Oh Allah! You are High in Your Position; Extremely Mighty; Strongly Able; Needless of creatures; Magnificent in Your Pride; Capable to implement what You will; Very Merciful; Truthful in Your Promises; Generous with bounties; Resourceful with goodness; Close when You're called; Omnipotent over Your creatures; Forgiving to those who repent; Able to do what You want; Capable of Reaching; Thankful when You're thanked; Attentive when you're remembered. In need, I supplicate to You. I desire Your proximity. I seek refuge in You from fear. I lament my plight to You. In weakness, I seek help from You. I rely on You to aid me. Oh Allah! Be the Judge between these people and us. They invited us but abandoned us. They then betrayed and killed us. We are the household of Your Prophet and the children of Mohammed, Your beloved Messenger, whom you entrusted with Your revelations and selected to deliver Your message. Help us out in this ordeal, and aid us out of it, for You are the Most Merciful.[42] Lord! I persevere on what You ordained. There is no God but You, the Helper of the needy.[43] I have no Lord except You, and I worship none but You. I persevere on Your verdict. You are the Help for the helpless, and the Eternal who never vanishes. You! Who accounts for every soul and its actions, be the Judge between them and me. You are the Supreme Judge."[44]

THE HORSE

Al-Husayn's horse rubbed its face on the Holy blood, and circled around the Prophet's grandson.[45] Omar Bin Sa'ad screamed, "Catch the horse! It is an offspring of the Prophet's horse." The horsemen encircled it. The horse kicked and stampeded quite many soldiers, killing forty men and ten horses. Bin Sa'ad screamed, "Let it go to see what it does." Once they stopped chasing it, the horse ran towards Al-Husayn. It sniffed the Holy blood, rubbed its forehead on it, and simultaneously neighed very loudly.[46] Imam Abu Ja'afar Al-Baqir narrated that the neighing of Al-Husayn's horse meant, "Oppressive indeed! Oppressive indeed is the community who killed its prophet's grandson." The neighing horse ran to the camp.[47] In his visit (Ziyarat Al-Nahiya Al-Muqadassa), the twelfth infallible leader said, "When the women saw the empty horse with the saddle twisted sideways on its back, they came out screaming; beating the cheeks of their exposed faces; wailing in grief. Completely devastated, they rushed towards Al-Husayn's body."

Zaynab, the Honorable, called, "Oh Mohammed! Oh my Father! Oh Ali! Oh Ja'afar! Oh Hamza! This is Husayn. He lay murdered on the open plains of Karbala."[48] She then yelled, "I wish the sky collapsed on earth![49] I wish that the mountains crumbled onto the plains."[50] She walked over to Al-Husayn, while Omar Bin Sa'ad and a group of soldiers were approaching her dying brother. She screamed, "Omar! How could you watch Abu Abdullah being murdered?" Omar turned his tearful face away from her.[51] She said, "Damn you! Is there a Muslim amongst you?" No one answered.[52] Bin Sa'ad screamed at his soldiers, "Get on with it and end his suffering!" Al-Shimr walked up to Al-Husayn, and kicked him. He then stepped on his chest, grabbed his Holy beard and struck him with the sword twelve times,[53] separating the Holy head from the infallible leader's body.

Robbing Al-Husayn

Bin Sa'ad's soldiers raced one another to rob Al-Husayn. Is'haq Bin Hawiyya robbed his shirt. Al-Akhnas Bin Marthad Bin A'alqama Al-Hadhrami robed his turban. Al-Aswad Bin Khalid robbed his sandals. Jamee' Bin Khalq Al-Awadi robbed his sword. It has also been narrated that Al-Aswad Bin Hanthala robbed Al-Husayn's sword. Bajdal saw a ring covered with blood in Al-Husayn's finger. He cut off the finger, and took the ring. Qays Bin Al-Ash'ath robbed Al-Husayn's velvet.[54] He always sat on it, until he became known as Velvet Qays.[55] Ja'ouna Bin Hawiyya Al-Hadhrami robbed his garment. Al-Raheel Bin Khaythama Al-Ja'afi, Hani Bin Shabeeb Al-Hadhrami and Jareer Bin Mas'oud Al-Hadhrami collectively robbed his spear and the rest of Al-Husayn's possessions.[56]

A man tried to untie a valuable band on Al-Husayn's waist to take it. This man narrated that he wanted to take the band, but Al-Husayn firmly held it. The man cut Al-Husayn's right hand off, because he was unable to remove it from the band. Al-Husayn firmly held the band with his other hand. The man cut off Al-Husayn's left hand, because he was also unable to remove it. The man said that, as he was about to take off Al-Husayn's trousers, he heard a very loud rumble. Breathless from fear, the man left Al-Husayn alone and passed out. While unconscious, the man saw the Prophet, Ali, Fatima and Al-Hasan. Fatima told Al-Husayn, "Son! They killed you. I ask Allah to destroy them." Al-Husayn told her, "Mother! This unconscious man cut off my hands." Supplicating to Allah to punish this man, Fatima said, "I ask Allah to rid you of your hands, feet and sight, and then chastise you in hellfire." Later in life this man said, "I already lost my hands, my feet and my sight. The only thing left from her supplication is the chastisement in hellfire."[57]

Notes & References

1. Al-Luhuf (P.65)
2. Al-Khassa'is Al-Husayniyya (P.129)
3. Al-Muntakhab (P.315)
4. Manaqib Bin Shahr Ashoub (V.2, P.222); Al-Bihar (V.10, P.305)
5. Majma' Al-Zawa'id (V.9, P.193); Al-Bihar (V.10, P.205)
6. Al-Luhuf (P.69); Tareekh Al-Tabari (V.6, P.259)
7. Al-Luhuf (P.65); Tareekh Al-Yaqoubi (V.2, P.218)
8. Al-Bihar (V.10, P.23); Maqtal Al-Khawarizmi (V.2, P.22)
9. Manaqib Bin Shahr Ashoub (V.2, P.222); Mutheer Al-Ahzaan (P.36); Al-Luhuf (P.66)
10. Al-Luhuf (P.66)
11. Maqtal Al-Khawarizmi (V.2, P.32); Mutheer Al-Ahzaan (P.26)
12. Tathallum Al-Zahra' (P.122)
13. Al-Muntakhab (p.313)
14. Tathkirat Al-Khawass (P.144); Al-Qamqaam (P.385)
15. Maqtal Al-Khawarizmi (V.2, P.32); Al-Ihtijaaj (P.163)
16. Mutheer Al-Ahzaan (P.36); Al-Irshaad
17. Maqtal Al-Awalim (P.97); Mutheer Al-Ahzaan (P.37); Maqtal Al-Khawarizmi (V.2, P.33)
18. Al-Bayan Wa Al-Tabyeen (V.3, P.171)
19. Manaqib Bin Shahr Ashoub (V.2, P.223)
20. Tareekh Al-Tabari (V.6, P.259)
21. Manaqib Bin Shahr Ashoub (V.2, P.223)
22. Al-Luhuf (P.67)
23. Al-Bihar (V.10, P.204); Maqtal Al-Awalim (P.98); Nafs Al-Mahmoum (P.188); Al-Khassa'is Al-Husayniyya (P.46)
24. Jala' Al-Uyun (Persian)
25. Al-Luhuf (P.67)
26. Maqatil Al-Talibiyyeen (P.47); Tahtheeb Tareekh Dimashq (V.4, P.338)
27. Maqtal Al-Awalim (P.98); Nafs Al-Mahmoum (P.189); Maqtal Al-Khawarizmi (V.2, P.34)
28. Nafs Al-Mahmoum (P.189); Maqtal Al-Khawarizmi (V.2, P.34); Al-Luhuf (P.68)
29. Maqtal Al-Khawarizmi (V.2, P.34); Tahtheeb Tareekh Dimashq (V.4, P.338)
30. Maqtal Al-Khawarizmi (V.2, P.34); Al-Luhuf (P.70)
31. Maqtal Al-Khawarizmi (V.2, P.35); Al-Kamel (V.4, P.31)
32. Tareekh Al-Tabari (V.6, P.258); Al-Bidaya (V.8, P.186)
33. Al-Khassa'is Al-Husayniyya (P.129)

34. Tareekh Al-Tabari (V.6, P.259); Mutheer Al-Ahzaan (P.38); Al-Luhuf (P.68)
35. Mutheer Al-Ahzaan (P.39); Al-Luhuf (P.68)
36. Al-Akhbar Al-Tiwaal (P.255); Al-Khitat Al-Miqriziyya (V.2, P.288)
37. Maqtal Al-Khawarizmi (V.2, P.35); Manaqib Bin Shahr Ashoub (V.2, P.222)
38. Al-Ithaaf Bi Hubb Al-Ashraaf (P.16)
39. Al-Luhuf (P.70)
40. Maqtal Al-Khawarizmi (V.2, P.35); Maqtal Al-Awalim (P.110)
41. Mutheer Al-Ahzaan (P.39)
42. Musbah Al-Mutahajjid; Al-Iqbaal
43. Asraar Al-Shahada (P.423)
44. Riyadh Al-Massa'ib (P.33)
45. Amali Al-Sadouq (P.98); Maqtal Al-Khawarizmi (V.2, P.37); Tathallum Al-Zahra' (P.128)
46. Tathallum Al-Zahra' (P.129); Al-Bihar (V.10, P.205)
47. Maqtal Al-Khawarizmi (V.2, P.37)
48. Al-Bihar (V.10, P.206); Maqtal Al-Khawarizmi (V.2, P.37)
49. Tareekh Al-Tabari (V.6, P.259)
50. Al-Luhuf (P.73)
51. Tareekh Al-Tabari (V.6, P.259); Al-Kamel (V.4, P.32)
52. Al-Irshaad
53. Maqtal Al-Awalim (P.100); Maqtal Al-Khawarizmi (V.2, P.36)
54. Al-Luhuf (P.73)
55. Maqtal Al-Khawarizmi (V.2, P.38); Al-Kamel (V.4, P.32)
56. Manaqib Bin Shahr Ashoub (V.2, P.224)
57. Maqtal Al-Khawarizmi (V.2, P.102)

Part IV:

Events after Al-Husayn's Martyrdom

"Kufans! You are abominable! Have you any idea how badly you broke the Prophet's heart? Have you any idea what blood of his you spilled? Have you any idea what daughter of his you abused? Have you any idea what sanctity of his you violated? You have committed a dreadful crime, for which heavens are about to burst, the earth explode, and mountains implode."
-Zaynab, the Honorable

The Eleventh Night of Muharram

The hardships of the eleventh night were unspeakable. Losing the Master of Youth in heaven, the reflection of the Prophet's light and character, was unbearably painful for the Prophet's daughters. Never having been abandoned or left on their own, the women and children of the Prophet's household longed for the glorious privilege of being continuously cared for and protected. Nonetheless, the sun set on that day, dragging the cloak of darkness and uncertainty upon the survivors of the Prophet's family.

The martyrs' bloody bodies lay in front of the burnt and looted tents. The dominant images of the aftermath were gruesome. The Prophet's daughters were left with no protector or supporter to fend off the imminent danger, or the potential abuse at the hands of their enemies. No one was around to console their hearts and ease their bereavement. The only voices that rang in their ears were the screams of little boys, the moans of young girls, the wails of mothers who wept on their martyred sons, and the grunting of women who wept on their brothers or husbands. Next to the emotionally devastated women and children lay the martyrs' mutilated bodies and their dismembered body parts.

The Prophet's daughters were helplessly trapped in the dry desert. Their emotional distress was horrendous. They were left to wonder whether the sun would rise on their own dead bodies, or on the shackles of their captivity. No man was around to defend them, except the extremely ill and helpless infallible leader (Zayn Al-Abideen), who, in addition to being a potential target for execution, was physically too weak to stand up.

Sadness and sorrow filled the earth and heaven on the eleventh night of Muharram. The beautiful maidens of heavens cried and screamed. The ascending and descending angels wept and wailed. The Jinn mourned Al-Husayn in their dwellings.[1]

The traitors and murderers, on the other hand, were boisterously joyful over their so-called victory. The enemies of the Prophet's household were unbelievably cruel and heartless. Bin Abu Al-Hadeed stated, "Obeydallah Bin Ziyad built four mosques in Al-Basra for the sole purpose of propagating enmity towards Ali Bin Abu Talib."[2]

On that night, Umm Salama saw the Prophet in her dream. He was covered with dust and dirt from head to toe. She asked him, "Oh Allah's Messenger! Why are you disheveled and covered with dust?" He answered, "My son Husayn has been murdered, and I have been digging graves for him and his companions."[3] She woke up terrified. She looked at the bottle the Prophet had given her to keep, and saw it bubbling with blood.[4] She also heard in the middle of that night a faint voice mourning Al-Husayn. The moaning voice said, "You! The ignorant who murdered Al-Husayn! Anticipate severe chastisement. Sulayman, Musa, Isa, the inhabitants of heavens and all the Prophets and Messengers have supplicated for a wrath to fall upon you."[5]

That night, Umm Salama also heard voices mourning Al-Husayn, but couldn't see anyone. The following was some of what she heard, "I call upon eyes to shed tears on Al-Husayn. I call upon them to weep on the honorable martyrs, who returned to the Omnipotent during the reign of an imbecile."[6] Bin Abbass rushed over and asked her about the reason for her crying. She told him that both of the bottles in her possession were bubbling with blood.[7] Bin Abbass also saw the Prophet in his dream on the day of Ashura. Holding a bottle full of blood, the Prophet looked disheveled and covered with dust. In his dream, Bin Abbass asked the Prophet, "May my soul be sacrificed defending yours! What is this?" The Prophet responded, "This is the blood of Al-Husayn and his companions. I have been collecting it all day."[8]

One can never overstate the significance and highness of Al-Husayn. His soul was a branch of Mohammed's, who in turn was an extract of the Divine Light. Al-Husayn's body remained on the sandy plains of the desert for three days, during which the sky was abnormally dark.[9]

People, at the time, believed that this phenomenon marked the onset of the Day of Judgement.[10] Some planets were seen colliding into others in broad daylight,[11] while sunlight was invisible for three straight days.[12] One should not find it difficult believe that the sunlight faded during the time period when the body of the Master of Youth in heaven was exposed in the open desert. Al-Husayn is a fundamental cause of the perpetual existence of the universe, because, as previously mentioned, he is an integral part of the Mohammedan reality, which is the core cause of all existence. Mohammed was Allah's first creation, and before this physical stage of existence, all of Allah's subsequent creatures acknowledged and submitted to the supremacy of the Prophet's household. A true believer should easily believe that the fundamental elements of nature were disrupted during these three days. These abnormal occurrence and supernatural phenomena further confirmed Al-Husayn's significance and high rank. Those who refute these miraculous signs have missed the opportunity of nourishing their faith.

It is narrated that the elements of nature were disrupted when a prophet's body was almost exposed. This occurred in the city of Samirra'a, when a Christian priest prayed by the prophet's grave and supplicated for rain. The sky filled with clouds and rain fell heavily.[13] It is crucial to keep in mind that throughout this whole event, this prophet's body was neither exposed nor mutilated. Having believed this authentic incident, we should easily absorb the fact that the sky changed color, and sunlight faded, when the body of the Master of Youth in Heaven was mutilated and left exposed to the elements.

All existing things and creatures were deeply touched by this heinous crime. Beasts wept and moaned on Al-Husayn. The Commander of the Faithful (Imam Ali) said, "May my mother and father be sacrificed for Al-Husayn, who shall be slaughtered behind Kufa! By Allah! I can foresee the beasts stretching their necks on his grave to weep all night until the crack of dawn."[14] The sky rained blood,[15] filling up crevices and jugs.[16] Red stains of blood were visible on walls and roof tops for a while. Red blood bubbled under rocks. Wherever a rock was removed, blood was seen bubbling underneath.[17] This phenomenon occurred everywhere, even in Jerusalem.[18]

When the Holy head was brought to the governor in Kufa, blood dripped from the walls of the palace.[19] Fiery flames streamed out from some of the walls towards Obeydallah Bin Ziyad. He ran away and told the attendants, "Conceal this."[20] Al-Husayn's Holy head simultaneously, and loudly said, "You are condemned! Where shall you run? If it doesn't get to you in this life, it surely is your destiny in the next." The head spoke until the flames receded. Everyone in the palace was startled. People saw blood stains on walls at sunrise and sunset for two or three months.[21]

Ahmad Bin Makki (d.568 A.H. = 1170 C.E.), narrated that a crow, covered with Al-Husayn's blood, flew to Medina and landed on the wall of Fatima Bint Al-Husayn Al-Sughra. It informed her that her father had been martyred. She conveyed the sad news to the people of Medina. They rejected her story, and commented, "She is another witchcraft advocate from Abd Al-Muttalib's family." Soon after this incident, the news arrived confirming her story.[22] It is highly possible that this story is true, because, in addition to the numerous super-natural phenomena that occurred after his martyrdom, Al-Husayn did have another daughter besides Fatima and Sukayna.

The Divine wanted the Community to realize the brutality of the Umayyads, and, at the same time, heed and acknowledge the significance of the Master of all Martyrs. The Exalted ordained to inform the contemporary community, and all coming generations, of the unprecedented atrocities that the tyrants inflicted on the Prophet's family in Karbala. The Omnipotent planned for Al-Husayn's martyrdom to become the role model, and the moral scale, by which humans would sort out good and evil. Al-Husayn's martyrdom, an implementation of the Will of the Lord of the Worlds, doubtlessly undermined all forms of aberration, and maintained the true path until the Day of Resurrection.

D'ubul Al-Khuza'ie narrated that his great grandmother, Sa'ada Bint Malik Al-Khuza'ie, saw the miracle of the dry tree in the house of Umm Ma'abad Al-Khuza'ieyya. This tree turned green, and bore a lot of fruit, after the Prophet performed ritual ablution over the bottom of its trunk. Less fruit grew on it after the Prophet's death, and none at all after Imam Ali's martyrdom. However, people used its leaves to treat their illnesses, but after a period of time, they noticed blood seeping out of its trunk. Never seeing something like this before, people were terrified. That night, they heard wailing and moaning, but could not determine the source of the voices. One of these voices said, "Your father is a martyr, and so is your uncle. He is the best uncle, for he is Ja'afar Al-Tayyar. How dare a sharp sword strike your dusty face?"[23] The news about Al-Husayn's martyrdom arrived shortly after this extraordinary phenomenon.

The Zafroun that the enemies looted from Al-Husayn's camp burned all those who touched it. The meat of the illegally confiscated camels was extremely bitter and flames streamed out of their flesh.[24] Redness in the sky was never seen before the day of Ashura.[25]

Bin Al-Jawzi stated: "When anyone becomes angry it usually shows on his face. The Real, however, is exalted from being a physical entity. He expressed His anger at the murderers of Al-Husayn, and conveyed His condemnation of their heinous crime, through the redness in the sky. Al-Abbass Bin Abd Al-Muttalib, the Prophet's uncle, was shackled as a prisoner of war after the Battle of Badr. His moans deeply touched the Prophet and kept him sleepless all of that night. One can only imagine how the Prophet would react if he heard Al-Husayn's moans. Wahshiyy killed Hamza, but later accepted Islam and was absolved of his past deeds. However, the Prophet told Wahshiyy to stay away from him, because he didn't like to see the killer of his loved ones. One can only imagine what the Prophet would do if he saw those who slaughtered his beloved grandson, and dragged his family on the backs of camels."[26]

The Prophet did attend the battle, and witnessed his cruel enemies trying to eradicate his family from the face of the earth. He also witnessed the women wailing on their loved ones, and the children screaming from thirst. Bin Sa'ad's army heard a terrifying voice say, "Kufans! You are condemned! I see Allah's Messenger holding onto his Holy beard (an expression of bereavement and anger), looking at you some, and gazing into the sky another." Ruthless and completely defiant, the Kufans convinced themselves that it was the voice of some maniac, and yelled at one another to ignore it. Imam Al-Sadiq said, "It must have been Jabra'eel's voice."[27]

Some angels yelled, "You are the confused community who had gone astray after the passing of its Prophet! Allah shall never aid you to enjoy the festive days of Fitr and Adha." Imam Al-Sadiq said, "Indeed! By Allah! They didn't enjoy them, and they never will, until the man who will eventually avenge Al-Husayn rises up."[28] Al-Sheykh Al-Bahai'e (d. 1030 A.H. = 1615 C.E.) narrated that one day his father, Shaykh Husayn Bin Abd Al-Samad Al-Harithi, entered the main mosque of Kufa, and found a ruby ring in it. The following was engraved on the bezel. "I am jewel, sprayed from heavens onto earth on Ali's wedding. I was brighter and whiter than silver, but Al-Husayn's blood dyed me red."[29]

Visiting Al-Husayn on the Eleventh Night of Muharram

Authentic traditions highly recommend that the followers of the infallible leaders (Shi'a) spend the eleventh night of Muharram at the site of Al-Husayn's grave. These traditions urge the believers to vent their intense bereavement, and to mourn their terrible loss. Once there, the believers should try to envision the horrific images of the mutilated victims, and simultaneously weep on them. The visitors should keep in mind that the eleventh night was loaded with agony and grief. The members of Mohammed's family were slaughtered and left exposed. Their Holy bodies lay scattered on the sandy plains after being crushed by horses. The visitors of the shrine should also remember that, throughout that night, the daughters of Allah's Messenger continuously wept and moaned. A sincere follower of the Prophet's household should console their broken hearts, and connect his tears to theirs. In addition to accruing immeasurable rewards, the believer who spends the eleventh night of Muharram at Al-Husayn's site would definitely console the heart of the purified Fatima Al-Zahra', and please the infallible leaders.

The following traditions confirm the importance of visiting Al-Husayn's grave on the eleventh night of Muharram, and emphasize the associated rewards. Narrated by Malik Al-Juhani, Imam Al-Baqir said, "Whoever visits Al-Husayn on the day of Ashura and stays overnight weeping, Allah shall reward him with bounties equivalent to performing two million Hajj, two million Umra, and fighting two million battles on the side of Allah's Messenger and the infallible leaders."[30] Some argued that the phrase "stays overnight" in the preceding tradition is not necessarily indicative of spending the eleventh night of Muharram in Karbala. The following authentic tradition defeats this argument, and further confirms our understanding of Imam Al-Baqir's words. Jaber Al-Ja'afi narrated that Imam Ja'afar said, "Whoever visits Al-Husayn on the day of Ashura, and spends the following night there, will be rewarded as if he was martyred with him."[31]

It is worth noting that Imam Al-Sadiq sequentially mentioned the visitation (Ziyara) on the day of Ashura, and spending the night. Had he intended otherwise, he would have explicitly mentioned spending the eve of Ashura, and then expounded on the visit next day (Ziyarat Ashura). The eleventh night of Muharram descended on the Prophet's daughters, the entrustment of infallibility, with unsurpassed difficulty and hardship. Basic common sense compels the visitor of Al-Husayn's shrine, on the day of Ashura, to stay there overnight.

The women of the Prophet's household were helplessly trapped in the dry desert. The bodies and body parts of their protectors and loved ones were scattered around them. This gruesome panoramic view stagnated before the eyes of the Prophet's daughters. In addition to their intense grief, the women and children were uncertain of the fate awaiting them at the hands of their enemies. Therefore, it is quite sensible that the follower of the Prophet's household, who visits on that day, should stay overnight. Once there, the believer should weep and wish to have been there so he could defend and console the bereaved members of the Prophet's household. It is highly recommended that the visitors utter, "We wish we had been with you to achieve the great victory."[32] Fatima, the Lady of all Women, would definitely be weeping on her beloved and thirsty son on that night. The believer in turn should participate in consoling the Prophet's daughter.

The following story highlights the importance of consoling Fatima Al-Zahra' as she mourns and weeps on her beloved son. Al-Qadhi Abu Ali Al-Muhsin Bin Ali Al-Tanukhi heard the following story from his father. Abu Al-Hasan Al-Katib once inquired about Bin Al-Na'ih. No one at the time recognized Bin Al-Na'ih (Bin Asdaq) except Ali Al-Tanukhi. Ali asked about the reason of this inquiry. Abu Al-Hasan Al-Katib replied, "My maid is a dedicated worshipper. Last night she woke up trembling and screaming for help. I asked her about it. In broken Arabic, she said that after her night prayers, she went to bed and dreamt that she was in an alley in Al-Karkh, where there was a clean and spacious room with many women crowded in its wide-open door. She asked these women about the reason behind their gathering. They collectively pointed towards the room. She entered the room, and saw in the middle of it a young woman with unrivaled beauty and radiance. The woman was dressed with beautiful clothes, over which she wore a white cloak, and on her lap was a man's head dripping blood. My maid asked the woman about her name. She said that she was Fatima, the daughter of Allah's Messenger, and that the head was Al-Husayn's." Al-Katib told Al-Tanukhi that the woman (Fatima Al-Zahra') told his maid in the dream to instruct Bin Asdaq to mourn Al-Husayn as follows, "How could I be content when I, his mother, did not tend to him in sickness? But why would I tend to Al-Husayn, when he was not at all sick?" Al-Katib said that at this point in the dream, his maid woke up terrified. He calmed her down until she fell back asleep. Abu Al-Hasan Al-Katib then requested from Ali Al-Tanukhi to convey Fatima's message to Bin Asdaq. Ali Al-Tanukhi replied, "I totally submit to the orders of Fatima, the Lady of all Women."

This happened in Sha'aban, where the visitors to Karbala suffered a great deal of abuse from the Hanbalis. Ali Al-Tanukhi kissed up to these bullies until he arrived to Al-Husayn's shrine in the middle of Sha'aban. He asked and looked around until he found Bin Asdaq. Ali told him that Fatima wanted him to quote her when he mourned her son. Ali instructed Bin Asdaq to chant the following, "How could I be content when I, his mother, did not tend to him in sickness? But why would I tend to Al-Husayn, when he was not at all sick?" Ali Al-Tanukhi was unaware that this was only one line of a long poetry. His unexpected message agitated Bin Asdaq. Al-Tanukhi told him the whole story. Bin Asdaq and the people around him wept. Bin Asdaq recited this piece of poetry throughout the whole night. Al-Tanukhi returned home and informed Abu Al-Hasan Al-Katib of his adventure.[33]

LOOTING

Bin Sa'ad's soldiers murdered Al-Husayn and attacked his camp immediately. They looted everything in the tents,[34] and set the whole camp on fire. The murderers attacked the Prophet's grandchildren and Fatima's daughters to mug them. The women and children were completely terrified. They ran away from the attackers screaming.[35] Some women had their cloaks snatched away. Others had their rings pulled off of their fingers. The criminals violently pulled the earrings and anklets from the ears and ankles of women and young girls.[36] A man violently snatched Umm Kulthoum's earrings, and badly wounded her ears.[37] Another man wept as he forcefully pulled out the anklet of Fatima Bint Al-Husayn. She asked him, "Why are you weeping?" He replied, "I am robbing the daughter of Allah's Messenger! How could I not weep? She exclaimed, "Let me go then!" He answered, "I am afraid that someone else would take it."[38]

One of Bin Sa'ad's soldiers maliciously whipped the women and children with the back of his spear after he mugged them. The young girls clutched onto their mothers and aunts. The women tried to shield the children, and simultaneously protect one another. From the spot where she was mugged, Fatima watched this horrific scene and became petrified. This man eventually saw her standing still and immediately attacked her. She ran away, but he brutally struck her with the back of his spear. Fatima fell unconscious onto the ground. Her aunt, Umm Kulthoum, wept and hovered over her until she woke up.[39] A woman from the family of Bakr Bin Wa'il happened to be with her husband in Bin Sa'ad's army. When she saw the daughters of Allah's Messenger being robbed and beaten, she screamed, "You! The tribe of Bakr Bin Wa'il! How could you allow the daughters of Allah's Messenger to be abused? Allah is the Supreme Ruler! Let us defend Allah's Messenger!" Her husband escorted her back to his camel.[40]

Extremely ill and unable to stand up, Ali Bin Al-Husayn lay down on a mattress. The enemies eventually encountered the infallible leader. A man yelled, "Young or old, kill them all off!" Another said, "Do not rush into things until we consul our commander, Omar Bin Sa'ad."[41] Al-Shimr unsheathed his sword to kill Al-Sajjad, but Hameed Bin Muslim interjected, "All praise is due to Allah! How could you kill boys? He is just an ill boy!"[42] Al-Shimr replied, "Bin Ziyad ordered us to kill all of Al-Husayn's sons." Zaynab, the daughter of the Commander of the Faithful, said, "You cannot kill him unless you kill me first. Leave him alone!" Having heard Zaynab, Bin Sa'ad intervened and repeatedly prevented the persistent Al-Shimr from killing Zayn Al-Abideen.[43] At this point, Bin Sa'ad's soldiers had virtually robbed everything, and never returned any stolen item.[44] Bin Sa'ad rode his horse towards the razed camp. The women and children looked at him and wept. Bin Sa'ad loudly ordered his soldiers to stop harassing the women and children. He then appointed guards to protect the women, and hastily returned to his tent.

The Horses

Bin Sa'ad called, "Who would like to stomp Al-Husayn's chest and back with his horse?" The following ten men volunteered: Is'haq Bin Hawiyya, Al-Ahbash Bin Marthad Al-Hadhrami, Hakeem Bin Al-Tufayl Al-Sunbussi, Amr Bin Sabeeh Al-Saydawi, Rajaa' Bin Munqith Al-Abdi, Salim Bin Khaythama Al-Ja'afi, Salih Bin Wahab Al-Ja'afi, Wakhit Bin Ghanim, Hani Bin Thabeet Al-Hadhrami and Usayd Bin Malik.[45] These men trampled the body of the Prophet's endeared grandson with their horses, and bragged about their performance to Bin Ziyad. The latter rewarded them very little for it.[46]

Al-Bayrouni wrote: "They (the Kufans) abused Al-Husayn with unrivaled cruelty. No community ever treated, or would ever treat, its worst villains with such brutality. They killed him with swords, spears, and rocks, and then stampeded his body with their horses."[47] Some of these horses traveled to Egypt, where people took off the horseshoes, and hung them as amulets on their doorsteps. This practice has become a tradition, to the extent that some people would buy horseshoes and hang them above their front doors.[48]

The Heads

Bin Sa'ad ordered the martyrs' bodies decapitated. Each tribe was assigned to carry a certain number of heads to collect hefty rewards from Bin Ziyad. Kinda tribe, under Qays Bin Al-Ash'ath, carried thirteen heads. Hawazin tribe, under Shimr Bin Thil Jawshan, carried twelve. Tameem tribe carried seventeen. Assad tribe carried sixteen. Mithhaj tribe carried seven and others carried the rest.[49] Banu Riyah, the tribesmen of Al-Hurr Al-Riyahi, prevented their comrades from trampling or decapitating Al-Hurr's body.[50] Later, on the day of Ashura, Bin Sa'ad dispatched Al-Husayn's head with Khiwilli Bin Yazeed Al-Asbahi and Hameed Bin Muslim Al-Azdi, and assigned Al-Shimr, Qays Bin Al-Ash'ath and Amr Bin Al-Hajjaj to keep the rest of the heads in their custody.[51]

Khiwilli's house was a few miles away from Kufa. He hid the head away from his wife, Al-Ayouf,[52] because she was a follower of the Prophet's household. A while after his arrival, Khiwilli's wife saw a bright light emanating from the furnace. Certain that there was nothing in it, she was totally perplexed. She approached it, and heard women weeping on Al-Husayn. The moans of the wailing women were heartbreaking. Al-Ayouf informed her husband and tearfully stormed out of the house. She mourned on Al-Husayn the rest of her life.[53] Early the next morning, Khiwilli took Al-Husayn's head to the governor's palace. Bin Ziyad had just returned from his military camp in Al-Nakheela. Khiwilli placed the head in front of Bin Ziyad, and said, "Fill me up with silver and gold, for I indeed killed the master of the world. I killed the man of unrivaled honor. I killed the son of the best father and mother." Extremely agitated at Khiwilli for praising Al-Husayn in the crowded forum, Bin Ziyad said, "If you knew who he was, why did you kill him then? By Allah! I shall never reward you at all."[54]

Notes & References

1. Tareekh Dimashq (V.4, P.341); Majma' Al-Zawa'id (V.9, P.199); Tareekh Al-Khulafa' (P.139); Al-Kawakib Al-Durriyya (V.1, P.56)
2. Sharh Al-Nahj (V.1, P.386)
3. Amali Bin Al-Sheikh Al-Tussi (P.56);' Tahtheeb Al-Tahtheeb (V.2, P.356); Thakha'ir Al-Uqba (P.148); Tareekh Al-Khulafa' (P.139); Sayr A'alam Al-Nubala' (V.3, P.213)
4. Mar'at Al-Janan (V.1, P.134); Al-Kamel (V.4, P.38); Maqtal Al-Khawarizmi (V.2, P.95)
5. Tareekh Dimashq (V.4, P.341); Taj Al-Ala'rous (V.7, P.103)
6. Tareekh Dimashq (V.4, P.341); Majma' Al-Zawa'id (V.9, P.199), Al-Khassa'is Ar-Kubra (V.2, P:127)
7. Ma'alim Al-Zulfa (P.91); Madinat Al-Ma'ajiz (P.244); Al-Muntakhab (P.235)
8. Tareekh Dimashq (V.4, P.340); Tareekh Al-Khulafa' (P.139); Mar'at Al-Janan (V.1, P.134); Musnad Ahmed (V.1, 242); Al-Kawakib Al-Durriyya (V.1, P.56); Thakha'ir Al-Uqba (P.148); Tahtheeb Al-Tahtheeb (V.2, P.355); Al-Kamel (V.4, P.28); Al-Sawa'iq Al-Muhriqa (P.116); Tarh Al-Tathreeb (V.1, P.22); Tareekh Baghdad (V.1, P.142); Al-Khitat Al-Miqreeziyya (V.2, P.285); Maqtal Al-Khawarizmi (V.2, P.94); Sayr A'alam Al-Nubala' (V.3, P.212)
9. Tareekh Dimashq (V.4, P.339); Al-Khassa'is Al-Kubra (V.2, P.126); Al-Sawa'iq Al-Muhriqa (P.116); Al-Khitat Al-Miqreeziyya (V.2, P.289); Tathkirat Al-Khawass (P.155); Maqtal Al Khawarizmi (V.2, P.90)

10. Al-Sawa'iq Al-Muhriqa (P.116); Al-It'haaf Bihubb Al-Ashraaf (P.24)
11. Tahtheeb Al-Tahtheeb (V.1, P.354); Al-Sawa'iq Al-Muhriqa (P.116); Al-It'haaf Bihubb Al-Ashraaf (P.24); Tareekh Dimashq (V.4, P.339); Maqtal Al-Khawarizmi (V.2, P.89)
12. Majma' Al-Zawa'id (V.9, P.197); Tareekh Al-Khulafa' (P.138); Al-Sawa'iq Al-Muhriqa (P.116); Al-It'haaf Bihubb Al-Ashraaf (P.24); Maqtal Al-Khawarizmi (V.2, P.89); Al-Kawakib Al-Durriyya (V.1, P.56); Kamel Al-Ziyarat (P.77)
13. Al-Khara'ij (P.64)
14. Kamel Al-Ziyarat (P.80)
15. Tareekh Dimashq (V.4, P.339); Al-Khassa'is Al-Kubra (V.2, P.126); Al-Sawa'iq Al-Muhriqa (P.116); Al-Khitat Al-Miqreeziyya (V.2, P.289); Tathkirat Al-Khawass (P.155); Maqtal Al-Khawarizmi (V.2, P.89); Al-It'haaf Bihubb Al-Ashraaf (P.25); Manaqib Bin Shahr Ashoub (V.2, P.206); Al-Kamel (V.4, P.29)
16. Al-Khassa'is Al-Kubra (V.2, P.126)
17. Tareekh Dimashq (V.4, P.339); Al-Sawa'iq Al-Muhriqa (P.116)
18. Al-Khassa'is Al-Kubra (V.2, P.125); Tareekh Al-Khulafa' (P.138); Maj ma' Al-Zawa'id (V.9, P.196); Al-A'qd Al-Fareed (V.2, P.315); Maqtal Al-Khawarizmi (V.2, P.90); Al-Kawakib Al-Durriyya (V.l, P.56)
19. Tareekh Dimashq (V.4, P.339); Al-Sawa'iq Al-Muhriqa (P.116)
20. Majma' Al-Zawa'id (V.9, P.196); Al-Kamel (V.4, P.103); Maqtal Al-Khawarizmi (V.2, P.87); Al-Muntakhab (P.338)
21. Al-Kawakib Al-Durriyya (V. l, P.56); Al-Kamel (V.4, P.37); Tathkirat Al-Khawass (P.155)
22. Maqtal Al-Khawarizmi (V.2, P.92)
23. Maqtal Al-Khawarizmi (V.2, P.100)
24. Tareekh Dimashq (V.4, P.339); Al-Kawakib Al-Durriyya (V.1, P.56); Al-Khassa'is Al-Kubra (V.2, P.126); Majma' Al-Zawa'id (V.9, P.196); Maqtal Al-Khawarizmi (V.2, P.90); Tahtheeb Al-Tahtheeb (V.2, P.354)
25. Al-Sawa'iq Al-Muhriqa (P.116)
26. Tathkirat Al-Khawass (P.154); Al-Sawa'iq Al-Muhriqa (P.116)
27. Kamel Al-Ziyarat (P.80)
28. Man La Yahdhuruhu Al-Faqeeh (P.148)
29. Kashkoul Al-Bahrani (P.17)
30. Kamel Al-Ziyarat (P.174)
31. Kamel Al-Ziyarat (P.137)
32. Uyun Akhbar Al-Ridha (P.66)
33. Nashwar Al-Muhadhara (V.8, P.218)
34. Al-Kamel (V.4, P.32)
35. Tareekh Al-Tabari (V.6, P.260)
36. Mutheer Al-Ahzaan (P.40)
37. Al-Dam'a Al-Sakiba (P.348)

38. Amali Al-Sadouq (P.99); Sayr A'alam Al-Nubala' (V.3, P.204)
39. Riyadh Al-Massa'ib (P.341); Tathallum Al-Zahra' (P.130)
40. Al-Luhuf (P.74); Mutheer Al-Ahzaan (P.41)
41. Tathallum Al-Zahra' (P.132)
42. Tareekh Al-Tabari (V.6, P.260)
43. Tareekh Al-Qarmani (P.108)
44. Al-Kamel (V.4, P.32)
45. Tareekh Al-Tabari (V.6, P.261); Al-Kamel (V.4, P.33); Muruj Al-Thahab (V.2, P.91); Al-Khitat Al-Miqreeziyya (V.2, P.288); Al-Bidaya (V.8, P.189); Tareekh Al-Khamees (V.3, P.133); Al-Irshaad; A'alam Al-Wara (P.888); Rawdhat Al-Wa'itheen (P.662); Manaqib Bin Shahr Ashoub (V.2, P.224)
46. Al-Luhuf (P.75); Mutheer Al-Ahzaan (P.41); Maqtal Al-Khawarizmi (V.2, P.39)
47. Al-Athaar Al-Baqiya (P.329)
48. Al-Ta'ajjub (P.46)
49. Al-Luhuf (P.81); Umdat Al-Qari (V.7, P.656)
50. Al-Kibreet Al-Ahmar (V.3, P.12)
51. Al-Irshaad
52. Ansaab Al-Ashraaf (V.5, P.238)
53. Al-Bidaya (V.8, P.190)
54. Mar'at Al-Janan (V.1, P.133); Al-A'qd Al-Fareed (V.2, P.213)

LEAVING KARBALA

After sending the heads to Kufa, Bin Sa'ad camped in Karbala until noon of the eleventh of Muharram. He gathered the bodies of his dead soldiers, performed funeral prayers and buried them. He deliberately left the Prophet's endeared grandson, the Master of Youth in Heaven, his family members and companions, without ritual washing and burial.[1] The Holy bodies were left exposed to the elements, and the visiting wild beasts.

After the noon prayers of that day, Bin Sa'ad marched towards Kufa. Alongside with him marched the survivors of the Prophet's family, and the women and children of some of Al-Husayn's companions. There were twenty women in total.[2] The entrustments and daughters of the best prophet were forced on unsaddled camels, with nothing to shield them from the blazing sun. The enemies treated the women and children like infidel prisoners of war. Twenty-three years of age, Ali Bin Al-Husayn Al-Sajjad was amongst the captives. The enemies forced him on a weak camel, despite his extreme exhaustion and severe illness.[3] Next to him sat his son, Imam Al-Baqir, who was only a little over two years of age.[4] Zayd, Amr and Al-Hasan Al-Mathna, Imam Al-Hasan's sons were also amongst the captives.

Al-Hasan Al-Mathna was captured after he killed seventeen men. He had eighteen wounds in his body and had already lost his right hand in the battle. Bin Sa'ad allowed Asma Bin Kharija Al-Fazari to save the little boy's life, because Al-Mathna's mother was from the tribe of Fazara.[5] Uqbah Bin Sam'aan, Al-Rabaab's servant, was also amongst the captives. After learning that he was just a servant of Al-Husayn's wife, Bin Ziyad released him. Al-Marqa' Bin Thumama Al-Assadi fought on Al-Husayn's side, but was not killed. His tribesmen rescued him, and took him home. Once informed, Bin Ziyad exiled him to Al-Zara.[6]

The women told their captors, "By Allah! Walk us by the

dead bodies." The martyrs' amputated limbs and bloody bodies were scattered all over the place. The marks of horseshoes on the crushed bodies were visible. The scene was horrific and heartbreaking. The women and children screamed and beat their faces as they looked at the mutilated bodies of their loved ones.[7] Zaynab vented her grief aloud, "Oh Mohammed! This is Husayn! He lay in the open desert; soaked in his blood and chopped into pieces. Your sons have been slaughtered, and your daughters are in captivity." Her sad words stirred up the dormant emotions of her enemies. Everyone around her wept.[8] Horses wept too; tears rolled down their eye onto their front legs.[9]

Zaynab slipped her hands under Al-Husayn's Holy body. She lifted him up, and said, "My Lord! Accept this sacrifice from us."[10] Zaynab's conduct clearly indicated that she, with a distinct role, had been Divinely selected and entrusted along with her brother in this Holy uprising. After her brother's martyrdom, the Honorable Zaynab stepped up to play her significant role. She was entrusted with the responsibility of completing the scope of this Holy uprising. She competently fulfilled her duties, one of which was to offer the Holy slaughter to the Divine. She, in addition to being the caretaker of the Prophet's family, was Al-Husayn's spokesperson. This reality should not be difficult to absorb, because Zaynab and Al-Husayn were but different rays emanating from the same light. Sukayna hugged her father's body. When it was time to leave, no one was able to separate her from him. Finally, a group of people forcefully pulled her away.[11] Sukayna often narrated that while she hugged her father, she heard him say, "My followers! Remember me every time you drink cold water. Also, mourn on me when your heart breaks for a loner or a martyr."[12]

The pitiful condition of the Holy martyrs had an immense emotional impact on Ali Bin Al-Husayn. Despite his patience, which could outweigh mountains, Al-Sajjad became extremely disturbed when he saw the mutilated bodies of his father and family members. His aunt, Zaynab Bint Ali, sensed his deep shock, and became concerned for her nephew's well-being. Attempting to ease his intense emotional reaction, she said, "Why are being too hard on yourself? You are all that is left for us. You are the extended presence of my grandfather, father and brothers. By Allah! This was Divinely ordained. Your grandfather and father were already informed of it. Allah had assigned people, unknown to the tyrants of earth, but known to the inhabitants of heavens, to collect these chopped limbs and bloody bodies and bury them. They shall erect a banner above your father's grave that shall never be destroyed or erased. The infidel leaders and the followers of evil will try their best to eradicate the grave, but their futile attempts will only add to its significance."[13]

Zajr Bin Qays screamed at the women to move onwards. They didn't. He whipped the Prophet's granddaughters while his comrades pushed them around, forcing them onto their rides.[14] Climbing onto her camel, Zaynab longed for the glorious days when she was always cared for and protected. All along and until that day, the brave and dignified sons of Abd Al-Muttalib formed a sanctified fortress around her. The Hashimite lions were always on alert, and immediately roared to defend her against any imminent danger. Zaynab was notably nostalgic to the bliss and peace of her grandfather's pure dwelling, where Allah's angels waited for permission to enter and serve the pious members of the Prophet's household.

Notes & References

1. Maqtal Al-Khawarizmi (V.2, P.39)
2. Nafs Al-Mahmoum (P.204)
3. Al-Iqbaal (P.54)
4. Riyadh Al-Ahzaan (P.49); Ithbaat Al-Wassiya (P.143); Tareekh Abu Al-Fida (V.1, P.203)
5. Isa'af Al-Raghibeen (P.28); Al-Luhuf (P.8)
6. Tareekh Al-Tabari (V.6, P.261); Al-Kamel (V.4, P.33)
7. Mutheer Al-Ahzaan (P.41); Al-Luhuf (P.74); Maqtal Al-Khawarizmi (V.2, P.39)
8. Al-Khitat Al-Miqreeziyya (V.2, P.280)
9. Maqtal Al-Khawarizmi (V.2, P.39); Al-Muntakhab (P.332)
10. Al-Kibreet Al-Ahmar (V.3, P.13)
11. Tathallum Al-Zahra' (P.135)
12. Al-Musbah (P.376)
13. Kamel Al-Ziyarat (P.261)
14. Tathallum Al-Zahra' (P.177)

IN KUFA

As the captives' caravan entered Kufa, people rushed out of their homes to watch the daughters of the Commander of the Faithful (Imam Ali). Umm Kulthoum loudly said, "You Kufans! Aren't you ashamed of yourselves? Allah and His Messenger are watchful of you staring at the Prophet's daughters!"[1] Touched by the captives' conspicuous agony and misery, a Kufan woman asked, "What kind of prisoners of war are you?" The Prophet's daughters replied, "We are the family of Prophet Mohammed."[2] Some Kufans gave the children dates, walnuts and bread. Zaynab yelled, "Charity is forbidden on us!" She threw all of it onto the ground.[3]

ZAYNAB'S SPEECH

The daughter of the Commander of the Faithful rose up to fulfill her Divinely assigned mission. She condemned the Kufans and successfully exposed Bin Ziyad's ill intentions and evil schemes. In the midst of incalculable chaos, calming the boisterous crowd and acquiring their complete silence seemed next to impossible. However, an extension of Mohammed's impeccable persona, Zaynab's powerful presence overwhelmed the unruly audience. She, with perfect posture and Divinely inspired bravery, silenced the huge crowd as soon as she gestured to them.

The narrator said, "Silence prevailed as soon as Zaynab Bint Ali gestured to the crowd. She spoke with tranquility, equanimity and an inherent bravery." She, peace upon her, said:

> "Praise is due to Allah, and blessings be upon my father Mohammed and his pure and righteous household. You Kufans! You are full of betrayal and disloyalty. How dare you weep? May your tears never stop and your moaning never end. You are just like the woman who undid her knitting after hard work. You only adopt faith when it suits

your lifestyle. You value judge others and love to be praised for your inadequacy. You are nothing but conceited liars. You are averse of righteousness, submissive like slaves to others, and only verbally abusive to the enemies. You are similar to the dead when told a story or a garbage dump that has become a grazing ground. You have dealt your souls a great mischief that invoked Allah's wrath. Your action shall beget you immortal chastisement.

How dare you wail and weep? Indeed and by Allah! You should weep plenty, and laugh a little. You have committed the greatest and most shameful crime, and you shall never be absolved from it. You have murdered the core of the message, and the son of the last Prophet. You have murdered the Master of Youth in Heaven, your light of guidance, the shelter of your righteous, and your shield against disasters. How could you ever be absolved from this heinous crime?

You are doomed and condemned! Your efforts have failed. You have lost a great deal and have become helpless, for you have invoked the wrath of Allah and His Messenger. You shall suffer humiliation and indignity for what you have done.

Kufans! You are abominable! Have you any idea how badly you broke the Prophet's heart? Have you any idea what blood of his you spilled? Have you any idea what daughter of his you abused? Have you any idea what sanctity of his you violated? You have committed a dreadful crime, for which heavens are about to burst. The earth is about to explode and mountains are about to implode because of your heinous crime.

Your ruthless murder rumbled the sky and caused rage on planet earth. Are you amazed that the sky rained blood? Well! The chastisement of the next life, where no support is fetched, shall be greater. Do not ignore the imminence of The Hour. It might seem far, but it is not. Vengeance against you has already been ordained. Your Watchful Lord shall absolutely settle the score."[4]

Imam Al-Sajjad said, "Aunt! Stop! Praise is due to Allah, Who blessed you with superior knowledge without the help of a teacher."[5]

Zaynab immediately stopped. Her speech astonished the confused and materialistic crowd. Her words awakened the Kufans, opened up their eyes, and provoked them to realize the immensity of their shameful crime.

THE SPEECH OF FATIMA BINT AL-HUSAYN

After Zaynab, Fatima Bint Al-Husayn rose up and addressed the crowd. She said:

"I praise Allah numerously, to match the number of sand grains and pebbles. I also praise Him to match the weight of the Throne and Heavens. I praise Him, believe in Him and rely on Him. I pledge that there is no God but Allah the One, devoid of any partnership, and that Mohammed, whose children have been unjustifiably slaughtered on the banks of the Euphrates, is His servant and Messenger.

My Lord! I seek refuge in You to avoid lies and altercations. You have blessed Ali Bin Abu Talib and entrusted him with the position of guardianship. Ali's rights were usurped and, like his son, he was murdered in the house of Allah the Exalted. The faith of Muslims around him was only lip service. They were ignorant because they did nothing to protect him in his life, and upon his death, until Allah the Exalted took his soul. He was pious, lenient, pleasant, and unrivaled with his dedication and miraculous achievements. He was fearless and never timid on the way of Allah, and despite the critics, he firmly adhered to the path of the Exalted. My Lord! You guided him (Ali) as a young boy, and praised his qualities as a man. He was devoutly loyal to You, and to Your Messenger. He had no interest in this life because he desired the next. He fought bravely on Your way. You accepted, selected, and guided him to the straight path.

Kufans! You are conceited traitors. Allah is testing us with your presence, and testing you with ours. However, His test has been a blessing on us. He deposited His Knowledge in our hearts, and selected us to be the medium of His justice and the residence of His Wisdom. He also appointed us the leaders of the earth and its inhabitants.

Allah ultimately blessed and favored us over all of his creatures because we are the family of His Prophet Mohammed.

You considered us liars and infidels, and daringly fought us and looted our possessions. You did all of this as if we were truly idolaters. This is not strange of you, since you slaughtered our grandfather (Imam Ali) in the past. The marks of our blood, that is the blood of the Prophet's household, are still fresh on your swords. You have done this because of your spite towards us. You are pleased, and your hearts are joyous for what you did. Be aware that you have violated Allah's ordinances, and have gone completely astray. You have schemed against Allah, but He schemes best. Do not be so elated for spilling our blood and looting our possessions. All of these disasters and atrocities, which have been inflicted on us, *were ordained in The Book before creation. Allah easily implements His ordinances. You shall never regret the past nor shall you be joyous for your gain, for Allah indeed despises the conceited and arrogant. (57:22)*

You are doomed! Anticipate wrath and chastisement! Wrath from the sky shall strike you like thunder and destroy you. Because you oppressed us, you shall plunge into the devastation of feudalism, and end up in severe and immortal chastisement on the Day of Judgement. Allah's wrath is definitely bound to befall the oppressors.

You are condemned! Are you aware of the gravity of your crime? Are you aware of the magnitude of your violation against us? What kind of humans are you? How dare you fight us? Your hearts are merciless, and your souls are innately evil. Allah allowed your hearts to become blinded, your vision to become blurry, and your hearing to become lame. Satan lured you, dictated your actions, and blinded your vision such that you shall never be guided.

Kufans! You are condemned! What kind of revenge have you had against Allah's Messenger? What score did you want settled with him? You have murdered my grandfather, Ali Bin Abu Talib, his sons and their pious and pure family members. I heard that an arrogant Kufan proudly bragged about killing Ali and his family. I also heard that he bragged about capturing Ali's daughters.

You! Whoever you are! How dare your dirty mouth brag about killing individuals whom Allah praised and purified from any mischief? Brag all you want. After all, you are a Kufan! I testify that every human shall be held responsible for his actions, and reap what he sowed.

Kufans! You envied us because Allah blessed us. Well! Allah blesses whomever He wants, because He is the sole source of blessings. On the other hand, the people from whom Allah withholds His light shall never be enlightened."[6]

People wailed, wept, and collectively said, "You! The daughter of the pious and the pure! Please stop! You have broken our hearts and set our guts on fire."

Umm Kulthoum's Speech

Umm Kulthoum said:

"Kufans! Do not say a word! Your men have murdered us, while your women are now weeping on us. This is preposterous! Allah shall be the judge between you and us on the Day of Resurrection.

Kufans! You abandoned Al-Husayn, murdered him, looted his possessions and unjustifiably captured his women and children! You should be ashamed of yourselves! You are indeed condemned! What has gotten in your minds? Are you aware of the enormity of your crime? Have you any idea whose blood you have spilled? Have you any idea whose women and children you have abused and captured? Have you any idea whose possessions you have looted? You have murdered the best of men after the Prophet. You are merciless and heartless! Nonetheless, Allah's party is definitely victorious while Satan's is the absolute loser."[7]

The forum turned completely tearful. The crowd wept aloud. Kufan women cried hysterically, beat on their cheeks, scratched their faces and loudly condemned the atrocities. Some said that people's constant weeping in that mournful forum was unprecedented.

AL-SAJJAD'S SPEECH

Ali Bin Al-Husayn was forced on an old and weak camel. He was firmly shackled with his hands tied around his neck, while his face bled constantly. Upon entering Kufa, Imam Al-Sajjad said, "You are an awful community, for you hold no regard for our grandfather! How will you justify your actions to Allah's Messenger on the Day of Gathering? We are the pillars of faith! How dare you force us on unsaddled rides?"

Imam Zayn Al-Abideen gestured to the crowd to calm down. As silence prevailed, he praised Allah and supplicated to Him to bestow countless blessings upon the Prophet. He then said:

> "You people! Some know who I am, but I shall introduce myself to those who don't. I am Ali Bin Al-Husayn Bin Ali Bin Abu Talib. I am the son of the man whose sanctity has been violated. I am the son of the man whose rights have been usurped, and whose possessions have been looted, and whose children have been captured and imprisoned. I am the son of the man who was unjustifiably slaughtered on the banks of the Euphrates. I am the son of the man who persevered until he was martyred. I am very proud to be his son.
>
> People! I ask you By Allah, are you aware that you wrote to my father and then deceived him? You, under oaths, had promised him your loyalty, pledged allegiance, and expressed your commitment to him. Instead of honoring your pledge, you turned against him and murdered him. You are doomed to have done this. You are indeed condemned to have chosen this path. How could you look the Prophet in the eye when he prosecutes you for murdering his family, and violating his sanctity? He will inform you then that you do not belong to his Community."

The crowd wailed and said, "We are in total loss, but we are yet to realize."

Al-Sajjad resumed, "Allah's mercy accompanies the person who accepts my advice and observes my proximity to Allah, my kinship to His Messenger and my position in the Prophet's household. Allah's Messenger is the best role model for all of us."

The audience collectively replied, "You are the son of Allah's

Messenger! We are all ears, submissive to your orders, ready to protect you, and shall not abandon you or turn you down. Issue your orders! May Allah's mercy be upon you! We shall fight your enemies and befriend your friends. We dissociate ourselves from those who oppressed you, and oppressed us."

Al-Sajjad responded, "It is impossible to trust you after you proved to be disloyal and faithless. Your desires have blinded your souls. You are telling me what you told my father before. By the Lord! I shall never believe you! The wound is still bleeding. My father and his family were slaughtered yesterday. The grief of Allah's Messenger, my father and his sons is still afresh. I moan on him (Al-Husayn) with every breath. I constantly choke on my tears. Bitterness is a constant taste in my mouth and throat. Grief has injected an excruciating and suffocating pain into my chest."[8]

THE BURIAL

Historians stated that the Master of Martyrs set up a special tent in the battlefield, and ordered that the martyrs from his family and companions be carried into it.[9] Each time a martyr was placed in it, Al-Husayn said, "A slaughter equivalent to that of the prophets and their families."[10] Abu Al-Fadhl Al-Abbass was the only exception. He was left on the bank of the Euphrates in the exact spot where he was martyred.[11] Imam Ali said that the martyrs of Karbala were the foremost; who have never been, and shall never be, surpassed by anyone. He also described them as the Masters of All Martyrs, in this life and in the next. Omar Bin Sa'ad departed to Kufa with the women, and left the Holy bodies of these martyrs on the hot sand under the blazing sun. It is important to know that, in that time being, no one visited the martyrs except wild beasts. Despite the wretched and heartbreaking condition, the Holy body of the Master of all Martyrs emanated bright rays of light, and diffused a sensational fragrance into the air.

A man from Bani Assad came to the battlefield after the departure of the troops. He said that beautiful a scent filled the air, and rays of light emanated from the martyrs' bloody bodies. He saw an incredible looking lion, jumping over the amputated limbs towards Al-Husayn's Holy body. The lion moaned and roared as soon as it reached the Master of all Martyrs. It then leaned close to Al-Husayn's body, and rolled around in his Holy blood. The man was amazed to see a predator do this. He hid, and carefully watched to see if it did anything else, but the lion did not. This man said that in the middle of that night, he witnessed things that were more startling. He saw lit candles all over the battlefield, and simultaneously heard heartbreaking cries and moans.[12]

Since only an infallible leader can bury his infallible predecessor, Imam Zayn Al-Abideen came to Karbala on the thirteenth of Muharram to bury his father.[13] The following authentic dialogue between Imam Al-Ridha and Ali Bin Abu Hamza attests to the fact that Ali Bin Al-Husayn, Al-Sajjad (Imam Zayn Al-Abideen), buried his father. (It took a few days to travel from Medina to Baghdad back then. Bin Abu Hamza was in disbelief that Imam Al-Ridha could have traveled to Baghdad, buried his father, and returned to Medina on the same day). Imam Al-Ridha asked the perplexed Bin Abu Hamza, "Was Al-Husayn Bin Ali an infallible leader?" Bin Abu Hamza answered, "Yes." Al-Ridha continued, "Who buried him?" Bin Abu Hamza replied, "Ali Bin Al-Husayn Al-Sajjad did." Al-Ridha asked him again, "Where was Ali Bin Al-Husayn?" He replied, "He was in Bin Ziyad's prison in Kufa, but he, without anyone noticing, left and buried his father then returned to prison." Al-Ridha explained, "Whoever enabled Ali Bin Al-Husayn to reach Karbala, bury his father and return (to Kufa), can enable the contemporary infallible leader, who is not in prison, to reach Baghdad and bury his father."

Al-Sajjad arrived to Karbala and saw Bani Assad restlessly wandering around the martyrs' bodies. Unable to identify the headless martyrs, Bani Assad seemed totally confused and helpless. Al-Sajjad informed them that he had come to bury the martyrs. The women of Bani Assad wept and wailed as Imam Al-Sajjad identified the bodies of Bani Hashim and their companions. Imam Zayn Al-Abideen walked to his father, hugged the Holy body and wept aloud. He then walked to where the burial site is now, lifted some sand, and found that a grave had already been dug. He placed his hands under Al-Husayn's back, and said, "In the name of Allah, on the way of Allah and on the path of Allah's Messenger. Allah is Truthful, and so is His Messenger. According to Allah's Will. There is no strength and power except that from Allah the Great." He lay him down without Bani Assad's help. He told them, "Someone is helping me." He rested the Holy body inside the grave, put his cheek on Al-Husayn's neck and said, "Blessed is the land that houses your pure body. You were our light! Your radiance receded from this life to shine on in the next. My nights are sleepless, and my grief is endless until Allah ordains for your family to join you. The son of Allah's Messenger! I greet you with peace, and I ask Allah to bestow His Mercy and Blessings upon you." He then wrote on the grave, "This is the grave of Al-Husayn Bin Ali Bin Abu Talib; who was abandoned and murdered thirsty."

After burying his father, he walked towards his uncle's body. Al-Abbass's condition astounded the angels, and devastated the maidens of heavens. Imam Al-Sajjad kissed Al-Abbass's neck, and said, "You are the radiant face of Bani Hashim! Life is worthless without you. You are a martyr indeed! I greet you with peace, and may Allah's Blessings and Mercy be upon you." He dug a grave for Al-Abbass, and as he did with his father, buried him without anyone's help. He told Bani Assad, "Someone is helping me." Imam Al-Sajjad allowed Bani Assad to help him bury the rest of the martyrs. He marked two spots and ordered them to dig two large ditches. He buried Bani Hashim in one, and the companions in the other. Al-Hurr Al-Riyahi was the only exception. His tribe had already buried Al-Hurr's' body in his current grave. Some narrated that Al-Hurr's mother was in Karbala, and when she saw the martyrs' bodies being mutilated, she transported her son to his current grave.[14]

In the mass grave of Bani Hashim, Ali Al-Akbar's body was placed closest to his father. Emphasizing this fact, Imam Al-Sadiq told Hammad Al-Basri, "Abu Abdullah was abandoned and murdered in an uninhabited land. Some visit him and weep on him. Others, who cannot visit him, are similarly grieved and deeply touched by his plight. The scene of his son's grave at his feet in that piece of uninhabited land is heartbreaking. The apostates usurped his rights. They then united against him; abused him, slaughtered him and left him for the wild beasts. They did all this after they denied him the water of the Euphrates, from which animals are allowed to drink. In his will, Allah's Messenger instructed his community to look after Al-Husayn and his family. Instead, people betrayed the Prophet and violated his will. His family members and followers were buried around him. Nonetheless, he lay lonely because he is far from his grandfather. To compensate for his loneliness, Allah inspired the faithful who honor and revere us to visit his site. My father told me that, since the tragedy of Karbala, Al-Husayn's Holy site has always been crowded with angels, Jinn, humans and animals. These creatures come to visit and commend Al-Husayn. Everyone envies the visitor of his grave. People, who want to gain blessings, should touch and look at the faces of his visitors. Allah, the Exalted, shows his visitors off to His angels. We, in our turn, supplicate day and night asking Allah to bestow His mercy upon his visitors. I was informed that some people from Kufa and its surrounding neighborhoods go to him in the middle of Sha'aban. Some of them recite Qur'an or weep. Others narrate the tragedy of Karbala or commemorate him in poetry, while some women wail on him." Hammad said, "I have definitely witnessed some of what you described." Imam Al-Sadiq continued, "I thank Allah, who guided some of the people to visit, praise and mourn us despite the abuse, prosecution and threats they receive from our enemies."[15]

IN THE GOVERNOR'S PALACE

Bin Ziyad returned from his military camp in Al-Nakheela to Kufa. Soon after he arrived at the palace, he placed the Holy head in front of him as if it were a prize. Blood dripped out of the walls, and fiery flames streamed out from some corners of the palace towards Bin Ziyad. The latter fled into the other room. The Holy head spoke loudly such that Bin Ziyad and some of his attendants clearly heard it. The head told Bin Ziyad, "Where shall you run? If it doesn't get to you in this life, it surely is your destiny in the next." The head spoke until the fire receded. This unprecedented miracle staggered everyone in the palace.[16] Seemingly unaffected by this awesome phenomenon, Bin Ziyad opened the palace to the public, and ordered the captives simultaneously brought to him. The family and women of Allah's Messenger were violently pushed into the palace in an incredibly pitiful condition.[17]

Bin Ziyad placed the Holy head in front of him, and repeatedly struck Al-Husayn's lips with a stick. Zayd Bin Arqam objected,

"Keep this stick away from these lips. By Allah, the only God! I saw the lips of Allah's Messenger kissing them." Zayd then wept. Bin Ziyad told him, "May Allah keep your eyes tearful. By Allah! Had you not been old and senile, I would have beheaded you." Zayd left the palace saying, "A slave has become in charge of his peers but only to exploit them. Arabs! You have become slaves from now on. You killed Fatima's son and pledged allegiance to Marjana's son (Bin Ziyad) so he would murder the pious and enslave the vicious. You have succumbed to humiliation. Whoever succumbs to humiliation is indeed condemned."[18]

Zaynab disguised herself, and stepped slightly away from the women. However, the inherent light of Prophethood and the radiance of infallibility attracted Bin Ziyad's attention. He asked, "Who is that disguised woman?" Someone answered, "She is the daughter of the Commander of the Faithful, Zaynab the Honorable." Adding insult to Zaynab's injury, Bin Ziyad deridingly said, "I thank Allah, who exposed you, killed you and destroyed your falsehood." Zaynab replied, "I praise Allah, who blessed us with Mohammed, and unequivocally purified us from any filth. The transgressor shall be exposed, and the shameless liar shall be destroyed, and we are neither." Bin Ziyad asked, "How do you view what Allah did to your family?" She answered, "I see nothing but glory. Allah preordained martyrdom for these men, and they gladly embraced their fate. Allah shall make you face them, where you shall be indicted and tried. Assess for yourself who shall be the loser then. You! Marjana's son! May your mother soon weep on you."[19]

Bin Ziyad became visibly irate at Zaynab for talking back to him in front of the crowd. He furiously jumped up to hit her, but Amr Bin Hurayth interjected, "She is a woman. A woman is never charged for mere talk. She should not be punished for her words, or blamed for any mischief." Bin Ziyad looked at her and said, "Allah had already soothed my heart when He destroyed the tyrant (Al-Husayn), and the disobedient rebels of your family." Zaynab tenderly commented, "By Allah! You have killed my protector, cut off the branches of my family tree, shaken its roots, and exploited its members. If this was your objective, then you should be totally satisfied."[20] Bin Ziyad then looked at Ali Bin Al-Husayn, and asked him, "What is your name?" He answered, "I am Ali Bin Al-Husayn." Bin

Ziyad asked again, "Didn't Allah kill Ali?" Al-Sajjad replied, "I had an older brother named Ali, but people killed him." Bin Ziyad emphatically reiterated, "Allah killed him." Al-Sajjad explained, "Allah takes the souls upon death, and no soul shall die without an ordinance from Allah."

Bin Ziyad became irate again at Al-Sajjad for talking back, and ordered his execution. Zaynab immediately hugged Al-Sajjad, and said, "Bin Ziyad! You have spilled enough of our blood. You have spared no one but him![21] You have to kill me first if you want to kill him." Al-Sajjad told Bin Ziyad, "Don't you know that we embrace death on the way of Allah, and that martyrdom is Allah's blessing upon us?"[22]

Bin Ziyad stared at Zaynab and Al-Sajjad for a while, and then said, "Leave him to her. The bond of kinship is amazing! She was willing to die with him."[23]

Al-Rabaab put her husband's head in her lap and said, "My Husayn! I shall never forget Husayn. The spears of the enemies killed him. They left him for dead in Karbala. I shall always be in grief for the tragedy of Karbala."[24]

The crowd in the governor's palace wailed and the forum became chaotic after Bin Ziyad's argument with Zaynab. Fearing that the turmoil might spiral out of control and lead to an instant reprisal, Bin Ziyad immediately ordered his police to imprison the captives in a house adjacent to the great mosque of Kufa.[25] Bin Ziyad's doorman narrated, "I happened to be close to them when Bin Ziyad ordered their detention. Kufan men and women gathered around, wept and beat their faces."[26]

Zaynab loudly told the large crowd, "No one is allowed into the prison except a former or a current concubine, because they similarly suffered the hardship of captivity."[27] Zaynab explicitly dictated the criteria of the women who were allowed access to tend to the captives in their prison. She prudently and publicly set this condition, because only a woman who had suffered captivity and imprisonment could be sympathetic and sincere in serving them.

Later on, Bin Ziyad put Al-Husayn's head in front of him and ordered the captives back into the palace. The women entered, and saw the Holy head radiating bright rays of light into the sky. Al-Rabaab could not help but fall onto it. She kissed it, and said,

"Our light of being has been left dead in Karbala without burial. The Prophet's grandson! I ask Allah to bless you and spare you all hardships. You were our shelter and fortress. Your company was faith and mercy. Who shall help the orphans and the poor now? Where shall the needy go now? By Allah! I shall mourn on you until my death."[28]

BIN AFEEF

Hameed Bin Muslim narrated that Bin Ziyad summoned the Kufans to the great mosque for congregational prayer. He stood on the pulpit and said, "I thank Allah, who aided righteousness and its adherents into victory, supported Yazeed and his party, and killed the liar, the son of a liar, Al-Husayn Bin Ali and his followers."[29]

Dormant in their aberration, no one in the audience raised an eyebrow or objected to Bin Ziyad's words, except Abdullah Bin Afeef Al-Azdi Al-Ghamidi from Bani Waliba. Bin Afeef stood up and said, "You! Marjana's son! The liars are you and your father, and the man who appointed you and his father. How dare you have the audacity to emulate the pious after you murdered the descendants of the prophets?"[30] Bin Ziyad loudly inquired, "Who was that?" Bin Afeef replied, "You! The enemy of Allah! It was I who spoke up. How dare you claim to be an adherent to Islam after you murdered the purified family, from whom Allah kept away all filth? I call upon the children of the Migrants and Supporters to avenge from your tyrant who, along with his father, has been cursed by the Messenger of the Lord of the Worlds." Extremely furious at Bin Afeef, Bin Ziyad ordered his police to arrest him.[31] Bin Afeef immediately yelled, "Oh Mabrur!" This was the slogan to which Al-Azd tribesmen rushed to rescue one another. A large number of his tribesmen attacked the police, freed him and escorted him home. Abdurrahman Bin Makhnaf Al-Azdi told Bin Afeef, "You are doomed! You have put yourself and your tribe into harm's way."[32]

Bin Ziyad imprisoned Abdurrahman Bin Makhnaf Al-Azdi and a group of men from Al-Azd tribe.[33] He then ordered his police to go after midnight to Bin Afeef's house and arrest him. Al-Azd tribe and their Yamani allies gathered to fend off the attackers. Informed of the Al-Azd's intent to resist, Bin Ziyad dispatched the tribe of Madhar under Bin Al-Asha'ath to do the job. A fierce battle ensued, during which both tribes suffered heavy casualties. Finally, Bin Al-Asha'ath and his soldiers reached Bin Afeef's house and stormed into it. Bin Afeef's daughter screamed, "They're here to capture you." He told her, "Just hand me my sword and do not worry." He put up a fierce resistance. He fought and simultaneously chanted, "I am the son of Afeef, the pure and blessed. Afeef is my father. I have always fought and killed your heroes." The girl told her blind father, "I wish I was a man to defend you from these transgressors, who murdered of the Prophet's pure household." His daughter navigated him through the battle, and for a while no one was able to subdue him. Finally, they encircled him. His daughter screamed, "What a loss! My father is being attacked, and no one is around to help him." Bin Afeef spun around with his sword and yelled, "By Allah! Had I not been blind, you would never arrest me."

Finally, a group of men overpowered him, pinned him down and took him to Bin Ziyad. The latter told Bin Afeef, "I thank Allah for disgracing you." Bin Afeef exclaimed, "How did He disgrace me? By Allah! Had I been able to see, you would have never arrested me." Bin Ziyad asked him, "You! The enemy of Allah! What do you think of Uthman?" Bin Afeef cursed Bin Ziyad and replied, "Whether Uthman did good or bad you have nothing to do with him. Allah is the Guardian over His creatures, and He shall rightfully judge between them and Uthman. Ask me about your father and yourself, or about Yazeed and his father." Bin Ziyad said, "I shall ask you nothing further. You shall choke tasting death." Bin Afeef said, "I praise the Lord of the Worlds. I have asked Him to bless me with martyrdom long before your mother conceived you. I have also asked Him to make it on the hands of His most evil creatures, but when I became blind I gave up my quest. Praise is due to Allah, who blessed me with martyrdom, and taught me that my old supplication has been answered." Bin Ziyad ordered him executed and crucified in Al-Sabkha.[34]

Jandab Bin Abdullah Al-Azdi was an old man. Bin Ziyad summoned him to the governor's palace and told him, "You! The enemy of Allah! Weren't you Abu Turab's companion in Siffeen?" He replied, "Yes indeed. I love him and I am proud to have been his companion. In contrast, I despise you and your father, especially now that you, fearless of the Omnipotent Avenger, murdered the Prophet's grandson, his family and companions." Bin Ziyad said, "You are more shameless than that blind man. I shall seek proximity to Allah by spilling your blood." Jandab said, "Allah shall definitely condemn you." Bin Ziyad, fearful of a reprisal from Al-Azd tribe, released him and justified, "He is old and senile."[35]

AL-MUKHTAR AL-THAQAFI

Bin Ziyad ordered the captives brought to his palace, and alongside with them, he ordered Al-Mukhtar Al-Thaqafi brought from prison. Shocked and touched by the captives' condition, Al-Mukhtar loudly condemned and cursed Bin Ziyad. The latter became angry and ordered the former to be taken back to prison.[36] It has also been narrated that Bin Ziyad whipped Al-Mukhtar and poked one of his eyes.[37]

Abdullah Bin Omar was married to Saffiyya Bint Abu Obeyd Al-Thaqafi, Al-Mukhtar's sister. Bin Omar personally requested from Yazeed to release Al-Mukhtar from prison, however, Bin Ziyad delayed it three days. Due to the intercession of his brother in law, Al-Mukhtar was freed after Bin Afeef's martyrdom. After murdering Bin Afeef, Bin Ziyad heavily cursed Imam Ali in his public address. Al-Mukhtar rose up, reviled Bin Ziyad, and said, "You are a liar and an enemy of Allah and His Messenger. Praise is due to Allah, who honored and blessed Al-Husayn and his army with paradise and forgiveness, and in contrast, disgraced you, Yazeed and his army with hellfire." Bin Ziyad struck Al-Mukhtar with a metal bar, fracturing his forehead. He then detained him.

Bin Ziyad's entourage reminded him of Al-Mukhtar's elite social status, and that Omar Bin Sa'ad and Abdullah Bin Omar were his brothers in law. Seemingly convinced, Bin Ziyad did not execute Al-Mukthar, but kept him in prison. Abdullah Bin Omar interceded for Al-Mukhtar again with Yazeed. The latter wrote Bin Ziyad ordering him to release Al-Mukhtar.[38] After his release, Al-Mukhtar began informing the followers of the Prophet's household of what he learned from Imam Ali's devout companions. He told them that he was bound to rise up to avenge Al-Husayn, and that he will kill Bin Ziyad and all the traitors who fought Imam Ali's son.[39]

The following authentic narration is only one of many in which Imam Ali foretold his loyal companions about Al-Mukhtar's uprising. Al-Mukhtar, Abdullah Bin Al-Harith Bin Nawfal Bin Abd Al-Muttalib and Maytham Al-Tammar shared one cell in Bin Ziyad's prison. After requesting a sharp blade to shave his body, Abdullah Bin Al-Harith explained, "I am worried that Bin Ziyad will execute me any minute now, and I would like to shave my body before it happens." Al-Mukhtar commented, "By Allah! He shall kill neither one of us, and soon you shall govern Al-Basra." Listening attentively to their conversation, Maytham Al-Tammar looked at Al-Mukhtar and added, "And you will rise up and avenge Al-Husayn. You shall kill the man who wants to kill us, and stomp his face with your feet."[40]

The description of Al-Mukhtar and Maytham was accurate, and the sequence of events unraveled exactly as they foretold. After Yazeed's demise, Abdullah Bin Al-Harith rose up in Al-Basra. Its people selected him to be their governor, and he subsequently ruled the province for one year. Al-Mukhtar in turn rose up and avenged Al-Husayn. He killed Bin Ziyad, Harmala Bin Kahil and Shimr Bin Thil Jawshan. Bin Nama Al-Hilli narrated that Al-Mukhtar killed eighteen-thousand of the Kufans who betrayed Al-Husayn, while ten-thousand of them escaped and joined Mus'ab Bin Al-Zubayr.[41] Shibth Bin Rib'ie was one of the escapees. He rode a bleeding mule, and as soon as he saw Mus'ab, Shibth yelled, "Please help! Lead us to fight the transgressor who destroyed our homes and killed our leaders."[42]

WORDS FROM THE HOLY HEAD

The Prophet's grandson, the Master of all Martyrs, was imbued with the Qur'an from the moment of his creation. Invaluable treasures, Al-Husayn and the Qur'an were integral pillars of the Prophet's Message, and the rightful leaders of his community (Ummah). The greatest of all Messengers had stated that the two are inseparable, until they reunite with him at the Pond. Throughout his life, Al-Husayn recited the Qur'an and lived by its codes, instructions and teachings. His articulate and categorical method of reasoning with the Kufans on the day of Ashura highlighted Al-Husayn's strong attachment to the Qur'an, and his unshakable adherence to its teachings.

Allah and His words occupied Al-Husayn's heart until his last breath. Al-Husayn's Holy head was heard reciting the Qur'an from the spear. This miracle occurred numerously. The purpose behind it was to awaken people, and attract them to the Divine light. Nonetheless, such a miraculous propagation of guidance and salvation was met with detrimental ignorance. The words from the Holy head fell on dysfunctional hearts and deaf ears, for *"Allah had sealed their hearts and ears while their vision is blurred. (2:7)"*

Having acknowledged Allah's Hidden Kindness, one should not be doubtful that this extraordinary phenomenon or miracle did occur. The Exalted Guardian assigned the Master of Martyrs to rise up in order to seal the door of aberration. Allah ordained a specific place and time for this Holy uprising. The Almighty revealed the scope and goal of this uprising to His Holy Prophet, and instructed him to inform Al-Husayn of all of its details. One can only submit to the Will of Allah, for *"He is never asked about what He does, but people are. (21:23)"* This Holy uprising embodied a Divine lesson. Allah wanted the contemporary community, and the coming generations, to learn from it, and subsequently, to be able to easily identify the transgressors who would try to distort the Holy revelations. Allah conveyed the lesson of this Holy uprising with pure blood on radiant pages, visible enough to the faithful in their struggle against the evil oppressors.

Miracles are more effective in electrifying their witnesses. The recitation of Qur'an by Al-Husayn's Holy head was one of many miracles that occurred throughout this Holy uprising. Even though incomprehensible to our minds now, the people who witnessed these miracles and heard verses of the Qur'an from Al-Husayn's Holy head should have been stunned and awakened. The speech of the Holy head verified before the eyes of its contemporaries that Al-Husayn was a manifestation of the true path. In addition to undermining the tyrant's evil schemes, this miracle occurred to sternly warn those who, swayed by their desires, had committed the atrocities. One should not deny the occurrences of miracles, even if their scope defies our logic and limited intellect. Al-Husayn was slaughtered in pure submission to the will of the Omnipotent. It suffices to mention that the Divine Power enabled Al-Husayn's head to speak, as It enabled the tree to converse with Prophet Musa Bin Imran.[43] Al-Husayn's significance, undeniably and by far, exceeds that of the tree. However, we employed this analogy only to elucidate our point, and to further support our argument.

Zayd Bin Arqam narrated that the criminals carried the head and passed by the room in which he was sitting. Zayd heard the head recite, *"Do you think that the people of the cave and inscription were highly wondrous among our miracles? (18:9)"* Having goosebumps all over his body, Zayd immediately replied, "You are the son of Allah's Messenger, and by Allah! Your head is much more wondrous."[44] They placed the head in the section of money exchange, which is the busiest and noisiest part of the market. The head of the Master of all Martyrs grunted very loudly to attract people's attention, and to compel them to listen to his advice. People were completely shocked because until then, no one had ever heard a voice from a severed human head. The crowd flocked towards it. The head recited the first thirteen verses of Surah "The Cave" and concluded with the following verse, "(Oh Allah) *Inflict more aberration unto the oppressors. (71:24)*" After that, the Holy head was placed on a tree. As people gathered around it to watch its staggering beauty and radiance, the head recited, *"The oppressors shall soon know where they end up. (26:227)"*[45]

Hilal Bin Mu'awiya narrated that he saw a man carrying Al-Husayn's head and heard the Holy head telling its carrier, "You separated my head from my body. I ask Allah to separate between your flesh and bones, and make you an example for His creatures as He chastises you." Hilal said the man furiously whipped the head until it stopped speaking.[46] Salama Bin Kaheel heard the head from atop the spear reciting the following verse. *"Allah shall aid you against them, and He is the Knowing Hearer (2:137)"*[47]

Bin Wakeeda said he heard the head recite Surah "The Cave." but he had a doubt whether it was Al-Husayn's voice or someone else's. Meanwhile, the head stopped reciting, looked at Bin Wakeeda and said, "Bin Wakeeda! Don't you know that we, the infallible leaders, are alive enjoying our Lord's bounties?" Bin Wakeeda decided to steal the head and bury it. The Holy head told him, "Bin Wakeeda! You can never do that. Spilling my blood is a greater violation than carrying my head on a spear. *Ignore them because soon they shall be dragged with the shackles and chains around their necks (40:71)."*[48]

Al-Minhal Bin Amr narrated that he saw Al-Husayn's head on a spear in Damascus, and in front of it, was a man reciting Surah "The Cave." As the man recited, *"Do you think that the people of the cave and inscription were highly wondrous among our miracles?"* the Holy head eloquently replied, "More wondrous than the people of the cave is murdering me and carrying my head around."[49] Moreover, when Yazeed ordered the messenger of the Roman emperor executed for publicly condemning the atrocities of Karbala, Al-Husayn's head loudly said, "There is no power and strength except Allah's!"[50]

AL-ASHDAQ'S TYRANNY

Bin Jareer Al-Tabari narrated that Bin Ziyad sent Abdul Malek Bin Al-Harith Al-Salmi to Medina to inform Amr Bin Sa'iid Al-Ashdaq of Al-Husayn's death. Abdul Malik claimed to be sick to avoid this mission. Bin Ziyad, a fiery dictator, did not buy his excuse. He ordered him to ride nonstop and to buy a new horse if the one in use became tired. Bin Ziyad warned him that he should be the first to break the news in Medina. Abdul Malek rode nonstop. Upon his arrival to Medina, a man from Quraysh asked him about the latest. He answered that the governor should know first. Abdul Malek told Bin Sa'iid Al-Ashdaq that Al-Husayn had been killed. Al-Ashdaq became vibrant and overtly joyous. Al-Ashdaq ordered his spokesperson to walk in the alleys of Medina and announce the killing of Al-Husayn. The women of Bani Hashim wailed in their homes. Their moans and cries echoed throughout Medina. Al-Ashdaq heard them from his house. He laughed and said wickedly, "Let them weep as our women wept." He then said, "We mourned on Uthman, and now we are even."[51] After that, he looked at the Prophet's grave and said, "You! The Messenger of Allah! Today we avenged the Battle of Badr." Some of the Supporters (Ansar) condemned him, and objected to his boisterous vindication.[52] He then stood on the pulpit and said, "People! An eye for an eye, and a tooth for tooth! Words beget more words! An utmost wisdom but no one heeds the warnings. He cursed us; we praised him. He was rebellious; we were kind to him. This is how we were in comparison to how he was. What can we do with someone who waged war to kill us? We had to defend ourselves."

Abdullah Bin Al-Sa'eb stood up and said, "Had Fatima been alive, and seen Al-Husayn's head, she would have wept." Al-Ashdaq scolded him and said, "We, and not you, are Fatima's family. Her father is our uncle. Her husband is our brother. Her mother is our daughter. Had she been alive, she would have wept. However, she would not have held a grudge against those who killed him in self-defense."[53] Al-Ashdaq was vulgar, rough and merciless. After Al-Husayn's martyrdom, he ordered his police chief, Amr Bin Al-Zubayr, to destroy the homes of Bani Hashim throughout Medina. Along with these homes, Amr destroyed the house of Bin Mutee'. Al-Ashdaq savagely beat and tortured the people of Medina. As a result, a large number of men ran away from the Prophet's city, and joined Abdullah Bin Al-Zubayr in Mecca.[54]

Amr Bin Sa'iid was nicknamed Al-Ashdaq because his mouth permanently turned to one side of his face. This happened to him because he incessantly cursed Ali Bin Abu Talib.[55]

Al-Ashdaq was a ruthless tyrant. Later in his life, Allah punished him with a taste of his own medicine. Abdul Malek Bin Marwan ordered him shackled and dragged to Damascus. Bin Marwan publicly reviled Al-Ashdaq before executing him.[56]

Accompanied by a group of women from Bani Hashim, the daughter of Aqeel Bin Abu Talib walked over to the Prophet's grave. She sat next to it and screamed. She then looked at the Migrants and Supporters and said, "You heedlessly abandoned the Prophet's household, and allowed the oppressors to murder them. What would you say to the Prophet on the Day of Judgement, when he tries or blames you for your complacency? The Prophet trusts and relies upon the Supreme Judge. You shall be deprived of his intercession on the Day of Gathering." The crowd wept hysterically. Some narrated that this was the most tearful day in the history of Medina.[57]

Zaynab Bint Aqeel Bin Abu Talib mourned Al-Husayn in a tender and a very sad tone. She complained about the lack of support that the Prophet's household received from the Muslim Community. She vented, "The Prophet's family members have been either imprisoned or murdered. How will you answer the Prophet when he asks about supporting his family? What will you say when he accuses you of being an accomplice in these crimes? What will you say when he holds you responsible for abusing his closest of kin? The Prophet shall complain about your lack of appreciation to his efforts in delivering the Divine Message!"[58]

UMM AL-BANEEN

I could not find a trustworthy source or an authentic narration confirming that Umm Al-Baneen outlived Al-Husayn and her son, Al-Abbass. There are only three different sources that may have contributed to the common belief that she did. The first is the statement of Mohammed Al-Qazweeni in page sixty of his book *Riyadh Al-Ahzaan*. He wrote: "A mourning session was held in the house of Umm Al-Baneen, the wife of the Commander of the Faithful and the mother of Al-Abbass and his three brothers." The second is Al-Samawi's statement in page-thirty-one of his book *Ibsar Al-A'yn*. Al-Samawi wrote: "In his *Sharh Al-Kamil*, Al-Akhfash quoted Umm Al-Baneen's words in expressing her grief. Her emotional poetry in mourning her son (Al-Abbass) breaks my heart. She carried his son, Abdullah, and went to Al-Baqee' every day to wail on Al-Abbass. The people of Medina, including Marwan Bin Al-Hakam, gathered around her and wept as they listened to her moans." The third is the statement of Abu Al-Faraj Al-Isfahani in his book *Maqatil Al-Talibiyyeen*. Describing Al-Abbass' martyrdom, Abu Al-Faraj narrated from Mohammed Bin Ali Bin Hamza, from Al-Nawfali, from Hammad Bin Isa Al-Juhani from Mu'awiya Bin Ammar, from Ja'afar, "Umm Al-Baneen, the mother of four martyrs, frequently went to Al-Baqee' to mourn her sons. People, including Marwan, gathered around her to listen to her tearful moans."

This is all we found about Umm Al-Baneen's life that pertain to the tragedy of Karbala. The first statement confirmed that a mourning session was held in her house, but provided no evidence that she was alive. The second statement was quoted directly from Abu Al-Faraj's work without proper investigation. Therefore, it cannot be considered an independent narration. I looked very hard for *Sharh Al-Kamil*, the book that Al-Samawi attributed to Al-Akhfash, but I could not find it. Moreover, I frequently asked Al-Samawi about the source of his statement, but he never responded. I ask Allah to reward him for his work. In his work, Al-Majlisi also quoted Abu Al-Faraj,[59] and this brings our discussion to the third statement.

Firstly, the men in Abu Al-Faraj's channel of transmission were all untrustworthy.[60] Secondly, Umm Al-Baneen was a devout follower of Prophet Mohammed, and extremely loyal to Imam Ali and the Masters of Youth in Heaven. Having acknowledged her loyalty to the Prophet's household, it is inconceivable that she would unnecessarily expose herself to male strangers (non-mahram men), and thus violate the rules of Islamic jurisprudence.

Women must, and at any cost, protect themselves from exposure to strange men. They are instructed to mourn on their deceased relatives in their homes. In an encounter with Abu Khalid Al-Kabili, Imam Al-Sajjad highlighted the Islamic perspective of women's sanctity. Explaining why the entry door should be completely shut, Imam Al-Sajjad told Abu Khalid, "Abu Khalid! A female neighbor of ours, not knowing that our door was half way opened, came out of her house. Moreover, it is not permissible for the daughters of Allah's Messenger to come out here to shut the door."[61] Therefore, people who lived amongst the Prophet's household and strictly followed their path of guidance could never violate the codes of jurisprudence that Allah mandated on women. Fatima Al-Zahra, on the other hand, was pressured by the people of Medina to go to Al-Baqee' to mourn her father. Nevertheless, Imam Ali built a house from the branches of palm trees to shelter her and protect her from exposure. It was called the House of Mourning (Bayt Al-Ahzaan).[62] Moreover, historians never mentioned that people gathered around Fatima to listen to her as she continuously wept on the Prophet.

Women go to the cemetery to weep over the grave of their loved ones. It makes no sense that a woman would go to mourn her son in a certain cemetery, while he is buried somewhere else. It is thus fair to conclude that Abu Al-Faraj fabricated this narration to cosmetically enhance Marwan's vile character. All along, Abu Al-Faraj intended to distort the truth and portray Marwan as a kind and loving believer. Having negated Abu Al-Faraj's feeble attempt, it is crucial to mention that historians had already depicted the evil image of Marwan Bin Al-Hakam. Historians narrated that he was overtly joyous for Al-Husayn's death. He looked at Al-Husayn's Holy head and deridingly commented, "I sure am glad that your cheeks have turned red from beatings. Spilling Al-Husayn's blood has definitely soothed my heart." Lastly, Abu Al-Faraj, in the same section of his book, contradicted his own fabrication. He stated that, on the day of Ashura, Al-Abbass inherited his brothers after they were killed. Mus'ab Al-Zubayry in page 43 of his *Nassab Quraysh,* and Abu Nasr Al-Bukhari in page 89 of his *Sirr Al-Silsila Al-Alawiyya* confirmed that Al-Abbass did inherit his brothers on the day of Ashura. Abu Al-Faraj fabricated that Umm Al-Baneen went to Al-Baqee' to mourn her sons. Later, in the same section of his book, he stated that on the day of Ashura Al-Abbass inherited his brothers. These statements contradict one another. Had Umm Al-Baneen been alive, she, according to the codes of inheritance in Islamic jurisprudence, should have exclusively inherited her sons. It is worth mentioning that, in addition to its numerous contradictions, Abu Al-Faraj's work is totally unreliable.

ABDULLAH BIN JA'AFAR

Bin Jareer narrated that when the news about Al-Husayn arrived in Medina, people flocked to Abdullah Bin Ja'afar's house to extend their condolences." His servant Abu Al-Salas complained, "Al-Husayn has brought us nothing but troubles." Bin Ja'afar smacked him with a shoe and said, "How dare you say this about Al-Husayn? By Allah! Had I gone with him, I would have been happy to be killed before him. By Allah! I lost two sons, and what consoles my heart is the fact that they were martyred with my brother and my cousin. It comforts me that my sons fought and persevered along with him." He then looked at his visitors and told them, "Losing Al-Husayn has devastated me. It is quite painful to me that I was not there to defend him. However, my two sons were."[63]

The story that Al-Balathri[64] and Al-Muhsin Al-Tanukhi[65] narrated is preposterous. They wrote that Abdullah Bin Ja'afar visited Yazeed after Al-Husayn's martyrdom. They also stated that Yazeed, surpassing his father's kindness, was extremely hospitable to Abdullah Bin Ja'afar.

Abdullah Bin Ja'afar's heart was burning with vengeance. He waited anxiously for an opportunity to destroy Yazeed and his corrupt family. It is unbelievable that Bin Ja'afar could have ever forgotten that Yazeed murdered Al-Husayn, his family and companions. It is also inconceivable that he could have ever forgotten that

Mu'awiya's son publicly whipped the Holy head of the Prophet's beloved grandson. How could Bin Ja'afar visit the murderer, whose sword was still dripping with the martyrs' blood? How could he visit the man who publicly denounced the Divine Message? How could he visit the man who articulated his enmity and vengeance towards the Prophet of Islam? Bin Ja'afar was fully aware that Yazeed said, "We killed their highest ranked leaders and avenged the Battle of Badr. Hashim sought to rule, but the truth is that the message and revelations are nothing but a lie." How could Bin Ja'afar ever forget that the Prophet's daughters were dragged in the dead heat and exposed to strangers? One should easily dismiss this accusation against Bin Ja'afar, because the source of it all was Al-Mada'ini, who was quite famous for his infatuation with the Umayyads. His book in which he praised the Umayyads and demeaned Ali and his family is full of fabrications. An intelligent reader should never be fooled by such deliberate contortions.

Bin Ja'afar was a pious man, and the story of this alleged visit is a clear fabrication. Al-Balathri and Al-Tanukhi quoted the story from Al-Mada'ini, who in turn stated it without mentioning its source. Human nature compels a bereaved man to develop animosity and a sense of vengeance towards the murderer of his loved ones. The following authentic stories prove that such an emotional reaction is a fundamental component of the human instinct.

Ubayy Bin Saloul insulted the Prophet. Subsequently, Allah revealed the man's derogatory description of Prophet Mohammed. Allah revealed in His Qur'an, *"Once we arrive to Medina, the elite one will kick out the low one (63:8)."* Abdullah Bin Ubayy learned the newly revealed words, and immediately went to see the Prophet. Bin Ubayy said, "You know that my father said this." The Prophet said, "Yes." Abdullah continued, "You also know that I am very kind to him. However, if you order his execution, let me implement it. I am afraid that if someone else does it, I'll eventually lose my temper and kill my father's executor, and consequently end up in hellfire."[66] Even though execution can sometimes be just, this story clearly indicates that human beings can become instinctively vengeful against the killer of their family members.

Omar Bin Al-Khattab employed this instinct of vengeance to provoke Sa'iid Bin Al-A'as against Imam Ali. Ali, Uthman, Bin Abbass and Sa'iid met at Omar's on one evening. Omar told Sa'iid, "You are being hostile to me as if I had killed your father. I did not, Abu Al-Hasan did." The Commander of the Faithful exclaimed, "Allah is forgiving! Islam prevailed while idolatry and all its relevant matters have become history. Omar! Why are you inflaming the hearts?" Sa'iid commented, "An honorable man killed him. It is soothing to me that a descendant of Abd Munaf, and not a total stranger, killed him."[67] An infidel, Sa'iid's father fought against Prophet Mohammed. Imam Ali killed him in the Battle of Badr. Sa'iid was uneasy about losing his father, even though the killer was an honorable man who implemented the orders of Allah and His Messenger. Sa'iid pretended to be content, but the fire of vengeance was raging in his heart. He was just waiting for an opportunity to avenge his father.

Sa'iid's son, Amr Al-Ashdaq, vented his deep animosity and raging vengeance towards the Prophet and his household. After the Battle of Karbala, Yazeed's governor in Medina, Al-Ashdaq, looked at the Prophet's grave, and loudly said, "You, the Messenger of Allah! Today we avenged the Day of Badr." Furthermore, when he heard the women of Bani Hashim weep on Al-Husayn, he said, "We mourned on Uthman, and now we are even."

Abdullah Bin Abbass

Bin Abbass refused to pledge allegiance to Bin Al-Zubayr. Once informed, Yazeed sent Bin Abbass a letter. Yazeed wrote: "I was informed that the atheist, Bin Al-Zubayr, asked you to pledge allegiance to him, and that you refused to become a supporter of evil and a participant in transgression. You refused because Allah blessed you and helped you recognize our significance. I ask Him to reward you for your loyalty to your kin. Your obedience, honorable status, and proximity to Allah's Messenger, compel me to revere and reward you appropriately. Utilize your unrivaled significance in the Community to influence your relatives and also strangers. Employ your indispensable significance to sway those who have been lured by Bin Al-Zubayr. People should definitely be more attentive and obedient to you than to that atheist and apostate. Greetings."

Bin Abbass replied: "I received your letter in which you mention that I refused to pledge allegiance to Bin al Zubayr because I recognize your significance. I did not refuse so you would reward me, but for a reason that only Allah knows. You also asked me to urge the people to abandon Bin Al-Zubayr. I shall never do this. How dare your filthy mouth ask me to do something? You are a miserable loser. You wrote promising to reward me. Keep your money, because you will never buy my love and support. By Allah! You offer us a little of our own money while you keep the rest. You are doomed! Do you think I will ever forget that you murdered Al-Husayn and the children of Abd Al-Muttalib, who were the radiant banners of piety? Do you think I'll ever forget that you looted them and left their bloody bodies in the desert without washing or burial? The wind covered them with dust, and the beasts visited them until Allah guided a group of people, who did not participate in the crime, to clothe them and bury them. Allah shall definitely chastise you for what you did. How could I ever forget that you delegated an inherently evil person and a prostitute's son to murder the Prophet's household? Your father committed a despicable sin, and acquired an eternal shame in this life and the next by claiming this man's father (Ziyad) to be his brother. The Prophet said an infant belongs to the dwelling in which he was born, and the adulterer should be stoned. Your father violated this rule because he was an adulterer and so is his son. Your ignorant father distorted the pure path and intentionally propagated corruption.

I shall never forget how you forced Al-Husayn out of his grandfather's sanctuary (Medina) to Allah's sanctuary (Mecca). You then sent your secret agents to murder him, and thus compelled him to leave from Mecca to Kufa. You recruited men and armed them against him just to express your enmity towards Allah, His Messenger and his household. You also wrote to Marjana's son (Bin Ziyad) to deploy his soldiers and intercept Al-Husayn with spears and swords, and to finish him quickly. You instructed Bin Ziyad not give Al-Husayn any chance to resist. You murdered him along with the children of Abdul Muttalib, whom Allah had purified from all filth. Unlike your evil and ignorant forefathers, we are purified like them; You knew that Al-Husayn was the most honorable man on the planet, and had he wanted the leadership of both sanctuaries, he would have easily acquired it. However, he left to protect the sanctity of both sanctuaries. He did not want his blood to be spilled in the Holy cities. He proposed a truce so he could return, but you, knowing how few his supporters were, ordered the murder and eradication of his family. You ruthlessly killed them as if they were infidels. How dare you ask me for friendship and support when my blood, which is the same as my brothers', hasn't dried up on your sword? I shall avenge from you, and Allah Willing, I shall do so before you murder me. And if you happen to beat me to it, then I will be a martyr, and Allah shall account for my blood along with the blood of His prophets. One day, Allah shall avenge us, for He is the Supporter of the oppressed, and the Avenger from the oppressors.

The most amazing part of it all is your belief that you humiliated us when you captured Abd Al-Muttalib's grand-daughters and the little children of their family and then dragged them to Syria. In contrast, Allah relieved you, your father and your mother from the burden of slavery because of us. My hands cannot reach over to kill you, but my sharp tongue and enmity to you shall definitely hurt you. Do not be very joyous because you murdered the family of Allah's Messenger. The Exalted shall soon drown you in your evil and destroy you. Moreover, Allah shall condemn you for as long as you live, and shall severely chastise you for what you have done."[68]

Notes & References

1. Al-Dam'a Al-Sakiba (P.364)
2. Mutheer Al-Ahzaan (P.84); Al-Luhuf (P.81)
3. Asraar Al-Shahada (P.477); Tathallum Al-Zahra' (P.150)
4. We put the speech together from the following sources: Amali Al-Shaykh Al-Tussi; Amali Bin Al-Shaykh Al-Tussi; Al-Luhuf; Mutheer Al-Ahzaan; Manaqib Bin Shahr Ashoub; Al-Ihtijaaj
5. Al-Ihtijaaj (P.166)
6. Al-Luhuf; Mutheer Al-Ahzaan
7. Al-Luhuf; Mutheer Al-Ahzaan
8. Al-Luhuf; Mutheer Al-Ahzaan
9. Tareekh Al-Tabari (V.6, P.256); Al-Kamel (V.4, P.30); Al-Irshaad
10. Al-Bihar (V.10, P.211)
11. Qamar Bani Hashim (P.115)
12. Madinat Al-Ma'ajiz (P.263)
13. Ithbaat Al-Wassiyya (P.173)

14. Al-Kibreet Al-Ahmar
15. Kamel Al-Ziyarat (P.325)
16. Sharh Qasseedat Abu Firas (P.149)
17. Akhbar Al-Duwal (V.1, P.8)
18. Al-Sawa'iq Al-Muhriqa (P.118)
19. Tareekh Al-Tabari (V.6, P.262); Al-Luhuf (P.90)
20. Al-Kamel (V.4, P.33); Maqtal Al-Khawarizmi (V.2, P.42); Tareekh Al-Tabari (V.6, P.263) A'alaam Al-Wara (P.141); Al-Irshaad
21. Tareekh Al-Tabari (V.6, P.263)
22. Al-Luhuf (P.91); Maqtal Al-Khawarizmi (V.2, P.43)
23. Al-Kamel (V.4, P.34)
24. Tathkirat Al-Khawass (P.148)
25. Al-Luhuf (P.91); Maqtal Al-Khawarizmi (V.2, P.43)
26. Rawdhat Al-Wa'itheen (P.163)
27. Al-Luhuf (P.92); Maqtal Al-Awalim (P.130)
28. Al-Aghani (V.14, P.158)
29. Al-Kamel (V.4, P.34)
30. Tareekh Al-Tabari (V.6, P.263)
31. Al-Luhuf (P.92)
32. Tareekh Al-Tabari (V.6, P.263)
33. Riyadh Al-Ahzaan (P.57)
34. Mutheer Al-Ahzaan (P.50); Al-Luhuf (P.92); Maqtal Al-Khawarizmi (V.2, P.53)
35. Mutheer Al-Ahzaan (P.51); Maqtal Al-Khawarizmi (V.2, P.55); Riyadh Al-Ahzaan (P.58)
36. Riyadh Al-Ahzaan (P.52)
37. Al-A'laaq Al-Nafeessa (P.224)
38. Maqtal Al-Khawarizmi (V.2, P.178 &179)
39. Al-Bihar (V.10, P.284)
40. Sharh Al-Nahj (V.1, P.210); Al-Irshaad
41. Al-Akhbar Al-Tiwaal (P.295)
42. Tareekh Al-Tabari (V.7, P.146)
43. Al-Darr Al-Manthour (V.2, P.119)
44. Al-Irshaad; Al-Khassa'is Al-Kubra (V.2, P.125)
45. Manaqib Bin Shahr Ashoub (V.2, P.188)
46. Sharh Qasseedat Abu Firas (P.148)
47. Asraar Al-Shahada (P.488)
48. Sharh Qasseedat Abu Firas (P.148)
49. Al-Khassa'is Al-Kubra (V.2, P.127)
50. Maqtal Al-Awalim (P.151)
51. Tareekh Al-Tabari (V.6, P.268)
52. Nafs Al-Mahmoum (P.222); Sharh Al-Nahj (V.1, P.361)
53. Maqtal Al-Awalim (P.131)
54. Al-Aghani (V.4, P.155)

55. Mu'jam Al-Shu'ara (P.231)
56. Jamharat Al-Amthaal (P.9)
57. Amali Bin Al-Shaykh Al-Tussi (P.55); Manaqib Bin Shahr Ashoub (V.2, P.227)
58. Mutheer Al-Ahzaan (P.51); Al-Luhuf (P.96); Al-Kamel (V.4, P.36)
59. Al-Bihar (V.10, P.201)
60. Tahtheeb Al-Tahtheeb (V.10, P.214)
61. Madinat Al-Ma'ajiz (P.318)
62. Wafa' Al-Wafa' (V.2, P.103)
63. Tareekh Al-Tabari (V.6, P.218)
64. Ansaab Al-Ashraaf (V.4, P.3)
65. Al-Mustajad Min Fa'laat Al-Ajwaad (P.22)
66. Usd Al-Ghaba (V.3, P.97)
67. Sharh Al-Nahj (V.3, P.335); Tahtheeb Tareekh Dimashq (V.6, P.134)
68. We constructed this letter from the following sources: Majma' Al-Zawa'id (V.7, P.250); Ansaab Al-Ashraaf (V.4, P.18); Maqtal Al-Khawarizmi (V.2, P.77); Al-Kamel (V.4, P.50)

The Captives to Syria

Bin Ziyad sent a messenger to inform Yazeed that Al-Husayn and his companions had been killed, and that the rest of his family, including the women and children, were imprisoned in Kufa. Bin Ziyad also wrote a note and threw it into the prison where the Prophet's family was detained. The note read, "We mailed Yazeed to ask him what to do with you. The mail went out and a response shall return soon. If you hear loud calls of 'God is Great,' then you should anticipate execution, otherwise you will live." A letter from Damascus arrived in which Yazeed ordered Bin Ziyad to send Al-Husayn's family[1] along with the martyrs' heads to Syria.[2] Bin Ziyad ordered Zajr Bin Qays, Abu Barda Bin Au'f Al-Azdi and Tareq Bin Thibyan to lead some Kufans and carry the martyrs' heads, including Al-Husayn's, to Yazeed.[3] It has also been narrated that Mujbir Bin Murra Bin Khalid carried Al-Husayn's head and delivered it to Yazeed.[4] Ali Bin Al-Husayn's hands were cuffed to shackles and tied around his neck. He marched behind the Holy heads, and along his side marched the rest of his family.[5] The scene was heartbreaking, and the condition of the women and children was chilling.[6]

Later on, Bin Ziyad ordered a group of men including, Shimr Bin Thil Jawshan, Mijfar Bin Tha'alaba Al-A'idi, Shibth Bin Rib'ie, Amr Bin Al-Hajjaj, to rush out and join the caravan. He instructed them to display the heads in every town they pass.[7] The men caught up with the caravan in a nearby neighborhood.[8]

Bin Lahee'a narrated that he saw a man hanging onto the cloak of the Ka'aba, and incessantly asking Allah's forgiveness. The man repeatedly said, "You shall never do it!" Bin Lahee'a pulled the man aside, and said, "You must be crazy! Allah is Forgiving and Merciful. Even if your sins were countless, Allah can delete them all." The man explained, "You should know that I happened to be one of the men who carried Al-Husayn's head to Syria. In the evening we would sit around the head and get intoxicated. One night, while I was guarding the head and my comrades were asleep, I saw a bright light and people encircling the head. I was stunned and terrified. The scene rendered me speechless." This man said that he heard weeping and wailing and a distinct voice calling, "Oh Mohammed! Allah ordered me to implement your commands. Would you like me to rumble the ground under these people and destroy them as I destroyed the enemies of Prophet Lut?" The Prophet responded, "Oh Jabra'eel! I shall have a stance against these people, and my Lord shall witness it all on the Day of Judgement." The man said that he screamed, appealing for salvation from Allah's Messenger, but instead the Prophet told him, Go on, I ask Allah to never forgive you." After narrating this, the man looked at Bin Lahee'a and exclaimed, "Do you think that Allah will ever forgive me?"[9]

Bin Ziyad's thugs set the Holy head down in some neighborhood. Before they settled, a metal pen suddenly appeared and wrote with blood on a nearby wall, "How could the community who murdered Al-Husayn hope for his grandfather's intercession on the Day of Judgement?"[10] Cruelty and aberration sealed these criminals' hearts, and none of them seemed affected by this miracle. Their repugnant sinfulness shall reap them severe punishment from Allah, the Supreme Judge. A few miles away from Aleppo, the men set Al-Husayn's head on a rock. A drop of blood fell from the Holy head onto the rock. This drop of blood bubbled on the tenth of Muharram of every year. Locals gathered around this rock, mourned and wept on Al-Husayn on the tenth of Muharram of every year. They maintained this ritual until Abdul Malik Bin Marwan (An Umayyad tyrant) ordered the removal of the rock. The rock was never seen again. Nonetheless, the locals built a dome on top of its original spot and named it "The Drop." Furthermore, there was a mosque near the city of Ramah known as Al-Husayn's Mosque. Locals often told that the rock, the print and the blood inside the mosque lay exactly on the spot where Al-Husayn's head rested before it was carried to Damascus.[11] There is another shrine near Aleppo known as the "Spot of the Miscarriage." The locals gave it this name because when the caravan of the Prophet's daughters arrived to that spot, Al-Husayn's wife miscarried a fetus named Muhsin.[12]

Later, on the way to Damascus, they placed the head on a spear close to a monastery. In the middle of that night, a Christian priest heard a voice praising the Lord and saw bright light emanating from the Holy Head. The priest also heard someone say, "Abu Abdullah! I greet you with peace." Oblivious to the unfolding events, the priest was totally perplexed at these abnormal phenomena. Early the next morning, he inquired about the head. The men replied, "This is the head of Al-Husayn Bin Ali Bin Abu Talib, whose mother is Fatima, Mohammed's daughter." He said, "You are all condemned! The prophecy that the sky will rain blood when he is murdered has come true." He asked their permission to kiss the Holy head. They refused until he paid them money. Shaken by the radiance of the Holy head, the priest instantly gave his testimony that Allah is the only God, and that Mohammed is His Messenger. After departing with the head, the men saw the following verse carved on each of the coins the priest gave them, *"The oppressors shall soon discover their miserable destiny. (26:227)"*[13]

IN SYRIA

As the caravan approached Damascus, Umm Kulthoum requested from Al-Shimr to walk them through less crowded roads, and that the heads be lifted high up to divert the spectators' eyes from staring at the women and children. Contrary to Umm Kulthoum's request, Al-Shimr tucked the heads away and led them through the most crowded roads.[14] Emotions ran high, and the scene of the helpless women and children was horrific and pitiful. The captive's caravan entered Damascus on the first of Safar.[15] Bin Ziyad's cruel soldiers stopped the Prophet's family, and lined them up at Bab Al-Sa'aat, one of the main gates of Damascus (known nowadays as the gate of Tuma).[16] Spectators celebrated and played their musical instruments joyously. A man approached Sukayna and asked her, "What kind of captives are you?" She replied, "We are captives from the family of Mohammed."[17]

All along, Yazeed had been waiting on his balcony in Jeeron. When the martyrs' heads appeared in the distance, a crow yelled. Documenting his elation, Yazeed poetically commented, "When the caravan appeared, and the heads radiated towards Jeeron, a crow yelled. I told the crow that yelling is pointless, because I have avenged from the Prophet." Based on this enmity and vindication towards the Prophet, Bin Al-Jawzi, Al-Qadhi Abu Ya'ala, Al-Taftazani and Al-Jalal Al-Suyuti ruled that Yazeed was an atheist, and concluded that it is permissible to curse him.[18] Sahl Bin Sa'ad Al-Sa'idi (a companion of the Prophet) approached Sukayna and asked, "Can I do something for you?" She replied, "Pay off the carrier of Al-Husayn's head, and instruct him to step away from the caravan so people would look at it instead of staring at the women."[19]

An old man approached Imam Al-Sajjad and said, "I thank Allah, who destroyed you and aided the commander of the faithful (Yazeed) against you." The infallible leader, like the rest of the Prophet's household, reciprocated with a glimpse of his genuine kindness, and emanated a ray of guidance upon the confused man. Al-Sajjad eventually cleared the distortion, and restored a pre-existing purity in the old man's heart. Al-Husayn's son exclaimed, "You are a respectable old man! Have you read the Qur'an?" The man said, "Yes." Al-Sajjad continued, "Have you read *Say, I seek no reward from you, except loving the relatives (42:23)* and *Learn that one fifth of whatever you profit must be allocated for Allah, His Messenger and the relatives? (8:41)*" The old man said, "I have read this." Al-Sajjad explained, "By Allah! We are the relatives meant in these verses." Imam Al-Sajjad resumed, "Have you read *Allah shall keep all filth away from you, the people of the Messenger's household, and thoroughly purify you? (33:33)*" The old man replied, "Yes I have." Al-Sajjad said, "We are the people of the Messenger's household, whom Allah purified." The man shockingly exclaimed, "By Allah! Are you the ones?" Imam Al-Sajjad, "By our grandfather, Allah's Messenger! We are undoubtedly the ones." The old man fell on Al-Sajjad's feet, kissed them, and said, "I ask Allah to be my Witness in dissociating myself from those who murdered you." Remorseful for slandering Imam Al-Sajjad, the old man declared his repentance in front of the infallible leader. Once informed of what the old man did and said, Yazeed ordered his execution.[20]

Shortly before the caravan entered Yazeed's palace, they tied the captives with more ropes. One was tied around Imam Zayn Al-Abideen's neck, from which an extension was tied around Zaynab, and so on, until all of the Prophet's daughters were tied together. From this point on, the captors brutally and continuously beat the captives until the caravan finally arrived to Yazeed's assembly. The Umayyad tyrant was sitting on his comfortable couch. Ali Bin

Al-Husayn looked at him and said, "What do you think the Prophet would do if he saw our condition?" The attendants wept. Yazeed ordered his guards to cut and remove the ropes.[21]

The captives were placed on the stairs of the mosque where prisoners of war usually sat. Al-Husayn's Holy head was placed in front of Yazeed. The latter looked at it and said, "We bravely held steadfast! However, our sharp swords won the war. We destroyed highly ranked men because they were oppressive rebels."[22] Yazeed looked at Al-Nu'man Bin Basheer and said, "I praise Allah because He killed him." Al-Nu'man replied, "The commander of the faithful, Mu'awiya, would have disapproved killing him." Yazeed said, "That was before he rose up. Had he risen up against the commander of the faithful (Mu'awiya), the latter would have also killed him."[23]

YAZEED AND IMAM AL-SAJJAD

Yazeed looked at Al-Sajjad and asked him, "Oh Ali! How do you see what Allah did to your father, Al-Husayn?" Al-Sajjad replied, "I saw what Allah has ordained before the creation of heavens and earth." After consultation, Yazeed's associates suggested the execution of Imam Al-Sajjad. The infallible leader interjected, "Yazeed! Their suggestion contrasts that of Pharaoh's advisors. When Pharaoh asked his associates what to do with Musa and Harun, they suggested that he grant Musa and his brother a grace period. Moreover, you are the son of a former slave, and you can never eradicate the Prophet's family." Yazeed quietly gazed down.[24]

A while later, Yazeed told Ali Bin Al-Husayn, *"Disasters befell you all because of what you have done. (42:30)"* Ali Bin Al-Husayn replied, "We were not implied in this verse. Allah says that *any disaster befalling earth or you has been ordained in a Book before We implement it. Allah easily does things. This happens so you would not regret what you missed, or be over-joyous for what you gained (57:21-22)*. We are implied in this verse because we neither regret what we missed, nor are we over-joyous for what we gained."[25] Irritated with Imam Al-Sajjad's response, Yazeed immediately quoted an old poetry of Al-Fadhl Bin Al-Abass Bin Utbah, "Cousins! Cool it down! Do not inflame the old feud between us."[26] The infallible leader then asked permission to speak. Yazeed said, "You can as long as you do not incite troubles." Al-Sajjad said,

"I am in no position to start any trouble. What do you think the Prophet would do if he saw me in this condition?" Yazeed ordered his guards to take the shackles off of Imam Al-Sajjad.[27] Yazeed instructed his spokesperson to praise Mu'awiya, and then to revile Al-Husayn and his family. The speaker heavily cursed Ali and Al-Husayn. Imam Al-Sajjad yelled at him, "You invoked the wrath of the Creator to please a creature. You are bound to hellfire!"[28]

He then told Yazeed, "Allow me to stand on this wooden structure so I may utter words that please the Exalted, and invoke His rewards for the audience." Yazeed vehemently rejected Al-Sajjad's request. The attendants insisted that he grant Al-Sajjad permission to speak, but to no avail. Yazeed's son, Mu'awiya, intervened, "Allow him! How articulate can he be?" Yazeed replied, "These people were inculcated with unrivaled knowledge and eloquence."[29] People nagged Yazeed until he finally gave in and allowed Imam Zayn Al-Abideen to speak. The infallible leader looked at the crowd and said:

> "I praise Allah, the Eternal who never dies, the First without a beginning, the Last without an end, and the Everlasting after the annihilation of all creatures. He ordained the days and the nights, and accurately parted between them, for He is the All-Knowing King, and the source of all blessings. People! We have been blessed with six insurmountable merits and favored with seven. We have been blessed with knowledge, perseverance, forgiveness, eloquence, courage and love in the hearts of the believers. We have been favored over all other creatures because the Prophet, Al-Siddeeq (Ali), Al-Tayyar, the Lion of Allah, the Lion of His Messenger and the two most honorable grandsons of this Community (Al-Hasan & Al-Husayn) are members of our family. You people! Some of you know who I am, but for those who don't, I shall introduce myself. People! I am the son of Mecca and Mina. I am the son of Zamzam and Al-Safa. I am the son of the man who carried the black stone with his cloak. I am the son of the best man to tread the earth and perform pilgrimage. I am the son of the man who was transported on Al-Buraq with Jabra'eel navigating him to the seventh heaven. I am the son of the man whose proximity to his Lord is indescriba-

ble. I am the son of the man who led the angels of heavens in congregational prayers. I am the son of the man who received the revelations from the Exalted. I am the son of the man who bravely fought in the Battles of Badr and Hunayn under the Prophet's command. I am the son of the man who never was, even for a blink of an eye, an infidel. I am the son of the most pious believer and the inheritor of prophets. I am the son of the Muslims' fortress, and the role model for the fighters on the way of Allah. I am the son of the man who destroyed the Traitors, the Transgressors and the Apostates. I am the son of the man who destroyed the idolater parties (Ahzaab). I am the son of the bravest and the most devout man. This man is the father of Al-Hasan and Al-Husayn, Ali Bin Abu Talib. I am the son of Fatima Al-Zahra, the Lady of all Women. I am the son of Khadeeja Al-Kubra. I am the son of the man who was left soaked in his blood on the sandy plains. I am the son of the man who was slaughtered in Karbala. I am the son of the man who was mourned by Al-Jinn in the dark, while the birds wept on him in the air."

At this point the forum turned loudly tearful. Afraid of a massive reprisal, Yazeed interrupted Al-Sajjad and ordered a man to start the call to prayers (Athaan). The caller yelled, "Allah is Great!" Imam Al-Sajjad loudly commented, "Allah is greater, more Exalted, Higher and more Generous than I can ever observe and understand." The caller resumed, "I testify that there is no God but Allah." The infallible leader said, "Indeed! I testify with every witness that there is no God or Lord except Him." The caller continued, "I testify that Mohammed is His Messenger." The infallible leader requested, "I ask you to honor Mohammed and be quiet until I talk to this man." Al-Sajjad then looked at Yazeed and said, "Is this honorable and generous Messenger your grandfather or mine? If you claim that he is yours, the audience will know that you are lying. If you acknowledge that he is mine, then why did you unjustifiably murder my father, loot his possessions, and capture the women of his family? My grandfather shall definitely be your adversary on the Day of Judgement, and you shall be condemned into hellfire thereof." Yazeed screamed at the caller to immediately utter the words (Iqama) to which people assemble for congregational prayers. The attendants were in total disarray. Some prayed while others dispersed.[30]

THE HOLY HEAD

The women and children of the Prophet's household sat behind Yazeed. The latter ordered the Holy head placed on a golden tray in front of him.[31] Sukayna and Fatima, Al-Husayn's daughters, stood up and tried to peek at the Holy head, but Yazeed repeatedly blocked their view. They finally saw it and wept aloud.[32] In the meantime, Yazeed opened the gates of his palace to the public.[33] As people entered, Yazeed mercilessly beat Al-Husayn's mouth with a stick.[34] He, while whipping the Holy head, numerously reiterated, "Today we avenged the Day of Badr."[35] He then quoted Al-Hasseen Bin Al-Hamam, "We bravely held steadfast. However, our sharp swords won the war. We destroyed highly ranked men because they were oppressive rebels."[36]

Yahya Bin Al-Hakam, Marwan's brother, was among the people who attended that forum. Yahya commented, "The people who were slaughtered in Al-Taff are closer in kinship to us than the wicked slave Bin Ziyad. It is quite shameful to live and see that Sumayya's descendants outnumber the Prophet's." Yazeed smacked Yahya on the chest and said, "Shut your mouth you damn fool!"[37] Abu Barza Al-Aslami told Yazeed, "I bear witness that I saw the Prophet sniff the mouths of Al-Husayn and Al-Hasan. After that I heard him say that the two are the Masters of Youth in Heaven. The Prophet then supplicated and asked Allah to destroy and condemn their murderers into the worst pit of hellfire." Yazeed became irate and ordered his guards to drag Abu Barza out of the assembly.[38]

The Roman Emperor's messenger looked at Yazeed and said, "The horseshoe of Isa's donkey was found on some island. We, from the world over, go to it as pilgrims to convey our respect, nourish our faith, and renew our commitment. We revere that place the way you revere your Holy book. However, I assert that you are in complete aberration."[39] Yazeed became furious and ordered the execution of his guest. The Roman Emperor's messenger walked to the Holy head, kissed it and loudly enunciated the two testimonies (There is no God but Allah, and Mohammed is His Messenger). While this innocent man was being executed, people in the assembly heard

Al-Husayn's Holy head loudly and eloquently say, "There is no power and strength except Allah's."[40]

The Holy head was then placed on the main door of the palace. It remained hanging in the same spot for three days.[41] Bright rays of light emanated from the Holy head and sensational fragrance filled the air.[42] Yazeed's wife, Hind Bint Amr Bin Suhayl, saw the radiant Holy head dripping blood at her door step.[43] She ran unveiled into the assembly and screamed hysterically. She told Yazeed tearfully, "How dare you place the head of the Prophet's grandson at our doorstep?" Yazeed covered her and said, "Hind! Wail and weep on Bani Hashim's loss! Bin Ziyad hastily murdered him."[44]

Yazeed ordered his police to place some of the heads at the main gates of Damascus, and some at the main gate of the Umayyad Mosque.[45]

Elated and vibrant, Marwan joyously articulated the true purpose of killing Al-Husayn. Describing the murder, Marwan said, "It was a perfect blow, by which the strongest pillars of our kingdom have been erected." Marwan repeatedly beat Al-Husayn's face with a stick and said, "I sure am glad that your cheeks have turned red from beatings. Spilling Al-Husayn's blood has definitely soothed my heart."[46]

A SYRIAN MAN AND FATIMA

Historians narrated that a Syrian man looked at Fatima Bint Ali,[47] and asked Yazeed if she could become his maid. Terrified at what she heard, the daughter of the Commander of the Faithful hugged her sister Zaynab very tightly and said, "How could I ever become a maid?" Zaynab replied, "Don't worry! This will never happen." Yazeed said, "I could make it happen if I want." She told him, "If you do, you'll publicly become an apostate." He replied, "Your father and brother are the apostates." Zaynab said, "It is Allah's revelations, and the religion of my grandfather, father and brother that guided you and your father, if you happen to be a true Muslim." Yazeed said, "You! The enemy of Allah! You just lied." Zaynab moaned and said, "You are an oppressive ruler. You use your position to degrade and oppress people."[48] The Syrian man reiterated his interest in Fatima. Yazeed snapped and yelled at the man, and then told him, "I ask Allah to grant you an irrevocable death sentence."⁴⁹

ZAYNAB'S SPEECH

Yazeed chanted in the crowded assembly, "I wish my grandfathers who fought (against the Muslims) in the Battle of Badr were alive to witness our victory. Surely, they would have ecstatically commended my efforts. We killed their leader and avenged our loss in Badr. Hashim monopolized kingship however there has been no revelation and no message. Had I not avenged from Ahmed's household, I would not have been loyal to my forefathers."⁵⁰

Having heard him, Zaynab Bint Ali immediately rose up and spoke. She said:

> "All Praise is due to the Lord of the Worlds, and I ask Him to bless His Messenger and the members of his household. Allah is always Truthful. He said the outcome of those who commit sins is that they deny and degrade Allah's revelations (30:10). Yazeed! Because you dragged us around the planet as captives, you think that Allah has somehow honored you and dishonored us! You also think that He favored you and ranked you high! This is your wishful thinking, and you are acting as if it were true. You usurped our rightful leadership, and you are happy that things seem to be going your way. Well, do not rush into false conclusions. Have you forgotten that Allah said *the infidels should not think that Our Respite is good for them: We postpone their punishment so they can add more loads to their sins, and then end up in disgraceful chastisement (3:178)*?
>
> You are the son of former slaves! How dare you tuck away your women and maids while you drag the Prophet's daughters around as captives? You have dislocated them and exposed their faces to strangers. Your thugs dragged them from one town to another, where strangers of all classes stared at their faces. They had no one to protect them, let alone a man to guard them. I never expect you to be remorseful or considerate, for you inherited the savagery of your grandmother (Hind), who chewed the liver of the pious (Hamza). Your flesh grew on the blood of martyrs! We, the Prophet's household, always anticipated ani-

mosity and hostility from you because you relentlessly coveted and dreaded us! You constantly beat Abu Abdullah's face with your stick. At the same time, you shamelessly bragged that if your forefathers were alive, they would have ecstatically commended your efforts. You have truly devastated us when you spilled the blood of Mohammed's household. You slaughtered the bright stars of this earth and Abdul Muttalib's pious descendants. You ostensibly called up on your forefathers from afar to share your joy. However, you forgot that soon you will join them and regret your actions. Soon enough you will wish that you would not have said and done this.

My Lord! Help us restore our rights. Destroy those who oppressed us. Spill Your wrath upon those who spilled our blood and murdered our protectors.

By Allah! You have invoked a wrath upon yourself. Allah's Messenger shall definitely prosecute for slaughtering his children, abusing the members of his household and violating his sanctity. This shall occur on the Day of Judgement, when Allah shall reunite the members of the Prophet's household, heal their wounds and avenge them. *Do not think of those who are slain on the way of Allah as dead, but alive with their Lord enjoying His bounties (3:169).* Allah shall be The Judge and Jabra'eel shall assist Mohammed in prosecuting you. The Prophet shall know then who empowered you and enabled you to abuse the Muslims. The oppressors shall then embrace their miserable outcome and be chastised in the worst place possible.

My words are too precious to scold and revile an imbecile like you, but I am compelled to compromise in order to expose your viciousness. I can slander you endlessly, but I am tearful and my heart is raging with grief. It is amazing that the former slaves and the party of Satan have audaciously murdered the pure party of Allah. Your hands are stained with our blood. Your jaws are chewing on our flesh, while wolves and wild hyenas visit the martyrs' pure and blessed bodies. You shall soon reap what you have sewn, and be severely chastised for dragging us around as a war gain. Your Lord, the Absolute Justice, is never oppressive to His creatures. I complain to Allah and seek help from Him. Scheme all you want and do all you can. By Allah! You shall never eradicate our message or bury our revelations. In contrast, the shame of your crime shall haunt you forever. Your scheme has floundered, your days are numbered and your possessions shall be squandered. The Day, in which the Caller announces that Allah's wrath shall befall the oppressors, is imminent. Praise is due to the Lord of the Worlds, who blessed our pious predecessors with eternal joy and forgiveness, and blessed their successors with martyrdom and mercy. We ask Allah to multiply the martyrs' rewards and grant them even more. Allah is Merciful and Loving. We ask Him to grant us a rewarding outcome. We count on Allah and on Him we rely."[51]

Yazeed said, "Such grief is justified. It is easy to weep on loved ones." Yazeed was a vulgar transgressor and an ignorant tyrant. He looked at his associates in the assembly, and shamelessly asked them, "Do you know why Fatima's son blundered, and what caused him to be self-destructive?" They collectively replied, "No, we don't!" Yazeed foolishly explained, "Al-Husayn claimed that his father, his mother Fatima, the daughter of Allah's Messenger, and his grandfather are superior to my father, mother and grandfather respectively. He also thought that he is superior to me and more qualified for the position of leadership. His claim that his father is superior to mine is easily refuted, because my father and his asked Allah to judge between them, and people know that Allah favored mine. His claim that his mother is superior to mine is definitely true. Fatima is the daughter of Allah's Messenger, and she is definitely superior to my mother. His claim that his grandfather is superior to mine is definitely true, for no one would ever believe in Allah and the Day of Judgement and dare to think that anyone could surpass the Prophet. However, Al-Husayn blundered because of his ill understanding of religion. It seemed like he never read the following verses of the Qur'an: *Say my Lord! You are the owner of kingship. You give it to whomsoever You will, and take it away from whomsoever You will, You exalt whomsoever you will and degrade whomsoever You will (3:26). And Allah grants the right of kingship to whomsoever He wills. (2:247)*"[52]

THE DILAPIDATED STRUCTURE

Zaynab's words fell on the audience like thunder. Her speech shook the forum in Yazeed's assembly. Men conversed and confessed to one another that they had been entrenched in aberration and confusion. In an attempt to absorb the turbulence and avoid an instant reprisal of the angry and remorseful crowd, Yazeed ordered the captives to be dragged out of his assembly and placed in an adjacent building. Old and dilapidated, this allocated structure provided no protection from the weather elements. The pure members of the Prophet's household were confined to these ruins for three days,[53] during which they continuously wept and wailed on Al-Husayn.[54]

One day, Al-Sajjad stepped out of the building to get some fresh air. Al-Minhal Bin Amr asked him, "The son of Allah's Messenger! How have you been?" Al-Sajjad replied, "We have been like the Israelis when Pharaoh slaughtered their sons and captured their women. The Arabs feel superior to non-Arabs because Mohammed was one of them. Quraysh feels superior to the rest of the Arabs because Mohammed was one of them. We, his household and family members, on the other hand, have been slaughtered or dislocated. We all belong to Allah, and to Him we shall return!"[55]

Al-Minhal narrated that while Imam Al-Sajjad was still talking to him, a woman ran after the infallible leader and asked him, "You are our guardian! Where are you going?" Al-Sajjad immediately stopped talking to Al-Minhal and rushed towards her. Al-Minhal inquired who the woman was. Someone told him that she was Al-Sajjad's aunt, Zaynab.[56]

Notes & References

---

1. Al-Luhuf (P. 95 & 97)
2. Tareekh Al-Tabari (V.6, P.262)
3. Tareekh Al-Tabari (V.6, P.264); Al-Kamel (V.4, P.34); Al-Bidaya (V.8, P.191); A'alam Al-Wara (P.149); Al-Luhuf (P.97); Al-Irshaad
4. Al-Issaba (V.3, P.489)
5. Tareekh Al-Tabari (V.6, P.264); Al-Khitat Al-Miqreeziyya (V.2, P.288)
6. Tareekh Al-Qarmani (P.108)

7. Al-Muntakhab (P.339)
8. Al-Irshaad
9. Al-Luhuf (P.98)
10. Majma' Al-Zawa'id (V.9, P.199); Al-Khassa'is Al-Kubra (V.2, P.127); Tareekh Dimashq (V.4, P.342); Al-Sawa'iq Al-Muhriqa (P.116); Al-Ka-wakib Al-Duriyya (V.1, P.57); Al-Ithaaf (P.23)
11. Nafs Al-Mahmoum (P.228)
12. Mu'jam Al-Buldan (V.3, P.173); Khareedat Al-Aja'ib (P.128)
13. Tathkirat Al-Khawass (P.150)
14. Al-Luhuf (P.99); Mutheer Al-Ahzaan (P.53); Maqtal Al-Awalim (P.145)
15. Al-Athaar Al-Baqiya (P.331); Misbaah Al-Mutahajjid (P.269)
16. Maqtal Al-Khawarizmi (V.2, P.61)
17. Maqtal Al-Khawarizmi (V.2, P.60); Amali Al-Sadouq (P.100)
18. Ruh Al-Ma'ani (V.26, P.73)
19. Maqtal Al-Awalim (P.145)
20. Al-Luhuf (P.100)
21. Al-Anwaar Al-Nu'maniyya (P.341); Al-Luhuf (P.101); Tathkirat Al-Khawass (P.149)
22. Mar'at Al-Janan (V.1, P.135)
23. Maqtal Al-Khawarizmi (V.2, P.59)
24. Ithbaat Al-Wassiyya (P.143)
25. Al-Aqd Al-Fareed (V.2, P.313); Tareekh Al-Tabari (V.6, P.267)
26. Al-Muhadharat (V.1, P.775)
27. Mutheer Al-Ahzaan (P.54)
28. Nafs Al-Mahmoum (P.242)
29. Riyadh Al-Ahzaan (P.148)
30. Nafs Al-Mahmoum (P.242)
31. Mar'at Al-Janan (V.1, P.135)
32. Al-Kamel (V.4, P.35); Majma' Al-Zawa'id (V.9, P.195); Al-Fusul Al-Muhimma (P.205)
33. Al-Kamel (V.4, P.35)
34. Tareekh Al-Tabari (V.6, P.267); Al-Kamel (V.4, P.35); Majma' Al-Zawa'id (V.9, P.195); Al-Fusul Al-Muhimma (P.205); Tathkirat Al-Khawass (P.148); Al-Sawa'iq Al-Muhriqa (B.116); Al-Furu' (V.3, P.549); Al-Bidaya (V.8, P.192); Manaqib Bin Shahr Ashoub (V.2, P.225); Al-Khitat Al-Miqreeziyya (V.3, P.289)
35. Manaqib Bin Shahr Ashoub (V.2, P.226)
36. Al-Kamel (V.4, P.35); Al-Fusul Al-Muhimma (P.205)
37. Tareekh Al-Tabari (V.6, P.267); Al-Kamel (V.4, P.35)
38. Al-Luhuf (P.102)
39. Al-Sawa'iq Al-Muhriqa (P.119)
40. Maqtal Al-Awalim (P.151); Mutheer Al-Ahzaan (P.55)
41. Al-Khitat Al-Miqreeziyya (V.3, P.289); Al-Ithaaf (P.23); Maqtal Al-Khawarizmi (V.2, P.75); Al-Bidaya (V.8, P.204); Sayr A'alam Al-Nubala' (V.3, P.216)

42. Al-Khitat Al-Miqreeziyya (V.3, P.284)
43. Maqtal Al-Awalim (P.151)
44. Maqtal Al-Khawarizmi (V.2, P.74)
45. Nafs Al-Mahmoum (P.274)
46. Riyadh Al-Ahzaan (P.59); Mutheer Al-Ahzaan (P.55)
47. Tareekh Al-Tabari (V.6, P.267); Al-Bidaya (V.8, P.194); Amali Al-Sadouq (P.100)
48. Al-Kamel (V.4, P.35)
49. Tareekh Al-Tabari (V.6, P.265)
50. Al-Luhuf (P.102); Al-Athaar Al-Baqiya (P.331)
51. Maqtal Al-Khawarizmi (V.2, P.64), Balaghaat Al-Nissa' (P.21)
52. Tareekh Al-Tabari (V.6, P.266); Al-Bidaya (V.8, P.195)
53. Maqtal Al-Khawarizmi (V.2, P.64)
54. Al-Luhuf (P.207); Amali Al-Sadouq (P.101)
55. Mutheer Al-Ahzaan (P.58); Maqtal Al-Khawarizmi (V.2, P.72)
56. Al-Anwar Al-Nu'maniyya (P.340)

To Medina

Yazeed was overtly joyous for murdering Al-Husayn and his companions. He was publicly elated for capturing the daughters of Allah's Messenger.[1] The Umayyad tyrant publicly expressed his joy in the general assembly. He shamelessly articulated his atheistic beliefs, and publicly denounced the Divine revelations of Mohammed's Message. Moreover, Yazeed asserted in front of the audience that he killed off Al-Husayn and the Prophet's family to avenge the Battle of Badr.

Yazeed's cruelty and viciousness surpassed that of his vile and infidel forefathers. Yazeed's main goal was to abort the significance of the Prophet's household from people's minds and hearts. Nonetheless, listening to frequent condemnations of his tactics and actions, Yazeed began to realize the severity of his crime, and his complete failure to achieve his goal. He also began to understand the depth of his father's will, in which Mu'awiya wrote: "The people of Iraq will insist on Al-Husayn until he rises up. Once he does, I instruct you to forgive him, because his kinship is honorable and his rights are insurmountable."[2] Yazeed's entourage, family members, and women condemned him for his shameful actions. The story of his cruelty and his cold-blooded murder of the Roman Emperor's messenger, and the subsequent speech of the Holy head *(there is no power and strength except Allah's)*[3] resonated throughout Damascus.

Yazeed began placing the burden of this crime on Bin Ziyad's shoulders in order to divert the attention of his critics. He unsuccessfully used his governor as a scapegoat to avoid a potential rebellion against his regime. Afraid that the uncontrollable unrest would escalate into a popular uprising, Yazeed hastily ordered Al-Sajjad and the rest of the family taken back to their home. Yazeed complied with all of the demands of the Prophet's household in order to ensure their expedited departure from Al-Sham. He ordered Al-Nu'man Bin Basheer to lead a group of men to escort the Prophet's household to

Medina. He also instructed his men to look after the captives and be kind to them until they arrive to their destination.[4]

The caravan passed through Iraq on the way to Medina. The Prophet's family requested from their escort to take them to Karbala. They arrived and found Jaber Bin Abdullah Al-Ansari with some Hashimites and other relatives of Allah's Messenger visiting Al-Husayn's grave. The caravan of the Prophet's family joined Jaber and his companions at Al-Husayn's grave. The men and women wept, screamed and beat their chests. Al-Husayn's family and the visitors from Medina spent the next three days in Karbala.[5] They constantly mourned and wailed on Al-Husayn throughout that whole time.[6]

Jaber Bin Abdullah Al-Ansari wept over Al-Husayn's grave. Jaber repeatedly said, "Oh Husayn!" He then said, "My love! Why aren't you answering your beloved? How could you answer after the veins of your neck bled all over your chest? How could you answer after your head had been separated from your body? I testify that you are the endeared son of the Seal of the Prophets. I testify that you are the son of the Master of all Believers, and that you are the son of the most pious man. I testify that you are the descendant of the banner of guidance. I testify that you are the fifth person under the cloak (Ahl Al-Kisa') and the son of the Master of all Successors. I testify that you are the son of Fatima Al-Zahra, the Lady of all Women. You have been ranked remarkably high, for the hand of the Master of all Messengers fed you, the pious nurtured you, the breast of ultimate faith nursed you and the purity of Islam weaned you. You were blessed in your life and upon death, but the believers' hearts are in total grief for losing you. I ask Allah to bestow His peace and blessings upon you. I testify that you were slaughtered like your brother in faith, Yahya Bin Zakariyya."

Jaber gazed around the grave and said, "I greet the souls who supported Al-Husayn and settled with him. I testify that you fulfilled the true goal of prayers, paid alms, commanded the good, forbade evil, fought the infidels and served Allah until certitude filled your hearts. I swear by the Creator, who entrusted Mohammed to deliver His Message, that we were included in your Holy uprising."

Atiyya Al-A'wfi exclaimed, "We never traveled the valleys and mountains, let alone wielded our swords to fight! These men have been decapitated and mutilated. Their children have become orphans and their wives have become widows. How could we be included with them?" Jaber answered, "The love of my heart, Allah's Messenger, said that a person will end up with whom he loves. He also said that a person who condones an act will be considered an accomplice. I swear by the Divine, who revealed His message to Mohammed, that our intention is in full compliance with the path of Al-Husayn and his companions."[7]

Notes & References

---

1. Tareekh Al-Khulafa' (P.139)
2. Tareekh Al-Tabari (V.6, P.180)
3. Maqtal Al-Awalim (P.150)
4. Al-Irshaad
5. Riyadh Al-Ahzaan (P.157)
6. Al-Luhuf (P.112); Mutheer Al-Ahzaan (P.79)

The Head with the Body

Having sensed that Yazeed was willing to comply with all of his demands, Imam Zayn Al-Abideen requested exclusive custody of the Holy heads so he could properly bury them. Yazeed immediately relinquished the heads of Al-Husayn, his family members and companions to Imam Al-Sajjad. The infallible leader buried the Holy heads with the respective bodies. The authors of *Nafs Al-Mahmoum* and *Riyadh Al-Ahzaan*, in pages 253 and 155 respectively, asserted that Al-Sajjad carried all of the heads back to Karbala. Regarding Al-Husayn's Holy head, Al-Fattal in page 165 of his *Rawdhat Al-Wa'itheen* and Bin Nama Al-Hilli in page 58 of his *Mutheer Al-Ahzaan*, narrated that it was returned to Karbala. Both scholars stated, "This is what the adherents to the twelve infallible leaders believe." On page 112 of his *Al-Luhuf*, Bin Tawouss wrote that Al-Husayn's head was returned to Karbala. He then stated, "The adherents to the twelve infallible leaders rely on this fact."

In his *A'lam Al-Wara* and *Maqtal Al-Awalim*, pages 151 and 154 respectively, and also in his *Riyadh Al-Massa'ib*, Al-Tabarsi mentioned that Al-Husayn's head was returned to Karbala. He then stated, "This is a common belief amongst the scholars." Al-Majlisi in his *Bihar Al-Anwar* stated similarly. On page 200 of the second volume of his *Manaqib*, Bin Shahr Ashoub stated, "Al-Murtadha mentioned in his work that Al-Husayn's Holy head was returned and buried with the body in Karbala." Al-Tussi said, "Al-Arba'een visitation ritual originated from this fact." On page 67 of his *Aja'ib Al-Makhlouqat*, Al-Qazweeni stated, "Al-Husayn's head was returned and buried with the body on the twentieth of Safar." In his *Bihar*, Al-Majlisi quoted Al-Hilli, and then stated similarly. On page 12 of his *Al-It'haaf Bihubb Al-Ashraaf*, Al-Shabrawi wrote: "It was narrated that Al-Husayn's head was returned after forty days."

In his *Commentary on Hamziyyat Al-Bussayri*, Bin Hijr stated, "Al-Husayn's head was returned forty days after his martyrdom." On page 150 of his *Tathkirat Al-Khawass,* Sibt Bin Al-Jawzi wrote: "The assertion that it (the head) was returned and buried with the body is highly reliable." On page 57 of the first volume of his *Al-Kawakib Al-Durriyya,* Al-Mannawi stated that there is a consensus amongst the followers of the twelve infallible leaders that Al-Husayn's Holy head was returned to Karbala. Al-Mannawi also emphasized that Al-Qurtubi was in favor of this opinion. On page 331 of the first volume of his *Al-Athaar Al-Baqiya,* Abu Al-Rayhan Al-Bayrouni wrote: "Al-Husayn's head was returned on the twentieth of Safar, and buried with the body."

Having learned this, one should not even consider an opposing argument. It was narrated that Al-Husayn's Holy head was placed in Imam Ali's grave. The previously mentioned scholars had definitely heard or read this narration, but rejected it because its authenticity was deficient, and the men in its channel of transmission were unknown. Responding to a question about the location of Al-Husayn's head, Abu Bakr Al-Alloussi said, "Seek Al-Husayn's head neither in the east, nor the west. Abandon your quest and come to me. It is in my heart."[1]

Notes & References

1. Tathkirat Al-Khawass (P.159); Al-Babiliyyat (V.3, P.128)

THE FORTIETH DAY

The practice of commemorating a deceased for forty days after his death is quite common. People hold special gatherings to praise the deceased, and expound on his good deeds and high moral values. Such gatherings are held to pay respect to the deceased and to keep his memory alive. Humans tend to forget their dead with the lapse of time. Nevertheless, some people employ poetry in an attempt to engrave the memory of the deceased in the minds, and implant love for him in the hearts. The lifestyle of the deceased is thus revived with each line of poetry or literature flattering him. The importance of the deceased and the associated blessings of such gatherings add more significance to this beautiful ritual (the fortieth). There is even more emphasis on the importance of these rituals, especially when the commemorated is a significant reformer and a role model on the path of guidance. These commemoration rituals serve as a media center in which people learn self-discipline and reflect upon the deceased's reform ideology.

Abu Tharr Al-Ghaffari and Bin Abbass narrated that the Prophet said, "Earth mourns the believer for forty days."[1] Zurara narrated that Imam Ja'afar Al-Sadiq said, "The sky mourned Al-Husayn. It drizzled blood for forty days. Earth mourned him. Darkness dominated the planet for forty days. The sun mourned Al-Husayn; its light dimmed and its brightness waned for forty days. The angels continuously wept on Al-Husayn for forty days. Also, no woman in our household dyed hair, used eyeliner or any make up until we received Bin Ziyad's head. However, we remained bereaved thereafter."[2] These traditions confirm the credibility that mourning the dead for forty days was, and still is, standard and common practice. On the fortieth day, the relatives and friends of the deceased usually gather at the site of his grave to mourn their loss. Commemoration rituals are not uncommon amongst non-Muslims. Some Christians hold a ceremony and utter the funeral prayers on the deceased forty days, six months and a year after a person's death. Some Jews commemorate their dead for thirty days, and then organize mourning ritual nine months or a year after death.[3] People from different faiths gather to pay respect and commend the achievements of the deceased, especially if he or she was a significant figure, or an exemplary model in his or her community.

Al-Husayn's Holy uprising and self-sacrifice outlined righteousness and true devotion. The Prophet's grandson preserved the Divine Message, and his lifestyle embodied its codes. An objective investigative study of our history would definitely yield the conclusion that the Master of Youth in Heaven was the best role model of the Community. Al-Husayn's martyrdom lit the path of true peace, and preserved the message of righteousness. His self-sacrifice maintained the genuine codes of harmony, ethics and self-discipline. Al-Husayn demonstrated to the masses the vitality of social order. He taught the generations timeless lessons of reform, moral values and wisdom. Al-Husayn's devotion to Allah, and his self-sacrifice in the process, earned him the honor of being commemorated annually. The ritual gatherings of the Fortieth Day, or Arba'een, have become an incredible opportunity for spiritual nourishment to people from all classes. A large number of believers flock to Al-Husayn's shrine on Arba'een to reflect upon the moral values of the Prophet's grandson. The faithful observe this significant occasion in order to quench their spiritual thirst.

Humans are limited in their achievements to time and place. Therefore, commemorating a person forty days after his death is usually a one-time event. The Master of all Martyrs, on the other hand, is a medium of indescribable merit and superior qualities. Humans in all generations need to learn lessons from him and his lifestyle. Holding an annual fortieth session in his shrine serves in the propagation of his uprising and the ideology of true reform. Moreover, this mourning ritual, a constant reminder of the Umayyads' cruelty, compels the believers to condemn tyranny and oppression. New venues of rewards and blessings open to the speaker or the poet, as he or she delves further into Al-Husayn's uprising and self-sacrifice. Upholding the Arba'een ritual, the followers of the Prophet's household annually renew their allegiance and commitment to their infallible leaders. Perhaps Imam Al-Baqir alluded to the commemoration ritual of Arba'een when he said, "The sky wept on Al-Husayn for forty days, during which it abnormally appeared ruby red in the morning and the evening."[4]

Imam Al-Askari said, "There are five signs in the believer. The first is to pray fifty-one rounds (Raka'as) of prayers. The second is to honor the visit of the fortieth. The third is to recite *In The Name of Allah, The Most Gracious and The Most Merciful,* loudly (in mandatory prayers). The fourth is to wear a ring in the right hand, and the fifth is to rub the forehead on the ground."[5] This authentic tradition endorses organizing mourning ceremonies on Arba'een to commemorate the Master of all Martyrs. The followers of the Prophet's household participate in this ritual to convey their love, loyalty and commitment to their third infallible leader. It is a sign of true faith to visit Al-Husayn's grave on the fortieth, and to mournfully remember the atrocities committed against him, his family and companions. Visiting Al-Husayn on the fortieth is an expression of strong attachment to the Master of Youth in Heaven, whose self-sacrifice preserved the Divine Message.

Some have argued that in the above tradition, Imam Al-Askari implied "visiting forty" believers rather than visiting Imam Al-Husayn on the "fortieth." Unfamiliar with the intricacy of the Arabic language, some people misunderstood and consequently distorted the true meaning of Imam Al-Askari's statement. The eleventh infallible leader enunciated Al-Arba'een which literally translates as "the forty" and not Arba'een which is "forty." Having said Al-Arba'een (by using *al* as a prefix), Imam Al-Askari implied a very specific ritual at a very specific time. Moreover, the subject, ritual visit (Ziyara), is one of five qualities that were cascaded in a special frame of faith on the path of the twelve infallible leaders.

The infallible leaders from the Prophet's household are undeniably the "Safety Ship" and the medium of Divine mercy. Loyalty to them and adherence to their path are exclusive characteristics of the true believer. The infallible leaders implemented the ordinances that Allah revealed to their grandfather, and sacrificed their precious lives to preserve the codes of Islam. Highlighting this fact, Imam Al-Hasan Bin Ali said, "Twelve infallible leaders, all of whom will be poisoned or slaughtered, shall assume the responsibility of implementing the Divine codes." Therefore, we should commemorate every infallible leader on the fortieth day after his martyrdom, because Imam Al-Askari did not specify that the believer should exclusively visit Al-Husayn on his fortieth. However, prominent scholars asserted such indication because Al-Husayn's self-sacrifice ultimately preserved the path of true Islam. Scholars emphasized visiting Al-Husayn because his Holy uprising became the most powerful tool in sorting out righteousness from aberration. Acknowledging this fact, the believer should easily absorb the following popular statement, "Prophet Mohammed propagated Islam, and Al-Husayn preserved it." The Prophet himself asserted this reality when he said, "Al-Husayn is from me, and I am from him." This authentic and splendid tradition clearly indicates that Al-Husayn endured the horrific abuse from his evil enemies to reinforce the foundation of true Islam on one hand, and uproot all forms of aberration and corruption on the other. In his statement, the Prophet reminded all of us that exposing the tyrants and combating their vicious crimes constitute the original path that he, the Messenger of Islam, treaded to deliver the Divine Message.

The infallible leaders focused on the emotional aspect of Al-Husayn's Holy uprising in order to attract kind-hearted believers to them. They informed the Muslims of the atrocities, and the level of cruelty and abuse, inflicted on the Prophet's household in Karbala. The infallible leaders' goal was to create an educational opportunity in which the masses would learn the facts, and conclude that Al-Husayn was the rightful and just leader, who never succumbed to the oppressors. The infallible leaders aimed to instill in people's minds and hearts the concept that the leadership was a Divine right passed on to Al-Husayn through his grandfather and father, and that those who oppressed and fought the Divinely appointed leaders represent tyranny and injustice.

After this elaboration on the crucial importance of Al-Husayn's uprising and self-sacrifice, one should easily understand the infallible leaders' emphasis on observing Al-Husayn's commemoration on Arba'een. The Divinely appointed guardians deliberately avoided observing the fortieth for any of them, including the Messenger of Islam. Nonetheless, they urged the believers to commemorate Al-Husayn on the fortieth because his uprising is a very strong factor in uniting the religious community. The infallible leaders knew that attracting attention to the events of Karbala was more effective in keeping alive the cause of all of the twelve leaders. They said, "Keep our cause alive, and discuss issues relevant to our lives." These words further assert the infallible leaders' pleasure with the believers who focus their discussions around the members of the Prophet's household.

Imam Al-Askari's tradition listed five characteristics of the believer. The believer in Al-Askari's tradition is the one who honors the rightful leadership of the twelve infallible leaders. To prove this exclusivity, let us now discuss the four remaining components of this authentic tradition. The first one is praying fifty-one Raka'as every day. This number was legislated on the night of ascendance (Mi'raaj). The Prophet interceded to reduce the obligatory to seventeen Raka'as in the form of what is known as the five daily prayers. Praying thirty-four recommended Raka'as, including the eleven Raka'as night prayers, is highly recommended. The order of these recommended prayers (Nafila or Nawafil) is summarized as follows: eight Raka'as before the noon (Thuhr) prayers, eight before the afternoon (A'sr) prayers; four after the sunset prayers (Maghrib); two after evening prayers (Isha) that are equivalent to one; two before morning (Subh) prayers, and eleven including *Shaf'* (two Raka'as) and *Watr* (one Raka'a) as the night prayers (Nafilat Al-Layl). The result of adding the recommended to the obligatory prayers is fifty-one Raka'as.

This practice is totally exclusive to the followers of the Prophet's household. The majority of the Muslims (Sunnis) agree with the followers of the Prophet's household on the number of Raka'as, and the format of the obligatory daily prayers, but disagree on the recommended ones. Bin Hammam Al-Hanafi, in Volume 1, page 314 of his *Fat'h Al-Qadeer*, stated that the recommended Raka'as (excluding the night prayers) are twenty-three. The Sunnis disagree with one another on the number of Raka'as in the night prayers. Some say it is composed of eight, some say two, while others say thirteen. Therefore, the total number of the obligatory and recommended Raka'as never adds up to fifty-one. This proves that such a practice is completely exclusive to the followers of the Prophet's household.

The second component is to recite *"In the Name of Allah, the Most Gracious and the Most Merciful"* aloud in the obligatory prayers.

The followers of the Prophet's household learned from their infallible leaders that it is obligatory to recite the above verse aloud in the loud prayers, but only recommended in the quiet ones. Al-Razi wrote: "Shi'as believe that it is the Prophet's tradition to recite In the Name of Allah, the Most Gracious and the Most Merciful (Bismala), or the opening verse, loudly in all of the daily prayers. However, Sunni scholars disagree with them. There is a consensus that Ali Bin Abu Talib recited the opening verse aloud. Furthermore, whoever emulates Ali has been truly guided, because the Prophet had asked Allah to keep righteousness on Ali's side in whatever he does."[6] Denouncing Al-Razi's conclusion, Al-Alloussi wrote: "A person claiming to be following the purportedly authentic traditions from Ali is an infidel, because it is blasphemous to believe in some traditions, while rejecting others. He (Al-Razi) mentioned that whoever emulates Ali has been truly guided. This is the case only if we can verify the reality or provide proof of Ali's practices, and it is impossible to do so."[7] The offensive language of Al-Alloussi and others would never diminish the true believers' loyalty to the Master of all Successors. The Prophet marked Ali's high rank when he told him, "Ali! No one truly knew Allah except you and I. And no one truly knew me except Allah and you. And no one truly knew you except Allah and me."[8] Sunnis strictly disallow loud recitation of the opening verse during the quiet prayers. Bin Qudama in page 478 of Volume 1 of his *Mughni*, Kassani in page 204 of his *Badai' Al-Sanai'*, and Al-Zarqani in page 216 of Volume 1 of his commentary on Malik's jurisprudence, stated that loud recitation is strictly disallowed during prayers.

The third characteristic or sign of the believer is to wear a ring on the right hand. The followers of the Prophet's household emulated their infallible leaders and maintained this practice. Some Sunnis expressed their opposition to this tradition. Bin Al-Hajjaj Al-Maliki wrote: "Traditions urge a person to handle all filth with the left hand, and to receive clean things in the right. Therefore, we understand that it is recommended to wear the ring in the left hand, because you receive it with your right hand and then wear it on your left."[9] Bin Hijr narrated that Malik despised wearing a ring on his right hand and insisted on keeping it on his left. Al-Baji ferociously defended Malik's practice.[10] In his *Aqd Al-Durar*, Al-Sheykh Isma'il Al-Baruswi wrote: "According to authentic traditions, the ring is supposed to be on the right hand. However, because this has become the practice of the corrupt and the oppressors (the Shi'a), the tradition was changed in our time to placing the ring on the pinky of the left hand instead."[11]

The fourth is rubbing the forehead or the face on the ground. Rubbing is the translation of "Ta'feer," which means to put something on dirt. In his *Al-Hadai'q*, Al-Shaikh Yusuf Al-Bahrani stated that this tradition instructs the believers to place their foreheads on dirt or clay during prostration. Sunnis were not as strict with prostrating on clay. Abu Haneefa, Malik and Ahmad allowed prostration on the turban,[12] the cloak, or on any piece of cloth.[13] Hanafis allowed prostration on the hand (but recommended against it),[14] wheat, corn, mattress, or the back of a person if they were both performing congregational prayers.[15] Rubbing the forehead was recommended in the tradition to alleviate arrogance and reinforce the sense of humility in the hearts of believers. However, prominent scholars like Sayyed Bahr Al-Ulum, and the author of *Al-Madarik*, stated that a person should rub his cheeks and forehead on the clay during the post prayer prostration of grace. Narrated traditions urge the believer to rub his cheeks during the prostration of grace.[16] Prophet Musa earned his proximity to the Divine through this practice.[17] Moreover, there is a consensus amongst the followers of the Prophet's household on this practice. The Sunnis were never committed to it, whether during or after the prayers. It suffices to add that Al-Nakh'ie, Malik and Abu Haneefa (popular Sunni scholars), despised the post prayer prostration of grace. Nevertheless, Shafi'es[18] and Hanbalis[19] performed it, but only at the arrival of a bounty or the end of a hardship.

Conclusion on the Signs of the Believer

We have proven beyond any reasonable doubt that these five signs are exclusive to the believers who strictly adhere to path of the Prophet's household. Therefore, Imam Al-Askari urged the followers of the Prophet's household to flock to Karbala on the fortieth to commemorate Al-Husayn, and to remember the unprecedented cruelty and abuse inflicted on him and his family. Visiting Karbala on the fortieth is the most luminous sign of the believer because Al-Husayn's Holy uprising, an epic of human struggle against injustice, embodied the pinnacle of true faith and devotion.

Some insist that the fortieth in this tradition implied visiting forty believers. Such interpretation is quite misleading and disturbing because there is no linguistic reason for such a conclusion. Visiting forty believers is recommended to all Muslims, and it is a common practice amongst Sunnis and Shi'as. This tradition depicts a complete picture, and one should not snatch one word from it and use it out of context. This tradition excludes all but the followers of the Prophet's household. Visiting Al-Husayn on Arba'een is the only interpretation of the "fortieth" in this tradition, because this practice is exclusive to the adherents or the followers of the Prophet's household. The scene of Al-Husayn's shrine on the fortieth of every year further attests to our illustration and understanding of this tradition. Believers from the world over flock to visit the Master of Youth in Heaven on that day.

Prominent scholars have emphasized that this tradition highlights the importance of visiting Al-Husayn on the fortieth (Arba'een). The statements of these scholars further prove our argument. Shaikh Al-Tussi in page 17 Volume 2 of his *Tahtheeb* detailed the rewards that a person accrues upon visiting Al-Husayn on specific occasions, including Ashura. Al-Tussi then narrated Imam Al-Askari's tradition. Furthermore, visiting Al-Husayn on the fortieth was detailed in page 551 of *Misbah Al-Mutahajjid*. In his *Al-Muntaha*, Al-Allama Al-Hulli wrote: "It is recommended to visit Al-Husayn on the twentieth of Safar." He then narrated Imam Al-Askari's tradition. Allama Al-Majlisi narrated Imam Al-Askari's tradition in the section *"The Blessings of Visiting Al-Husayn on the Fortieth"* of his *Mazar Al-Bihar*. In his *Al-Hada'iq*, Shaikh Yusuf Al-Bahrani commented that visiting Al-Husayn on the fortieth is a sign of the believer. In his *Mafateeh*, Sheykh Abbass Al-Qummi narrated Imam Al-Askari's tradition from *Al-Tahtheeb* and *Musbah Al-Mutahajjid*, but did not elaborate on it. Al-Qummi might have believed that visiting forty believers is the true interpretation.

Some have argued that whenever the infallible leaders encouraged their followers to visit Al-Husayn, they simultaneously mentioned the associated rewards. They thus concluded that had visiting Al-Husayn been meant in this tradition, the eleventh infallible leader would have mentioned the associated rewards of this visitation ritual on Arba'een. This argument is flawed and easily refuted. Imam Al-Askari only stated the signs that distinguish the believer. He deliberately avoided the rewards of any particular one, including that of the "fortieth visit." Shaikh Al-Mufeed in his *Massare Al-Shia*, Allama Al-Hulli in his *Al-Tathkira Wa Al-Tahreer*, and Mulla Muhsin Al-Faydh in his *Taqweem Al-Muhsineen*, asserted that it is highly recommended to visit Al-Husayn on the twentieth of Safar (Arba'een). In his *Tawdheeh Al-Maqassid Al-Arba'een*, Shaikh Al-Baha'ie stated a similar opinion, but violated the consensus on the date of the visit. Beginning his count from the tenth of Muharram, Shaikh Al-Baha'ie concluded that the fortieth is on the nineteenth of Safar, instead of the twentieth.

Notes & References

1. Majmou'at Al-Shaykh Waraam (V.2, P.276); Al-Bihar (V.2, P.679)
2. Mustadrak Al-Wassa'il (P.215)
3. Nahr Al-Thahab (V.1, P.263 thru 267)
4. Kamel Al-Ziyarat (P.90)
5. Al-Tahtheeb (V.3, P.17); Misbah Al-Mutahajjid (P.551)
6. Mafateeh Al-Ghayb (V.1, P.107)
7. Ruh Al-Ma'ani (V.1, P.47)
8. Al-Muhtadhar (P.165)
9. Al-Madhkhal (P.46)
10. Al-Fatawa Al-Fiqhiyya Al-Kubra (V.1, P.264)
11. Ruh Al-Bayan (V.4, P.142)
12. Al-Mizan (V.1, P.138)
13. Al-Hidaya (V.1, P.33)
14. Al-Fiqh Ala Al-Mathahib Al-Arba'a (V.1, P.189)
15. Al-Bahr Al-Ra'iq (V.1, P.319)
16. Al-Kafi (V.3, P.129); Man La Yahdhuruhu Al-Faqeeh (P.69); Al-Tahtheeb (V.1, P.266)
17. Man La Yahdhuruhu Al-Faqeeh (P.69)
18. Kitab Al-Umm (V.1, P.116); Al-Wajeez (V.1, P.2)
19. Al-Mughni (V.1, P.626); Al-Furu' (V.1, P.382)

In Medina

Imam Al-Sajjad and his family members spent three days in Karbala before returning to Medina. Throughout their stay, the women and children of the Prophet's household oscillated from one grave to another, and continuously wept and wailed on their beloved martyrs. Worried for the well-being of the bereaved and emotionally distressed women and children, Imam Al-Sajjad planned to depart from Karbala towards Medina as quickly as possible. Basheer Bin Hathlam narrated that as the caravan of the Prophet's household approached Medina, Ali Bin Al-Husayn stopped and assembled a tent to shelter himself and the women. The infallible leader then looked at Basheer and said, "Basheer! Your father, may Allah bless his soul, was a poet. Are you? Basheer replied, "The son of Allah's Messenger! Yes I am." Al-Sajjad continued, "Go into Medina and mournfully announce Abu Abdullah's martyrdom."

Basheer rode in to Medina. As he arrived to the Prophet's mosque, he wept aloud and yelled, "People of Yathrib! I call upon all of you! How could you enjoy life after Al-Husayn has been murdered? I am weeping on him. His body was left bloody in Karbala, while his head was carried around on a spear." Basheer then announced, "Ali Bin Al-Husayn, his aunts and sisters are camped in the outskirts of Medina. He sent me to inform you of his location." People, including women and children, rushed out of their homes towards the campsite of the Prophet's household. Men and women tearfully extended their heart-felt condolences to Imam Al-Sajjad. Imam Zayn Al-Abideen came out of his tent wiping his tears with a handkerchief. A servant of his held a chair and walked behind him. The infallible leader sat down as tears rolled down his face. People wailed hysterically. Some described this gathering as the most tearful in the history of Medina.

Al-Sajjad gestured to people for calm. As silence prevailed, Al-Husayn's son said:

"I praise the Lord of the Worlds, the Beneficent, the Merciful, the Holder of the Day of Judgement, the Creator of all beings who distanced Himself above the highest heavens, but is still so close as to witness the faintest whisper. We praise Him for the great tests and the associated difficulties and hardships. We praise Him for the excruciating pain of suffering, and the grief from the appalling atrocities. We praise Him despite the great loss that rendered us in everlasting agony and bereavement.

Oh People! Allah, the Exalted to whom all praise is due, tested us with an indescribable tragedy, and a major blow to the path of true faith. Abu Abdullah Al-Husayn, and his family, have been slaughtered. His women and children were captured and dragged. Along their side, the murderers carried Al-Husayn's head on a spear into towns and cities. Such cruelty is unrivaled.

Oh People! Who amongst you could ever be happy after this heinous crime? What heart could not be saddened for Al-Husayn? What eye of yours can withhold its tears? The earth, the oceans and their waves, heavens and their pillars, planet earth and its contents, trees and their branches, whales in the deep waters, the closest angels and the inhabitants of heavens all wept on him. Oh people! Who wouldn't be heart-broken after the killing of Al-Husayn? What soul would not be emotionally devastated at this loss? What ear would hear such a belligerent blow to faith, and not become deaf?

Oh people! We were exiled and dislocated. We, without committing a crime or inciting trouble, were treated like rejects and infidels. We endured an unprecedented level of cruelty and brutality. What they did to us was an abominable and flagrant violation. By Allah! The Prophet ordered the members of his community to look after us. Had he ordered them to kill us instead, they would not have done what they did. We all belong to Allah, and to Him we shall return. The magnitude of our grief is immeasurable. We complain to Him about this horrendous, painful and devastating loss. We ask Allah to account for our pain and suffering. We also ask Him to reward us for the brutality and abuse we endured, for He is the Dignified and the most

Capable Avenger."

An old and handicapped man, Sawhaan Bin Sa'asa'a Bin Sawhaan Al-Abdi stood up and apologized to Al-Sajjad. Sawhaan explained that his legs were crippled, otherwise he would have joined Al-Husayn and defended the Prophet's household. The infallible leader accepted his apology, thanked him, and commended him and his father. After the tearful gathering, Imam Zayn Al-Abideen entered Medina with his family and children.[1] Ibraheem Bin Talha Bin Obeydallah approached Al-Sajjad and sarcastically asked him, "Who was victorious?" The infallible leader replied, "When prayer time is due, recite the major call to prayer (Athaan) and then the minor one (Iqama), and you shall know then who was victorious."[2]

Umm Kulthoum chanted, "Our grandfather's city! How could you welcome us? We are back, but with agony and bereavement. We left with our honorable family, but we returned without our men and sons." Zaynab Bint Ali held onto the handles of the gate of her grandfather's mosque, and screamed, "Grandfather! I announce to you the loss of my brother Al-Husayn." Sukayna yelled, "Grandfather! We lament our suffering to you. By Allah! I have never seen a person more vicious than Yazeed. No infidel or idolater is as harsh or vile as he is. He continuously beat my father's face and deridingly asked him if he liked the beating."[3] The honorable daughters of Allah's Messenger wore black and mourned the Master of Martyrs around the clock, while Imam Al-Sajjad prepared food for them.[4] Imam Al-Sadiq said, "The women of Bani Hashim did not wear any eyeliner, or any sort of make up or ornamentation, for five years until Al-Mukhtar avenged Al-Husayn, and sent them the head of Obeydallah Bin Ziyad."[5]

Al-Rabaab wept on Al-Husayn until her eyes dried up. A maid of hers told her that eating Saweeq (food made of barley and wheat) would restore the functioning of her tear glands. She ordered some Saweeq made to resume weeping.[6] The following is only some of what Al-Rabaab chanted as she mourned on Abu Abdullah. "The one who was the light of guidance is now dead in Karbala without burial. The Prophet's grandson! I ask Allah to reward you with goodness, and spare you any hardship. You were my fortress and shelter. Your company was mercy and faith. Who shall look after the orphans and the needy? Where will the impoverished go now? By Allah! I shall mourn you for as long as I live, and until my last breath."[7]

Ali Bin Al-Husayn withdrew and became reclusive in order to avoid the pervasive division and factionalism of that time. He spent all of his time worshipping Allah and mourning his father. He wept day and night. One of his followers exclaimed, "I am afraid that what you are doing is self-destructive!" Imam Al-Sajjad replied, "I vent my agony and grief to Allah, and I know from Him what you, ordinary people, don't. Prophet Yaqoub had twelve sons. Allah ordained one of them to be temporarily separated from him. Yaqoub knew that his son was alive, but still wept on him until his eyes dried up. He cried on his son and eventually lost his sight. I, on the other hand, saw my father, my brothers, my uncles and my companions slaughtered around me. How could my bereavement ever end? Every time I remember the mutilated bodies of Fatima's children, I choke on my tears. Every time I look at my aunts and sisters, I remember how they were bewildered and ran in terror from one tent to another."

Oh Allah's Messenger! To you we lament the acts of oppression and tyranny that your community committed against the pure members of your household.

Notes & References

---

1. Al-Luhuf (P.116)
2. Amali Al-Shaykh Al-Tussi (P.66)
3. Riyadh Al-Ahzaan (P.163)
4. Mahasin Al-Barqi (V.2, P.420)
5. Mustadrak Al-Wassa'il (V.2, P.215)
6. Al-Bihar (V.10, P.235)
7. Al-Aghani (V.2, P.158)

CPSIA information can be obtained
at www.ICGtesting.com
Printed in the USA
LVHW022322180523
747455LV00027B/645